T. H. JONES

T. H. JONES

Poet of Exile

P. BERNARD JONES *and* DON DALE-JONES

UNIVERSITY OF WALES PRESS
CARDIFF
2001

British Library Cataloguing-in-Publication Data.
A catalogue record for this book is available from the British Library.

ISBN 0–7083–1707–3

Published with the financial support of the Arts Council of Wales

THE *A*SSOCIATION FOR
*W*ELSH *W*RITING IN *E*NGLISH
*C*YMDEITHAS *L*LÊN *S*AESNEG *C*YMRU

Typeset at University of Wales Press
Printed in Great Britain by Dinefwr Press, Llandybïe

For
Madeleine, Sian, Rhiannon and Ruth Myfanwy

Contents

 confused

Preface

❧

T. H. Jones achieved little recognition in Wales or Britain during his lifetime. He did, briefly, gain notoriety in Australia from the bitter irony of his untimely death, but was then largely forgotten through the 1970s and 1980s. He re-emerged eventually as the semi-mythic anti-hero of what Meic Stephens termed 'the second flowering' of Anglo-Welsh poetry.

A writer of significance requires champions – Ian Hamilton, in his seminal study of literary estates, terms them the 'keepers of the flame'. Unashamedly partisan on the subject, we reject the view of T. H. Jones as a transitional figure or literary John the Baptist prophetic of the revival of Welsh poetry in English. We seek to reposition him as one of the defining poets, alongside Dylan and R. S. Thomas, of mid-twentieth-century Welsh culture, his distinctive contribution being an early postmodernism. Modernism, in which his work is deeply rooted, emphasizes the signifier over the signified, connotation over denotation; T. H. Jones's poetry engages also with the search for personality: 'the Welshman in exile', the 'Taffy' who 'was transported', 'spoiled preacher', 'poor colonial's Dylan Thomas'. The deliberate tensions that lend fascination to his work derive from the poverty of his childhood, the stifling ideology of the chapel, the typical dislocating effects of a middle-class education and world war which transformed this grandson of a shepherd, son of a road-man, into academic high-flyer and campus poet.

Postmodernism frequently asserts the primacy of the nomadic, questioning those values that define the traditional kind of Welshness that focuses on home, hearth and hiraeth. The family is dismantled by the postmodern as surely as war completed the dismantling of those 'certain certainties' of which Jones's childhood was 'assured'. We have examined the poet's attempt to rebuild his life: in post-war Aberystwyth upon a basis of romantic nationalism; in poverty in London through vain pursuit of an academic career; during the grey 1950s, as an unwilling schoolteacher in Portsmouth – and contrast this with the intoxication of the sharp colours of the new academic life in the New World of Australia, the sun, the wines of the Hunter Valley, the assured status and sexual freedoms of campus life.

This book is a total collaboration. Its obvious genesis was the biographical research undertaken by P. B. Jones for his Ph.D. thesis, 'Home and the Fictions of Childhood in the Works of T. H. Jones'; its less obvious one an accidental moment when Don Dale-Jones was astonished and delighted to discover, in 1966, on a shelf in the library of Trinity College, Carmarthen, an Anglo-Welsh poet of sexual love. Joint authorship is still unusual in literary biography and joint literary endeavour fraught with broken friendships, but this work arose and developed from a friendship which has matched its progress. Neither of us has been able to understand why nobody has wished, in the more than thirty years since T. H. Jones's death, to forestall our endeavour; each of us has consistently desired to be a 'keeper of the fame' alongside Jones's widow, Madeleine Mitchell, his sister, Pat Power and her family, and professional enthusiasts such as Meic Stephens, Julian Croft and the late Harri Webb. A major decision was whether to write conventional literary biography or, in the spirit of postmodernism itself, proceed by means of a dialectic that foregrounded our differences rather than the large area of consensus that is our joint reading of Jones's life and work. The further we proceeded in the enterprise, however, the smaller the degree of disagreement: by the time the final version was achieved there remained no differences significant enough to be worth foregrounding. At the heart of our reading is Jones's clearly postmodern assertion that 'all my poems lie' with its inevitable corollary that the life that is our text lies too.

How could we, looking back on the life and work of a mid-twentieth-century man from the perspective of the beginning of the twenty-first century, fail to address the fictions of self in this writer's world and work? These 'lies' and shape-shiftings challenge directly the ethical problem all biographers confront. How much should we tell, how much conceal? How much, in any case, could we 'know', and in what sense? At the time of his death Jones may have published all he intended at that point – yet there remained (and remain) unpublished more than two hundred poems, several stories, some criticism and the draft of a book on Yeats. Thanks to the unfailing generous support of Madeleine (Jones) Mitchell we have had access to all of this material.

The manuscript which holds the key is the extraordinary (as far as we know unique) 'complete poems' – the Black Book which, in an older, kinder world would have pride of place in the National Library of Wales. In a real sense the 'autobiography' T. H. Jones refused to write, this contains, written out in a fair hand that changes little over more than thirty years, virtually all of his poems in chronological order. That this and so much else remains for the biographer/critic is due to Madeleine and to Pat Power, keeper of a family archive. Much, unfortunately, has gone, including all of the post-war letters between Jones and his wife. Sadly departed also are several of the friends and colleagues interviewed by P. B. Jones, most significantly Gwyn Alf Williams, Gwyn Jones, Jim Smith, Mrs Hammonds (T. H. Jones's teacher at primary school) and Donald John Jones, one of his two closest schoolfriends. We very much regret our inability to make contact with T. H. Jones's first love, Clara Jones.

We would like to believe that this biography will stimulate further critical attention from perspectives which we have not chosen or been competent to adopt. A feminist view of this very male man (his particular maleness is an important aspect of his mid-century significance) with his 'chauvinistic' view of women and sexual relationships would be important. There is also the post-colonial angle, which would foreground the fracturing of the complex interaction of history, language and environment which 'made' T. H. Jones and seek to deconstruct the Australian 'lie' of the poor colonial poet who could not return to live in his own country 'like a bloody Englishman'.

T. H. Jones, had he lived, would have been seventy-nine in the year of the millennium, not a great age for an Anglo-Welsh writer of the twentieth century. Not long before his drowning he had arranged a sabbatical year in the USA and projected a return visit to Wales. He might have become – he undoubtedly had ambitions to do so – an icon comparable to Dylan Thomas. He possessed the required qualities, the poetry and the performances. Give him a stage, rostrum, bar or party and he was, at once, vibrantly alive. He had acute critical ability (most evident in his wise and very readable study of Dylan) and academic clout. Even in his cups he was, at the time of his death, writing better than ever; he was on the verge of yet another shifting of shape. Pointless to speculate over what might have been when what actually exists has been so long and so incomprehensibly undervalued.

The authors and publishers are grateful to Madeleine Mitchell for her kind permission to quote from the works of T. H. Jones.

PROLOGUE

Precedents in Unlikely Places

Stand on the summit of the low volcanic hill, Allt-y-clych, 'hill of bells', that 'small hill' which dominated the mind and dreams of the poet for more than thirty years, and you can, on one of those rare clear days in mid-Wales, make out the mass of the Brecon Beacons to the south, and the stark shoulder of Hay Bluff. To the east broods the blackness of the Radnor Forest; the military ranges of Epynt echo to the south-west, and northward the Cambrian Hills are shaped by the man-made waters of the Elan Valley. Ted Richards, in his *Homage* to T. H. Jones, describes this area as:

> the spine of Wales . . . Older than Testaments,
> the first, the Cambrian Rock.
> Here all is spare, sparse, primitive.[1]

Metonymic Allt-y-clych dominates all, a Welsh Ben Bulben under whose bare head the ashes of the poet were scattered and whose 'dictionary of vowels' was always, to the living poet, 'open at Alpha and Omega'. 'Bedraggled with wet fern/And stained with sheep',[2] it held, for him,

> like a threat
> The wild religion and the ancient tongue,
> All the defeated centuries of Wales.[3]

Allt-y-clych is the hill of a legendary bell buried, with an equally legendary treasure, by monks at the very edge of the lands of the Cistercian Abbey of Strata Florida. The hill separates the twin rivers, Chwefri and Hirnant. Draw a seven-mile circle with Allt-y-clych as its centre and you encompass the entire landscape of the actual, and the imagined, childhood of T. H. Jones.

1

Close to the centre are the churches of Llanafanfawr and Llanfihangel Brynpabuan, and the Baptist chapel of Pisgah excoriated by the poet in his satire, 'The Welshman in exile speaks' (13 April 1961), as 'the ugliest building I have ever seen'.[4] Enclosed in the circle are the village of Newbridge-on-Wye and the small market town of Builth, that 'spa of no renown'.[5] The landscape of Llanafanfawr into which T. H. Jones was born on 21 December 1921 is vast and empty; it has rarely figured in recorded history. The pre-Christian circular churchyard contains 'the sepulchral stone of Bishop Afanus . . . the most pious and reverend of the county in his day'.[6] He was the son of Cedig ab Caredig; his feast has been commemorated each year on 13 November since his martyrdom by Vikings early in the sixth century. Giraldus Cambrensis records an apocryphal story of the Lord of the Castle of Radnor in the reign of Henry I entering Llanafan church 'without sufficient caution or reverence'[7] and passing the night there with his hounds:

> Arising early in the morning, according to the custom of the hunters, he found his hounds mad and himself struck blind. After a long, dark and tedious existence he was conveyed to Jerusalem, happily taking care that his inward sight should not in a similar manner be extinguished; and there being accoutred and led to the field of battle on horseback he made a spirited attack upon the enemies of the faith and, being mortally wounded, closed his life with honour.

The legendary bard, Mab y Clochyddyn (sexton's son), was Llanafanfawr's first literary hero. He flourished (obscurely, for little more is known about him) between 1340 and 1380; one of the two poems that survive in *The Red Book of Hergest* is about a young and beautiful girl. Thomas Huet (ob. 1591), first translator into Welsh of the *Book of Revelations*, is buried in the churchyard. At the end of the eighteenth century were born two quintessentially opposite personalities, each in his way truly remarkable: the antiquary, Thomas Price (better known under his bardic name, Carnhuanawc), at Pencaerhelm Farm in 1787, and, at Builth in 1790, Thomas Jeffery Llewelyn Prichard, journalist, poet, novelist and actor.

The exploration of historical antecedents raises important

questions about the extent to which 'biographical' texts 'represent real life'. This study will not attempt any simple equation between even 'obviously biographical' texts and the 'reality' of the writer's life. It is essential to distinguish clearly between lived experience and experience mediated into words, to have always in mind what Jacques Derrida calls 'the paradoxical problem of the border'.[8] T. H. Jones's predecessors in the Llanafan landscape are important because, like him, they straddled significant borders and were interpreted, historically, as defining literary 'boundaries' and embodying contrary forces in the fragmenting cultures of *their* time.

As far as English literary history is concerned, Thomas Price is remembered as a minor character in the life of the proto-feminist and adventurer, Lady Hester Stanhope (1776–1839). On one of her forays into forgetfulness and rurality among the peasantry of Powys, she took him under her wing as one of her 'young men'. In Wales, however, he was recognized, almost as soon as he died, as a passionate advocate of the Welsh language and Welsh culture. He was educated at the Dame School in Llanafan and then by the vicar, Harry Beynon: 'he learned with great facility to spell and read in his native tongue'.[9] Later he helped Lady Charlotte Guest with her translation of the *Mabinogion* and worked to establish a close relationship between Wales and Brittany. Like T. H. Jones, Price acknowledged the influence on his life of his place of birth:

> Brought up as I have been in the remotest parts of the Principality often I do dwell with pleasure upon the recollections of my infancy; when in the winter's night I sat in the circle around the fire under the spacious chimney piece and listened to the songs and traditions of the peasantry, or to the poetry of David ap Gwilym read by the firelight; and if but a harper should chance to visit us happy was the day.[10]

The fine biography of Price by Jane Williams (Ysgafell) is an important point of reference for an understanding of T. H. Jones, born only a mile from Pencaerhelm. She chose to read her subject as a noble savage, a romantically innocent child who grew up to be great and good. Emyr Humphreys places him as: 'Somewhat in the traditional manner of Brân the Blessed . . . possessing the bridge building capacity which has to be cherished in any society that is by nature fissiparous and contentious, given to sectarian arguments, easily divided but not so easily ruled.'[11] He links the triumphs of Price with those of Iolo Morganwg 'in the series of remarkable eisteddfodau held in Abergavenny between 1834 and 1853' and identifies him specifically with the valley of the Usk, which is seen as the last outpost of a lowland Celtic world. 'Carnhuanawc, like Old Iolo, was a myth-maker . . . his platform eloquence moved his eisteddfod audiences to strive to live up to the flattering picture he painted of the Welsh gwerinwr and gweithiwr.'

It was Price and Iolo Morganwg who, under the influence of the German philosopher, Herder, manufactured the myth of an educated Welsh peasantry:

> Show me another country in the world in which the peasantry and the lower classes feel such an interest in literature and intellectual pursuits as the people of Wales do . . . show me another race of men on the face of the earth among whom the labouring classes are the patrons of the press.[12]

Jane Williams promoted the myth that Price was a product of the very peasant culture which he had himself invented.

> Thomas Price was habitually attentive to reading and eager in the acquisition of knowledge of every kind, but he applied himself with particular diligence to the study of Geometry, Astronomy and Mechanics, and appeared to derive great satisfaction from his frequent practise of the self-taught art of drawing.[13]

It is interesting to compare the attitudes of T. H. Jones and Thomas Price to the landscape in which they had spent their formative years a century and philosophical poles apart in their sensibility. Thomas Price, the romantic conservative,

> would contrive to steal away down to the summit of a neighbouring hill or to some secluded dell or memorable spot, where he could enjoy the scenery and the changing aspects of the sky in perfect solitude; sometimes inviting one or other of the most thoughtful from among his school fellows to accompany the quiet ramble and share his pensive pleasures. Standing one day upon a high rock on the brink of the river Chwefri with a

small spy glass in his hand, he lamented audibly that he did not possess a telescope such as Sir Isaac Newton had used with which instead of merely getting a view of Llandrindod he could also have seen the planet Saturn.

From the same rock, the disillusioned socialist, T. H. Jones, would contemplate:

> The sideland farms precariously
> Clinging among the bracken to an old
> And often defeated hope.[14]

and conclude:

> You must believe
> In some impossibly glorious promise
> To mow meadows and milk cows in such
> Unlikely places.[15]

The poem, with its ironic postmodernist echo of Wordsworth's 'Resolution and independence' ('This morning gives us promise of a glorious day'[16]), exemplifies what Raymond Williams calls the privileging of 'mental' over 'manual' labour. T. H. Jones's vision is rather that of Blake's Golgonooza than Price (who poses, having effectively dispossessed his countrymen of their individual voice, as the sole representative of Welshness). Jones insists that 'the landscape never sweetened us, / Nor all our mouthings brought us nearer God.'[17]

Jane Williams is anxious to emphasize Price's rural roots:

> he was fond of all manual arts and would stand watching craftsmen at their work, occasionally practising the handling of the tools with such accuracy of observation and natural dexterity that he acquired these easily and as a pastime the ability to rival their performance.[18]

Her concern is to present Price as simultaneously a peasant and a detached observer of peasant life. His chief characteristics, detectable, she asserts, in most men of genius 'who do not by birth belong to the upper classes of society, and consequently stand unshielded by courtesy and exposed to . . . shafts of envy and resentment', are sanity, unaffectedness, lack of self-absorption and cheerfulness. He owes his ascent to gentility equally to the support of his family, in particular his mother, with her 'discriminative sense', and to the fact that in his youth there was nothing

> in the conduct of his rural companions to counteract the congeniality of his familiar associates. The Welsh peasantry have ever been remarkable for gentle and cheerful suavity of manners, for an acute perception of distinctions and differences and for readiness in yielding respect to every sort and degree of real superiority.[19]

Price's vision of a rural society is mediated by reflection and requiem: the Cymro knew his place, but he had his own language. A century later T. H. Jones would feel the loss of Welsh as deeply significant: 'I am tongue-tied, having not gratitude enough / To speak in my own language or to hold my peace.'[20] Resented by his contemporaries at primary school as 'mouthy'[21] in English, and as a result frequently bullied, Jones was to find Llanafan distinctly less ready to yield respect to his *real superiority*. Not for him 'the spontaneous tribute of esteem and admiration – won from his neighbours'[22] that moved Price to extend 'for ever towards his countrymen . . . a boundless gratitude and self sacrificing love'. Nor would he detect any general veneration 'for every thing belonging to departed centuries'.

His enthusiasm for his 'nation's ancestral monuments' was markedly more ambivalent than that of Thomas Price. For Price the landscape had been specifically, harmoniously and divinely provided for the enrichment of his sensibilities:

> Mountains with their ever changing aspects of majestic serenity, hills clothed with rich woods of varied hues and outline, rivers and brooks with broad cataracts and spouting waterfalls, wild crags and embattled cliffs with their sparkling crystals and antediluvian trilobites, fertile valleys and luxuriant grasses and fields with mineral springs of curative repute, all being round him greatly pampered by Divine Providence to meet the capacities of his soul.[23]

T. H. Jones ('A Welsh poet finds a proper story', 4 October 1964) in contrast reworks Blake's

> I went to the Garden of Love,
> And saw what I never had seen:
> A chapel was built in the midst,
> Where I used to play on the green.
>
> And the gates of this Chapel were shut,
> And 'Thou shalt not' writ over the door . . . [24]

into an account of the existential poet as a fallen Adam obliged to manufacture from words and paper his own paradise:

> In a garden beginning he finds a proper story
> And lets the paper bellow, bark and build it
> For him while he cradles in the treetop in Wales
> His silence and the serpent and the woman
> And all that glory.[25]

The natural landscape of Llanafan which, with its complement of empathetic 'naturals', had miraculously gentrified Thomas Price, worked no such transformation upon his rebellious contemporary, Thomas Jeffery Llewelyn Prichard. History records no meeting between Price and this journalist, bookseller, librarian and strolling player, author of the first Anglo-Welsh novel, *The Adventures and Vagaries of Twm Shon Catti, Descriptive of Life in Wales* (1828),[26] but they were born less than five miles apart and within three years of one another. It is interesting to speculate what this alienated wanderer, disaffected rebel and quintessentially Anglo-Welsh writer might have said to the proudly Welsh literary champion. Did they, perhaps, encounter one another at Lady Augusta Hall's Llanover when Prichard, sporting a grotesque wax substitute for the nose either lost in a theatrical duel or rotted by the pox, was snuffling over his catalogue of the library?

Prichard

saw fame in the distant future and comfort and rest. But his patron, who scrupulously examined his manuscript, began to find fault. He had to choose between historic accuracy or the entire withdrawal of his patron's support. He was not required to make false statements but to slur over facts. And this he would not do.[27]

Did Price, Lady Augusta's trusted adviser and frequent guest, play some part in Prichard's dismissal? 'I was turned adrift', he complains, 'too poor to go on unaided and then began my downward course.'[28] Like T. H. Jones, Prichard and Price were myth-makers, but the rootless Prichard (a T. H. Jones prototype) would have no truck with Price's construction of Welshness. He hated 'Fanatics of Welsh nationality'[29] and had a consuming preference for the English over the Welsh language, asserting, in his introduction to *Heroines of Welsh History*, that the disappearance of Welsh in the cause of 'the greatest of blessings . . . the union of all Britain under one sovereign'[30] would make him quite happy. A quarrel with the fiercely nationalistic Price would have been unavoidable. Nor would his stance have been likely to secure him patronage from a Welsh aristocracy defining its identity in terms of the fictions of Iolo Morganwg.

For Emyr Humphreys, Carnhuanawc's legacy was his success in impressing on the Welsh aristocracy 'the value of the Welsh language as a social lubricant'.[31] Prichard, precursor of a distinctive Anglo-Welsh literature, was expelled from the emergent establishment and, too old and disfigured to find employment in an English-medium Welsh theatre that was in serious decline owing to the antipathy of the Nonconformists, with his *Twm Shon Catti* pirated and earning him nothing, went into a rapid downward spiral. He died a horrific death at World's End, Swansea, tormented and then incinerated by young thugs among a chaos of dirty and dusty books, pamphlets and manuscripts in prose and poetry.[32] Thomas Price met his very different end shortly after Prichard's dismissal from Llanover Hall and was buried with some ceremony; Jane Williams sums up his life with 'He was born to little, lived upon little, grasped at no more than he possessed'.[33]

Son of a labourer, grandson of a shepherd, both of them Welsh-speakers, T. H. Jones had to contend with a sense of guilt and a problem of identity characteristic of the Wales of the twentieth century. It is a remarkable coincidence that the rural backwater which formed him should also have provided the example, consciously drawn upon, of two such contrasting, seminal figures as the 'Cymro', Price, and the 'Anglo', Prichard.

1

1921–1933

Childhood – Some Frosty Farmers Fathered Me to Fare

T. H. Jones's mother, Ruth Teideman, was sixteen years old when she met her future husband, Llewelyn Morgan Jones, in Hannah Street, Porth, south Wales. She had been born on 25 May 1904, one of the sixteen children of Henry and Rhoda Teideman. Her father was a Cockney. His father had been a whaler, and his own life was even more colourful: he ran away from home to join Lord George Sanger's Circus, where he doubled as lion-tamer and bare-fist boxer with a speciality in knocking out kangaroos. An intemperate life on the road ceased to appeal, however, when he met Rhoda Jones, a Welsh-speaking servant girl from a family of Rhondda Salvationists. The couple settled in Barry, where Henry traded in coal 'in a small way'[1] until the Depression put him out of business. According to family tradition, Henry Teideman preferred to avoid his Salvation Army duties and put his boxing skills to more militant use as a bodyguard for the miners' leader, Arthur Cook.

Ruth, an early example of what Gwyn A. Williams referred to as the 'maiden tribute' went 'out to the servants' quarters of the English'[2] in 1917, when she was thirteen years of age. She was employed at a Yorkshire boys' school in Halifax, and it was on her first home holiday from this that she met her future husband. Llewelyn Morgan Jones was the sixth of the ten children of Thomas (1853–1950) and Mary (Mari) Jones (1855–1938) of Cwm Crogau, a 34-acre smallholding tenanted from the Venables Llewelyns of Llysdinam, Newbridge-on-Wye, on the Radnorshire/ Breconshire border. Thomas Jones 'Crogau' was a prodigious 'character': shepherd, rate-collector, deacon of his Baptist chapel, he is recorded on the census of 1871 as 'scholar'. In his later years he taught reading and writing in his second language, English, at

1*d*. per night to those of Pisgah Chapel, Llanafan, and community who wished to learn it; he charged 2*d*. a night for Welsh. A large man in every sense – 'beast big', his grandson was to call him – he was a patriarch who came to symbolize for T. H. Jones much that was best about his childhood:

> proud then
> And prouder now to call myself only
> Young Crogau, old Crogau's grandson.[3]

Thomas's brother-in-law, Daniel Jones of Bwlchciliau, was Llanafan's Bardd Gwlad – the last of his kind.

Llewelyn Morgan Jones (1891–1976) had been born at Old Cwm Crogau, today a vestigial, overgrown ruin in a wildlife reserve high up the Hirnant Valley. By 1891 it had degenerated into an insanitary hovel, and shortly after Llewelyn's birth the family moved down to a newly constructed house, also, confusingly, known as Cwm Crogau. The location, chosen because, being drier, it was more healthy, lies beside the drovers' track which runs up from the rolling country bordering the gentle pastures of the Wye Valley, through the narrow and in parts steep-sided Cwm Hirnant to the Elan Valley.

From boyhood, Llew Jones had much self-belief. He had been fostered out, in the manner of the times, to childless relations at Cefn Gorwedd, taking with him, as a condition of the deal, two shirts; in return he had learned to knit his own stockings, obtained some rudimentary education and acquired independence. T. H. Jones's boyhood friend, Donald Jones, describes him as a man who rather fancied himself,[4] and photographs of him as a young man show a figure remarkably dapper for a mountain shepherd's son. One of these catches him in the driving-seat of a De Dion Boution owned by an encyclopedia salesman who chanced to stop in Builth Wells on his way to the Venables Llewelyns. He appears only slightly out of place in the fine vehicle, nervous in his Sunday best but with the flat cap typically well back off his face. As he hated wearing a hat, this underlines his often-stated ambition to become a chauffeur to the gentry, and there is a painful yearning on his open, countryman's face. The reality was that he lacked the social graces to match his ambition: he was offered a job as farm labourer on the estate.

When war broke out in 1914, Llewelyn, the first of the local young men to volunteer for military service, joined the Glamorgan Yeomanry. Here was an opportunity to escape the servitude, crushing boredom and total obscurity of menial toil in north Breconshire. Because of the family tradition of folk poetry, his enlistment was honoured in the *The County Times and Brecon and Radnorshire Gazette* with a praise-poem, a piece of jingoistic doggerel which appeared under the pseudonym, Afan, and was almost certainly composed by Uncle Daniel Jones:

> Our friend The Old Cwmcrogau,
> Has reared a gallant son;
> Who joined the Territorials
> To fight the cruel Hun.
> This brave and sturdy farmer
> Has power and a will;
> So on a stone will carve his name
> Upon the Gorllwyn Hill.[5]

Deacon Daniel Jones rejects the pacifism of the Nonconformist, Henry Richard, who had declared that 'every war is contrary to the spirit of Christ', for something close to Lloyd George's speech to the London Welsh the following month, a speech that was so influential in persuading the rural Welsh, as the poem puts it, to stop 'slacking, talking' and 'learning Welsh' and leave their cosy hearths to fight for Britain 'as Welshmen did of yore'. It is (perhaps inadvertently) realistic enough to visualize the almost certain death of the volunteers, for which it offers the conventional solace of 'a patriot's grave' and the honour of a bardic epitaph.

Afan's verses did not galvanize other Llanafan boys to follow Llewelyn Jones to glory and the grave – it was not until Lloyd George became Minister of Munitions and specifically Welsh and Welsh-speaking regiments were created that recruitment became, in the eyes of the government, satisfactory. They were, however, moved 'to try their hands as poets for the first time' and in *The County Times* that summer, poem challenged poem in traditional bardic combat. Llanafan Lad's effort was accorded the crown:

> All honour to Cwm Crogau's son
> The shepherd from the hill

> Who readily answered England's call
> With a determined will.
> Like him the boys of Afan's hill
> Will join the fighting line
> To do their share for hearth and home
> Where England's banners shine.

Here is the wild optimism characteristic of Britain at this time, different from that of England only in its emphasis on the heroic Welsh as saviours, in the manner, presumably, of Henry Tudor's army.

Llewelyn Jones saw service in Egypt, Palestine and France, but we know nothing of his experiences or his feelings about them because, like many veterans of that brutal conflict, he refused to discuss the matter. He returned home cured of wanderlust and, ambitions crushed, made his last journey of significance – the fifty miles from Llanafan to the Rhondda to find work and a wife.

To the inexperienced Ruth Teideman, Llewelyn Jones not only was physically attractive, but appeared to offer salvation from her own drudgery; he was also romantically different by virtue of his experience and background. She looked forward to the move to Llanafan because, for members of the mining communities, it was the holiday country in which, at Llangammarch, Llanwrtyd and Builth Wells, in cheap guest-house or tented village, the miners and their families spent their single week of freedom. Jack Jones, in the first volume of his autobiography, *Unfinished Journey*, described pre-1914 Builth as:

> the little Mid Wales spa to which colliers went to get an annual clearing out of the coal dust swallowed during the year. A seven day night and morning course was supposed to clear a collier out as clean as a whistle, but it wasn't for that I cycled there. There were attractions in addition to the waters, racing, purging and soothing. Lovely country, a clean unpolluted river, home made bread and home cured bacon, impromptu concerts in the moonlight, girls on holiday who liked a bit of fun . . .[6]

Jack Jones met, married and buried his beloved Laura at Builth.

Whatever dreams Ruth had were soon stifled in the isolated hill country above Builth where Thomas Henry Jones was born six months later, on 21 December 1921, into a tiny farmhouse already overcrowded with Welsh-speaking grandparents and aunts. Family mythology has it that he was delivered by the legendary Llanafan midwife remembered even today for smoking her clay pipe throughout her deliveries, but the prosaic truth is that the wife of a neighbouring farmer assisted at the birth. Ruth suffered badly from what we recognize today as post-natal depression, and gave serious thought to escaping back to south Wales.

Llewelyn Jones obtained employment as a roadman with Breconshire County Council. His disappointed ambitions led him to drink; like Iago, the fictionalized version of his father created by T. H. Jones in his seminal rites-of-passage story, 'Home', he was physically violent towards his wife. In real life he ill-used his son also. On one occasion Ruth left him, but he soon persuaded (or blackmailed) her into returning. Llewelyn felt trapped by his marriage and disappointed with a wife too soft and gentle, 'biddable as a shepherd's bitch'.[7] Certainly his son's poems frequently criticize women for these characteristics (in real life it was strong, independent, artistic women who attracted T. H. Jones's love). Slowly, however, Ruth came to terms with her circumstances, working hard to keep the family together on a very small income. Llewelyn handed his wages over to his parents each Friday, and family rows were frequent when (like Walter Morel) he spent some of the money on drink. Ruth, denied any vestige of economic independence, was trapped in the middle and it was some time before she became reconciled to her husband and his family through her children. Three daughters were born: Brenda (1924) at Ivy Cottage, and Myra (1926) and Valerie (1932) at Cwm Crogau.

Cwm Crogau in the 1920s was a typical hill smallholding. Subsistence living could be supported on a tiny flock of sheep, a cow, pigs and chickens only if supplemented by a regular wage. The survival of his growing family trapped Llewelyn Jones in menial employment. On winter evenings there was little to look forward to in returning to the candle- and oil-lit home (mains power did not reach Llanafan until the late 1950s). There was farmwork to be had in summer: extra money could be earned from hedging, 'tushing' timber and ploughing, the last a pleasure as he had the knack of it. Amenities were few. The lavatory was some distance from the house, set over the Crogau stream which runs down into the Hirnant. Water came from a well so deficient in iron that Ruth developed a goitre that was cured only by the sinking of a sweeter one.

A pair of photographs taken in 1926 reveals a striking contrast between husband and wife. Llew stands between two friends, very much 'one of the boys', rubbing his hands, the centre of attention. The companion snap shows Ruth with her children. She is at work, not play. Bucket in hand, she feeds the chickens. A rough tunic covers a dress that has seen better days. Her sleeves are rolled up, her hair lank, her neck goitred. She refuses her face to the camera. Young Harri, foregrounded, wears a smile which mirrors that of his father.

Ruth's daily life, though never easy, did become more tolerable over the years. If she was but gradually and grudgingly accepted by her in-laws, neighbours quickly appreciated her Valleys warmth and hardworking ways. Her routine included the weekly trudge to Llanfihangel Church, two miles away, to collect groceries from the delivery wagon of Down's Stores of Builth. On Fridays she rode the family pony eight miles to Llandrindod to sell the small-holding's meagre surplus of butter, eggs and vegetables. She was so badly depressed by Myra's birth and the continuing coldness of her in-laws that she returned with the children to Porth, whence only Brenda's homesickness brought about an early return (Harri, it seems, had felt quite at home in the Valleys atmosphere). Poor though they were, the children were not without toys – but these came from their mother's parents, not, as in 'Home', from their father's.

In the 1920s the Hirnant Valley was not the 'hole in the middle of Wales' portrayed by Harri Webb in the 1960s.[8] At Upper Cwm, the farm nearest to Cwm Crogau, the Davies family had boys of T. H. Jones's age. Glyn, a sensitive, musical boy, today the last Welsh-speaking native of Llanafan, recalls that T. H. Jones did not mix readily. Glyn and his brothers preferred Brenda 'because we did not have a sister of our own'.[9] The young T. H. Jones's best friend and role model was his grandfather, Old Crogau. Every Monday the boy would get up early to catch Bess, the pony, so that the old man could ride to Builth market where he would spend the day collecting rents at the Swan Hotel, socializing at the sales and drinking. 'Old Crogau' was a local legend and his grandson was honoured to become 'Young Crogau' – a title which, except in the pre-war poem, had bypassed its rightful recipient, Llewelyn. The short story, 'My grandfather would have me be a poet', is an extraordinary fictionalizing of the relationship between the seven-year-old boy and his grandfather.

Although Llewelyn Jones was not a religious man, the combined influence of the Salvationist Ruth, the grandparents and Uncle Daniel Jones sent the children to Pisgah Baptist Chapel. The preacher, Revd Davies, was nicknamed 'Jelly Belly' because of his habit of visiting parishioners at meal times. His major contribution to divinity was not subtlety of theological discourse but volume of voice: his hell-fire sermons were said to be capable of penetrating the chapel walls to convert any literal and metaphorical lost sheep that had strayed into the graveyard. The Jones children observed the traditional Sabbath as a statutory day of rest and they attended at least one service as well as Sunday school. T. H. Jones and his sisters became talented performers on the chapel circuit, and he seems to have enjoyed the society which chapel offered.

John Berger (in the essay 'Understanding a photograph') suggests that 'photographs bear witness to a human choice being exercised in a given situation. A photograph is a result of the photographer's decision that it is worth recording that this particular event or that particular object has been seen.'[10] The Jones family photographer was Auntie Maggie, unsympathetically portrayed in 'Home' but remembered by T. H. Jones's sisters with affection. In later years, when she lived at Crossroads Cottage, on the road from Newbridge to Beulah, the girls never failed to call on their way home from school. She became their favourite aunt and a focus of Llanafan folklore (the Welsh National Museum holds in its archives an audio recording of her childhood reminiscences in her native Welsh). Her Box Brownie snaps of T. H. Jones's early years may not be works of art, but they are worth a biographer's attention because, as Berger puts it, even the most banal of photographs may explain a message, 'make the photographer's decision transparent and comprehensible'.[11]

Aunt Maggie's record opens with a blurred snap[12] of T.H. and Brenda Jones at Ivy Cottage, Llanafan, to which the family had moved so that Llewelyn's elder brother Jack and his new bride could live at Cwm Crogau. Harri and Brenda, tiny figures, are dwarfed by a broken gate; washing hangs on the line in the background; the garden is overgrown and the steps on which they stand are badly in need of repair. The dispossessed children are poorly dressed and Aunt Maggie has caught them *au naturel*, just as they were on the day of her visit from Cwm Crogau. In sharp contrast is the posed photograph taken by the excellent Abery Studio of Builth.[13] Here the children are in their Sunday clothes against a painted backdrop: Brenda's hair has been carefully combed and tied with a bow and her white frock is clean, if not pressed; five-year-old Harri fixes the camera with an apprehensive stare and his right arm is protectively around his sister's shoulders. What these two photographs have in common are the expressions, and the boots – the children possessed but the one pair each and Harri's are noticeably muddy even in the studio.

Jack's wife, Annie, hated Cwm Crogau as bitterly as Ruth. The couple soon moved to Hirwaun. With their departure and with Mari now blind, Ruth was persuaded back to the smallholding. She had spent her meagre savings on renovations to Ivy Cottage, 'Old Crogau' having promised to make good the loss. He never did so, however, and her situation was exacerbated when the spinster aunt, Maggie, and the unemployed bachelor uncle, Fred, moved in to take advantage of Llewelyn's wages and her industry. A third photograph, the first one to be taken at Cwm Crogau, shows Ruth, Harri and Brenda with Mari, their grandmother, in a frozen field of broken earth dusted with snow. Landscape dominates – the human figures disappear into the powerfully foregrounded frozen earth, the low, fecund, feminine hill ('like Mam's breasts, homely and tremendous'[14]), the flimsy barn. In 'A refusal to write autobiography',[15] T. H. Jones would write 'Nothing is more difficult for me than to get any really accurate picture of the boy I was among those hills' and 'Home' can be seen as a kind of snapshot of that boy.

From 1927 to 1933 T. H. Jones attended Llanafan Primary School. The five-mile walk from Cwm Crogau can be traced today through a landscape which, though it has seen some significant changes over the sixty years since last he trod that way, still retains something of the wild bleakness variously recalled in so many poems – 'broken landscape of regrets'[16] or 'loved sky and humped hills'[17] or 'cold splendour';[18] the 'beginning garden'[19] or 'improbable land'.[20] Cwmchwefri is now a timeshare complex until recently overshadowed by a dense conifer plantation, but if you follow the footsteps of the schoolboy along the poorly surfaced drove-road you soon climb out onto unaltered moorland. To reach Llanafan village, you follow the bridle path, the 'Rhiw Ierthu', up through waist-high gorse to Cwmchwefri Rocks where

> In the cold splendour of that rocky place
> I killed a rabbit with a stick, and stood,
> Exultant, virile, dominant,
> And ten years old.[21]

It was a favourite place, and a savage one:

> I have been walking above Cwmchwefri
> Where the hills slant sharply into rock
> And nothing, not even a kite, hopes to live.[22]

A steep descent takes you to the Chwefri Valley and along the now-metalled lane to where Aunt Emily once kept the Post Office at Crossroads. He would sometimes take the long way round and call, but Emily Jones, though she preferred him to his sisters, was not noted for her hospitality. Usually he took the short-cut down the steeply sloping path through deciduous woodland to the footbridge. The badly potholed track then ascends between high blackthorn hedges to Brynieuau Farm and follows the ridge to the Llanafan Road. The final part of the journey is considerably changed: featureless new agricultural bungalows with satellite dishes and the much-widened B4686 have coarsened the approach to the school, which remains relatively unmodified as the Llanafan Community Centre. T. H. Jones recalled it (two rooms, three teachers, eighty pupils sitting three to a desk) without affection:

> I miched from school occasionally too, but not very often because of Proud Salop or schoolie . . . a man who walked always looking up at the heavens, and taught with a hazel stick, thick as my wrist, which he applied impartially to hand, back or arms. His blows bruised and crippled, so that it did not pay to mich from school. For one exercise he would promote a young child to the top standard, and next day send him down again with a beating for writing untidily or making a blot. I hated Proud Salop and his school more than I hated our snuffling little

preacher and his Sunday school, because I had been allowed to break away from the latter, but I was a rabbit in the last rows of corn before that red faced bully from Shropshire.[23]

Ethel Lewis, who taught Standard One from 1928, remembered the bullying Mr Edwards as a physically big, imposing man with a 'little twittering wife'.[24] Born in 1911 at Eppynt Villa, Garth, Ethel was the daughter of a Llanafan farming family. Her father had farmed Dolfallen until an injury made this impossible and he became Relieving Officer for the Builth Board of Guardians, administrators of the busy Builth Workhouse which served the many tramps and itinerant workers who travelled the Llandovery–Welsh Hay (Hay-on-Wye) route into and out of England. A very intelligent scholarship girl at Builth County School, she had upset Rhys Thomas, its headmaster, by failing to persuade her father to let her go with her cousin to Swansea Teacher Training College. She confirms the atmosphere imposed by Mr Edwards:

All the children bar a few had their dinner at school, they munched their sandwiches and Mrs Evans, the other teacher, and myself made cocoa for them. Well, they would be chatting away quite happily, then Mr Edwards would come through and you could hear a pin drop; we would stop eating and talking immediately. We were all afraid of him . . .

For a short time Ethel Lewis was T. H. Jones's teacher: 'He was a scrappy writer – it was like a spider going up the page. He was always in trouble with Mr Edwards for not doing tidy hand-writing. I thought, "How ridiculous!" because Harri's ideas were so good, so handwriting didn't matter.' He suffered under the 'Proud Salopian' for the first three years of his school-life:

I learned to read, write, do sums and to recite a long fatuous poem called 'The Leak in the Dyke'. Books and words and stories were, however, beginning to fascinate me though I had only a meagre diet on which to feed. We had four books at home: the Bible, and Sankey and Moody . . . the *Pilgrim's Progress* which I liked . . . and Mrs Beeton which was exotic and unfailing of delight . . . [25]

These books were the staple fare for all the Jones children, and the youngest sister, Pat, still has the Bible and the very battered Mrs Beeton in her possession. D. H. Lawrence, a strong influence on T. H. Jones's early short stories, also knew every word of the Salvation Army tunes and the Sankey and Moody revivalist songs, wrote about the importance of hymns in a man's life, and explained that he had 'been familiar with Apocalyptic language and Apocalyptic image . . . because I was sent to Sunday School and to Chapel, to the Band of Hope and to Christian Endeavour, and was always having the Bible read at me'.[26]

T. H. Jones came to hate school, but luckily Edwards retired in 1929 and was replaced by Mr Swan. 'He was a very good teacher', says Ethel Lewis, 'and broadened the children's outlook.' He introduced football, netball and cricket and even tried to create a swimming pool. T. H. Jones's younger sister, who also attended school in Mr Swan's time, remembers sledging in the winter – the whole school would go down to the frozen Chwefri, where the older boys would pull the young girls across the ice. 'Proud Salop' had discouraged the speaking of Welsh by the few children whose first language it was; Swan was merely indifferent. Ethel Lewis taught 'a few Welsh airs', but cannot recall Welsh being spoken in the playground; she remembers that Llanafan had been a Welsh-speaking area in her own youth. Her great grandfather, the famous preacher, David Williams, had been minister of Troedrhiwdaler Chapel, where services continued wholly in Welsh until his successor, D. A. Griffiths, introduced a monthly English service, 'but I have the family Bible of my mother's family, the "Tynrallts", and although it is a Welsh Bible, all the entries for the christenings are in English.' Troedrhiwdaler Chapel was a focus – the only one – for Welsh culture well into the 1920s and retained a resident preacher until the late 1980s.

T. H. Jones did not 'mich' school while Mr Swan was head-master. Indeed, assisted by the Breconshire scheme that gave the children a half-holiday on one Friday each month if attendance targets had been met, the attendance of all children was excellent:

Mr Swan sold the idea to the children. They would come whatever they felt like. But Harri was a bit of a loner, a withdrawn child. His ideas were so much in advance of the others'. He wasn't thinking the same things they were thinking.

An important feature which served him well was the termly library box. Ethel Lewis remembers the library boxes starting when she was a pupil at Garth School – 'it was wonderful'. At Llanafan too the arrival of the box was an event and T. H. Jones seems to have read widely. In his Writers of Wales monograph, Julian Croft correctly recognizes the significance of these books, but he is wrong to accept the poet-in-exile's boast that he read Prescott's *History of the Conquest of Mexico* at the age of nine – in fact this book would figure significantly in his reading as a sixth-former at Builth Wells County School.

A typical day at Llanafan School went as follows:

> Assembly with lots of hymns. Then we started the classes and our main topic was 'nature'. We would take a particular plant or animal as the main feature and work around it for the week. Mr Swan introduced cookery. We got an oil stove, and on Fridays we taught cookery. I was astounded that only a few years ago a lady who helped my aged aunt said to me, 'I've been making some cakes and I'm still using the recipe book you gave us at Llanafan School.' Mr Swan said to us, 'Try to introduce a bit of variety into the children's diet' (which largely consisted of 'stump', and, of course, the constantly-topped-up boiled pot of soup or 'cawl').

Both T. H. Jones and his sisters had great respect for Mr Swan.

In 1932, while travelling by train to Builth, Ruth learned from Tom Williams, who had replaced 'Old Crogau' as shepherd on the Llysdinam estate, that she had become homeless. Without informing her, her in-laws had given notice on their tenancy to move into a less remote house, Rhiwolau. Llewelyn went to see Sir Charles Venables and in consideration of his war service the latter arranged for Trefelin, a small, landless cottage on the Beulah–Newbridge road, to be renovated for the family. Their last child, Patricia, was born there in 1934. Although there was at first no money for furniture, Ruth and the children were happy with the move: she was free at last from uncongenial in-laws and had supportive neighbours nearby; they enjoyed a wider community of friends and the inclination of the family away from the ascetic hill people towards the more liberated lowlands and the intimate cosiness of Newbridge. Not that their life seemed at all easy to an outsider from a higher social class – T. H. Jones's wife, Madeleine, would recollect in 1965 that:

> Ruth worked so hard when the children were young carrying water up the slope from the brook to fill the copper, wringing out everything by hand (it was only about 1946 when she had the luxury of a wringer and later tapped water in the kitchen) and trying to dry the clothes in competition with the seemingly endless rain. All the cooking was done on the fire, even the first kettle of water for a brew of tea could only be boiled once Dad lit the fire. All the labour saving devices came later. A wonderful woman and the nicest Mother-in-law one could wish for.[27]

For a while Jones, scrawny in body and pale of complexion, was taunted with the nickname 'Harry Palethorpe' (after the famous brand of sausages). School was still at Llanafan and the walk remained three miles each way. During his last years at primary school he was so seriously bullied that the log-book records the names of boys thrashed for tormenting him – and there remained a perception, amongst those members of the community who chose to remember him, that he was an unpopular boy who grew up to take revenge in his writing (Eastwood retained similar notions of D. H. Lawrence). Glyn Davies, however, who, in spite of his natural intelligence and musical talent did not go on to secondary education, is more charitable, recalling as more characteristic an incident on the cricket field when T. H. Jones, dismissed as usual to field on the boundary, became so lost in daydreams that he was hit in the face by the ball and knocked unconscious.

Fictions of Childhood

It was at secondary school that T. H. Jones discovered his talent for fiction. We can begin to trace the writer's transmutation of biographical reality as early as his publications in *The Wyeside*, the magazine of Builth Wells County School. 'The Welsh hills', published when he was in the sixth form, is already shaping *The story told in the beginning garden*.[1] The landscape and people of Llanafan are prettified in the manner of a Georgian belles-lettrist. Hills 'look down with a smile on the Welshman's home'; from Allt-y-Clych 'one can see many miles of pleasant countryside around'; the 'fine men' who farm there 'smell cleanly of the honest earth' and 'have their simple and unswerving belief in God'.[2] The short stories 'Home', 'My grandfather would have me be a poet' and 'A day at the seaside', all of them written in the unhappy 1950s, and a number of poems, many of them written near the end of his life, also fictionalize the experience of childhood, but the mature writer transforms his material in the opposite direction, consciously shunning the 'rehearsed response'.

'Home'[3] opens on the day when Hannah, unable any longer to endure her brutal husband and spiteful in-laws, makes a final effort to escape. The previous day, pay-day at the sawmill where he works, Iago, her husband, has failed to return home for his evening meal because he is boozing in the village pubs. Hannah and the in-laws ('Gransir', 'Grannie' and 'Auntie') wait up for him. They are all 'tense' and 'irritable', the women quarrel, the grandfather shouts them down. When Iago returns, there is a public quarrel between husband and wife; when they retire she reproaches him until, brutal in his drunkenness, he beats her and throws her out of bed. She looks back on her courtship, her young illusions and the reality of her marriage. She has long given up her early dream that a home of their own would give her a chance to reform her husband, but has now come to feel that her son, Huw, is being alienated from her: it is this that drives her, the following day, to find an empty cottage, arrange to rent it and borrow a 'gambo' (two-wheeled cart) to move her furniture. She is too late: although Iago does not oppose the move, Huw bursts into hysterical weeping that neither she nor anyone else can stop. She holds out against him until the last box – her son's toys and books – is being loaded; then, when the hysterical child says, 'I'm not coming . . . I'm stopping with Gransir', she gives in, crying, 'I canna go. The boy's breaking my heart.'

T. H. Jones's fictional account of his parents' marriage and his own young reactions to it, based in part on what his mother had confided to him, is obviously influenced by D. H. Lawrence's *Sons and Lovers*. Hannah takes her name from the street where Ruth Teideman chanced to meet and fall in love with Llewelyn Jones:

> It had been the end of the war and Cwmbach like every other mining village had been for a while both gay and prosperous. Hannah was seventeen, short, fair, not quite plump, very ready to be amused, very ready to be warm and loving to everybody.

He is given the name Iago which, although its significance is less sinister in Wales[4] than England, appears significant:

> [Iago] was very dark and quiet, a man from the mountains, not at ease in the brightness and colour of the towns. He had been a boy just starting to plough four years ago when some obscure impulse had made him volunteer; he was a man older than he should have been. He talked very little and hardly at all about his war experiences. This gave him an air of reserve and mystery

and Hannah 'loved him from the moment she saw him. Two days after their first meeting she almost welcomed his rough seduction.' Three months later, pregnant, 'She made him marry her and they departed for the hills . . . she had given away her youth.' Taking, as Lawrence had, his mother's side, T. H. Jones presents the court-ship as loveless on the man's side and self-deceit on that of the inexperienced young woman.

Hannah, like Gertrude Morel, soon becomes disillusioned. She manages to cope with the disappointment of a wedding for which neither her husband nor her family show much enthusiasm: 'Despite the lack of colour and romance and communal emotion at her wedding, Hannah had felt happy with her dark mysterious husband who was taking her up to his own country and whose child was excitingly alive beneath her heart', but the 'loneliness and the bareness and the silence of the hill-country terrified her from the beginning' and she finds herself living with in-laws she comes to hate, in an overcrowded small house, claustrophobic, chapel-dominated and Welsh-speaking. The neighbours are 'withdrawn, clannish, sly', and she

> an exile, an outsider, not welcomed or wanted. Iago remained mysterious and remote: his reserved silence became sullenness, and the brutality with which he had first taken her became the norm of his behaviour. His drinking had begun early in their life together, even before the child was born. She was six months pregnant when he first struck her.

At first, Hannah dreams that 'if only Iago and she could live on their own with Huw, away from the internecine bitterness of the overcrowded house on the hill, she might by love and patience soften and reform her husband', but she soon realizes that he will never change and, like Mrs Morel, transfers her hopes of happiness to her son – and is robbed by her husband's family of even that consolation.

In fictionalizing his parents' marriage, his boyhood self, his paternal grandparents and his Auntie Maggie, Jones as author clearly sympathizes with Hannah. Jones as Huw, however, rejects her in favour of Gransir. This provides us with a starting-point for an exploration of the complex issue (important because it is habitually and consciously foregrounded by the mature writer himself) of 'truth' and 'fiction' in his work. In the unpublished essay, 'A refusal to write autobiography', roughly contemporary with 'Home', he affects to exclaim:

> Those writers who confidently, with assurance recall and depict their childhoods amaze me. I am reluctant to call them liars or even imaginative reconstructors. All I will say is this: their childhoods were different from mine, their lives too were different from mine . . . my childhood, actually as it was, is as unreal to me as Alice's.

Reality, in T. H. Jones's view as in that of the declared post-modernists, is made of multiple and often irreconcilable realities.

The framing narrative in 'Home' is the search for a community of discourse, an issue foregrounded by Hannah's inability to employ the home-language of her in-laws. Hannah has not found it and, within the artifice of the story, never can. The Jones figure, Huw, 'who could not imagine and did not desire a life anywhere else', has sensed it and chooses it rather than to go with his mother. The Ruth figure, Hannah, is not the well-scrubbed controlling manager of her family and bustling community organizer remembered by her contemporaries, but the woman-as-victim-and-martyr archetype, 'shapeless in a sacking apron, hair stretched in worrying rolls across her strained and sweating face'; Auntie (Maggie, in real life an ambiguous figure) is 'maliciously absent . . . watching that the mother took nothing belonging to the family from the house'. Iago (Llewelyn) is also characterized by physical absence.

The representation here of T. H. Jones's grandfather is quite different from both the fact and a number of other fictions. In 'My grandfather going blind' he is a noble figure:

> When the cataracts came down, he remembered
> Verses, grew grumpier, but did not cry or break.
> His bulk sagged, shrunk a little; he would have liked
> The comforting presence of Mari, even as she was . . .
> Was sometimes peevish, liked to talk in Welsh,
> Was for the most part content with his old dog,
> Blind, deaf, rheumatic, and pretty daft,
> His firm stick, strong pipe, his memories – and me.[5]

The poem was written ten years later, in the very different social and emotional framework of Australia, and is coloured by the *hiraeth* of exile: this grandfather is reminiscent of Wordsworth's Michael,[6] he possesses the virtues of frugality, patience and perseverance. In the story, 'Gransir' is a coded male opposition to Hannah, and his heavy drinking, admired elsewhere as a sign of machismo, is linked to hypocrisy: 'with the fretful righteousness of one whom age has now limited to drinking bouts once a month and who in all his sixty-eight years never tasted beer on the Sabbath', he accuses his son of 'drinking like a pig'.

T. H. Jones aims at a triple narrative perspective: the antipathy of Hannah, the moral contract sensed by the growing Huw and the dislocation of the man who once was that boy and is now an unhappy, exiled middle-class teacher of naval apprentices in Portsmouth. The writer's ego is divided between the remembered child and the remembering creator and this, as Freudian critics have pointed out, permits the rational ego to observe the experiencing self and shape what it recollects into art. Mari, the grandmother, is neither the 'tiny woman in a big chair, / Talking mostly to her small boy sons' of 'My grandfather going blind' nor the person eulogized in 'My grandmother died in the early hours of the morning' (10 December 1961):

> A little woman was dead, a little old woman
> Who had long confused me with her youngest son.
> I did not even think, how small she looks.
> And certainly had no thoughts for her life of labour,
> Nor wondered how she who had always been old to me
> Had once been whatever beauty the world has
> To the old man I now led out of the room . . . [7]

She is 'softened by age except in malice to her daughter-in-law' and she mumbles 'the bitter comfort that all men were beasts anyway'. Granny and Auntie represent the closed, indifferent hill community, and Hannah would rather 'be struck by her husband than . . . be verbally tormented by the women of his family'. She appeals to Gransir, but 'Shut your mouth,' he said. 'Quarrelling like crows.'

Huw is more comfortable with the community he knows than the imponderable new home over the hill. In the real world the new home would have meant the warmth of the extended family at Porth, the energy of the industrial valleys and the matriarchy of 'Mam'; the grown man remained fascinated with what the child might have experienced. The poetry sees Llanafan as a place of penance – 'Thorn', for example, one of the last poems, images the poet as the twisted tree punished by the winds, 'The thrashed and lonely thorn'.

According to T. H. Jones's sisters, it was his Uncle Dan who prophesied that he would be a famous poet. Daniel Jones Bwlchciliau is memorialized in one of the most powerful and mythopoeic of the poems which comprise the 'Hiraeth' section of *The Beast at the Door* (1963).

> See Daniel wear the sky
> Like a sodden overcoat, the earth weighing down
> His feet, as he wrestles again with an old text
> And wonders why his sheep are so obstinate about dying.[8]

According to those who knew him, the real Daniel was a cultural dinosaur on the verge of extinction, a hill-farmer who spoke in Welsh long after the frontier of Englishness had pushed to the west of his home. The poem mythologizes him into an Old Testament prophet:

> Sometimes, picking stones off an old, thin field,
> Or riding, wet to the waist, through the bracken
> In search of old, thin sheep scarce worth the saving,
> His mind would be lifted from perverse sons and daughters,
> His head kestrelled in space towards Allt-y-clych,
> And he felt he could prophesy like Isaiah.
> Or he would see somewhere towards Abergwesyn
> The city that had no need of the sun, neither
> Of the moon, to shine in it.[9]

No poem that centres on a poet/peasant/hill-farmer can avoid what J. P. Ward calls 'the figure rooted in landscape',[10] that voiceless archetype of R. S. Thomas's early work. Many of the poems in *The Stones of the Field* (1946) and *Song at the Year's Turning* (1955) present the peasant as a solitary contemplated from above by a poet physically, emotionally and culturally distanced. T. H. Jones's poems in this kind are a riposte to Thomas: although 'In memoriam' (9 August 1962) sets off from the epigraph 'Where you may see how God blessed husbandry in this land', it opens with the sharp contradiction, 'But not in mine'. R. S. Thomas habitually begins with the pointed finger, the act of observation – 'Ah, but you should see Cynddylan on a tractor' is the best-known example – and goes on to view his specimen through the framing device of a break in the clouds, or under a star-filled sky. But in T. H. Jones's poetry the poet is, like T. H. Jones himself, *of* not *in* (himself born into) a landscape which is a version of his heart's country. The reader is thrust into the presence of either the peasant-as-worker/poet or that of a child threatened/terrified by his surroundings. In a land where the struggle to scrape a living is always predominant, the persona is often collective, a family bending their backs, for example:

> – You have to plough the furrows I have ploughed,
> Or pick the stones off the bitter fields
> Before they're fit for ploughing, all day, all day
> Or lift potatoes until your back is breaking.[11]

Daniel 'wears' the sky, believing himself to be at ease with/in possession of his environment, but in reality it, in an opposite sense, wears him: its soddenness weighs him down even as he lifts his eyes to the hills of his salvation. Riding his pony through bracken which soaks him to the waist, he searches for worthless sheep as an escape from the perverse youth of his family, 'the cramped house' with 'too many / Sons and daughters' in it. Pertinacity in uncomfortable physical labour sets his mind free to 'kestrel in space' or visualize, beyond Abergwesyn, the New Jerusalem. Daniel would not have welcomed a more 'blessed husbandry' because it is only in the sweat for survival that post-lapsarian Adam can explore the boundaries of self and approach God. 'Boundaries', writes Keith Tester,[12] 'make sure that the human does not have to confront the ambivalent sublimity of the infinite space of our worlds.' Boundaries enable us to define meanings and, making yet another attempt to define his own experience, T. H. Jones found a paradigm in the hymn-writer, poet and visionary who 'Dared to be a Daniel, / Dared to stand alone' and who throve on an 'unprofitable husbandry' that included the siring of so many children.

This late Australian period poem seeks intertextual resonances (T. H. Jones strongly believed that 'poems talk to poems') in the writing of Puritan New England. It concludes with the poet identifying himself with his uncle. Even 'stones off . . . sour fields'[13] can be emblems of hope to the exile, and imaginatively reliving the old man's physical experience might enable the poet, in his own old age, to continue to 'Lift my head to sudden visions and prophesyings'.[14]

In 'My grandfather would have me be a poet', written at Portsmouth in the 1950s, the grandfather is not Old Crogau, but a synthesis of him and Daniel:

> Two days after I was born my Grandfather came down from the
> hills to have a look at me. 'Call him Gwilym,' he said, 'he's going
> to be a poet.' My father, who had hoped to make me as good a
> poacher as himself, spat his disappointment into the fire, and my
> mother sighed at this abrupt dissipation of her vision of me as a
> preacher . . .

This curt minimalizing of the parental contribution is biographically unfair, though it is true that the young T. H. Jones did not
enjoy a close relationship with his father, but it is significant that
poet and preacher are thrown into opposition. In T. H. Jones's
world, you might entertain, or entertain yourself with, the idea of
ordination,[15] but you knew that you could not be an R. S. Thomas.

Gwilym grows up 'slim and kindly neglected and full of endless
tremble of wonder. For five or six years I confused my Grandfather with God.' The Old Crogau figure of the fiction does not
live with the family, but in his own shepherd's house at the top of
the valley. He is no deacon, but an elemental force – 'I found that
he was bigger than the mountains and moved about more than
they did' – an unregenerate pagan diametrically opposed to 'God
incarcerated in the dirty little white chapel which smelled of soap,
lamp oil and deacons, and was always uncomfortable and cold,
even in summer . . . my grandfather was magnificent and free like
the wind about the hill tops'. From this grandfather the child
learns, symbolically at the age of seven, to understand 'the triple
intoxication of knowledge, power and freedom of choice. I
preferred my grandfather, who smelled of sheep and tobacco and
sometimes of drink, to God cooped in Bethel.'

In the fiction the boy and the old man are allies in the
glorification of God-free liberty while everyone else is 'cooped up
like silly sheep with God in the Chapel down below. We were
sinners and loved each other and the mountains were ours.' They
seal their brotherhood in potato whisky which makes Gwilym long
to 'knock down the bloody preacher' and sends the old man to
sleep. The transformation of biographical fact is so radical here
that a critic must take care to avoid over-reaction. No writer of
fiction can altogether avoid an autobiographical element, just as
no reader can avoid the temptation to take too much of the fiction
as fact. Where the writer – again one thinks of D. H. Lawrence –
operates rather close to verifiable reality it is only too easy to

misinterpret his art. Post-structural critical theory is helpful here in its suggestion that there are as many versions of a text as there are readers to read it.

'My grandfather would have me be a poet' has many identifiable departures from verifiable fact. 'The old man could neither read nor write': Old Crogau taught these skills. 'He knew much Welsh and English verse by heart and could compose in both languages': biographically this was Uncle Dan – Old Crogau enjoyed reciting poetry and coached his grandchildren in their eisteddfod pieces, but he was no poet. 'He had sixteen legitimate children, whom he tyrannized or neglected according to whim': Thomas Jones Crogau had ten legitimate children and no illegitimate ones, and neither neglected nor tyrannized them. And he was far from being an 'enemy of the chapel', let alone a 'proclaimed' one. Old Crogau fascinated his grandson because he was a character, albeit a more conventional one: he had had the reputation, in his youth, of 'possessing the strength of a young horse, the neatest fashion of slitting a pig's throat and a barrel's capacity for beer'; and there were interesting contradictions in his life between the decorous deacon, heavy drinker, founder of sheepdog trials and rate-collector. These biographical facts offered the exiled academic manqué a basis for wish-fulfilment – by building on the security of selected undeniable realities, he could create an uninhibited pagan figure, secure (unlike himself) in self-approval, able flamboyantly to defy established religion in life and rout it in death by persuading his young ally to give him a kind of Viking funeral.

> As the flames shot merrily upwards, and the house collapsed, I heard my grandfather's laughter, and was content to know that he had had his way in death as in life, and that his chapel-ridden enemies would never have him in their power to shut in a box, and bury in damp earth, and give over to the possession of worms and the God of the preachers.

In reality, young T. H. Jones appears to have enjoyed the social side of the chapel; the wild boy of the story is made instinctively as anti-chapel as his grandfather: 'When I lay in bed that night supperless and sore from the belt because I had not been to Sunday school I was convinced of the rightness of my judgement and cared less than ever for burning in Hell . . .' This self-assured rejection is a feature of adolescence, not childhood, and is imagined by a man who can neither refrain from contravening chapel-teaching, nor avoid suffering the effects of 'the original and withering worm . . . within my blood'.[16] What began as dilemma culminated in neurosis: it is summed up in 'The Welshman in exile speaks' (13 April 1961):

> Being a boy from the hills, brought up
> Believing that fornication is a sin,
> Adultery abomination, what should I do
> But fornicate until I'm caught, and then
> Commit adultery in my dreams.[17]

'Portrait gallery' (24 October 1961),[18] a better poem, is a savage satire of the hypocrisy of the regular attenders at (Pisgah) Chapel. When it became known in Llanafan, this caused much resentment because the portraits were readily identifiable. Each character has his or her particular vice. Davies hates his wife because 'at least once a week she makes him forget / He is a deacon'; Welsh-speaking Tomos is 'resentful of everything English, especially / Money, which he needs'; Isaac 'seems to have an orgasm when he sings' (perhaps this is the only way he can manage it?); blue-eyed John Pritchard 'looks / As if he takes every woman in the parish' and Bill Beynon 'with the accent dropping thick / From his lips' denies that he is Welsh – delusion, deception, hypocrisy, and the gallery, (theatrical, rogues' or picture) is the onomatopoeically suggestive Pisgah.

So much for the men. The first of the four women is Mary (Mari) Jones, T. H. Jones's grandmother:

> Mary Jane, tiny
> And eighty, who's had ten children, and milked
> The cows immediately before and after
> Each birth.

Next, the *virgo* not quite *intacta*, Sarah

> who got lost once
> On a mountain, and noted for her good works
> Ever since

and the promiscuous Megan 'who has three children, / Two she thinks may be her husband's'. Miriam, in the eyes of a man obsessed by words, is the most duplicitous of all, for she is a dissembler with the language itself: she has been going 'properly' to chapel for fifty years 'and never understood a word'.

Finally, but not finally, because the poet's venom ultimately, and typically poisons himself: 'Look on this gallery, boy, and wonder / What these, your ancestors, would think of you.' These people are his stock. Who has more right than they to stand in judgement on him?

These, and other all-too-identifiable Llanafan characters feature in unpublished poems. 'Worthy is the Lamb' (15 April 1962) contains 'Glyn' who 'walks for miles / To conduct an indifferent rehearsal of The Messiah'; in 'Bronwen' (2 March 1962), Bronwen marries old 'Tomos Tymawr and his lies', betraying (as the poet sees it) a girlhood when

> There was nobody sweeter, nobody,
> Neither in the hay nor the honeysuckle . . .
> Nobody sweeter to us starved boys . . .

These poems have more in common with Caradoc Evans than R. S. or Dylan Thomas, and in his *Dylan Thomas*[19] T. H. Jones finds in the short stories of the latter a fusion of elements of James Joyce and Evans, whom he describes as:

the product of the Welsh Sunday School, brought up on the Welsh Bible and the rhetoric of the Welsh pulpit. He reacted violently against what he regarded as the pharisaism and hypocrisy of Welsh chapel goers, but when he came to express this revolt in words could only do so in an extraordinary prose based on the rhythms and idioms of Welsh Nonconformity.[20]

T. H. Jones acknowledges a debt to the vision of Caradoc Evans, who writes in 'a virile, exuberant, nonconforming prose that has influenced almost every subsequent Anglo-Welsh writer'.[21]

T. H. Jones's fictional persona rejects formal education in favour of the oral tradition: 'From my grandfather I learned many verses . . . and he told me many stories . . . mostly of drinking bouts and trotting matches, and sheepdog trials and women he had known and the iniquity of religious people. I began to make up my own stories.'[22] Julian Croft believes that it is to childhood memories that 'the adult poet continually returns, and not to those of his adolescence'.[23] The truth seems more complex – in both short stories and poems the very meaning of the term 'adult' is brought into question as the changeable, often unstable state of childhood is explored. Even when physically prepubescent, the Gwilyn character of the stories is imbued with the angst-ridden dreamy romanticism of adolescence, and there are echoes of Joyce's 'Araby': 'My life became a continuous dream; my only contact with reality was my grandfather and I was never sure where dream ended and reality began. It did not matter.'[24] The characters of *Dubliners* are part of Joyce's reshaping of his home-ground into art and he calls the collection 'a chapter in the moral history of my country'.[25] T. H. Jones transfers to real sisters and fictional brothers something of his own emerging sexuality: 'My brothers and sisters were writhing delightedly in the sticky grip of religion, they sang with smug lugubrious piety of the unattractive joys of salvation and the certain terrors of Hell.'[26] But the Gwilym of the second half of the story is not the boy of the Llanafan Primary School years, he is the sixth-former of Builth County School: 'Soon I would leave school, but it would be to exchange a known servitude for an unknown and perhaps unendurable one as a farm servant' – a not unlikely destination for a poor roadman's son. In 'A refusal to write autobiography' the time of creative awakening is confirmed as 'nine or ten . . . though I don't remember giving the disease a name for another five or six years'.

'A day at the seaside',[27] though written at approximately the same time as the previous story, could hardly be more different. Tailored to an Anglo-Welsh audience familiar with the short stories of Dylan Thomas and with frequent deliberate overtones of his prose style, it captures the intellectual openness of the nine- or ten-year-old child with the 'disease' alluded to above and his growing impatience with his peer group and, even more, with chapel-folk. It opens with the boy waiting at the foot of the Cwm for the Sunday school outing to begin. (Pisgah) Chapel had never previously ventured on the seaside: the elders had felt that

> journeys to the seaside were very well for coalgrimed and contaminated chapels from down the valleys: but for Pisgah . . . a

tea on the chapel meadow in full view of the admonishing and decorous gravestones was all that was required by way of concession to the spirit of youth and its demand for some sort of nibble at the fleshpots of Egypt.

The sensibility here is that of adult-author-as-adolescent, but the story soon shifts into the imagination of a younger child. 'Aberystwyth! The name made Gwilym puppy-sick with delight.' This story, with its domestic-market appeal, derives further resonance from the reader's knowledge, playfully appealed to, of its author's wartime seafaring experiences and from an appreciation of Aberystwyth as a kind of 'last' resort. T. H. Jones's sister, Brenda, remembers the occasion fictionalized here and it is recorded in a photograph in the family album.

During the charabanc journey Gwilym feels 'wonder at the country they were passing through' (for the young T. H. Jones this was the only journey of any significance made between the ages of nine and eighteen, when he would return to Aberystwyth as an undergraduate). The power of the boy's expectation is built up with the few scraps of literary knowledge about the sea (he has never seen it) which the naïve Gwilym has acquired at school, from his grandfather, from recitation at eisteddfodau and from the Bible (Psalm 107, Byron, Barry Cornwall: 'they that go down to the sea in ships' – 'To sea! To sea! The calm is o'er' – 'Roll on, thou deep and dark blue Ocean' – 'The blue, the fresh, the ever free'). At last the crest of the final hill is attained. Standing, peering, gripping the seat in front of him like a captain on his bridge, the boy sees 'only a thin strip coloured like the blade of a scythe just after sharpening' (the image is of all-too-familiar workaday reality). He refuses to admit disappointment, but the contrast between his fictionalized seaside and the actual Aberystwyth makes a liar of imagination.

The trippers disembark into a 'larger version of the school playground' and nobody else is interested in seeing 'the wonders of the Lord in Cardigan Bay'. Drizzle begins to fall and the boy finds himself confined to a town different only in size from the few others of which he has had experience. 'The long grey morning passed, slow as a poor sermon' – he might as well be in chapel. He alone has risen to the occasion; everyone else behaves 'exactly . . . as they did on market and fair days at home!' At last, miraculously, the sun comes out and Gwilym manages to prevail on his uncomprehending mother to take him to the shore: 'Gwilym did not try to explain what the sea meant to him, nor that he thought the words "And there shall be no more sea" the most terrible in the whole Bible.' When they reach the shore, the tide, of course, is out: 'This was not as he had imagined it. The strip of water, dulled blue with frothy bits here and there, seemed not at all significant or wonderful.' It seems that reality has triumphed over the nine-year-old's fiction, but suddenly he realizes that the tide is coming in, the apparently insignificant strip of water 'stretched away for miles and miles right across the whole round globe' and for one fleeting, golden moment, imagination is justified: 'The gulls made music in his ears, and the half-dozen pleasure boats that he could see were argosies and armadas.' Almost at once the rain returns and his mother hustles him away from the 'dreaming beach' to the pedestrian reality of the town – his first encounter with the hard fact that fiction is the triumph of hope over experience.

The snapshot taken on that day shows T. H. Jones, hand in hand with his three sisters, ankle-deep in a murky sea on a mucky day. The girls seem quite happy in the water; their brother is awkward and knock-kneed. The fact appears to be that he would rather have been somewhere else.

Once again in a deconstruction of a real occasion in his early life, the writer structures his narrative to emphasize his difference from the other children and consequent isolation. For them 'Woolworth's with its lights and colours was fairyland.' This consumers' paradise of the hungry 1920s, with its temptations to the deadly sin of Avarice, is not for the fiercely different Gwilym: 'He despised the purchases of the other children – the sweets and ice cream, the coloured and lettered rock, the gimcrack toys, the balloons, the hooters, the comic postcards.' The text resonates with hints of the outcast Ishmael, both the Old Testament and the Melville character. With something of the sternness of an Old Testament prophet, Gwilym feels that 'His money was a mockery to him, like a stone given to a hungry man who had asked for bread'.[28] How crass the offer of seven pence when 'all he wanted was the sea which no money could buy'.

Gwilym's dream of the sea is an act of the creative imagination, however, 'which no disappointment could kill', and, fortified by this realization, he makes his self-assertive statement, purchasing, much to the disgust of his unimaginative contemporaries, 'a shiny blue notebook costing one penny and a red New Pocket Dictionary of the English Language, price 6d', obvious signifiers of the birth of the writer.

The romantic whimsy mischievously hinting at Dylan Thomas is part of the controlling ironic subtext. The narration largely foregrounds the sensibility of the child who, on the homeward journey, wrestles with disappointment and frustration and cuddles his books for comfort. At least he has seen the sea, and T. H. Jones now intervenes as omniscient narrator with a comfort the child could not have imagined:

> the time would surely come when he would see [the sea] properly – would see it in all its beauty and majesty, its pride and power, in all its moods and colours, in all parts of the world, in terror and delight, in storm and calm – would himself go down to the sea in ships and do business in great waters and see the wonders of the Lord.

And now the child returns, to feel 'the resolute comfort of his thoughts' lull away 'his disappointment' on the homeward journey as his first poem shapes itself in his mind: 'I have gone walking on the ancient hills . . . / I will go walking on the ancient seas . . .' He has good reason to be 'content with his day at the seaside', and when he wakes up the next morning, at home 'the hills were all a green tide'.

The child's day at the seaside, though not fictionalized in words until 1954, was shaped in the mind of the man who went to sea in 1940, returned thence to university at Aberystwyth, and later, teaching naval apprentices at Portsmouth, juxtaposed his naval experiences with those of the child in the story. Echoes of this formative experience often resurface in the poetry, most notably in the seminal elegy, 'Lucky Jonah' (12 September 1959), where it is used to give perspective to the more dangerously formative wartime experience:

> A small boy in a small Welsh school
> Dreamed over books that he would go to sea
> Knew schooners, barques and brigantines,
> The names of sails and rigging,

Dreamed of being a captain, proud and almighty,
Pacing the quarterdeck, and taming
Weather and mutiny with eyes reflecting
Glitter of seas, the seas
Of all the world – he knew them all.[29]

1933–1939

Spa of No Renown

In September 1933 the focus of T. H. Jones's life shifted nine miles or so, down to Builth Wells, the small market town on the River Wye. He was one of three boys that year at Llanafan School to 'pass the Scholarship' for a free place at Builth County School – even so, the Jones family found it hard to manage the 15*s*. book-fee and in 1935 his father had to ask to be excused payment.

We can form some idea of the Builth of that time from Robert Gibbings's *Coming down the Wye*, the best of the many tourist guides published in the 1920s and 1930s. The town, he writes, is

Modest in the sense that it is shy and retiring. Until you close upon it you do not realise that there is a town there at all, its grey roofs being hidden by the surrounding trees. But like many shy and retiring people it has a charm of its own once you are admitted to its intimacies. The streets are narrow and winding, but that is all the better for passing chat. Vehicles of any description are seen as an intrusion in those streets: they interfere with pedestrians.[1]

Gibbings, a friend of Eric Gill's, was a wood-engraver and illustrator with an eye for the picturesque native; he found the farmers assembled at Builth market distinctly picturesque:

For the most part they wore either hats pulled over their eyes or caps on the backs of the head. Old mackintoshes covered their shoulders, and with few exceptions brown breeches led the way to black leggings and muddy boots. Each man carried a stick. Some of these were stout and strong, others were slight and tapering and delicately balanced as a rapier. The men of Mid Wales take great delight in a good walking stick. They will wax lyrical about the golden colour of a hazel or the deep red of a blackthorn. The handles, whittled through many a winter's evening, are rich in character and craftsmanship.[2]

When, at the age of thirteen, T. H. Jones wrote (for the County School magazine) his own brief tourist's guide to the Wye Valley, he found little to say about Builth: 'Builth Wells also has a reputation as a mineral water spa. Here, the Irvon meets the Wye just above the town. Builth Wells is well known in the sporting annals of Wales.'[3] The following term an essay on Builth Castle catches the tone and style of the polite essay as surely as 'The River Wye' had caught that of the tourist guide:

> As I went slowly away my thoughts were of the past, and of great stone castles and all their grandeur, of pompous barons and the pride with which they regarded their castles, and of the wonderful works of Nature which outlast anything man can make or do.[4]

Nearly thirty years later, looking back from his Australian exile, he wrote the poem 'Builth Wells':

> A picture of a town beside a river:
> Schoolcaps, girls' knickers, French letters,
> And French teachers, beside the sylvan Wye:
> How beautifully my memories lie.
>
> Builth, Buallt, spa of no renown,
> But sprawled about the grassy Groe,
> Along the brawling reaches of the Wye,
> Where I'll go home to die:
>
> Small town, home of a great footballer
> And of a greater choir, O Builth.
> Stay small beside my memoried Wye
> Where all my poems lie.[5]

The ironic echoes of the schoolboy pieces ('well known in the sporting annals / wonderful works of Nature') are both typical and appropriate because it is the poet's adolescence that is being evoked ('Schoolcaps, girls' knickers, French letters'). His feelings about Builth are ambivalent: 'sylvan Wye' (an ironic nod to

Wordsworth[6]) is the kind of tourist-bait displayed on railway posters; the 'spa' is 'of no renown', and it sprawls about the Groe (the municipal park and main recreational and courting area – the popular promenade was along the riverbank from the town bridge to Jane's Parlour, the small café and sweetshop frequented by senior pupils of the school). It was not the river that 'brawled' here (the reach was used for boating) – the transferred epithet refers to the fist-fights and petty schisms typical of small-town life. The very name of the place, 'Builth, Buallt' is made ambivalent. There were several 'great footballers', both soccer and rugby union, and the choir, particularly under the famous Llew Buallt (E. Evans), had won the National Eisteddfod as far back as the 1880s (but can we take seriously anything so characteristically 'Welsh-small-town' as this?). It was at Builth that T. H. Jones first encountered and first attempted to compose poetry and the poem's heaviest ambiguities are to be found in the threefold rhyme 'Wye/lie', 'Wye/die', 'Wye/lie' and the words 'memories' and 'memoried'. Initially the reader, moving from 'sylvan Wye' to 'memories lie' supposes himself in the familiar Georgian world. This first 'lie', however, acquires quite another sense from its near association with 'girls' knickers, French letters', we cannot take seriously the sentimental cliché 'Where I'll go home to die', and the 'poems lie' of the final line brings in a characteristic postmodern cynicism: poetry is fiction, 'made up' and not to be mistaken for truth.[7]

Builth Wells County School had been built in 1899, to house ninety pupils. By 1930 it had 134 boys and girls, and over-crowding was not its only problem. The provision of free education (the Evans Exhibitions) for farmers' sons had caused an imbalance: these boys, said one 'Headmaster's Report',[8] seemed to think that the scholarships existed 'to enable them to pass pleasantly the interval between leaving the elementary school and taking up seriously the business of farming'. Their attendance and academic achievement were poor, and they tended to leave after three years, but they were the dominant peer group and their example had a bad effect on the rest: in 1930, only six out of nineteen managed to pass the School Certificate.

By the time T. H. Jones entered the school, however, a new and energetic headmaster, P. G. Davies, B.Sc., MA, appointed in 1929, was beginning to bring about improvements. A graduate of Oxford University, he was Welsh-speaking and had played first-class rugby for London Welsh and cricket for Gowerton. He found a school with virtually no corporate life: no morning assembly; no pastoral care; virtually nothing in the way of extra-curricular activity. Davies restructured the timetable and the curriculum, introduced an assembly, the termly magazine (*The Wyeside*), a dramatic society, eisteddfod, dominoes, draughts, chess and boxing and set up an Old Students' Association.

Like most country children, T. H. Jones was boarded out, during the week, at the expense of the county council. There were numerous large houses built to accommodate visitors to the spa, but its popularity had declined and many married women were happy to supplement their income by offering accommodation to schoolboys (unmarried women and widows were restricted to the accommodation of girls). His week began at 4.30 a.m. each Monday at Trefelin when he was awakened by his father. The fire was lit and breakfast made before he began the steep descent between the high hedges of the poorly surfaced road to Newbridge station to join other children from the upper Wye valley and Newbridge itself on the thirty-minute journey by single-track railway to Builth. Landladies did not provide food, so breakfast and evening meal during the week consisted of bread and cheese (eggs if Ruth had any to spare). Lunch was at school, cooked by the girls as part of their domestic science curriculum.

The Depression helped P. G. Davies raise academic standards. F. J. Anthony, the energetic young teacher of history and English, remembers how difficult it was, in those days, to get a teaching job: 'Builth was not an academic school . . . the agricultural influence was very strong . . . [but] . . . Even at a school like Builth . . . I was one of *fifty* applicants.'[9] (For grammar schools and state schools there has never been a better period for the appointment of well-qualified staff.) On the other hand, the 10 per cent cut in salaries imposed in 1933 (the 'Geddes Axe') naturally had a bad effect on staff morale. Overcrowding – pupils who would have left stayed on because there were few jobs in the area, and pupils were transferred in from other schools because their parents had moved in search of work – meant that 'Science was taught to classes of thirty-five in a laboratory intended for fifteen'.[10] In 1933 the school governors refused to admit any new pupils until the 'issue of accommodation had been satisfactorily addressed by Breconshire Education Committee',[11] and £1,875 0s. 8d. was spent on new buildings.

T. H. Jones came close to missing secondary education altogether. The May Committee, which had reported in 1931, had strongly suggested that all secondary pupils should be self-financing, and from April 1933 the Free Place system had been superseded in Wales by the Free and Special Places system. Breconshire, however, had won approval for 100 per cent Special Places, so admission continued to depend on academic ability rather than financial circumstances.[12] Gwanwyn Lewis, an exact contemporary who would later become political agent to Tudor Watkins, MP, attributes Breconshire's policy to the influence of Labour councillors from Brynmawr and Ystradgynlais, with their 'personal experience of the deep poverty of industrial South Wales'.[13] Of the new entrants in 1933, twenty-four (T. H. Jones among them) paid no fees, one paid £3 6s. 8d., two paid £5 and two £7 10s. 0d. and there were two Evans Exhibitioners at £7 10s. 0d. On the other side of the Wye, in Radnorshire, children were less fortunate. Gwanwyn Lewis 'played tennis and hockey and paid nothing . . . My violin was purchased from the County for £1. Pupils at Llandrindod had to buy all their sports equipment . . . it was much more difficult for working class children to continue school there.'[14] Times were hard all over Wales:

> most of the small farms had become pensioners of the Milk Marketing Board and there was a general *sauve-qui-peut* into teaching, any nice clean jobs that were going, and into the shadow world of 'No Good Boyos' . . . thousands were left . . . to scrub along under the fish-eyed scrutiny of under managers, Means Test Men, public assistance boards, in a purgatory of sustained and inquisitory humiliation which burned itself into the memory.[15]

Robson Davies, one of T. H. Jones's closest schoolfriends, recalls:

> I first met Harri in class in September 1933 – I remember the school was incredibly cold, there was no central heating, but there were fires in the grates, and the teachers had a marvellous time sitting in front of the fires rubbing their arms in ecstasy while the pupils were chattering in the cold.[16]

Central heating was installed in the new 'temporary classrooms' in January 1934 (it is indicative of the national concern about investment in state education that at Builth, as in many other schools, this accommodation remained in use until 1988). Robson Davies remembers 'the famous new woodwork room which smelled of boiled glue' and the excitement when rugby was introduced in 1934:

> Harri particularly liked it because the finesse required to control a soccer ball did not go well with the slopes of Allt-y-Clych. The ruggedness needed to play rugby was well developed in him. He became a very formidable wing forward. He was quite furious, he had a flash in the eye, those deep-seated dark eyes, he was quick on his feet and he was a tigerish tackler.[17]

Although he played with enthusiasm, T. H. Jones did not take his rugby too seriously. He joked about it in another contribution to *The Wyeside*:

> When fifty heavyweights form a scrum,
> He stands behind like a calf,
> And when they all decide to fall,
> They fall on the stand-off half.[18]

Robson Davies reflects that 'It is hard to realise . . . we had not seen rugby at Builth – or anywhere else, for that matter . . . we didn't actually know what the game . . . looked like: no television, of course. We played on the Groe; there were no playing-fields.'[19]

In class T. H. Jones was a law unto himself. Robson Davies remembers him as

> a bright pupil . . . he took things very much in his stride. He had his own style of doing things – he didn't consider French grammar was worth bothering with, he just read Molière and anything else in the French library. The result was he could do French with consummate ease. He didn't know the rules, he just knew how to use the language – and this was the key to Harri's character: he was a reader, a voracious reader, he read absolutely everything he could find, English and French.[20]

T. H. Jones's other good friend, Donald Jones, son of a solicitor, was also an avid reader; they both loved literature from their first year, though in different ways: Davies remembers that

Harri was a great all-rounder, not a bookworm – you don't often think of poets as violent wing forwards! Harri had one very curious black spot – he was the most unmusical person in the school. He admitted to me one day, 'I don't think I'd recognise "God Save the King" unless they were actually saying the words.'

P. G. Davies made it a policy to employ staff who could offer music and drama as 'extras'. His own children were talented musicians and a hothouse of creative arts flourished in the school until the outbreak of war split up the teaching team.

Many of the staff were remembered as 'characters'. The rugby enthusiast, Whiteman,

> was a Major in the Territorial Army and after weekend camp he always repeated his pet speech, 'It's all very well for you, being comfortable in your desks, doing your Maths., but if you're squat under a hedge, and it's pouring with rain, and you're trying to calculate how much pepper per man per day, it's not so funny!'[21]

'Geogger' Evans struck Robson Davies as a man of great panache:

> Staff always wore gowns teaching. I remember when Harri and I first met him. He came into class, he just looked at us, and he picked up his gown and a piece of chalk and he turned round to the board and with a very quick movement he drew a perfect circle and then he said, 'That, boys, is the world.' We also knew him as The Cyclone Kid – for his speed in the corridors . . . we thought him extraordinarily clever. Gwanwyn and the girls were less enthusiastic – he compared unfavourably with their heart-throb, the handsome, immaculate Frank Anthony. Anthony says that Evans used to compare Builth, with its old-fashioned customs and lack of privacy, to 'Cranford'. Although Anthony found Builth 'a friendly place . . . it didn't attract me except for the summer. . . But Builth was cut off.'[22]

He agrees with the 'Cranford' analogy.

T. H. Jones's thirst for knowledge had, as we have seen, already established itself at Llanafan School, but it took him a year or so to appreciate the greater resources of a new, and larger school.

[Anthony] became conscious of Harri only in the third year, when I taught him History and English. At this time the only thing that struck me about him apart from the way he used to write (which was well above average) was the intense interest he took in the English lessons. But he was keen on history as well. He was not, of course, an outstandingly snappy dresser, but, talking to him, you would have thought he came from a well-educated family with a good background . . .[23]

Gwanwyn Lewis puts it more bluntly:

He was a boy whose jacket sleeves were always too short for him. He had these long, bare wrists, so his hands always looked cold. He never wore a tie, so he didn't conform. He wore this wide-open-necked shirt over an ill-fitting jacket. He had lank, long, straight, heavily pomaded hair, with thick strands invariably hanging over his face . . . he was always flicking them out of his eyes. His two front teeth were very badly decaying . . . we liked him, but he was gaunt, and cold, and an academic.[24]

F. J. Anthony was responsible for *The Wyeside*, which he produced with the assistance of a constantly changing committee of senior pupils. T. H. Jones contributed to it regularly from his third year. 'I always used to look to Harri. And he always turned up with something that was worth printing.'[25] He also figures regularly in eisteddfod, sports and debating society reports.

In the autumn term of 1934, a cheaper milk-scheme improved the diet of the pupils, blackboards were for the first time attached to walls and the Dorian Trio began the first of three decades of concerts suffered rather than enjoyed by unappreciative pupils. Anthony remembers that 'the three ladies, they played a romantic type of classical music, which was well received by the girls, but by the boys not so much'.[26] According to Donald Jones, the tone-deaf Harri used to concentrate on what lay between the cellist's legs – 'and I don't mean the cello'.[27]

T. H. Jones's first contributions to *The Wyeside* were schoolboy-humorous poems: 'Chinese football' and three limericks. On 18 October 1934, the debating society resolved, by 13 to 11, 'That this house considers that expenditure on boys and girls in secondary schools is a waste of money' and on 1 November comprehensively denied 'That Wales is a home of lost causes'. T. H. Jones was present and soon began to play a more prominent part. He spoke (tongue-in-cheek, perhaps?) against the motion 'That modern clothes are unhygienic'.

By Easter 1935 T. H. Jones had written the 'brief tourist guide' already referred to.[28] Almost every one of his contributions to the magazine demonstrates, in the light of his subsequent career, a different aspect of a writer's apprenticeship. Here he has evidently done a good deal of research and is trying out the style thought appropriate to travel-writing at the time. He catches it so well that one suspects him of plagiarism:

> St. Mary's Church in Monmouth whose graceful spire is a common landmark was built in 1881 by Street. According to tradition, the bells were a gift of Henry V who brought them from Calais. Monmouth's only other church of ancient foundation is dedicated to Sir Thomas Beckett, and is distinguished by a great deal of Norman work.[29]

Like most of his contemporaries, T. H. Jones had not been to Monmouth. F. J. Anthony recalls that

> One of the things I particularly noted about the pupils at Builth was how very little they travelled . . . It was very difficult to get them to understand such things as the Industrial Revolution, what it meant: they had no conception because they had seen no industry.[30]

By 1935 the debating society had become 'The Literary and Debating Society', but there was too little contribution from the 'floor' of the somewhat conscripted 'House'. The subjects debated were less insular than might have been supposed. In 1935 there was discussion of measures to protect the town from Nazi attack in the event of war. The debate on 21 February – 'If four people were entrapped in a submarine and there were only one life-saving apparatus, to whom should it be given' – saw Wells (eight votes) defeat the pacifist Gandhi (seven), the proto-feminist aviatrix Mrs Mollison (Amy Johnson) (three) and the fascist Mussolini (two). Pacifism was not the issue in Breconshire that it was in socialist south Wales or the Nonconformist north. On 7 March the motion 'That England should disarm' was lost by 13 to 8.

Prize Day saw Jones beaten into second place for the Year 2 Form Prize by his friend, Donald. The highlight of the occasion was the award of the Meyrick Scholarship in Modern Languages at Jesus College, Oxford, to R. Anthony Sayce, the school's star pupil. As Principal Thomas Lewis of Aberystwyth remarked in his address to the packed hall, 'I have access to the Central Welsh Board inspectors' monthly report, and few schools reveal more general progress than Builth Wells.'[31] Emrys Evans, Director of Education for Breconshire, endorsed this, and added that it was obvious that 'a tremendous amount of brain-work and skill had been put into such apparently dry subjects as woodwork and drawing'.[32] This would be patronizing today, but it is refreshingly free of contemporary educational jargon and merely reflects the bias characteristic, even in rural areas, of the grammar-school philosophy.

By Christmas 1935 Donald, Robson and Harri had entered the fourth form and their contributions to the magazine foreshadow their future careers. Robson had written a long piece about a visit to a steelworks, and Harri, who spent his holidays working on neighbouring farms, contributed the mannered literary piece quoted earlier, 'The castle ruins and the streamlet'.[33] Donald, meanwhile, was concentrating on music: he was leader of the orchestra and played Bach's Suite in D with the Dorian Trio.

The autumn term of 1935 ended with the school's first major dramatic production, *The Rivals*. T. H. Jones, who had enjoyed playing Puck in Jones House's scenes from *A Midsummer Night's Dream* in 1934, was unable to take part as he was not available to rehearse at weekends. The division of his life – Monday to Friday at Builth; Saturday and Sunday at Trefelin – was limiting his social activities and, unlike Donald Jones, he had no girlfriend. According to F. J. Anthony, this was not unusual – he can recall virtually no 'steady' relationships during the 1930s, even in the sixth form; Gwanwyn Lewis, however, remembers that 'there were several sweethearts right through the school, innocent enough, though, but Harri was anything but attractive to girls'.[34]

'The poet', T. H. Jones's first short story, appeared in *The Wyeside* of summer 1936,[35] and will thus have been written when he was about fourteen and a half years old. The narrator, a Cambridge graduate and 'Young Squire' type, resembles Cyril in *The White Peacock*, and 'Gipsy Jack', the poet, is characterized not only by description, but by a bold attempt at his spontaneously produced poems:

> The silver moon bequeaths
> To the pinewoods by the sea
> A blaze of silver light
> That glories me.

'Little Puddlecombe', the setting for the country fair at which the two men meet, is probably Newbridge-on-Wye, and although the signifiers are commonplace (roundabouts, swings, coconut-shies, giggling girls and their 'rustic swains'), and there is hardly a hint of the real Newbridge, with its hard-drinking men, wild women, horse-traders and 'pound-doctors' (knackers' representatives), the achievement is a remarkable one.

In September 1936 T. H. Jones entered the fifth form and began to be considered a rather special pupil. 'I really noticed him as someone out of the ordinary by the time he came to Form 5', says F. J. Anthony.

> I thought, 'This boy is very interested in everything you do in class . . .' I would mention something which the class should have known, but lots of them didn't, and Harri would look up and half wink . . . or, if I repeated something, Harri would look up and nod his head as if to say, 'I've remembered.'[36]

This is the year of the two humorous rugby pieces and a sharply contrasting poem, 'The fairies' dance':

> In meadows green
> The fairies dance,
> With golden sheen
> On gossamer wings
> And soft, soft steps
> Unheard, unseen . . .[37]

Adolescent, over-alliterative and precious, it is nevertheless a not unaccomplished attempt at a recognized form. Over the next two years he would experiment with various other traditional lyric modes introduced to him by F. J. Anthony.

On 24 March 1937 Anthony, now founder and chief producer of the Builth Dramatic Society, directed *She Stoops to Conquer* with Robson Davies as Hardcastle, Donald Jones as Tony Lumpkin and T. H. Jones (typecast) as landlord of The Three Pigeons.[38] There was an additional performance at the Victoria Hall, Llanwrtyd Wells, where he scandalized younger members of the cast and teachers by unashamedly drinking, afterwards, in the Neuadd Arms with some farming friends. Not even teachers, let alone schoolboys, visited public houses openly in those days. F. J. Anthony recalls:

> If, as a member of staff, you wanted a drink, you didn't dare go into a pub in Builth, because of general talk. P.G. [Davies] was very strict. I remember after a production for the town's dramatic society bottles of wine were brought out backstage for the cast. I had a drink or two. P.G. had me on the carpet next day . . . [39]

That T. H. Jones established, as a schoolboy, a reputation for enjoying a pint of beer, separated him only from his middle-class friends. For men of the farming community, his father prominent among them, heavy drinking was the main compensation for the harshness of everyday life.

The short story 'Nellie's disappearance'[40] is a trite and pretty account of an old man and his cat:

> the lonely old man loved his cat. For a year . . . the two had lived together, the one feeble and half blind, the other young, strong and clear-sighted, the one in an almost pitiable state of senile decay, the other in the full flower of youth, and a considerable depth of affection existed between them.

There is some sophistication of technique in the double antithesis, and the relationship hints at the boy's relationship with his blind grandfather (the mature poet would return to this[41]). He is learning to deploy the resources of language. 'Next morning there was no sign of *le disparu* so Old Simon jammed his battered hat on his snowy head, and, gnarled stick in gnarled hand, set off down the village to look for his kittiken':[42] '*le disparu*', 'jammed', the repetition of 'gnarled' and the consciously disparaged diminutive modify the inevitable sentimentality of the cat's proud return with three kittens.

T. H. Jones entered the sixth form, over his father's serious objections, in the autumn of 1937, and was provided with a bedroom of his own for study purposes. He contributed two contrasting poems to the autumn magazine: 'Memory', a poor Keatsian stab ('To that rich garner-house of treasures sweet / We call up from the past in reverie') at a Shakespearean sonnet (signed 'Henry Jones'),[43] and a Newbolt parody, 'To those who do not like school' (signed 'H.J.').[44] It is possible, at this stage in his development, to tease out three strands of influence. The first is material copied out and prepared for eisteddfod recitation by him and his sisters and including such characteristic pieces as 'The navvy's prayer':

> They were holding a gospel mission, and into the crowded
>   hall,
> There came one night to the meeting a navvy rough, big and
>   tall,
> What had brought him into the gathering it would have been
>   hard to say –
> Whether he came to listen or to just pass an hour away . . . [45]

and other Band of Hope reworkings of the popular ballad typical of the work of Robert Service. Next, a mass of verse printed in tuppenny leaflets with such titles as 'The children's popular reciter' and 'The gem children's reciter'. Two examples of material known to have been performed by T. H. Jones are remembered within his family. 'A child's prayer'[46] was recited at Pisgah Chapel in 1931:

> God make my life a little hymn
> Of tenderness and praise,
> Of faith that never waxeth dim
> In all His wondrous ways.

Then there is Alfred Briggs's robust Salvationist adaptation of Longfellow, 'The modern village blacksmith':

> In the Army Hall on Sunday with the villagers he meets . . .
> With a note of triumph tells them how each day he gladly greets,
> Asks the Lord to help him use it for his fellows' greatest good
> That his forge may be a temple, sanctified tho' rough and crude.[47]

Finally, there was the poetry accessible in newspapers such as the *Western Mail*, with its long-running 'Wales day by day' miscellany in which, on 7 March 1951, T. H. Jones's 'Poem on St David's Day' would appear. The following:

> Beneath the moon on Margam Hill
> The Roman bugles stir and call
> The legion's fallen, proud and still
> Within the fastness of the wall.

(11 May 1933) is typical of the column. Rooted in Welsh history, traditional in subject and technique, patriotic and portraying rural or once rural Wales, it is the work of the genial, influential poet, critic, historian and educationist, Arthur Glyn Prys-Jones (1888–1987).

Most potent is the lyric poetry encountered at school. Julian Croft suggests that it was the work of Noyes, Longfellow and Shelley,[48] but the key text ('that bit of Victoriana that haunted my youth and almost killed my poetic ambition'[49]) is *The Golden Treasury of the Best Songs and Lyrical Poems in the English Language* by Francis Turner Palgrave (1824–97). This anthology, still popular in the 1960s as a school and examination text,[50] was first published in 1861, revised in 1896 and reprinted, in the 'World's Classics' series alone (with additional poems bringing it 'up to date' to the death of W. E. Henley in 1907), at least twenty-five times.

The Golden Treasury contained none of the work of living twentieth-century poets. It is perhaps most interesting as a reflection of the inhibitions of its age – 'You can look in vain for Chaucer!' observed Donald Jones. There is a strong representation of Shakespeare, Shelley, Wordsworth and Herrick, but no Blake, no Donne – nothing, indeed, to hint of, or foster, modernist inclinations. Julian Croft is certainly right to assert that T. H. Jones 'had still to be exposed to the main trends of English poetry in the 1920s and 1930s',[51] but there can have been very few pupils in the Welsh grammar schools of the period lucky enough, like T. H. Jones's contemporary and close friend, Tom Sallis, to be taught by an Alun Lewis. F. J. Anthony remembers that:

> There was no study of contemporary poetry – we studied one classical, two or three Romantics (in French as well for

comparison). But Harri was good at practical criticism, where we had some freedom: he generally spotted the gist of the thing and the style. I remember I gave them a passage, Harri looked up and said, 'Excuse me, is this D. H. Lawrence?' I didn't know how he knew. We had no Lawrence in the school library.

In fact T. H. Jones *had* read some Lawrence: Donald Jones had provided him with *Sons and Lovers* and a collection of short stories. Lawrence was a major influence on the stories he would write in the 1950s.

'Nocturne' is a musical and, in metre and rhyme, much more accomplished Shakespearean sonnet whose picture of sunset and moonrise:

> the young moon from some far-off shore
> Sails like a graceful, full-rigged ship on high.
> Now in the palely-silver, soft moonlight
> Behold th'undying beauty of the night.[52]

is pure Prys-Jones (although 'distant rim', 'starry fleece' and 'raise the evening hymn' hint at Gray and Cowper). The same issue of *The Wyeside* contains a second short story, 'The revenant', which looks forward to the mature 'What's become of Waring',[53] and, in its thinly disguised versions of T. H. and Donald Jones ('We had been boyhood friends: we had been at school together') also to 'Saturday night' (1955).

In 1938 T. H. Jones became co-editor of *The Wyeside*. In his first issue he printed an account by R. A. Sayce, then working on his D.Phil. at Oxford, of Vienna at the time of the Anschluss. Set between a painful schoolboy attempt at humour and an incompetent sonnet, it is a remarkable intrusion of *realpolitik* into the still-comfortable world of small-town mid-Wales:

> At Cologne, a member of the S.S. . . . was being seen off on the Vienna Express by his friends. He appeared to have been drinking heavily; his singing and shouting was quite deaf to the entreaties of his friends to remember his new dignity.[54]

This is the first sign in the magazine of a sense of the wider and increasingly threatening European political scene and an indication that older pupils of the calibre of T. H. Jones were beginning to develop political interests.

> Of course we teachers were conscious of the war through our social contacts in the town. I knew the local parson and the other teachers, and we used to meet together, and conversations would inevitably come around to Hitler. We were all radical in those days. The inevitable outcome of war was a question we discussed, but I don't think this was a question generally understood by the pupils themselves, except one or two like Harri, because he was a historian – we studied modern or European history to 1914; he understood the background: in fact I thought at one time he would become a historian.[55]

Something of T. H. Jones's embryonic political thinking can be detected in the prose piece which he contributed to this same edition. 'The Welsh hills',[56] his first attempt at a picture of the landscape which would inspire many of his best poems, is, on the surface, a conventional meditation, but references to 'hidden' sheep-paths, 'timid mountain ponies', 'buzzard', 'fox', iconic 'hills' ('So I have grown to love Allt-y-Clych from whose rocky summit one can see many miles of pleasant countryside around') and a vengeful, Calvinistic deity are, in retrospect, significant. There is some experimental diction – 'a buzzard will hover in the cerulean air above Chwefri Rocks' – and a telling awareness of the insularity of the farming community. The Welsh hills are offered as a barrier against horrors such as Guernica (27 April 1937) and the essay's imaginary Celtic paradise as a balance to Sayce's Europeanism. Years later T. H. Jones would reflect, wrily, 'it occurred to me that I might say that it was being Welsh that started it all, being Welsh and having those hills'.[57]

It was difficult for sixth formers to find somewhere to spend free evenings. There was the Kino, which F. J. Anthony describes as 'a flea-pit, school staff never used it. We went to the cinemas at Llandrindod', but which had attractions for adolescents on a Saturday night and was cheap. But Hollywood fictions, so important to Emlyn Williams at the same age, seem to have meant nothing to T. H. Jones. He was usually isolated at Llanafan over the weekend and had little pocket money, but it was easy enough to gatecrash the Kino and the true explanation appears to be indifference. As an adult, certainly, he did not take cinema seriously and his works contain few, if any references to any of the media. Nor did radio play any part in his development. Few farms had one; the radio age did not reach mid-Wales until the outbreak of war convinced the community that a wireless was worth the hard-earned price.

Builth's Kino was above the bookshop frequented in the 1930s by Jack Jones, but his path and T. H. Jones's seem never to have crossed: books, bought or borrowed from Boot's or W. H. Smith's library, were something else that the latter could not afford. Donald Jones, however, bought many books, in particular the 6*d.* Penguin paperbacks which began to appear in the summer of 1935, and he was happy to lend them to his friend. Donald recalls that a favourite weekday evening haunt was the usually deserted waiting-room at Builth railway station. The two rather serious sixth formers huddled over a tiny Turtle stove for informal seminars on the latest Penguin or current politics[58] and Harri's readings of his pastiches of poems from *The Golden Treasury*. They were disturbed occasionally by a foul-mouthed porter anxious to find out which of the County School girls 'had, did' or 'soon might be willing to: [he] had a perverted delight in accusing us of having come to this waiting-room *hot* from some incredible sexual encounter'.[59] *The Wyeside* 'Editorial' of Christmas 1938 suggests something of the nature of the young men's conversations, but their experience is best recalled in the short story 'Saturday night'.

This was written at Portsmouth and remained unpublished until Bernard Jones discovered it among T. H. Jones's surviving papers.[60] Written, with the Welsh market very much in mind, in the style of Dylan Thomas, it is a synthesis of memories of a mid-Wales adolescence of the 1930s. It is set at 'Llanfihangel . . . the windiest town in the world', a synthesis of Builth Wells, Newbridge-on-Wye and that part of Llanafan which centres on the Red Lion. The co-heroes of the story are Dai, 'tall and thin enough to be mistaken for a lamp-post by a market-night farmer if not by his dog', and the first-person narrator, Gwilym. Both Dai and Gwilym are aspects of T. H. Jones himself, with elements of Donald Jones incorporated. The psycho-narrative explores conflicts that T. H. Jones recognized in himself.

Harri/Gwilym both leads and is led by Dai/Harri. Dai attends the County School and intends to become a writer: 'he had recently abandoned the Bible for the writings of Lenin and he lived a hunted life in the middle of a great and historically necessary conspiracy which They organised to keep Us down.'[61] The two young men are engaged in the inevitable occupation of small-town youth in every age – hanging about on a street-corner, hoping that something will turn up. The author as teller-of-the-tale is buried – an ingenious device – within a fiction about a boy who, conspicuously ill-equipped to become a writer, had managed to do so. The writer, intentionally or not, reveals a psychological ambivalence that would later be the prime cause of his drive to self-destruction.

> A gaggle of girls went by on their way to the twice-weekly cinema. Seeing me rush after them, Dai reproached me on the shoulder with his long preacher's hand (borrowed from 'The Peaches') – 'Look, boy,' he said in the wise old voice he had got from neither Solomon nor Marx, but had been born with. 'We've only got one-and-sixpence between us.'[62]

Nothing happens, and the wind blows, and Dai curses Llanfihangel for not being all those other towns 'where things happen all the time'. He speaks with the authority of the thirteen-year-old T. H. Jones, who liked to discourse at large of London, Rome, Constantinople and Chicago. The source of Dai's insights is a whole fortnight spent with an 'Uncle who was a Marx-and-Engels-reading cobbler in Merthyr, and last year Dai had been to Cardiff to see an International (only he had been knocked over and trampled on in the excitement . . .)'[63]

The irony that pervades this story, in particular that which surrounds Dai's 'socialist' politics (his source, occupationally a cobbler, may be presumed to have been talking 'cobblers') tells of the T. H. Jones of the 1950s, beginning to reject his earlier Stalinist opinions, rather than the adolescent of the late 1930s. The point about the latter is his naïveté, in politics as Dai, in sexual matters as Gwilym. As the two friends wait for stop-tap to trigger some action, a range of thinly fictionalized local characters is mentioned: 'Jack Lie Down, a farmer at the bald top of the valley', was bald in real life and his main function and great delight really was 'the nurture and mating of Llanfihangel Emperor, the biggest Shire stallion anyone had ever seen'. Jack's name derived from his Saturday night habit of returning home 'drunk as David's sow' and commanding his horse to '"Lie down, Emperor," and the two of them would sleep, on the clean stable straw'.

Another character of this amoral world is Will Twenty:

> A quarryman who on some desperate occasion in his youth had counted his Saturday pints . . . and every Saturday since had obstinately drunk the same number . . . Will, who was still a quarryman, but neither as young nor as pint-proof as he had been, could be relied on to be spectacularly sick on his way home, or even, if we were in luck, to pee a splendid private Niagara over someone's respectable front door.[64]

Whatever the differences between the Saturday night culture of the Valleys and that of the small towns of mid-Wales, hard-drinking and urination in public evidently was not one of them. Nor was wife-beating. Here it is treated off-handedly: the victim's circumstances are different from those of Ruth Jones: 'Gypo Rowlands might have a fight with his wife – we were connoisseurs of these bloodstirring, bloodspilling, all-in, to-hell-with-the-Queensbury-Rules-and-police-interference encounters.'[65] Adolescent male machismo is well captured. Women are stereotyped as passive victims of male power. And although there are moments that recall Llaregub and a whole tradition of Welsh short-story whimsy, in general 'Saturday night' seems authentic.

Gwilym, 'despondent as a dipped sheep', starts his climb back to the hills – and at last something does happen. Through an uncurtained window the archetypal adolescent male voyeur sees a naked girl combing her hair by the light of a paraffin lamp which makes her 'glow like the yellow, yellow butter or imagined gold'. The scene is evoked in an apt mixture of striking imagery and the clichés of soft porn: 'Her young breasts yearned towards the mirror' and she 'held her body in the proud cup of her hands for the mirror's inspection'. She is 'a princess in an old story, asking the traditional question, "Mirror, Mirror . . ."' And then, the deflation of 'I remembered my responsibilities and ran back to the square to find Dai'. Together, the two friends watch the drama to its end – a man enters the room, the girl pulls down the blind: 'Behind that darkened window everything in the world had happened, was happening, was going to happen.'

The poetry-readings and discussions in the waiting-room enabled T. H. Jones finally to put aside eisteddfod performance in favour of creation on his own account. F. J. Anthony does not remember him as much of a performer: 'I used to read a lot of poetry aloud to the class myself, but generally the performance of poetry was left to the eisteddfod. I don't remember Harri being outstanding therein anyway.'[66] This view is contradicted by others and by T. H. Jones's successful public readings in Australia.

Weekends were usually spent at Llanafan in the small roadside cottage full of adoring sisters. There were occasional visits from schoolfriends. Robson Davies recalls 'visiting Harri at Llanafan at weekends. It was great fun too, because it was lovely country and we used to go out on our bicycles and join him there and I have one special memory of meeting Harri's grandfather, a marvellous character.'[67] More usually, though, there was work on local farms at Penrallt and Dolfallen.

The attractions of Dolfallen, which lies between Rhayader and the Elan Valley, are easy to understand. There the Price family ran a successful lowland dairy farm and T. H. Jones was able to earn pocket money helping the sons with their milk-round in Rhayader, with the harvest, and in the farm's plantations. As the farm was near the River Elan, he was able to do some fishing. Life there was softer than that of the hill-farms and appealed to the sensitive sixth former. Mrs Price, an imaginative cook and a kind of second Mam, was fond of him: during the war Mrs Price caused some consternation in her family by asking for news of him before that of her own children.[68] He wrote to her regularly and always included regards for her in his letters home.

Other attractions of Rhayader were the many pubs and the presence of young, if usually unachievable, women. 'The riding strangers',[69] the first of the 'Gwilym' stories, recalls 'girls with foxglove cheeks' and the adolescent's longing 'to be a tall violent man to do all things easily'. Strangers in masks enter a remote valley where 'All night Gwilym had lain across four counties in the heat of love' (a powerful image of frustration only partly relieved by onanism). They are dressed in black, a man and a woman who bear terrible power to destroy an Eden already imperilled by an emerging awareness of the knowledge of good and evil that only woman can provide. When Gwilym returns home, his grand-mother is on her death-bed and 'the house in his mother's care and domination'. There is some of the alienation here of the boy in 'Home',[70] but the adolescent has begun to recognize her 'knowledge, a wise woman, old as the hills', and to hate her for it and transfer his love to his grandmother, as in life T. H. Jones transferred some of his affection to Mrs Price, Old Crogau and the real Mari. With the death of the grandmother comes recognition of adolescent morbidity, 'loving the old and mindless, the withered flesh' in preference to young 'palpitating life'.

Gwilym, realizing that, if the one rider brings death, the other offers carnal delight, walks, whistling, to the farm that clearly represents Dolfallen, where he is restored with 'apple tart and milk . . . it was a warm house of life'. The girl of the farm takes him out and, in the orchard, encourages him to lie with her in the grass. 'Except a corn of wheat fall into the ground and die . . . He was a corn of wheat, fair and dying' – John Barleycorn, the earth mother, the White Goddess: the moon rises and the lovers are revealed, naked and shivering. Gwilym weeps against a symbolic apple tree and is reluctant to return home.

'Holy deceptions',[71] another short story evocative of adolescence, is written in a style heightened and evocative of the Bible, yet also simple and concrete. It explores the emergence of adolescent sexuality and the formation of a writer. Its hero, half-dreaming, agonizedly sensitive, lives within parameters only in the most literal sense set by clock and barometer: 'Voices spoke and sang through all the lifeladen minutes of the twice-twelve hours on the ponderous, erect grandfather clock that fought with the lying barometer for pride of place where the porch cheated you quickly into the kitchen.'[72] All his senses overwrought, he dreams his way towards maturity. The first deception, as in 'My grandfather would have me be a poet', is God, 'the greatest trickster, the cunningest cheat of them all', unavailable when you seek him in his chapel, but ready to pounce 'with sudden dexterity' out of nature or on the edge of sleep. The second is language ('In the beginning was the Word, and the Word was with God'[73]) which sometimes the embryo writer sees 'run before his eyes, dancing intricately in patterns he could yet see clearly, and making the meaning of everything plain' and at other times finds 'grey, stubborn, and worthless'. Then there is sex, embodied in the goose-girl out of folk- and fairy-tale, who appeals to the poet, uses him and rides away 'with a lout'. Girls, like words, could lie, cheat, trick and disappoint and 'had to be studied, fought, outmanoeuvred, mastered'.

The hero tries, successively, for God's love and the love of women, imagined in the signifiers of Celtic mythology – flowers and stars and trees, then animals and birds and fish. When the girl fails him, he confides in the schoolmaster, but they part in anger and misunderstanding. Finally, when he no longer knows the difference between flowers and stars, words and thoughts, a woman 'expected and unknown' comes to his bedside and the 'last and holiest deception' is played upon him. This is, again, the White Goddess, the Muse. 'Forget your dreams', she says, 'and I will show you the beauty of the world' and 'I am your slave', he replies. But she will not tell him how he is to see or embody the world's beauty, and the story concludes with a passage central to the understanding of T. H. Jones as a writer, and as a man:

> When he awoke from a long sleep, he remembered the visit and knew his doom, knew for a moment of certain vision that his life was to be one of endless wrestle with the angel, of ever increasing mastery of craft to be faced with ever increasing complexity of problems, of commerce with the heart of the mystery that must for ever remain mysterious. He saw that he would acquire knowledge, experience and even wisdom, and remain a fool to the last. He would know the feelings of sappy buds stretching out into the light, and of roots cunningly sucking existence out of darkness, would feel in himself the thrush's bubble of song and the hawk's power of wing and relentless sight, would be both the weasel thirsty for blood and the spelled hare giving up its life, would travel in all lands and all regions of the past, love many women and all for different qualities . . .[74]

The intense awareness of this specific rural background, hinted at already in that early prose piece, will always be characteristic, as will be the many women, desired early and, attained, with their individual passions leading always back to the One: Mother, Goddess, Muse.

T. H. Jones's sister, Myra, joined him at the County School in the autumn of 1938, the only pupil in her year at Llanafan to pass the scholarship. She recalls the time vividly:

Harri in the Sixth Form, standing very often in the door, and I felt very proud because we had both come from a small school. Harri always went with me to school, but although we lodged in Builth, it was never at the same house because boys and girls were not allowed to. I remember our dinner at school was paid at that time by the British Legion. Harri and the rest of the Sixth Form sat at the head table, Harri next to P. G. Davies. To me Harri always looked as though his hands were cold, probably because he had very thin hands. In our lodgings we ate our own food. I usually bought a loaf for breakfast and tea, which lasted all week. I usually had 3/- for the week. Most of the children were much better off than Harri and me, but they were never any different with me. I suppose I felt a bit envious of their clothes, but never their money. But the business people of Builth were like Margaret Thatcher's family, not poor like she pretends, the small businesses were quite prosperous even in the Depression. When Mrs Thatcher goes on about being poor, they weren't like we were, a big family with only one wage: you were short of money. My father liked a drink; the other brothers didn't. He went out on a Saturday night. He couldn't really afford that, but he had to have a smoke and a drink. It was my mother who went short, not us: we had plenty to eat and we were always clean and clothed. I was in Builth in school uniform from the beginning, but not the school coat until I was 14. But nobody laughed; the children were never spiteful. Harri was the same: he wasn't dressed as well as Donald Jones and Robson Davies – professional people.[75]

The photographic evidence supports this. In official sixth form photographs, T. H. Jones stands or sits with his patched clothes hanging loosely on his thin frame. His hair is crudely styled and rebelliously over-pomaded compared with that of wealthier schoolfellows. It is also rather long, but not, surely, as Julian Croft claimed, 'for lack of fourpence'.[76] Compared with today's victims of 'youth-culture', they seem an unfashionable group. Middle-class contemporaries, and teachers, remember T. H. Jones as spectacularly scruffy – a very 'angry young man', says Donald Jones (there is some evidence that he exacted revenge on those who had bullied him at Llanafan by himself bullying their younger siblings). According to F. J. Anthony, 'Harri was untidy: his tie would be down there, his shirt opened at the front, his hair would be flying all over the place'. As adolescence turned to manhood, T. H. Jones's heavy, dark eyebrows seemed to underline his increasingly serious personality, and his penetrating eyes diverted attention from the jug-handle ears that displeased the conventional majority of Builth girls.

Three more apprentice-pieces were printed in *The Wyeside* during his final year at school. 'The night raid'[77] reworks an episode from the *Iliad*, book 10 (the raid of Odysseus and Diomedes on the Trojan camp and the killing of the Greek spy, Dolon). Apart from altering the plot in favour of Troy (the two Greeks, Meriones and Socus in T. H. Jones's version, having killed Dolon are themselves slain 'by a steely ring of Thracians'), he contrives a striking first line: 'A heron swung crying into the night air, alarmed by the approach of the two Greek spies' and a neatly plangent conclusion: 'away on the forsaken battlefield, Dolon's armour swung in the mournful breeze, creaking on the tamarisk tree, while his headless corpse rotted on the scene of the carnage below. The heron cried mournfully again, as if Athene herself mourned the dead.' It would be interesting to know the inspiration for this original version of part of a very old story.

'The Wye in flood',[78] thirty-three lines of blank verse, is an extraordinary experiment in styles. Pre-Romantic poetic diction ('rage', 'flood' (for 'river'), 'fray' and, above all, 'finny prey') echoes 'Nocturne', but 'The salmon quiver in ecstasy, and leap' and 'Raises man far above Nature's brute force' are close to contemporary speech. A series of epic similes for the river's violence suggests Homer, perhaps via Milton – but logs float like crocodiles and plunge like torpedoes. Such eclecticism foreshadows the postmodernist development of the mature work.

Finally, and one might say inevitably, in the Summer 1939 number of *The Wyeside*, there was a Petrarchan sonnet. Entitled, as were several of the mature poems, merely 'Sonnet',[79] it is the most contemporary of the juvenilia. Its subject is a definition of the poet, who sees, 'in the white light of the bursting dawn . . . more beauty than his heart can hold', prizes 'russet leaves' more highly than 'gold / Of Ind', sees fairies in the dew of a lawn and Robin Hood and his Merry Men in the woods – has, in short, an 'aching tenderness of soul'. If the later poetry is post-, this is pre-modernist, Georgian again. It is perfect of its kind, handling the difficult rhyme-scheme with ease and rounding off with a neat couplet. The young man who wrote this is the young man retrospectively portrayed in 'Holy deceptions' – servant, lover and victim of the White Goddess, poet through and through, even unto death.

The Higher School Certificate had now to be negotiated. 'He contemplated Oxford', says F. J. Anthony, 'but I expect he never could have afforded it.' It was not, in fact, unheard of for a working-class Welsh schoolboy to go to Oxford. Emlyn Williams had managed it half a generation earlier by winning a scholarship to Christ Church and being, thanks to the efforts of Sarah Grace Cooke and an energetic, well-connected headmaster at Holywell County School, as we should now put it, 'sponsored', by a circle of well-wishers. T. H. Jones had to settle for the top County Major Scholarship and a place at Aberystwyth.

He celebrated with Robson Davies, who recalls their

> marvellous holiday camping at Llanwrtyd. There was Donald and Harri, Alan Jones and Jack Daft. To teenage boys from Builth at this time, Llanwrtyd was rather as Dublin City (if you know the words, you'll know what I mean). We went off there on our bicycles. Donald had a marvellous drop-handlebar bike. I had a 1929 Humber which weighed about a ton. Harri had an even older bedstead of a thing.[80]

One photograph survives of this last pre-holocaust holiday in the elegiac sunshine of 1939. Robson Davies's sisters sit outside a bell-tent by Abernant Lake. The sky is summer-clear. Four of the boys are standing. T. H. Jones alone, his expression profoundly thoughtful, is seated.

1939–1946

The Lecherous and Griefless Sea

As soon as T. H. Jones's holiday was over, he returned to the realities of farm-work to help pay for Aberystwyth. His scholarship covered fees and allowed £40 a year for keep, but, even with a loaf of bread at 4*d*. and postage still 1*d*., he doubted whether that would be sufficient.[1] His father had made it clear that he could not help. Having failed to prevent his son from attending the County School in the first place, he was trying to talk him into a 'safe' job in a bank. He told his Red Lion drinking companions that things were going to be 'damned hard' for Harri and that he would rather have extra money coming into the household than a 'layabout student son'.[2] He was probably speaking with affectionate, if rough, irony: he had not forgotten his own dreams of better things and, with his dapper ways, was regarded by Llanafan people as quite the gentleman.

At about this time T. H. Jones submitted another Petrarchan sonnet to a local eisteddfod.[3] The last of his 'schoolboy' pieces, it is a conventional response to a relationship broken off by the girl who used to 'bend / Her fair head over me, and "To the end / My love," would say'. The disconsolate poet who 'would gladly go / To Hell for her if I could be her friend' must content himself with 'her sacred mem'ry':

> her golden hair and eyes
> Of candid blue still from the mists above
> Bend over me when I'm asleep at dawn,
> Her shadow rises with me when I rise.

The complex form is handled effectively, the conclusion is neat and there is an attempt to balance poetic diction with more colloquial language – 'Is over now', 'gladly go / To Hell for her', 'in actual fact' and 'when I'm asleep'.

All Builth's thirteen pubs were fuller than usual, that baking August, as were the chapels, the churches and the Kino. For Llewelyn Jones and his fellow veterans of the first war, though, its twenty-fifth anniversary was nothing much to celebrate. The imminence of a second conflict with Germany became clear with the signing of the German/Soviet pact, and the recently established Civil Defence Organization circulated information leaflets throughout Wales. 'Your gas mask' and 'Masking your windows' hardly seemed relevant to Trefelin, but they gave T. H. Jones a nightmare based on the image of panicking civilians in the film of H. G. Wells's *The Shape of Things to Come*.[4] Uppermost in the minds of people at Builth, Newbridge and Llanafan was the problem likely to be created by the evacuation of thousands of children from the cities. By the end of August the newspapers were full of the migration of people from London and the South Coast and strange cars began to appear in Llanafan's lanes: middle-class people from Liverpool, Manchester, Birmingham and south Wales were looking for safe houses to rent for the duration.

Sunday 3 September was 'a lovely sunny morning in Builth'.[5] Gwen Davies attended chapel as usual and missed the radio announcement of the ultimatum that would expire at 11 a.m. She returned after Chamberlain's cryptic broadcast at 11.15 to find 'The house already . . . full of soldiers'.[6] In fact there were only four of them, members of the Territorial Army called up a few days earlier. At Llangattock Church the congregation had heard the speech on the vicar's wireless. That evening, at Horeb Chapel in Builth, the Reverend Caradog Owen declared: 'Europe will become a continent of bloodshed on a greater scale than the First World War, but nevertheless the gospel of love and peace will be preached to the whole world . . .'[7]

Caradoc Evans, who had made his own escape to mid-Wales, predictably took a more cynical view:

God never meant me to live in the country. Here you see the same persons every day, and hear the same war grumbles although the war has not touched the farmers yet except to put more money into their pockets and to exempt their sons. One never hears a word about the sacrifices of other people. The war is being fought for certain persons who are not in it . . . [8]

In 1939 there were still in Builth people who felt that the real threat came from the dwellers in the Gogledd, the north Walians, rather than the 'Krauts'. The greatest threat to Builth, to its women at least, would be the GIs, and the nearest it would come to war, the race riots between black and white US servicemen from their segregated camps on opposite sides of the Wye. Even before he began his first term at university, T. H. Jones, according to his friends,[9] was much of Caradoc's mind: 'In all wars the idealist fights for the imagined golden lands, while the practical man gathers the harvest at home. It is easy to be a rebel or a pacifist when one knows . . . the hiding places.'[10]

Soon a party of mothers with young children descended on Builth. They were evacuees from Bootle, and caused consternation by drinking unaccompanied in public houses, fraternizing with local men and creating chaotic queues at the only fish-and-chip shop. As soon as this news reached Llanafan, T. H. Jones and other young men from the villages altered their drinking routines to taste the pleasures of the city women before the latter, bored, homesick and disorientated, returned to perilous Liverpool.

His horizons somewhat broadened, T. H. Jones set off for pastures new with his mother's gnomic advice echoing in his ears: 'Don't take up boxing, and have nothing to do with actresses',[11] and with some of her excellent apple tarts among his luggage. Aberystwyth was still very much The Welsh People's University, its founding transformed into a national epic of the struggle of the *gwerin*. For Gwyn A. Williams his scholarship was of iconic significance, along with: 'The Labour Council noted for both heroic service and unheroic nepotism and petty corruption . . . T.B. (*y ticai*) and dyphtheria ('the dip') . . . of *noson lawen* . . . fights with the fascists on the Bont, and how difficult it was to discuss the performance of the Spitfire in Welsh.'[12] When the war was over, 'Gwyn Alf' would be a co-digger of T. H. Jones's. In 1939 the town was suffering a 'painfully severe dislocation'.[13] Dyfnallt Morgan, president of the SRC, regretted, in a letter to *The Dragon*, magazine of the student body, the evacuation to Aberystwyth of University College, London (UCL):

It makes it difficult for us to maintain our integrity as a community and to preserve our individuality as a Welsh college . . . we are faced with the sad prospect of a dwindling number of men students as the age groups are called up . . . the continuation of a full university life will become increasingly difficult as the war proceeds . . . [14]

T. H. Jones experienced a touch of sweetness almost immediately. He fell in love with a fellow student, Clara (she preferred 'Claire') Jones, daughter of a Carmarthen bank manager. It has been argued that what people were fighting for in the Second World War had far more to do with the security and sense of values represented by their families and loved ones than with abstract notions of anti-Fascism, freedom or patriotism. The threat and the realities of war, for the first time shared more evenly between civilians and the services, facilitated the expression of love, perforce liberating many women and men from traditional inhibitions. Many women gained economic freedom and a degree of sexual liberation. In *Reflections on War and Death*,[15] Freud had made the connection between violence and eroticism: the exigencies of war encourage, even impel, the individual to disregard civilization's inhibition of the natural sex-drive. But 'war aphrodisia' was hardly yet an epidemic at Aberystwyth: *The Dragon* ruefully commented that 'Aber women don't mind hostile hostel restrictions in the least'.[16] Not so the cosmopolitans of UCL: they presented a petition of complaint at being required to be back in Alexandra Hostel by 10 p.m.:

Is it reasonable to expect grown women in their early twenties in this year of grace, 1940, to pack up dancing, pictures, meetings and whatnot when the night is still young, and they are so beautiful, and run along home? . . . at 22 she has to risk heart-failure to get in by 10 . . . at 23, she will amble erratically along, grunting alcoholic ditties, blind to the wide. [17]

T. H. Jones's relationship with Claire lasted on and off until 1944. The second important influence in these early months was the Peace Pledge Union. The Aberystwyth and UCL groups united in a joint Pacifist Club with ninety members, sixty-two of them registered conscientious objectors. Then there was the Labour

Club, a combination of the traditionally moderate Aberystwyth
socialists and the Marxist UCL Socialist Society, 200 members in
all, which T. H. Jones joined during his first few weeks. The
immense and self-confident Roy Evans, another product of Builth
County School, was its president. By no means universally
popular, he was regarded by many as a Welsh front for London
Marxism. 'No gentleman ever weighs more than 200 pounds',[18]
commented *The Dragon*, epigrammatically, and 'Assumes the God,
Affects to Nod'.[19] He was a good friend to T. H. Jones, who
immersed himself in study-circles 'on Marxism and Imperialism',[20]
and a powerful influence, as was the staff representative, Sydney
Herbert. The Labour Club had an excellent programme of
speakers, including Arthur Horner, Jim Griffiths and Krishna
Menon.

The effect of war on the college and its traditions is easily
traceable in the pages of *The Dragon*. After Christmas 1940, a more
serious mood emerges. Parochial commentaries have to make way
for discussions of India, China and Scandinavia. Even 'The College
by the Sea' was obliged to concede that when 'the nation's armed
for battle, when men are faced with killing and being killed and
personal hopes, ambitions, plans are being shattered . . . we are fools
if we do not change our perspective accordingly'.[21] T. H. Jones
engaged in frequent and animated conversations, usually at the
public house, on such issues as the 'mobilisation' of the university
system: 'If, as the government threatens, the universities become
merely technical schools serving the war machine, we students have
no hope of serving the society that made us.'[22] Some students
lamented the loss of the old college spirit as enshrined in archaic
customs such as 'Quadding' (the enforced segregation of the sexes
between lectures by requiring them to circulate in opposite
directions around the college quad). Among other current topics
was the locking away of national art treasures in the now massively
fortified (if not always very well-guarded) National Library.

By January 1940, T. H. Jones was sufficiently established to have
become secretary of the Labour Club and the driving-force
behind its implementation of the tasks set out at the Party's
Liverpool Conference:

> to extend the anti-war movement of the college, to give support
> to the Indian people in their struggle for independence, to assist

in the fight for the preservation and extension of student liberties, and to run campaigns against the spread of the war into Finland and the Scandinavian neutrals.[23]

He signed the secretary's report Harri Jones, the first time he had employed, in print, the name under which he was known to family and friends, but by the time of his next report he had returned to T. Henry Jones. This uncertainty over the appropriate name for public use, already noticed in his schoolboy publications, is an aspect of his search for established identity: all of his mature work would eventually appear as that of T. H. Jones.[24]

Between January and March, under the influence of W. B. Yeats and, to some extent, of T. S. Eliot, he was working on 'The pacifist',[25] his own lament for the gap between the ideal world and the real:

> I think of all who vainly died
> to make the world more fit for men,
> and with a broken-hearted laugh
> I mutter underneath my breath:
> Let all the grain be free from chaff
> in God's good granary after death.

This is the first poem to show signs of maturity, a considerable advance on the love-sonnet. On the reverse is a more interesting love-poem in free verse, 'Acrobat':

> Your heart is an acrobat that will not stand still
> but swings in mad evolutions from the earthfast trapeze
> you have made of my heart. When will you learn
> that stillness is desirable? that the whirl of movement
> is maddening? that I am not to be spurned?
> For, one day, if your acrobatics cease not, the trapeze
> will vanish, you will crash to earth, all movement gone,
> all motion ceased for ever.

The content may be pedestrian, but the conceit is worked out neatly and at length, the rhythm appropriate and the playing off of the sentence unit against the line effective. The influence this time is surely Robert Graves?

The police prevented the anti-war clubs from demonstrating on the promenade, and the university authorities refused to permit the sale or distribution of literature from the Peace Pledge Union, Plaid Cymru, the Socialist Society, the India Society and the Labour Club. Their excuse was that they wished to prevent Communist propaganda. 'Rule by the Red Bogey once more', said T. H. Jones,[26] and paraded the streets with copies of the *Daily Worker*.

His feelings for Claire were serious enough for him to introduce her to the family during the Easter vacation of 1940. Llewelyn was now a corporal in the Home Guard (established as the Local Defence Volunteers – 'Look, duck and vanish'[27] – in 1939). Broomhandles for guns gave way to rifles, uniforms and a modicum of training with regular soldiers on the Eppynt range. The Builth Home Guard had greater pretentions, with its two platoons, gun emplacements and the Wye bridge, fully prepared for demolition, to patrol. Several family photographs show Llew proudly posed in khaki with his First World War stripes up; a particularly striking one shows him, rifle slung, beside a colleague mounted on a pony. The only action Llanafan saw during the entire conflict amounted to clearing up the effect on some sheep of a few jettisoned bombs and an attempt by a fellow member of the platoon to shoot Llew when he pulled rank rather too emphatically.

Signposts had been removed, in mid-Wales as elsewhere, a problem for visitors out on lonely roads. Petrol was rationed, but most farmers managed to secure enough coupons to keep their vehicles running. T. H. Jones took Claire to Builth on the crossbar of his bicycle, to find the kerbs painted white to assist dimmed headlights and air-raid shelters constructed. The Dig-for-Victory Campaign had transformed flowerbeds into vegetable patches. There were no funfairs now on the Groe, but the *Brecon and Radnor Express* reported 'all seats . . . taken by 9 p.m. and the blackout much appreciated'.[28]

Summer 1940 was an acrimonious term at Aberystwyth, with increased tension between UCL students and their more conservative Welsh colleagues. The registrar's *Annual Report* papered over the cracks: 'Undoubtedly many London students have now a nobler conception of Wales and of Welsh university life while our own students are given the unique opportunity of exchanging ideas with a wide selection found in the largest modern British university.'[29] The barriers between townspeople and students had begun to break down. YMCA and YWCA residents began to share aspects of student life; students found themselves drawn into social work, often in connection with the numerous children evacuated from the slums of Liverpool. Claire was a member of the group which discovered that, of 3,000 children evacuated in September 1939, only 411 remained by June 1940. Accommodation was inadequate, no entertainment whatever was available, schooling was very limited because too few teachers had accompanied the children and there was a shortage of textbooks and equipment. The relationship between the LEA and the Liverpool authorities was hampered by excessive bureaucracy, and this was compounded by the insistence of evacuated schools on maintaining their autonomy – 'In one school there are six headmasters with only a few children in their charge'.[30]

T. H. Jones's continuing political activities gave him an unusually high profile for a fresher. In a debate between the United War Movement Society and the Pacifists, he was singled out for particular criticism. He spoke for a Charter of Student Rights and against staff who were slow to modify their pre-war attitude that 'Students hold no rights, only privileges'.[31] When *The Dragon* complained of prison-like conditions at Alexandra Hall, threats of legal action were made and an apology demanded. None was made, and the matter was eventually dropped, but the dispute convinced T. H. Jones that it would be worth surviving the war 'just to return and edit *The Dragon*'.[32]

The aim of the United War Effort Society was to suppress 'subversive elements within the college'.[33] It regarded the local Pacifists' Tribunal as too soft on conscientious objectors, savaged the Peace Pledge Union for 'assisting the spineless specimens who, angelically waving a bible . . . gave their answers as practised at the PPU mock tribunals', and insisted, in direct reference to T. H. Jones and a few of his friends from south Wales, that 'The propaganda disseminated by the Communists through their medium, the *Daily Worker*, must be stopped'.[34] With the approach of examinations, the college authorities were more than ready to accept complaints from the police and ARP about lax blackout and late-night noise at Alexandra Hall. They responded by insisting on 'the use of candles only' after 10.30 p.m. – very petty, T. H. Jones thought, against the background of war in Europe. There were a few compensations, the Labour Club's private production of Odets's *Waiting for Lefty* among them, but, tired and disillusioned, he was happy to escape for the summer vacation.

Summer dragged by. Very short of money, he had to apply for a further loan. His occasional term-time sessions of poker had been of little help, but luckily, with many men now called up, there was no shortage of employment at Newbridge. He worked for Hope's, a local building firm, and at weekends 'tushed' timber with his favourite cousin and drinking-partner, Afan Bwlchciliau. Sometimes he got in to Builth or Rhayader at the weekend. The Enniskillen Dragoon Guards had been moved there directly from the Dunkirk beaches and an apocryphal story went round the pubs about a soldier who had discarded a fortune in gold to swim for his life. There was no shortage of female company, partly because Hilda Vaughan, the Builth-born writer of romantic fiction, had returned there to organize young women from all over Britain into the Brecon and Radnor WLA Battalion. The Kino opened on Sundays now, in spite of a letter of complaint from the town council to the home secretary.

Michaelmas term saw an event of epochal significance for Wales in the appointment of the young, but distinguished editor of the *Welsh Review*, Gwyn Jones, to the chair of English. T. H. Jones would later establish a fruitful, if uneasy relationship with him. Some of the tensions of May and June had evaporated. T. H. Jones returned as an established character and became the somewhat unlikely treasurer of *The Dragon*, which honoured him with the aphorism, 'I drink when I have occasion and sometimes when I have no occasion'.[35] Roy Evans wrote that 'One of the good things the war has done is to mix up various student bodies. In this way, any amount of provincialism, local prejudice and snobbishness is eliminated.'[36] Students now enrolled in the ARP, the OTC and the STC. T. H. Jones ceased to be secretary of the Labour Club, though he remained a member of its very active committee. He was fully involved in study-groups: 'A.B.C. of Socialism' (alternate Thursdays) and Idris Bell's 'British Foreign Policy' group. The club started its own periodical, *The Clarion*, but it ran for a few issues only.

Student numbers were, inevitably, reduced. The mood shifted from pacifism to almost universal support for collective security. T. H. Jones's mood shifted too: he took up boxing, trained intensively and, although imperfectly co-ordinated, fought like the devil and made full use of the height/weight advantage conferred by his excessively lean frame. As the only student of English in the UCL/UCW Boxing Club, he naturally became secretary. Less naturally, he penned for *The Dragon* excessively boring accounts of its activities. The first part of his mother's advice had gone by the board. Eric Corfield was one of the magazine's targets that term: 'I want to be a sheikh, I do, I don't want to be a school-teacher',[37] and never forgave T. H. Jones, a member of its inner circle, for the innocent jibe. After the war Corfield, as senior English master at Builth County School, blocked all moves to honour 'yet another Anglo-Welsh windbag'.[38]

T. H. Jones occasionally drank with Tom Sallis, from Bargoed, an old boy of Pengam School. Alun Lewis was a name to conjure with at Aberystwyth, and Tom told stories of walking to school with his English teacher 'who used to take the mickey out of me something dreadful'.[39] One weekend, T. H. Jones, only there for the beer, accompanied the rugby team to a match against the Royal Artillery at Tywyn. When the train stopped at Dyfi Junction, Tom recognized, and called out to, an untidy figure in worn battledress:

Alun Lewis came up, and in his quiet voice said to me, 'What are you doing, Sallis?' 'Playing rugby, sir.' 'Still being the blood, Sallis, are you?'

He was a lovely man, a superb, sympathetic teacher, always with a wry smile on his face. In school, he would sit with his feet up on the table and read out from our Sixth Form essays – 'I've got a beauty here: "Voltaire harnessed the horses of reason; Rousseau unleashed the tigers of emotion".'

In retrospect, Harri and him were so much alike.[40]

On Friday 25 April 1941 Vera Brittain, on the slow train from Shrewsbury, enjoyed the late spring. 'Railway banks covered with primroses, anemones and celandines, going into this unbombed, unimpaired country from England was like entering another world.'[41] At Aberystwyth she delivered the annual Foundation oration, taking as her subject 'The shape of the future'. The hall was crowded, and the students, she recalled:

listened attentively, without shuffling their feet, and hardly anyone left, which showed their interest. But though everyone seemed pleased afterwards, I did not feel it was one of my best speeches. There was too large a space between the platform and the audience for easy contact and, after sherry, we went on into a town café. All the hotels were crowded with army, R.A.F. and university.[42]

T. H. Jones was so impressed that he began, in an eventually prize-winning essay, 'Visions', to explore some of his own ideas. 'Visions' won in the inter-college eisteddfod, and it is a remarkable achievement for a nineteen-year-old from a rural background, an enormous advance from the prose of *The Wyeside*.

It begins with the premise that modern man has lost the ability to be, in Blake's sense, visionary, and then seeks to disprove it with a series of utopian visions of the post-war world:

Our visions are of a new world, whence ugliness and war, if not pain and death, have vanished, a world cleanly, ordered, decent, where each works for all, and yet each individual personality has every facility for the fullest expansion and development . . . For prophets and kings we substitute in our visions power and planning. We see these two things utilized, so that war and ugliness and dirt and disease are banished, and a new, confident civilization rises, phoenix-like, from the ashes of the old.[43]

That the defiant optimism of this is founded in Marxism is evident from 'each works for all . . . power and planning', and from the quotation of Auden ('New styles of architecture, a change of heart'[44]) and Spender ('The pylons'), but it is the Marxism of a poet, for the essay ends, as it began, with William Blake: 'Perhaps in the morrow of that new world, some new Blake will arise, who will see the International Brigade walking among the haymakers, and with whom Marx and Lenin will dine.' And a wry touch typical of the mature writer warns us to take a small pinch of salt: 'I began this essay by saying we have lost our faculty for seeing visions: I have spent the greater part of it in making statements contradictory to that assertion. That is because I do not really believe in it.' It is not only the poems that 'lie'.

From time to time, throughout his life, T. H. Jones produced, rather in the Welsh bardic tradition, performance pieces ('The first Christmas'[45] is a prose, and 'The enemy in the heart'[46] a verse example); 'Visions' is his first performance piece. Its prose is, in turn, lyrical, resonant and colloquial. Its range of reference is wide: Blake, H. G. Wells (whom he patronizes as 'too essentially bourgeois'), Eliot, Proust, Lenin, Moses, Pericles, Hegel, Marx, Joan of Arc. He quotes from, or alludes to the Bible, Yeats and Chaucer ('The house of fame') as well as Auden and Spender, and the future for which he hopes is, in consequence, deeply rooted in the past. Chaucer's dream-vision, derived from Dante, concludes with the bearers of false tidings about to be confuted; Blake's 'Albion' derives from Celtic legend. T. H. Jones's vision relates to the Eden of David Jones's paintings, populated by transcendental beings walking in a garden paradise, and to those of Ceri Richards, with their bounding sensuality. Amid the savage military setbacks, he has found something worth his fighting for.

He spent part of the summer of 1941 working at Dolfallen, and in July volunteered for the Royal Navy:

> The lecherous and griefless sea
> Was always more beckoning than gardens
> To a boy from bare, exciting mountains.

he was to write, in 'But if it be a boy you shall put him to the sea'[47] (11 October 1962). His family, who had not read 'Visions', were mystified.

He was sent to HMS *Ganges*, the shore-based training establishment at Harwich, for initial assessment, and then to Gloucester for basic training. He made many friends there, and it is a pity that no letters have survived from that period because it was one of the formative experiences of his life. There he came to understand and appreciate that close comradeship unique to naval service. From Gloucester he went to HMS *Scotia*, at Ayr, to complete his training as a telegraphist. This job, which required intelligence but carried no privileges of rank, was one for which the services frequently chose clever working-class men. Unfortunately for the biographer, T. H. Jones was never much of a correspondent and most of the letters which survive are of the protective/uninformative kind which all men on active service are obliged to write, by censorship or out of consideration for the anxiety of their families back home. There were certainly other letters – to Claire Jones, for example – but it has been impossible to trace any of them.

The first to survive is from Ayr, dated 'Saturday' (10 or 17 January 1942) and, apart from domestic matters (receiving cigarettes, sending clothes home to be washed and enquiries about his sisters – Brenda joined the WRAF, Myra the Land Army and Valerie (aged ten) and Pat (aged eight) were still at school), contains an anecdote which reveals something about the Home Front at the time:

> another chap and me went for a walk along the beach. After we had gone a few miles, we went up a path and came to a house. We were feeling thirsty, so we called and asked for some water. They took us in and gave us some tea and cake. It was very nice I can tell you.[48]

On Thursday 29 January, his training complete, he set out from Ayr, supposedly for Portsmouth: 'We started from Ayr at 8 o'clock last night and arrived here at 4 o'clock this afternoon. That's the longest journey I have ever been on.'[49] He was not at Portsmouth, but at HMS *Mercury* at Petersfield, and went on leave the following day, visiting Claire at Aberystwyth before returning to Trefelin. A family photograph celebrating the occasion shows Llew in his best suit, with polka-dot tie, watch and silver chain, smiling broadly. Ruth, in her best frock, is looking serious. The sailor stands between his two elder sisters; Valerie and Pat complete the group. It was the last time the whole family would be together.

The period in this transit camp was the low point of his naval experience. Although it was 'like our old Gloucester home, right out in the country', it had the usual disadvantages of the transit-camp: 'temporary, everybody is always coming and going. Nobody settles down properly. Also everything is much dirtier than it has been in other places.'[50] The next letter reports that he is 'expecting to be drafted any time, as out of 17 of us 15 have already had ships.' Only he and Bill, 'the boy from Aberaeron . . . one of my old pals',[51] remained. Ruth had forwarded the family photographs and, remembering Mrs Price, Dolfallen, he asked for her to be given a copy of the group. Like his companions in limbo, he was being kept occupied. On one occasion at least he was able to put his Dolfallen skills to good use:

> I've done all sorts of jobs since I've been here except the one I've been training for for the last 6 months. I even had the job of

working a horse and cart the other day when we were shifting some huts and I was the only bloke who had ever been near a horse. It was a grand job compared to some we get and I wouldn't mind having it every day. I've also been a sentry in the middle of the night. Luckily it was a fine night. [52]

Shortly afterwards a hasty note from the Royal Naval Barracks, Portsmouth announced: 'I'm off to my destroyer (HMS *Airedale*): I've no idea where I'll be going except that I am going abroad . . . Write regularly even if you don't hear from me, I'll get the letters some time.' [53] He managed a farewell drink with 'Mick and a couple of the boys' and the following day he wrote at greater length:

After an all night train journey I'm on board ship. This is a last minute letter we're allowed to write. I'm not allowed to tell you anything as to where I'm going or where I am . . . please put the enclosed letter in an envelope and post it to Miss Claire Jones, 17 Spilman Street, Carmarthen. I believe that when you write to me now, you will only need to put a 1½*d.* stamp . . . and remember, I'll be home again some time. [54]

He was probably at Liverpool, aboard one of the six large passenger liners commandeered as troopships because they were fast enough to travel without escort and could accommodate as many as 15,000 men. Because the Axis dominated the western Mediterranean, the route was via Freetown, Sierra Leone and the Cape, where, like many another serviceman, he thoroughly enjoyed a few days of South African hospitality before changing ships to travel via the Indian Ocean, Red Sea and Suez Canal to Alexandria.

Four letters, two of them dated 20 April (one to Myra, the other to his parents and younger sisters), survive from the voyage. They show that his first real experience of the sea which had fascinated him from an early age[55] was a pleasant one. He did not suffer from seasickness:

I feel very fit and healthy, and my face is quite sunburnt. I love being at sea . . . We have a very free and easy time but life is very dull at sea when you have nothing to do . . . . fags 10 for 4*d.* and beer 4½*d*. a pint. We are only allowed 2 pints a day by the way . . . We get plenty of food here, and it's of better quality and better cooked than any I've had in the Navy. Also, in the canteen we get loads of chocolate and sweets, which I wish I could give to the kids. I don't eat them myself, because I think it is wrong that we should have them, when the children can't. [56]

Further complaints follow: there is not enough hot water to wash himself and keep his clothes clean, and he is missing his Welsh pals. The letter to Myra regrets that he cannot help her find a pen-pal and comforts her for lack of success with young men. 'Be patient, you'll meet some nice lad one of these days.' He signs off, jocularly, '*Au Revoir*, Harri.'[57]

The voyage was uneventful, but T. H. Jones's first letter from Alexandria reveals a narrow escape. 'I am safe and well, and on a ship at last, although it is not the one I was sent out here to join.'[58] His widow, Madeleine Mitchell, explains that 'While on a brief leave in Alexandria he caught 'flu and was sent to the sick bay at the naval depot. He missed the sailing of his ship . . .'[59] He was reassigned to HMS *Seaham*, a recently built, newly arrived mine-sweeper. *Airedale*, which had left Alexandria on 13 June to escort Malta convoy MW11, was bombed on 15 June by German and Italian aircraft, set on fire and had to be scuttled by torpedo and gunfire: 133 of her crew were rescued; 42 lost their lives. His parents, who had heard of the sinking from a radio news bulletin, had been left in cruel suspense for a considerable time.

T. H. Jones served aboard *Seaham* until October 1943 and in shore bases at Algiers, Bougie and, possibly, Naples until October 1944, when he returned to Britain. The overwhelming impression conveyed by the letters is of deep concern for, and interest in his family and friends at home, anxiety to keep in touch with his Gloucester pals and the crushing boredom and discomfort of life at sea. Although the letters give not the slightest hint of this, 1942 is the year of the Malta convoys:

During the short period at the turn of the year when Rommel had been driven out of Cyrenaica five supply ships reached Malta, but with Rommel's first forward moves at the beginning of 1942 the Luftwaffe was able to reoccupy North African airfields which, together with its bases in Crete were used to

interdict the passage of east–west convoys. In February an entire
convoy, attempting to make this passage, was destroyed; its last
surviving ship was scuttled in desperation. In March a convoy of
four vessels, attacked from the air and by the Italian surface fleet,
managed to get two ships through . . . In June an attempt was
made to run convoys simultaneously from east and west. Of the
eastern convoy no ship reached the island but from the west two
out of seventeen merchantmen made port. In August a further
convoy of fourteen merchantmen sailed from the west. Five of its
ships reached Malta; one of them, the American tanker Ohio,
torpedoed on two successive days, arrived lashed between two
destroyers. In both these operations the escort fleets suffered
very heavily. The losses included the British aircraft carrier Eagle
which went down with a squadron of spitfires on board.[60]

Madeleine (Jones) Mitchell gives an idea of her husband's true
feelings: 'it was terrifying escorting convoys between Africa and
Malta. He dreamed for the rest of his life of the attacks by Stuka
bombers on their ship.'[61] An unpublished poem inspired by the
question, 'Have you ever been frightened?', records such an
incident:

> Stukas screaming down
> While I repeated mechanically, meaninglessly,
> 'Get the bastards, get the bastards,' for once
> *En rapport* with our gunners – I was trapped
> In a box with dot-dash dash-dot hammering
> My head.[62]

As we know,[63] T. H. Jones had been fascinated by the sea from
an early age. His initial interest, a straightforward boys' adventure
fiction, was a dream brutally transformed to nightmare by the
reality of war. Their war service was the supreme experience for
men of his generation. Some would test the patience of their
families for the rest of their lives by compulsively retelling one
story. T. H. Jones never did this, but the condition of his
subconscious mind might have been healthier if he had. In his
great war-poem, 'Lucky Jonah',[64] he refers to 'all of life' as 'a long
survivor's leave' and the mature poetry is full of imagery drawn
from the sea, its unifying thread danger, in particular the
nightmare, death by drowning. The epigraph of 'Lucky Jonah'

would be 'A man born to be hanged cannot be drowned'. 'Sailor' (19 February 1954) contains the stanza:

> Remembered tides at once roar in his ears
> And ride him down beneath his frightened eyes.
> Scrabble and gasp among the plunging fears
> Betray the nonchalance with which he lies.[65]

Ronnie Roantree, T. H. Jones's great friend on HMS *Seaham*, recalls one of the many incidents that could not be written home about – sailing out of Benghazi on a clear, moonlit night:

> We didn't like being at sea in those conditions – the phosphorescent wake of the convoy was so easy to pick up. We were all at action stations. The *Snapdragon* was sunk with the convoy captain on board. We went to pick up the survivors. The captain kept shouting out from the blazing ship, 'Carry on with the convoy!', and then another stick of bombs took him away. Ollie, Harri and myself would often put one in three of our rum ration away neat in a bottle to use after we'd been in action, to steady our nerves. Harri had been on watch and seen it all. We'd come below a little earlier and had had tinned fish, putting our vinegar in a rum-glass on the table. Harri came in, shaking, and hit the glass straight back in one. Typically, he kept a straight face and said, 'I think I'll have my rum now.'[66]

In quiet intervals between storms of this kind, T. H. Jones learned to swim, using ship's lifebelts as water-wings. He read a good deal: Shakespeare, *Penguin New Writing*,[67] *The Welsh Review*,[68] *Horizon*[69] and, precious in a different way, the *Brecon and Radnorshire Gazette*, which he swapped with a friend from Kington for the *Hereford Times*. He introduced Roantree to Wordsworth and Shelley. Roantree 'never saw Harri write poetry during the war, at least not on board ship. After the war Harri said to me, "I might just have a couple of books in me"'[70] but Madeleine Mitchell recalls that he drafted poems during the boredom of the long watches at sea and during quiet moments in the signals room:

> There are many poems worked out on naval message pads – he tried unsuccessfully to place some of them – A great shortage of

paper and the few poetry magazines received more poems than they could publish. He was always trying and was never too disappointed with reject slips.[71]

Twenty-two poems/drafts from the period April 1942–December 1945 survive in manuscript, including one of 'This hero now' sent by air letter to *Horizon* on 2 February 1944 (it was rejected and returned but published, unaltered, in 1947[72]) and three which, since they have a return address on them, may be presumed to have been sent to that or other literary magazines.

He would later, in his Oliver & Boyd monograph, quote with approval Dylan Thomas's assertion:

War can't produce poetry, only poets can, and war can't produce poets either because they bring themselves up in such a war but this outward bang bang of men against men is something they have passed a long time ago on their poems' way towards peace. A poet writing a poem is at peace with everything except words, which are eternal actions; only in the lulls between the warring work on words can he be at war with man. Poets can stop bullets, but bullets can't stop poets. What is a poet anyway? He is a man who has written or is writing what he, in his utmost human fallible integrity, necessarily communal, believes to be good poetry. As he writes good poetry very rarely, he is most often at peace with the eternal actions of words and is therefore very likely to be caught up in any bang bang that is going. When he is fighting he is not a poet. Nor is a craftsman a craftsman. I think capital lettered WAR can only in subject-matter effect poetry. Violence and suffering are all the same, and that it does not matter how you are brought up against them.[73]

A powerful reason for not being seen to write poetry was the way that the navy maintained, indeed reinforced, both the decencies and the injustices of British society. For intelligent working-class young men the class system was in no sense levelled up. According to Roantree, the effect of this on his leftist friend was to encourage him 'to be an inverted snob . . . You didn't take a commission, just in case you had to mix with the officers.'[74] On one occasion T. H. Jones, known to be the mess-scribe and interpreter of letters to the illiterate, was detailed to write up a court-martial. In an act of conscious defiance, he made a mess of it and was taken to task by the first lieutenant, who asked whether they had taught him to write in paragraphs at school. This was neither the time nor the place to play the university man, or the poet either. The officers were decent enough by their own lights (he was asked by a couple of them to teach them all the French he knew and 'accepted because, though I don't know if I can do it, I believe in having a try. It ought to be quite interesting, and a very good experience for me'[75]) but they would not have shared his intellectual interests even if they had been able: they tended to look on educated ratings as the stuff of which barrack-room lawyers were made. In the First World War, as T. H. Jones would later maintain in conversation with Donald Jones, educated men had died leading the uneducated into oblivion; in the Second, the ranks were full of bored, defiant, disaffected intellectuals, many of whom would become influential radical instructors during the demobilization period.

One way of coping was simple bloody-mindedness. 'We drank hard, we got paid for six weeks, went ashore, and that was that – the release', says Roantree.[76] He and his friend deliberately failed their promotion examinations. On one shore-leave in Algiers, T. H. Jones encountered an old acquaintance, John Elwyn Williams, 'one of the bright Dowlais boys of his generation'.[77] Williams was a commissioned officer, but he was a working-class Welshman first, and they swapped uniforms for a night of mischief and misrule.

The letters home show a young man with a profound loving concern for family and friends: although most of the surviving letters are to 'Mam, Dad and All', he also wrote individually to Myra and Brenda, to Grandpa and Auntie Maggie and to Valerie and Pat. He inquires minutely about his parents', grandfather's and sisters' health and the latters' progress at school, commiserates with a neighbour for the death of her baby and with other neighbours for bad or tragic news of their sons. They show also (extremely important for this poet) a young man deeply in love for the first time. Thirty letters survive for the period of fifty-six weeks from 11 June 1942 to 25 July 1943 (an average of one every two weeks, excluding the weekly letters to Claire Jones, none of which we have been permitted to trace). There is then a gap of nearly a year (but no reason to suppose that he wrote less regularly during that time) and eight letters from the period 3 June 1944 to 28 December 1945. Although, for obvious reasons, the authorities made every effort to deliver correspondence regularly, it was subject to the vicissitudes of war: T. H. Jones did not receive his first letter from home until 1 August 1942, nearly four months after it had been posted. On 6 March 1943 he reports that photographs sent to his friend, Ollie, have arrived stained with sea water; and there are frequent complaints that no letters have been received for extended periods. Almost all of his own letters are short and often the strain imposed by essential omissions shows through – 'I guess this isn't much for 1*s*. 3*d*. but I'm afraid it will have to do as I have nothing more to say' is a typical, recurrent comment.

References to Claire treat her as already a member of the family. She is mentioned twelve times, usually as having written or been written to, and it is clear that she was writing as regularly as he was. Writing to Valerie and Pat in 1943, he says: 'I am going to see *Gone with the Wind*[78] tomorrow night, the very long film, you know, all in colour. I'd like to take you with me to see that, though I'd rather take Claire!' In June he 'has had a lovely photograph of Claire in her graduation gown yesterday'.[79] There is no alteration of tone in the first letter after the long gap.[80] In it he hopes that Val has 'passed for the County this year' because 'Claire says you are very much like me'. The relationship survived, on his part, until at least 9 July 1944, when he has 'just written to Claire'. At some time thereafter we know, from Ronnie Roantree, that he 'got a letter from Claire. The usual sort of thing, "I'm sorry etc . . ."'[81] But, although this must have caused great distress, the nearest we have to a direct reaction is in the reference to another woman in a letter to Donald Jones in 1945: 'I have been indulging in a grand passion for the past three months – very soothing and gratifying to my soul and body after three womanless years.'[82]

Several of the war-period poems throw light on the relationship with Claire Jones. In the song, 'Calling within us the spring . . .' there are conventional equations between passion and the seasons:

> Calling within us the spring
> Answering itself in the blood
> Foretelling function of summer
> Pregnant with increase of autumn
> Nescient of winter's decay;

> Calling within us the spring,
> Poetry leaping to answer
> The call of the flux of us the blood
> Love, a bacchanal dancer . . . [83]

The 'bacchanal dancer' recalls the hyperactive heart of 'Acrobat'; the whole poem is very much in 1930s style, almost pastiche.

'In the duality of man . . .',[84] inspired, presumably, by sexual frustration, explores the conflict between man as rutting stag and worshipper of chastity. 'No more for you and I, my love . . .' reflects nostalgically on courtship at Aberystwyth:

> No more for you and I, my love, the warm retreat
> In pub or cinema; the privacy of the sheet,
> The intimate coffee, or the long, slow walks
> Around the old town, or the quiet talks
> Watching the moonlight silver all the beach . . .[85]

This is an unsuccessful, incomplete draft whose very conventionality and failure serve to emphasize a strength of feeling for which no objective correlative has been found.

'Similes in exile',[86] in contrast, was sufficiently achieved to be sent to a literary magazine. It also is very much in 1930s style:

> Similes of sunlight at thought of you occur,
> Patterning their brightness on the parched air
> Of this exile like birds' song descending
> From its high tower, or waves befriending
> A lonely beach.
>   Within this envelope
> Of flesh, this crumbling keep
> Of bones and blood, are images
> Of you; symbols are in the sky; and these
> Are timeless though your beauty's mortal.
> Time is a prison; and its granite portal
> Opens upon eternity; the key is love,
> And though we love now at remove
> Of space and time, I still hold in my hand
> Your heart fluttering like a caught bird.
> We are out of focus; but adjust your mind,
> Tune in the wavelength of the whispered word,

And you shall hear me: the mutual response
Of our two hearts will outlive our mere romance.

Here again is an apprentice poet, struggling to escape, one might suggest, from an excess of Palgrave's *Golden Treasury* at school (clichés abound): Shakespeare clashes with Auden and MacNeice, the assonantal rhyme indicates an awareness of Wilfred Owen and the image of 'tuning in' is highly suitable in a poet whose daily occupation is wireless telegraphy. The first two lines of another fragment are the apt comment of a conscious apprentice: 'The loose leaves of the poems I have read, / Remembered, drift like ghosts of autumn, down'.[87]

The contrast between 'The singing wonder of the stars . . .'[88] and 'Nostalgia'[89] may perhaps reflect the reception, at some time between the two, of the letter to which Ronnie Roantree referred. The former is a perfectly achieved exercise in a conventional form:

> The singing wonder of the stars
> Shall heal these scars,
> The shadowed beauty of the night
> Yet give delight
> To mind and body, ease
> Be found beneath tall trees,
> And all lost joys
> Recaptured in her face and voice.
> The singing wonder of the stars
> Shall heal these scars.

The latter expresses love for a place – Wales, unusually for this poet, industrial south (his mother's country) as well as rural mid-Wales. Its 'nostalgia' is for a return to the womb:

> Waves whelm me westwards from this antique sea
> to read my own land's verdant scripture.
> Time is here a mirror
> for its own failures.
> I would see a river
> and a mountain lonely in the sky,
> and the dark friendliness of trees.
> Antiquity's monotone
> is reflected in this changing, unchanging sea.
> I want to feel again a modern fever

> and see a pithead, a town's crucifix,
> and the long street straggling down the mountainside,
> the huddled cottages,
> and the twin comfort of the pub and chapel.

The emotion is under control and the form, free verse controlled by sentence-units of two, two, three, two and five lines, creates an effective movement and a satisfying climax. The play of vowel-sounds and assonances is prophetic of the mature work. The main influence here is, not surprisingly, Idris Davies although 'Antiquity's monotone' echoes Eliot's 'Capricious monotone'.[90] The 'mirror' image is characteristic of the early mature poems of the 1940s.

Two days after T. H. Jones's first letter from *Seaham*[91] the Eighth Army had lost 230 tanks. Eight days later Tobruk had fallen and a week after that the British had retreated to within sixty miles of his base at Alexandria. Only five months later Rommel had been defeated at El Alamein (23 October), Operation Torch (8 November) carried out and Tobruk retaken (13 November). By the end of the period covered by the surviving letters, the Germans had surrendered in North Africa, Mussolini had fallen from power and the Allies had entered Rome and landed in Normandy. Little of this was, or could be, reflected in them. On 23 June 1942, writing to Grandpa and Auntie Maggie, he reports meeting Ned Hughes:

> I was ashore the other night, and having a glass of beer with a couple of the lads, when some other sailors came in and started talking to us. After a bit one of them asked me if my name was Jones. I took a good look at him, and it was Ned Hughes. He had just been sunk, but was quite alright, though very fed-up at being out here again so soon.

On 30 August, not long after the loss of the aircraft carrier, HMS *Eagle*, he describes his situation as 'fairly safe, which is a good thing, but I would rather put up with a bit of risk if only I could get home now and again'.[92] By 20 September, he is spending most of his time at sea and on 7 November reveals that, for the first time since he joined the ship, the whole crew have been given three days' leave. After D-Day he looks forward to the end of the war:

Every day brings good news now, and there are grounds for hoping that it may not be so very long now before this war is at last over, and we can all go back to the ways of peace again, which is the fervent hope of every one of us.[93]

And that is all.

With only a few exceptions, it is the people and surroundings of Llanafan that provide the high points of the correspondence: his grandfather's increasing blindness; births, marriages and deaths; whether Valerie will get to the County School and Pat has recovered from a problem with her hands; his father's achievements in the Home Guard; the seasons and the rural activities that go with them. 'You all seem to have done very well at the whinberry picking. Wish I could be there to eat some of those tarts.'[94] 'The kids must be enjoying themselves with all these holidays for potato picking. Tell them I want to know exactly how many potatoes they have each picked.'[95] 'Thank all the Ystrad people for their kind thoughts, and tell them that I hope to be coming round for supper again one of these days, and I hope there'll be some cider there!'[96] 'You seem to be having a lovely spring at home. I wish I was there to see it.'[97] This astonishing spring was still vividly in his mind nearly twenty years later when he wrote, for his youngest sister, Pat, the Edward Thomas-like lines

> A wind blew, warm as loving, from the west
> And the girls came out like berries. The old hedgerows
> Were sprung and blossomed to life, and could not rest
> Till the hawthorn was subdued by one torn rose.[98]

On two occasions he makes a memorable contrast between this world and the one in which war service forces him to exist:

It is Sunday morning and there is just the same air of rest and quiet around as there is on a Sunday morning in summer at home, though perhaps this peaceful atmosphere is somewhat deceptive here. It is already quite warm. By the time I go on watch again this afternoon it'll be really hot. I like the sunlight but I often wish I could exchange the heat for a nippy frost. One is continually thirsting and, as Dad says he used to, I often think with longing of the cold, clear water at home. We have been lucky in getting a few lemons so that we have been able to make some lemonade and also to make tea with lemons instead of milk

– a most refreshing drink. This is the first fresh fruit we have had
for a long time though we have heaps of tinned pears and
peaches. That probably makes your mouths water but just think
that mine is watering quite as much at the thought of the fresh
food I could get at home.[99]

It's funny to think of it being shearing time now back home,
because it's so long since I have really seen sheep. I have seen
them, even here, but it is only an occasional specimen, rather as
one might see a goat at home, and never a flock; and anyway a
sheep on a lead in the street with an Arab at the other end of the
lead is very different from a sheep on the hillsides at home.[100]

The three-day leave in November 1942 was based at what is
euphemistically described as 'an army rest camp on the beach . . .
I went with Ronnie and a couple of others, and when our money
ran out after two days we returned to the camp and had a lot of
fun, chiefly bathing and drinking beer.'[101] This is how he reports it
in his letter of 7 November, under the impression that censorship
does not permit him to describe what had really occurred. By 13
December he has learned that he can reveal that two days were
spent in Jerusalem, and the letter of this date is perhaps most
interesting of all. Knowing that his mother will be interested to
hear about the Holy Places, he made a special effort and produced
something close to a consciously literary effusion:

the town is built on four hills and the surrounding country is
very wild. In places on the bus ride there and back I could almost
imagine myself going over the [Brecon] Beacons . . . In the
morning we went to Bethlehem, and saw the Church of the
Nativity, where is the crypt where Christ was born. Like all the
churches there, it is very beautiful, full of lovely things. I bought
a couple of small presents in Bethlehem,– a small book with the
cover made of olive wood from the Mount of Olives for you,
Mam, and some handkerchiefs marked Jerusalem and
Bethlehem for the girls . . .[102]

The gifts were posted home, arrived safely and remain in the
family's possession. The letter goes on to mention the Pool of
Siloam, the church of St Peter built 'on the spot where Peter
betrayed Christ . . . we also saw the House of Caiaphas where
Christ was imprisoned and scourged', and rounds off with

Solomon's Quarries and the Garden of Gethsemane. But just before writing, he had heard of the tragic, ironical death of his friend, Elwyn Davies, who, having survived two shipwrecks, had been killed in a road accident.

The invasion of Sicily on 10 July 1943 was a seminal experience. It would be sixteen years before this, the convoy experiences and the whole Mediterranean episode found their full artistic expression, in 'Lucky Jonah',[103] the finest war-poem never to be anthologized. A delay of this length in coming even partially to terms with the appalling events of modern warfare is neither surprising nor unusual: the great prose works of the First World War took ten years to emerge. Ronnie Roantree remembers the episode which was to form the controlling centre of the poem: 'For some reason, a mistake probably, an Italian submarine surfaced. Certainly it was unaware of the British ships that surrounded it, and we went in to ram it. At the last moment, the skipper brought us round. Harri was up on deck.'[104] The submarine was the *Bronzo* and a series of graphic photographs taken by another of T. H. Jones's shipmates survives to supplement the poem's account. 'One day we caught a submarine, trapped like a fish / In the relentless circle of sixteen ships.' Its attempt to surrender was ignored in an instinctive act of revenge:

> and still our gunners
> Pressed their automatic fingers
> To make her run with blood.

T. H. Jones's friend, Ollie, went aboard, and on his return the effect of the experience was obvious to everyone:

> He had gone down into the conning-tower, and bits of bodies were everywhere. The captain of the submarine was not an Italian, but a German. He was badly mutilated, but still conscious. The officer in charge was called 'Piggy', a bank clerk before the war. He just took out his revolver and shot the German through the head.[105]

The wounded were laid out on *Seaham's* upper deck. One man was dying – 'Like a butchered sheep',[106] it seemed to the country-boy looking on. Although he 'tried for it', he could feel no pity.

The *Bronzo* was towed to Syracuse; strategic charts discovered on board assisted the successful and relatively bloodless attack on Taranto in September.

'Lucky Jonah' will be examined in more detail in its proper place – the escape from schoolteaching at Portsmouth and the voyage back through the Mediterranean on his way to Australia. However, it is worth referring, at this point, to the aspects of this, and one or two other later poems relating to the whole Mediterranean experience, which supplement the limited bio-graphical information afforded by the letters and the recollections of Ronnie Roantree. 'Lucky Jonah' is an elegy, by the man who 'cannot be drowned',[107] for those who have been, or have other-wise lost their lives. Central among them is Elwyn Davies, the friend with whom the poet, as a boy, had dreamed of ships although (or perhaps because) they 'saw the sea [only] once annually when the Sunday School / Charabanced us . . . to the . . . coast / Of Wales'. As we know, Davies did not drown, in spite of being twice sunk, an irony which intensifies the tragedy. The convoys are evoked first by means of understatement – 'I saw a ship go down, / Quietly in the middle of the afternoon' – and then with the specific horror of 'The scalded stokers and the sick, singed smell'. The tensions that could not be mentioned in letters home, but haunted T. H. Jones's nightmares for the rest of his unquiet life, are conveyed by:

> The mad, forgiven captains – 'Clear Lower Deck.
> I have to tell you that we probably sha'n't
> Set foot on land again. Men, I rely on you.'

and the lookout brought up at Defaulters because 'He sees a submarine / In the undershadow of every blasted wave'. Character-istically, even in their worst moments sailors do not wish to exchange places with their fellow combatants in the army: 'Thank God / We're not poor bloody pongoes in the sand.'

Boredom is hinted at only as an overtone in the opening line's 'blue yawn of the sea', but shore-leave features prominently. Elwyn Davies is encountered 'in a brazen bar / In Alexandria'. Brawls, rum and 'offered sisters – "Nice girl, very clean"' develop the picture, and a haunting passage, reminiscent of *Under Milk Wood*, remembers the 'Jacks who are not jolly any more':

Remember me, mate? Had a run ashore
With you in Alex. once. We found a girl
And christened her the Nut-Brown Maid.
Remember me? I hit a gharri-driver once
Because he wouldn't let me have his whip.
Remember me? I fell out of the motor-boat.

And the poet's tongue lingers lovingly on Mediterranean place-names: 'Alex., Benghazi, Tripoli, Algiers, / Beirut, Valletta, Famagusta.'

'Lucky Jonah' is consciously related to the childhood experience of 'A day at the seaside' explored in Chapter 2. Many poems would develop out of the destruction of childhood innocence by young adult experience. 'Mediterranean: wartime'[108] looks back to 'the corrupted patterns of the war . . . Drinking in bars around the sunlit harbours . . . [holding] the middle sea in a glass of wine / And [listening] to the vowelled bawdiness / Hiding a world of longings'. 'Sailor', 'Voyages' and 'Adrift' evoke the combination of boredom and fear that characterizes seafaring in time of war:

Witness the longdrawn watches of the night
He drowns again in a remembered sea.[109]

The ballad in my breast
Persisted in its hurt, and drove
My green pursuit
Over the endless waters of unrest.[110]

Companioned so by ghosts
I ride this burial sea
Away from the living coasts.

And so remain dumbfound
With the sound of the sea, and the sea
Of the sound I sound.[111]

In October 1943 T. H. Jones, who had been the last to join HMS *Seaham*, was disembarked, 'The old ship' sailed away 'to do the invasion of Europe'[112] and he was transferred to a shore establishment, HMS *Hannibal*, at Algiers. Although he did not much enjoy living in barracks, it gave him a chance to relax, throw off the tensions induced by a war which had moved elsewhere and give sustained attention to his writing. All of the poems known to have been submitted to magazines bear the *Hannibal* address, and the few surviving letters speak of bathing and socializing.

At about this time he writes to Pat, the sister who always took the closest interest in his writing and who, after his death, has been most energetic in keeping his memory alive, from 'a place you would love – a library, – stacks of books all round. I've got one book in front of me, a volume of poetry I'd like to buy for you some day. Here is one poem – I'm sure you will like it.' And he copies out Hilaire Belloc's 'Tarantella' from Palgrave's *Golden Treasury*. Necessity makes strange bedfellows!

Madeleine (Jones) Mitchell records another incident from this period:

Another wartime nightmare, which woke Harri frequently to the end of his days, was being chased through the Casbah of Algiers in the early hours of the morning. The naval barracks were situated on the other side of this . . . and there was a strict rule that no ratings should pass through it unaccompanied after dark. Harri had spent the evening talking with a couple of French poets (I cannot recall their names) – a wonderful escape from the dull naval routine. Poetry was always his passion, so you can imagine how loath he would have been to leave this congenial company. Suddenly it was dark, so he had to risk breaking the rule. A couple of Arabs loomed out of a side-street. 'I've never had to run so fast in my life,' he told me later. [113]

One of the poets was the Henri Hell mentioned in a letter of 9 July.[114]

This is the appropriate place to deal with those poems of the war period not explored already in connection with Claire Jones. 'Cool pity covers us'[115] is in the manner of John Pudney:

> Cool pity covers us
> to hear the sorrows of the amorous
> nightingale.
>   What for the story
> of their sudden glory
> who flashed kingfisherwise
> across the unrecording skies?

> They have gone beyond lament
> who had for element
> the bare bright air
> and wrote their honour there.

'Reaching towards the light'[116] is Imagist, a beautifully realized evocation of a peaceful moment in the midst of tension:

> Reaching towards the light;
> Only the heat of the afternoon, and the sea,
> The still sea, and the unmoving sky;
> And all the restlessness of mind diluted
> To this thin fluid delicately dropping
> In contemplation even.

Derivative, perhaps, but none the less beautiful for that – the underlining of the sense by contrast, in movement and sound, between 'restlessness of mind' and 'thin fluid delicately dropping / In contemplation even', hinged on 'diluted' is beautifully done. This is understandably one of the poems thought worthy of sending to the magazines. Only the last six lines, unfortunately, have survived of another in the same category:

> Holds the sun leering to a rippled sea.
> Behind the glory; dream
> Is dissipated, epitaphs
> Contain us; shall we be forgotten
> When no more the bird laughs, laughs
> The wave; shall we be forgotten?[117]

The mood – disillusion, exhaustion after strenuous effort – is memorably conveyed.

The Petrarchan sonnet 'When we were young we felt the tortured cities'[118] is so typically 1930s and so reminiscent of Auden (the frequency of the sonnet in T. H. Jones's early work owes a great deal to Auden's use of the form) that it must be quoted in full.

> When we were young we felt the tortured cities
> Writhe in our bowels. Austria and Spain
> Were more than symbols to us. Our own pain
> And China more than a theme for heroic ditties.

> More than the object of our too-ironic pities
> The people dying on the huddled plain,
> The dreamer's loss the manufacturer's gain.
> But in our blood the feuds and aunties.
> Where are we now who sang that tortured time?
> What is the mask now of our tragic mime?
> Compassion still the fluid in the vein
> And in our bowels still the cities weep
> And through our thoughts the tortured peoples creep
> And the world is still our personal pain.

This is poetry analogous to a painter's copying of the work of a master: T. H. Jones assumes the persona of a member of the Auden Group, places his own poetic maturity back several years and with some skill manipulates the characteristic phrases ('too-ironic pities'/'feuds and aunties'). In terms of his development it is an important poem: it was the influence of Auden more than any other that saved him from being engulfed by that of Dylan Thomas.

'This hero now', datable because it survives as an air letter dated 2 February (1944) is an important link in the chain of development because, refused by *Horizon*, it was published three years later, unaltered, in *The Dragon*.[119] It is probable that a number of the *Dragon* poems had been drafted, even, like this one, completed during the war (the first four lines of 'Two Poems, I, In the shop front of your magnificence', Michaelmas 1946, survive on a Naval Message sheet). 'This hero now' is too long (fifty-seven lines) to be quoted in full, but its opening and closing lines are sufficient to establish its provenance:

> This hero now, a gauche cynic
> holds Europe helpless in the hollow of hand and skull . . .

> This now is our decision:
> Rear up the pillared hours
> against the principalities and powers . . .
> and let his heirs inherit
> the flowering of his fine spirit.

The influence is, again, Auden, who, notably in 1939, was writing poems biographical of actual 'leaders' (Yeats, Toller, Freud) and imaginary ones ('Epitaph on a tyrant', 'Like a vocation'). The opening and closing lines of the latter are:

Not as that dream Napoleon, rumour's dread and centre,
Before whose riding all the crowds divide . . .

But somewhere always . . .
                          is always standing
The one who needs you . . .
Alone among the noise and policies of summer,
His weeping climbs towards your life like a vocation.[120]

If Auden's tyrant was, or might have been, Adolf Hitler, Jones's 'hero', 'heavy booted and browed' with his hunger for 'those bright pavilions of his domestic ease, / his hearth of comfort' is the common fighting-man. Jones's 'hero' desires 'no vision of glory, / but only cessation of this battle-folly; / he is the hero, the cynic / the clumsy guard behind a sullen wall / of universal hopes and dreams'. It is typical of T. H. Jones's practice that this poem was published unaltered: once he had finished a poem he very seldom revised by so much as a comma.

Before moving to the last years of T. H. Jones's war, it is necessary to explore the perspective given by later poems which relate closely to this period. The very striking 'Brothel in Algiers: wartime'[121] reveals experiences naturally omitted from the letters. Donald Jones, a sergeant in the army, recollected visiting T. H. Jones in hospital at Algiers and Donald's native-servant had a sister who worked at one of the town's brothels, the resonantly titled 'Sphinx'. The poem evokes a visit to, and the atmosphere of the brothel, calling in aid echoes of Dante, Yeats and Auden.

It is in two almost equal parts (twenty-seven/twenty-five lines). The form is free-verse lines in stanzas comprising from three to nine lines. Part I evokes the brothel; part II the visit to the whore. The brothel is a place of 'humbling anonymity', 'furtive observance' and 'unexultant rites' performed in 'small rooms / Where dirty beds invite'. Its customers, 'Meek brutes and arrogant / And the world's wandering sons . . . sons of violence' will enjoy only 'short delight'. The young sailor seeking relief must

> Walk nonchalantly up the crowded stairs
> Through the smell of sweat
> The smoke patterns and the stale, sour wine-breath

to join the 'Sisters of mercy . . . in the dance'. Although their customers, 'The sons of fear' are 'violent, / The sisters of display are charitable'. Climax is achieved in six wonderfully laconic short lines:

> Noise
> And many smells
> And coin changing hands
>
> The deed
> The dance
> The darkness.

Stripped so to essentials, the story is commonplace enough, but there is far more to the poem. Its opening stanza, with its references to 'dark sisters', 'charities', 'heresy' and 'ritual' might appear to suggest that the brothel was formerly a religious house (enabling a rich irony by playing off spiritual against physical love). Equally, 'Lust's younger season / And the ritual denied / The dance' suggests the shipboard auto-eroticism of frustrated sailors, even, perhaps, adolescent masturbation. One of the meanings of the recurrent 'dance' is sexual intercourse, though the Herodias/Salomé overtone of 'Dance, o my daughters / For their short delight' indicates the broader sense of seduction linked with violent death. With the third stanza of part I a profounder meaning is introduced:

> Ithyphallic demented choirs
> Perform their unexultant rites
> The sad priest blesses.

The Ithyphallus (erect penis) was ritually carried in Dionysiac processions, the companions of Dionysus were the Bacchantes, the festival of Dionysus involved dithyrambic choruses ('ithyphallic' refers also to the hymns sung and metres used in the processions), sacrificial rites involving priests were part of the worship of the god, and his companions, before he became associated with the Bacchantes, were the Charities. As 'the fruit of Dionysus' is the grape, and wine the natural symbol of his intoxicating power, we are not surprised to find, in part II of the poem, a reference to 'sour wine-breath'. As 'ithyphallic' refers also to the stinkhorn fungus, this enormously significant word focuses the suggestions, throughout the poem, of the poet's disgust at his own sexuality and this particular indulgence of it.

Dionysiac ritual, certainly (and appropriately); self-disgust likewise – but there is yet more to this, the first of T. H. Jones's elaborately complex mature poems. Sad priests who bless, sisters of mercy and of charity – these cannot help evoking the contrast of religious and secular, and the self-disgust of the poet is readily attributable to his chapel upbringing[122] (we find here, indeed, the first manifestation of that damaging conflict between what the Bible taught and what the weak flesh demanded that is so characteristic of this poet). Part II opens with the customer on his way, it appears, to 'the top floor [where] they keep the rarities'. He pauses on the landing, leans over and 'look(s) down the gyres'. He sees 'the great tree in the court', he comes to the 'Sisters of mercy' with a prayer and 'the plucked fruit'. A few lines later we have 'the circles descend / And narrow / And the dance goes on'.

'Gyres', 'great tree' and 'dance' all allude to Yeats, the first seeing this 'simple' visit to a brothel as part of a pattern of Mediterranean history which includes Greek, Roman and Christian ritual. The tree from which a fruit has been plucked is T. H. Jones's first reference to the Eden myth, but it is also Yeats's 'chestnut tree, great-rooted blossomer',[123] just as the Dionysiac dance is also Yeats's 'dance, an agony of trance'[124] and the dance of life ('How can we tell the dancer from the dance?') and perhaps also Auden's ('Time breaks the threaded dancers'[125]). And with circles which 'descend / And narrow' we have reached the 'Inferno', that part of the *Divina Commedia* which best fits this poem's mood and intention.

'Ennui: Mediterranean', published in 1948,[126] is worth a mention because, no less indebted to Yeats, it appears to represent the opposite side of the same coin. Making his 'immemorial rendezvous' with 'These violent waters and the heart's decay', the poet evokes 'The Second Coming'.[127] The 'anarchy . . . rampant and tide of blood to drown the shrinking light' of its second stanza are extremely close to Yeats's:

> Things fall apart; the centre cannot hold;
> Mere anarchy is loosed upon the world,
> The blood-dimmed tide is loosed, and everywhere
> The ceremony of innocence is drowned . . .

There is no guilt or self-disgust here, though: T. H. Jones's final stanza accepts, even revels in anarchic passions:

> O innocent passion, loose the bloody tide
> Of anarchy, let the rich waters ride
> In savage triumph round the frenzied world,
> And let my hands sing what my heart has cried.

Temporarily, at least, he has escaped from chapel into the Dionysiac procession. Throughout his life he was always capable of doing this – but never for long.

Both of these poems show that already T. H. Jones is 'post-modernist' in the obvious and limited sense that he has digested the early work of T. S. Eliot and borrowed from it the kind of close allusiveness that characterizes *The Waste Land*. He has also responded creatively to the later work of Yeats (itself influenced by the modernist, Pound) and that of his older contemporary, Auden. Neither 'Brothel in Algiers: wartime' nor 'Ennui: Mediterranean' was thought worthy of inclusion in his first collection, *The Enemy in the Heart*,[128] even though he clearly recognized the quality of the former. Undoubtedly this is because the influences ('lies', we might call them in one of the senses that Jones uses that word) are too obvious.

From *Hannibal* T. H. Jones was posted, at his own request – 'I am quite pleased at the prospect of moving', he wrote in July 1944,

> new scenes, new work, new faces, help to make the time pass more quickly and make this life more bearable. I am sorry of course to have to be leaving John Elwyn, and Henri Hell, but I am getting used now to parting from friends.[129]

He went to HMS *Byrsa*, another shore establishment, at Bougie (now Bejaïa), east of Algiers. Nothing is known about the ten weeks he spent there (if, indeed, he did spend all ten there – the dating of 'Nostalgia' at Naples may mean that the base had been moved there by October).

Later in October he had come full circle back to *Mercury*, Petersfield, the signals school from which he had departed for the Mediterranean. Here he wrote the poem that might be said to sum up the disillusions of war hinted at in 'This hero now . . .', the first of a number of works titled simply 'Poem'. Its three carefully crafted stanzas with their sharply contrasted images ('knives of time', 'green tide of peace') evoke spiritual exhaustion and hark back to the pacificism of 1940:

> Nothing is left within my emptied acres.
> The razored tongues of time
> Have cut away the fragrance of my youth.
> A lonely ploughman in the barren pastures
> Turns me the haggard face of truth
> And calls me Crime.[130]

Always, in the mature work, it is to the images of his heartland – the lonely thorn thrashed by the wind, the old, thin field, the hills sodden with rain – that he will turn in such moods of despair.

After three months he was transferred to HMS *Cochrane*, Rosyth (this was where his pay came from – in fact he was on the destroyer HMS *Westminster* which was running the courier-service to Norway). Out of the frying pan into the deep-freeze, one might say. A letter to Donald Jones[131] reveals that, like many other servicemen, he was afraid of being sent east (Germany had capitulated on 7 May): 'At the moment life is rather good, but tense. My present cushy number may come to an end any day, and the Damoclean sword of a Far East draft descend . . .' The atom bombs spared him that, though he would not be demobbed for ten months yet.

He came in from the cold to a Britain made (temporarily) safe for socialism by the Labour landslide of 26 July, but was unable to get home for Christmas from HMS *Collingwood*, the education unit in Hampshire to which he had been transferred. From there he wrote, to his sisters, the first of his many occasional poems.[132] The apparent banality of this side of his output, baffling to academic friends in particular, can be understood partly in the context of the honourable tradition of the 'Bardd Gwlad' which he had inherited from his Uncle Daniel and T. H. Jones's roots in local eisteddfod performance, but there was a more contemporary model in the verse-letters of W. H. Auden[133] (themselves owing something to the octosyllabics with which Augustan poets had been accustomed to unbutton and to Byron's satires).

> Darlings,
>   Once again I sit,
> And rack my brains, and stretch my wit
> To write a little note to you . . .
> Outside it's lovely. Overhead
> The stars are shining; from her bed
> The silver moon has stolen slow
> To watch those brave star-captains go.
> Outside it's lovely. – Here's the *but* –
> Within this barren, oblong hut,
> The fact must really now be told,
> It's bitter, wicked, freezing cold,
> And I lie writing in my bed,
> With a jersey pulled up round my head.

For his youngest sister he is the adventurous big brother, the sailor home from sea with stories to tell:

> I'd tell you lots of wondrous stories
> Of all the marvels and the glories
> I've seen while roaming o'er the seas . . .

a world of the imagination to offer:

> I'd get up, and down would take
> Some old book from the shelves above
> Full of those poems that you love
> And you would read, with eyes a-glisten,
> While I would sit and smoke and listen.

This kind of thing is similar to (for example) parts of *New Year Letter*:

> No matter where or whom I meet,
> Shopgazing in a Paris street,
> Bumping through Iceland in a bus,
> At teas where clubwomen discuss
> The latest Federation Plan,
> In Pullman washrooms, man to man,
> Hearing how circumstance has vexed
> A broker who is over-sexed . . .[134]

Auden was adept at pastiche and this side of him is an obvious influence on T. H. Jones's serious poetry and his less serious ballads.

Nothing came of the 'grand passion'. T. H. Jones spent the final period of his service at HMS *Wildfire*, Sheerness, teaching English and history on one of the educational vocational courses designed to keep young servicemen and women occupied and prepare them for their return to civilian life.

1946–1951

Post-war Blues and Critical Encounters

At Sheerness T. H. Jones taught English and history. He was one of a team of five whose work included play-readings and discussion groups. Another member was Madeleine Scott, formerly a transport driver in the WRNS, who taught craftwork and French conversation. Madeleine was to become the true 'grand passion' of his life.

Her father, William McDonald Scott, had been born in 1884 at Bandaw, on the shores of Lake Nyasa in Central Africa, the eldest of the ten children of a medical missionary. William was sent to Edinburgh University to study divinity, but switched to medicine. After graduating with first-class honours in 1905, he chose pathology as his specialism and spent the next three years working with leading pathologists at Edinburgh, Munich and Paris. There he met Madeleine's mother, Alice Mollard, whose family came from Franche Comté but had moved to the capital when her father, Antoine, Radical *député* for the town of Dôle in the Jura mountains, became a senator. Alice was highly educated for a French woman of her time: she studied German and English at Besançon and the Sorbonne. They were married in 1914, and she abandoned without regret the political high life of Paris for a cottage in a small village near Cambridge, where her husband had obtained a university post. Madeleine was one of eight children.

In William's family, as in that of Antoine, daughters and sons were given equal opportunity of higher education. Six of his children chose medicine; his eldest daughter took a degree in English at Cambridge. Madeleine, the odd one out, would choose art school, but by that time her father, who Madeleine is certain would have disapproved,[1] was dead, a victim in 1941 of the Blitz.

Socially and intellectually the gap between the Jones and Scott families could hardly have been wider. 'It was a wonderful coincidence that your father and I ever met', she reflects.[2] 'He was a man from the mountains of Breconshire and I was brought up in Dulwich.' But the war had brought about a temporary disruption of the English class system, and the Wren and the telegraphist 'became good friends and I was amazed at the number of interests Harri and I had in common . . . Politically left wing, interested in the visual arts and music, and both keen francophiles.' The relationship was instant, passionate, stormy and, in spite of love affairs, for ever. On 1 April 1951, the poem which would stand first in T. H. Jones's first published volume, *The Enemy in the Heart*,[3] as 'Poem for Madeleine'[4] was entered in the *Black Book*:[5]

An ocean or embrace away
The weeping of my love fulfils
The sensual vision and the prayer.
Lost in the clarity of day,
Bewildered in the hurt of air,
My words are rain her sorrow spills.

A century or kiss ago
The generations in her eyes
Answered my urgency of prayer.
Now with the words I do not know
The vision in the random air
Of absence casually dies.

O love upon the distant shore,
O love so absent from my nights,
O image of my ecstasies,
O love, grant pardon to me for
Estranging time, estranging seas,
And all refusal of delights.

And grant me pardon, love, for pride
Expert in disobedience.
Forgive me that I could not reach
You when your longing cried.
And grant me pardon, love, for each
Failure of will, deceit of sense.

Eleven years later, in 'Cwmchwefri rocks'[6] she is identified with the Muse:

Ceridwen, in your arms I can forget
Cwmchwefri rocks and the stern face of God,
So that you come to me by night and night,
Blot out those images and those stricken cries,
And promise, promise that I may be yet
A poet worthy not to be refused.

Poets of sexual love need to fall in love repeatedly: the lyric impulse is renewed in the excitement each new passion engenders. As Graves has pointed out,

> No Muse-poet grows conscious of the Muse except by experience of a woman in whom the Goddess is to some degree resident . . . the real, perpetually obsessed Muse-poet distinguishes between the Goddess as manifest in the supreme power, glory, wisdom and love of woman, and the individual woman whom the Goddess may make her instrument for a month, a year, seven years or even more. The Goddess abides; and perhaps he will again have knowledge of her through his experience of another woman.[7]

For T. H. Jones, Madeleine would always represent the White Goddess/Muse, the eternal mistress and inspiration behind every passing fancy.

Serving below decks had confirmed for him, as it did for Roy Fuller, that there must be some sort of a social revolution, 'not least for the middle-class intellectual. It extricated me from the great problems of the thirties – how to live and write for a class to which one didn't belong.'[8] He was looking forward to his return to Aberystwyth, but first he must play his part in what, son and heir of the radical rural poor, he sensed was a charade: the slight shift of the political system to accommodate the philosophy of the welfare state. The Labour government seemed to offer barely enough of what he had been fighting for, but there was an undefined period to pass before formal demobilization, with its visit to the dispersal centre for the tweed demob suit, the shirt with two collars and the never-to-be-worn cufflinks, tie and trilby. There was a lot of drinking, talking and loving to catch up on.

'Nostalgia'[9] revealed how, at Naples in 1944, his thoughts had been turning towards a definition of his roots; at Sheerness he completed the process with 'Poem for Wales',[10] published, before his return to Aberystwyth, in *The Dragon*. A self-consciously bardic performance, this ode of six sixteen-line stanzas with a complicated rhyme-scheme, addressed to the 'Dark hills for which I feel this chemic love', is an epithalamium celebrating nothing less than holy matrimony between the returning poet and his native land. After confessing 'weakness' and 'lost faith' it characterizes his ancestors as 'proud and violent and passionate' and promises to revive, maintain and advance the 'splendour of [their] ancient name', and to strive to ensure that 'when I die I may with honour say, / Dark fathers, O in me you have not died'.

Unashamedly Blakean, this poem can be seen to grow out of the prize-winning essay, 'Visions'.[11] It acknowledges an obligation to honour his native land, and opens with an apology for personal 'weakness' and 'lost faith'. As heir to the 'foundering passions' of his proud ancestors, he will 'Be proud and violent and passionate, / And sing the joy of love's returning seasons'. He will 'suck the wonder of . . . those antique sounds / That trumpet me to darkening towers . . . And with a bardic fury proud proclaim, / In me my fathers are not dead'. Love and war, the bard's traditional themes, are brought together in a clarion call:

> when I lie in proud and perfect peace
> With a dark-haired woman of my race
> Whose raven eyes will never cease
> To lighten my hell-murky earthly place,
> In me my fathers have not died;
> And in the loftiest eyrie of my pride
> My soul – my fathers' soul, and hers –
> Sings in a towering exultation,
> Making a vast reverberation
> Through the dim centuries its singing stirs . . .

Uneven it certainly is – borrowed metaphysical conceits, Shakespeare, Yeats, Auden's 'neural itch', Dylan Thomas's craft of moulding sullen words – but magnificent in the sound and rhythm of its ringing phrases. Postmodernist in its unashamed eclecticism, 'Poem for Wales', like so many of the most interesting poems by so many poets, is about language itself, its 'thundering tongues and tower of words', the 'trumpeting' and 'triumphing' of the 'darkling syllables'. It asserts a central place in Wales for the Welshman who writes in English, an Anglo-Welshness (familiar today, but less so in 1946), deeply rooted in *Welsh* language and culture. Those capable of appreciating him – Professor Gwyn Jones, for example, who would shortly publish his work in the *Welsh Review* – must have looked forward with great interest to his return to Aberystwyth.

The war had inflicted some changes. University College had returned to London, but numbers were substantially inflated: the 750 at the beginning of the Michaelmas term had risen by a further hundred before the end of the academic year. Almost half of these were hard-bitten, world-weary ex-servicemen, but T. H. Jones was happy to see some sweetly innocent young women straight from school. A start had been made on the hillside campus at Penglais, but the focus of college life was still by the sea.

Mature students with a grasp of economic realities realized that there was little hope of building a socialist New Jerusalem, at Aberystwyth or anywhere else in Albion. The Attlee government played the Great Power abroad while at home it faced crisis after crisis. This was an impoverished, colourless period – clothes-rationing would remain in place until February 1949 and on 21 July 1946 a world wheat shortage caused bread to be put on the ration, where it remained until July 1948. Peter Richmond's 'Editorial' in the Michaelmas *Dragon*[12] summed up the first impressions of the 'returning wanderers' as, however,

> Encouraging . . . The town clocks, if they have hands, tell different times. The end is still off the pier. Change comes slowly to Aber though it is a balm to the wanderer who has had enough turmoil and strange and foreign sights to find Aber still sunk in its familiar dilapidation. [The demobbed student] may feel nothing, he may feel relief at having made it, he may feel that he no longer fits in or he may feel that he has never been away . . . life flows on and theirs is a new generation . . . college life has not changed very much, it is the ex-serviceman who has changed . . . as a fresher he entered college with practically the identical ideas of generations of his predecessors. He had the dreams and hopes that they had and asked the same questions of life that they did but in the light of his more recent experiences, he no longer has rose-coloured spectacles and now takes a more cynical view of things than he would otherwise have done . . . The wanderer once more finds himself confronted with the gruesomeness of

organised education . . . the library may appal him, the sight of earnest creatures who pore over massive volumes and make copious notes and who give him sharp looks if he makes too much noise turning over the pages of his *Daily Mirror*.

T. H. Jones, while in Malta, had met Tom Sallis, son of an ironmonger in Bargoed, a friend from pre-war Aberystwyth days. As they passed each other, the one embarking and the other disembarking, Tom suggested,

'How about going into digs together after the war?' Harri said, 'Fine.' We ambled to Aber together and found some terrible Dickensian digs at 8 Powell Street . . . For that year, wherever Harri went, I went – but we didn't go very far. [It was] a lost weekend that lasted a year.[13]

Many members of the academic staff, particularly those who remembered the aftermath of the Great War, were apprehensive about student indiscipline, but quite a few of the mature students of 1946 were married and intent on 'getting stuck into studying, and earning some money as quickly as possible. They were ambitious. Then there were the layabouts like Harri and myself who just intended to uncurl a bit.'[14]

The Powell Street digs were squalid. Their bedroom contained a double bed and a single one occupied by a farm-lad from Carmarthenshire. He had terribly smelly feet and T. H. Jones used to maintain that his only reason for getting drunk was to escape the odour. He shared the double bed with Sallis and neither of them thought anything of it.

The idea of two fellows sleeping together today has sexual overtones, but at that time it was more like it was in the eighteenth century when someone like Sterne would tour the Continent and you just fell into bed and you had no idea who slept alongside you. Just because we had been in the Navy, we had no intention of carrying out the tradition of rum, sodomy and the lash![15]

The rest of the lodging-house was occupied by an assortment of other bright boys from south Wales: Graham Rees (later vice-principal at Aberystwyth), Martin Jones from Gowerton (professor of Arabic at the American University, Cairo) and Wyndham Jones (also to achieve a chair). All went hungry: most days they breakfasted on pickled cabbage. A layer of dust covered everything and 'The lady of the house had a Pekingese called Queenie who crapped behind our sofa on the first day of term. The crap was still there at the end of term, but slightly harder. A terrible place for terrible students.'[16]

T. H. Jones assumed the regulation uniform for students at the time: grey flannels and sports coat, but honoured his naval past with a black polo-necked sweater. These appear to have been the only clothes he possessed: when, later that year, he got married, he had to borrow a shirt from Tom Sallis. He packed it in a tiny Gladstone bag with his only clean pair of socks. He was always superbly scruffy and sometimes very smelly, for the digs possessed no bathroom.

Attendance at lectures was perfunctory. It was more usual to get up late and go immediately to the Ship and Castle, the navy pub run by Bill Lewis, an ex-policeman. Bill had a collection of cap-badges from ships all over the world and was a great raconteur. T. H. Jones's favourite story was the one about the time when Bill had arrested an infamous murderer. Standing one day on the steps of Aberystwyth Police Station, contemplating the rain-lashed promenade, he had been approached by a shuffling old tramp who attempted to give himself up. Bill questioned him and it emerged that forty years earlier he had killed a night-watchman during a break-in at a Preston factory. He had fled to Ireland, but the killing had haunted his dreams. Finally he had made up his mind to make a clean breast of it, taken the ferry to Fishguard and tramped up the coast until overcome on Aberystwyth promenade by the Welsh weather.

Bill Lewis was regarded by ex-servicemen as the ideal landlord and had a soft spot for Tom Sallis and T. H. Jones, often the first through his door at 11 a.m. Bill advised drinking on a full stomach and his prescription was two eggs in a glass of brandy to be taken while he washed the previous night's empties. The Ship and Castle was a free house, important to serious drinkers like T. H. Jones. There were only three of them in the drinkers' desert that was Aberystwyth in 1946. On the last day of Michaelmas term, staggering out of the Ship and Castle, Jones turned to Sallis and observed, 'You know, we haven't seen the sea so far this term.'[17] They had hardly seen the lecture-room either.

T. H. Jones had been writing poetry, though – indeed, it was in circumstances like these that, throughout his life, he appears to have composed most fluently. The Michaelmas edition of *The Dragon*[18] printed what he called 'Two poems', the first, 'In the shop-front of your magnificence', another Petrarchan sonnet of which the opening lines had been jotted down at *Hannibal*, and the second, 'Believing in no grief save that alone', a variation on the sonnet (four triplets clinched by a couplet). Both are exercises in unrequited love. He had now been published extensively in his school and university magazines, but had yet to achieve the wider recognition of a literary magazine – that epoch in the life of the young writer. It was accorded when Gwyn Jones published 'The enemy in the heart' in the autumn number of the *Welsh Review*.[19]

Gwyn Jones ('Prof. Gwyn' to generations of Aberystwyth students) was professor of English and dean of the Faculty of Arts. He was happy to have T. H. Jones in his department – indeed, he became his mentor – but feared that the presence of too many ex-service students would swamp it with cynicism and fecklessness. Tom Sallis had tried to get in, but the professor asked what his future career was likely to be and when Tom replied that he would be entering the family hardware business, said, 'English is not for you, then, Mr Sallis. You need law to be a businessman.' That was the end of the matter. 'I did attend some of Gwyn Jones's lectures', Sallis recalls.[20] 'He was a star performer, an influence on Harri, and many students came just to listen to the flow.' Gwyn Jones was an accomplished writer of short stories, and a novelist as well as a distinguished scholar in the field of Icelandic and Early Norse, but his interest in Anglo-Welsh literature did not influence his English course, which was highly conservative in the Oxford style. He had founded the *Welsh Review* in 1939, the year before he got the chair at Aberystwyth, suspended publication during the war, and resumed it as a quarterly in March 1944. He defined it as 'a journal for the English-speaking Welshman which though conducted in English will recognise and champion the unique importance of the Welsh language and the distinctive national culture inseparable from it'.[21] He had published Caradoc Evans and Alun Lewis along with such distinguished outsiders as T. S. Eliot, H. E. Bates, Tolkien and Rowse.

The correspondence between the above declaration of intent and T. H. Jones's 'Poem for Wales' is evident, and Gwyn Jones certainly helped him to discover the particular kind of Welsh-poetry-in-English he wished to compose. Something of a patrician himself, he remembers T. H. Jones as 'a handsome hatchet-headed kind of South Wales collier type,[22] and their relationship was not always harmonious. On one occasion, having just completed a poem, T. H. Jones spotted him having dinner with his wife in a restaurant, barged in and thrust the composition, its ink barely dry, under his nose. Gwyn Jones found this entirely unacceptable from a man who, poet or not, was, after all, 'only an under-graduate'.[23]

'The enemy in the heart' is worlds away from the 'Two poems', though all three are in the universe of love. One of those landmark creations which, in prose and verse, define stages in T. H. Jones's development, this stretched sonnet is extraordinarily complex, a performance-piece in the bardic tradition which manages to cram far more into its sixteen lines than 'A poem for Wales' into its ninety-six:

> In the heart alone is the last enemy
> The fatal friend who in the dim cathedrals
> Of the towered and toppling waves
> Makes you an image of all lost remembered loves
> And kills the corn with terror of the sea
> Rapes the rich earth with his sea-green betrayals.
> Cast out romantically that spent savour
> That lurking enemy whose glaucous veins
> Spoiled the rich promise of your spousal saviour
> And drowned your green blades in his greener veins.
> But when you come to that last house of bone
> His are the last embraces you discover
> Though you go to your narrow bed alone
> In no fond convoy with a friend or lover
> That is the last speck on the unfolding chart
> The murderer the foul the vulture heart.[24]

If our first approach is, as it always should be with difficult poetry, a reading aloud, the first thing we notice is the echoing interplay of vowel sounds. The opening line alone uses five (in/heart/alone/last/enemy); the whole poem uses virtually every one available in English. The most notable sound in the first part of the poem is that of 'fatal' (fatal/waves/makes/rapes/betrayals), and it is used to enforce a chain of meaning. Language and imagery are heavily charged with ambiguity pushed as far as it is possible to go without producing an indecipherable code. The 'enemy' is the 'last' enemy, but also a 'fatal *friend*'.[25] As 'enemy' it kills, rapes and betrays; it is a 'friend' because it has to do with acceptable as well as hurtful emotion, and a 'fatal friend' because excess of emotion makes us vulnerable and brings neurosis and violence – but also, since 'heart' has physical as well as emotional implications, in the end puts us out of our misery. By juxtaposing 'dim cathedrals' (comfort/sanctuary) with 'towered and toppling waves' (danger/death, imagery habitual to T. H. Jones and deriving from wartime experience) the poet sets off religious echoes. This is not mere contrast: wave-shapes suggest the arches and vaults of the cathedral. With 'rapes' and 'betrayals' he underlines the sexual implications of 'heart', and with 'corn' and 'rich earth' evokes a related complex of fertility rituals and religious overtones.

This is a bardic performance in competition with Dylan Thomas. Controversy and competition were central to the Welsh bardic tradition (more than 5,000 lines of verse were penned in the debate between Edmund Prys and William Cynwal between 1581 and 1587). Dylan Thomas was the obvious Anglo-Welsh poet to be challenged at that time.[26] T. H. Jones would honour him later by referring to himself as 'the poor Colonial's Dylan Thomas'[27] and by writing the best short critical study of the poet.[28] We have already seen what might be described as contests with 1930s poets (Auden in particular) and shall see a notable one with W. B. Yeats. The relationship with the Metaphysicals (T. H. Jones's MA thesis would be on their imagery) is more complex, but Donne and Marvell are certainly echoed here.

T. H. Jones and Madeleine Mitchell had been separated for a whole term, 'but we wrote to each other every day, and he often mentioned his ideas for poems'.[29] Madeleine was following the four-year National Diploma in Design course at the Camberwell College of Art. She came up to Aberystwyth for the final week of term and when he returned home for Christmas T. H. Jones told his Mam that they were to be 'wed immediately'.[30] Ruth's reaction was the instinctive one of the careful Welsh Mam. 'You can't marry her, you've never had a job!'[31] But he was persuasive, a quick registry office ceremony was performed in London and the couple travelled north to placate the startled Scott family in Aberdeen. They

> found a little flat in Asylum Road,[32] Peckham, SE15, a neighbouring suburb to Camberwell. Harri spent each term at Aberystwyth, while I persevered with my Art School course . . . We married at Camberwell Town Hall on 14 December 1946, with my sister Peg and her husband Helio the sole witnesses. We celebrated afterwards at the Prospect of Whitby . . .[33]

T. H. Jones's reputation and circle of friends continued to develop. The latter included Ted Richards, ex-naval officer, part-time antique dealer, café proprietor and published short-story writer; Rachel Roberts, future actress, known to everyone as Ray, and her wild friend, 'Coming shortly – the Incendiary Blonde',[34] Mair Roberts, another daughter of the manse who, although less outrageous than Ray, was the one to be sent down.

> If Harri had a cloven hoof it was perhaps his sexual conceit – among the acres of rye these pretty, country folk would lie. He never gave it much conscious thought, he just assumed he had a certain magnetism for women. He was fond of women, was Harri. I remember when my girlfriend came up from South Wales one weekend and Harri and I had to move out of the double bed, he was so wonderfully solicitous to her. He hadn't thought of me as a romantic character, just his drinking-companion. He was really very motherly, and nurtured our relationship. He seemed to take far more interest in its success than I ever did.[35]

T. H. Jones became obsessed with Ray Roberts; many men did.

> She wasn't a noticeable beauty. She had a retroussé nose, very self-conscious about it she was, but her legs were good.[36] She was proud of them. She once did a highland fling in the Union wearing a kilt which she even seemed to have abbreviated just to display her limbs.[37]. . . Open and flirtatious, funny, candid about her relationships, she was essentially an innocent affecting worldly wisdom. Heavily made up, provocatively dressed even when not performing, she quickly acquired, among those who did not know her, what used to be called 'a reputation'.[38]

Most women students adored her, trying to match her dress-sense and the independent strength she displayed in her relationships. 'She had the talent to make things happen around her – like a whirlpool – exciting to be with.'[39] Her sad diaries record Aberystwyth as one of the happiest periods of her life:

> I was full of confidence and vitality. I was liked and thought colourful. Yes, I pretended to be a sophisticated, know-it-all, sexually experienced woman, when I was only a totally frightened virgin . . . I put on rouge, I wore red. I discovered the opposite sex, however, found me attractive when I stopped these practices . . . I stayed in bed in Alexandra Hall and did my hair and went to refectory to eat Welsh rarebit and play my amateur seduction act. The arrogance was there. I was different of course and mysteriously better than my fellows.[40]

Rachel sought the company of the ex-servicemen, the drinking boys and the serious womanizers – Bill Adams, for example, son of the vicar of Llangrannog, making a 'rake's progress'[41] through the local virgins. He and his friend, Dai Butch, were 'a real pair of shockers':[42] *The Dragon* summed Bill up with 'I have often regretted what I have eaten, never what I have drunk'.[43] Ray's friend, Mair, failed to take precautions and was sent down; Prof. Gwyn warned Ray that if she carried on as she had begun she would never get a degree. Exhausted and emotional after a party, she replied, 'I don't want a degree; I just want to go to bed'.[44] *The Dragon* made it the quotation of the year.

The first of T. H. Jones's 'Two poems'[45] characterizes its subject as magnificently and consciously beautiful, but having 'no warm humility to share' and being 'Aloof in your displayed indifference' and imagines forcing her 'to a sharp, complete surrender'. Sensing the virginity beneath 'that facade of bright disdain', the poem concludes with the potentially disastrous reaction that real sexual experience will bring, the cold beauty paradoxically marred 'with a spreading stain / Of tenderness my human hands have made'. The second poem plays in a metaphysical manner with love, death and the lesser death of lost virginity. While the lady mourns the latter, the poet, 'love's lord', turns, ironically, *in* poetry *to* poetry. And concludes that

> when necessary night
> Replaces this despairing, clarifying light
> Build we again our tiny world and bright.

> And never till the flesh fade from your bone,
> Again, dear wanton, shall you lie alone.

That 'lie' carries the usual connotations.

T. H. Jones found the English Society, of which he became student president in the Michaelmas term of 1946, the only place you could meet the staff with any ease or sense of equality. His presidential address was on Dylan Thomas. Enid Johnson records that 'we were given a close insight into the life and personality of the man and Harri's lecture was followed by a lively discussion'.[46] As we have seen, Dylan Thomas was an important stimulus to T. H. Jones's work, but as a challenge, not a warm bath to wallow in.

Other subjects for discussion included whether Plato was right to ban poets from his republic. New poetry by T. H. Jones, Haydn Williams and others was read and criticized. The liveliest discussions took place after the meetings when most of the participants adjourned to the Ship and Castle or the Prince Albert. The latter, run by the reigning Queens of Aber, Marks and Mann, closed in honour of every Edith Evans first night, when they headed for London. It offered opportunities for after-hours drinking in company with such regulars as Lady Mercy Martyr, the tipsy sister of the earl of Warwick, and her companion, the louche wife of Brigadier Bones. As T. H. Jones emerged, one dawn, sporting a seven-day stubble and stinking of beer and cigarettes, a vigilante from one of the local chapels accosted him with the suggestion that the pub was really not the place for a nice college-boy. His reaction is not recorded.

Haydn Williams was there for the poetry rather than the beer.

> The evenings were like another seminar, and more lively and productive than the official academic ones . . . Harri would read his own work and rave on about . . . Dylan Thomas and W. B. Yeats . . . but his tastes were pretty catholic, including Donne, all the Metaphysicals . . . but he also favoured the Hopkins of 'cliffs of fall / Frightful, sheer, no-man-fathomed'[47] . . . he resisted Eliot enough to admire Milton. Of course, Eliot was also one of Harri's heroes, although Harri was too much of a romantic to follow Eliot and Pound all the way. Eliot was simply in the drinking-water of all students in the post-war years.[48]

This is valuable testimony to the influences which had been playing on T. H. Jones since he escaped the *Golden Treasury*. If we are to describe his formation in bloodstock terms, we might call him 'out of Dylan Thomas by Yeats, Eliot, Auden and the Metaphysicals', but he is one of the most eclectic of poets and Hopkins would be only *one* of the lesser influences. What he took from Eliot was the past/present tension of *The Waste Land*, the modernist mythic method and the cultural pessimism. As David Jones had taken Eliot's fertility archetypes and quest as points of departure for visual discourse (the mapping of the interior Celtic landscape of his Arthurian project), so Jones, the postmodernist, would create a kind of verbal palimpsest by employing a collection of signs reflexively reworked from many texts in his companion-piece to 'A poem for Wales', 'In my returning':[49]

> In my returning, the proud, flowered walking
> Again in the loved, remembered land,
> The valleys and hills of fact and legend . . .
> The flowered and feathered landscape
> No longer a fading map of unloving strategy,
> But a weight and wonder of words . . .
> Wales wears an air, a grace, as a loved face
> Motions to kisses on the letters of exile;
> And the intricate maps of farms
> Welcome me back to a singing service,
> A wonder of work, and the toil of love
> In the green cathedrals of the sea-lapped,
> Lovely, enduring landscape of fact and legend.

Dylan Thomas ('Fern Hill') is the strongest influence here, but Auden is powerfully present ('Motions to kisses on the letters of exile'/'intricate maps of farms'), and so is Hopkins ('wears an air, a grace, as a loved face'). History is mythologized onto nature to underline continuity and assert the heart of the nation in an organic community. An interesting comparison is the function of landscape in Michael Powell's Neo-Romantic films, most remarkably *A Canterbury Tale* (1946). T. H. Jones's representation of landscape in this poem operates within verbal conventions untroubled by the ways in which social, economic and industrial developments had altered it. The mature poet will present his community in a manner very different from what is implied by 'a singing service' (see, for example, 'Portrait gallery'[50]) and work on the land will not be the Romantic 'wonder of work' or 'toil of love', but 'Torn timber lugged down cold and bleeding hillsides,'[51] 'In comfort on harsh rock / Or lacerated pine, / Never out of the wind / Or the thin nails of rain'.[52]

As early as the spring of 1947 T. H. Jones's reputation had been established at Aberystwyth: 'we'd rather find a short-story writer, an essayist, and a couple of poets to share the field with Harri Jones' wrote *The Dragon*.[53] He had shocked college staff at the debating society with his put-down of a doe-like undergraduette in political debate: 'But that was in another country, and besides, the wench is dead.'[54] Bill Adams borrowed the quotation as epigraph for a typically machismo piece dedicated to his poor, lost Mair, with her 'blonde hair mutated with the serried gold of the sand, long closed lashes and softly aggressive mouth; her incomparable body and limbs'.[55] As he abandons her, she challenges his ex-service alienation and nihilism: 'why don't you believe in God, why don't you believe in me, why don't you believe in any woman (and she was frightened then). Christ, man, why don't you believe in life, or being, or hurting, or hating, or dying or killing?'[56] T. H. Jones's 'This hero now', though written during, not after the war, is printed on the opposite page and makes a suitable companion-piece with its 'gauche cynic' of a hero racked by 'horror of guts and blood'.

Some of the strains that terms of separation and temptation were placing on T. H. Jones's marriage are to be detected in the 'Three love poems' published in the summer of 1947.[57] 'Invocation', rich in sea-imagery and full of Freudian allusions, is a pastiche of an Elizabethan lyric. The lover begs his mistress to 'Unlatch those lids' to reveal the 'deeper magic of a coral dream to which I plunge, / seeking a rich sea-change'. It concludes with lines youthful and wonderfully evocative, full of brilliant light and liquid sounds:

> Let your waves break over
> me, your bright waves cover
> me with tang and glitter
> of sun and wind and water;
> in your sun- and water-shine
> let me, o let me drown;
> deep in your multitudinous waves
> reap the rich harvest of our loves.

The final line contains, however, a sinister echo of 'kills the corn . . . Rapes the rich earth' ('The enemy in the heart'); the equation of sex with the sea will be characteristic of the mature love-lyrics.[58]

The second lyric, 'You', is a combination of the Metaphysical and the Dylanesque: its subject, with her 'black depth of hair', could seduce the poet's art to 'making idols of your heart / a hawthorn metaphysic, turn sonnets sacrifice' and make him 'forget / my craft the reason of it' – an extraordinary combination of Auden and Dylan Thomas.[59] It will be echoed in *The Weasel at the Heart*. The third, 'A wish', echoes Marvell and Keats in its desire for summer gardens of forgetfulness 'with flowers, / And the voices of dark women, / And an uninterrupted dream'.

In July 1947 T. H. Jones was awarded first-class honours in English. Madeleine celebrated by taking him to Marseilles and Corsica. Tom Sallis, arriving late for the Michaelmas term of 1947, found that T. H. Jones had unilaterally changed lodgings and moved in with the Merthyr boys in Portland Road. Tom moved into 'Llwyn Haf, better known as Llwyn Belsen. Harri sometimes stayed. We'd all rush down to breakfast to find that Gordon Thomas from Abercynon had eaten it all.'[60]

Among the Merthyr contingent was a young man of below average height, Gwyn Alfred Williams, reading history and later to become the distinguished broadcaster and academic better known in Wales as 'Gwyn Alf'. He remembered T. H. Jones as

a fantastic man. He seemed tall (mind you, everyone seems tall to me). Gaunt, craggy and permanently stooping, with a lock of dark, dank hair falling over his forehead like something out of the Celtic twilight. He was a lovely man, though very *secret*, inward – always withdrawn, even when making a speech in public, which he often did, usually in the street. The rumour was that he wanted to be seen as the man who drank himself to a First. He was certainly in the pubs all night and then up all through the small hours working himself to death. That, of course, was nonsense. What the bugger used to do was wake me up at about 2 a.m. and read me a poem. 'Gwyn, Gwyn, what do you think of this? The third line, man, you stupid bastard, do you think the third line works?' And God help you if you said, 'That's lovely, Harri, let me sleep.' You had to present reasoned and constructive criticism, and at 2 a.m. it was hell. Then he used to listen in as my mates and I would discuss history.[61]

The next morning he would present Gwyn with a poem on the Fall of the Roman Empire. This was more acceptable than his other irritating habit of bursting into Gwyn's room in the middle of the night in search of a condom. Family planning was a concern even if planning ahead was not.

Prominent among this early circle of friends was another Merthyr boy, R. G. Evans – 'Arge'. Another noted drinker, he was a biologist who had done his war service 'by devising a radically new sheep-dip'.[62] Intellectually perhaps the brightest of his generation, he went on to become reader in biology at Reading. His mother was to be embarrassed by the neighbours in her mining village who kept asking, 'When's your Ron going to get his Chair, then?':[63] five members of his primary school class were full professors already.

Haydn Williams was another member of the circle. A school-friend of Tom Sallis and another *protégé* of Alun Lewis at Pengam, he went up to Aberystwyth in 1947 anxious to meet the man about whom he had heard so many tall tales. He expected a physical presence to match the legend, but

> Instead Harri was thin and slightly stooping, very pale and very shy. He had vivid black hair and attractive, piercing eyes, though he was always bubbling over with news about his poetry. He'd just had one published and was very proud of the fact. He was nevertheless gracious, kind, and interested in other people. When he found out that I had written some verse that had been broadcast over the Forces Radio . . . this sealed the bond . . . and he was generous enough to consider me a fellow-poet and I was rather flattered.[64]

Haydn, never the complete insider, saw T. H. Jones's bohemianism and reckless *joie de vivre* as always tinged with melancholy, thought him 'much possessed by death' and closer to A. E. Housman than Dylan Thomas.

> He never darkened the door of a church or chapel when he was a student, few of us did, but he always shared a kind of vague religiousness, Christian, mystical, and would often express admiration and sympathy for the Roman Catholic Church . . . although his conversation on religious matters was usually

anecdotal and centred on Hopkins, Yeats or even Wilde . . . like Caradoc Evans who we much admired, Harri had an intense dislike of Nonconformity.[65]

The pub meetings had become formalized into the legendary Aberystwyth Honourable Philosophical and Philological Society (a jibe at The Honourable Society of Cymmrodorion). A flavour of its meetings may be obtained from the 'cod' report by its 'Philosophical Correspondent', Joss Davies, and 'Theological Correspondent', T. H. Jones:

> At the first meeting this session Officers were elected, and the healths of Adam Smith and David Hume were drunk . . . the most erudite meeting was that in which the Honorary President gave his address (brightened by his well known acid humour) on 'W. B. Yeats – an Internal View'. Other addresses were equally interesting, however. I need only specify the Staff President's lecture (with lantern slides) on 'The Lesser Gasteropods of Bitter Waters', [and] the Student President's learned and humorous disquisition on 'The Chemical Constitution of Nelson's Blood with Some References to its Physical, Psychological and Psychical Properties' . . . [66]

On one memorable occasion Mair Jones became one of the few women to be allowed into this all-male society. Daughter of the director of the Welsh Plant Breeding Station, she is described by Jim Smith, late professor of English at Southampton University, as 'Harri's particular *protégé*'.[67] She was the first aspiring young poet to receive his rather acerbic advice on technique:

> [these poems] get nearer to poetry than the earlier stuff you showed me, but there are still too many clichés not only of word and idiom but also of thought and emotion. Beware of machinery – it is so new, and has never been assimilated into the tradition of poetry other than in the Kipling way. 'Voluable Wheels' e.g. is journalese. 'The loom and the pattern' are clichés. 'Hypocenibe loom' is meaningless . . . in both of these you seem however to be trying to say something you really feel, and their forms – this pseudo verse – will get you nowhere . . . All this is harsh but I did find them interesting and I have hopes for you. Read Yeats's later poems and any criticism of Yeats you can find . . . Read Auden too and small doses of Hopkins and Dylan Thomas. These of course in addition to Spenser, Milton, Donne, Pope and Keats.[68]

A better description of the influences which formed T. H. Jones himself could hardly be found.

He was reading widely and experimenting all the time. Ray Roberts was distinguished in *Arms and the Man* and brilliant as the eponymous heroine of *Juno and the Paycock*: 'A new standard of college drama has been set.'[69] Despite problems with Joxer Daly's trousers, and Irish accents with more than a trace of Cardiganshire, Ray gave the student audience a glimpse of the greatness to come: 'The fervour and emotion shone through my performance and like my grandfather before me I held my audience as I was to do in later professional days – sometimes.'[70]

Although resisting the temptation to write 'an abandoned eulogy', T. H. Jones allowed himself to 'rave here about the vigour of the production as a whole . . . the undoubted histrionic genius of Juno'. The 'outstanding thing about the performance', he wrote, was 'that it deserved serious criticism'.[71] As a poet, he was as much in love with the art and passion of the performance as with the woman herself. He declared that the production of Ibsen's *Ghosts* was 'an unexhilarating trip over the grey northern waters', largely because the producer had failed to cast 'the best actress we have seen in College in our time'.[72] Obsessed by Yeats and remembering, no doubt, the inspiration and heartache caused by Maud Gonne and that she had acted in Yeats's famous play, *Cathleen ni Houlihan*, T. H. Jones decided to write for Rachel Roberts a play of her own.

He called it *The Weasel at the Heart*, a deliberate echo of the poem, 'The enemy in the heart',[73] and invited Scott Nesbit to design the set and a close friend of Ray's, Ronnie Cass, to compose the music. Cass was already establishing a reputation as musician and composer – he had performed on radio and produced semi-professional revues at Swansea. 'Harri had a terrific aura', he remembers, 'and he was very close to Ray as they were both rebels. A misused word: they were both different people who lived on their own plane.'[74] When he enthused about it to the Merthyr boys they christened it (by no means ineptly) *The Rat at the Testicles*.

T. H. Jones's copy of the play, no doubt amended during rehearsals, has been lost, but Donald Jones provided a copy of the twelve-page first draft which T. H. Jones discussed with him 'over a few pints in The Lion in Builth one weekend'. There are photographs in the summer 1948 *Dragon* of the Expressionist set and we also have the memories of the cast and some of the audience. Gwyn Alf Williams recalled 'young girl, old man and young poet, with a backcloth of two pillars and a cloud'.[75] Ronnie Cass remembers the music as the best he had written so far.[76] John Edmunds, straight out of school, played the poet: 'I was in awe of the ex-service students . . . the verse seemed full of "dung"[77] and what I thought were unpoetic concepts – but I was bowled over acting with Rachel.'[78]

Getting funds to produce the play precipitated a row between T. H. Jones and the conservative staff representative on the English Society, J. M. Nosworthy, who thought it wrong for the society to support new work. Haydn Williams, 'naturally cautious',[79] was one of the few members to support Nosworthy, but Jones forgave him and the cast had a whip-round to raise the cash. Haydn thought the play's genesis was the pub seminars on Yeats, and it was written for the most part in the pub. Beer and company were always a creative stimulus for T. H. Jones. His wife found it 'amazing how [he] could settle to writing late at night after a heavy evening of socialising'[80] and Julian Croft confirms this: 'He would write poems on small record cards in the pub at lunch time, or stay up into the small hours of the morning after a party.'[81]

It is said that every dramatist at some stage writes a 'Christ Play'. Emlyn Williams is an obvious Anglo-Welsh precedent with *The Wind of Heaven* (1945). H. L. Mencken's collaborator, George Jean Nathan, suggested that the intellectual and emotional maturity of a dramatist may be determined by the age at which he does so:

> Almost every writer for the theatre does a play about Christ some time in his life. Usually it is his first play, conceived while he is still at college . . . the Christ play seems to have a curious appeal to young men in their early twenties and old dramatic hacks. This is perhaps because, of all themes, the Christ theme is easiest to handle. It is impossible to fail . . . all he has to do is to darken his stage, bring on a bad actor in a white night-shirt and coincidentally bring up the lights again – the house is impressed as a score of Shaws and Synges could never impress it.[82]

The Weasel at the Heart evidently meets most of Nathan's criteria. It owes much to Yeats's *A Vision* with its theory that history is a cyclical process operating in 'gyres' of 2,000 years, each arising from the disintegration ('Things fall apart, the centre cannot hold'[83]) of the previous one and introduced by the coming of an initiate or Messiah. Its world is not Christian; rather it is coloured, thanks to Yeats's theosophical and hermetic studies, with spiritualism and magic. It owes something also to the bleak poetic prose plays of J. M. Synge, in particular *In the Shadow of the Glen* and *Riders to the Sea*. And it can be said to mark the beginning of T. H. Jones's engagement with the White Goddess.

Graves's fascinating, stimulating, exasperating book was published while Jones was working on his play and could not fail to influence him. It is deeply rooted in the Welsh history, literature and legend to which he had trumpeted his allegiance in the 'Poem for Wales';[84] it offers a 'key to all mythologies' and source of much imagery, and he was working on the imagery of the Metaphysical poets; its author's unusual temperament – loathing machinery, despising technological developments, desiring intensely to live close to nature and in accord with the seasons – attracted, and to some extent matched, that of the country-boy who had survived a high-tech war at sea. Graves, too, was a poet of sexual love inspired by a succession of lovers, each of them a manifestation of the eternal Goddess.

Like Wyndham Lewis, Graves disbelieved in 'progress', like Yeats he believed life to be cyclic, not linear. He believed also that when matriarchy was supplanted by patriarchy the quality of life and art was impaired. The assertive romanticism of *The White Goddess* appealed to T. H. Jones, as did its dismissal of 'pure' reason and its playful teasing out of the metaphysical conceits that he was researching. It seemed that there might be credible answers to Donne's apparently unanswerable questions about 'who cleft the Divel's foot' and 'what secrets were woven into the Gordian Knot'. For Graves, anthropology is queen of the humane sciences: through it a poet can get his facts right and facts are not truths but a power by which untruths can be confuted.[85]

For T. H. Jones, the magic of the Goddess as a power for structuring the poet's personality was probably of more importance than the thesis about the Goddess herself. He responded immediately to Graves's insistence that poetry is written in a trance-like state by a truly mad, truth-possessed, *male*, torn by conflicting feelings of sexual exaltation, disgust and horror, and to his interpretation and synthesis of the familiar Celtic myths – above all to the idea that each loved woman is a version of the Goddess as Mother, Lover and Layer-out. We have already seen, in 'Cwmchwefri rocks',[86] how these ideas would appear, stripped to their bare essentials, in the mature poetry of the Australian period.

The Weasel at the Heart does indeed open in darkness. Only the Poet's voice is heard, love's evangelist, asserting sunlight and summer love, tenderness and sweetness – but in ominous contrast with winter, 'that sharp satirist', cold, darkness and death. By the end of the opening lyric assertion has turned to prayer: 'End not their summer love'. The lights come up gradually, 'revealing a rough, simple hearth. Suspended above the fire a large, black pot. R. an old ragged man, seated. L. a handsome woman, also seated. At her side the young poet. The wind can be heard without.' Shadows of *Shadow of the Glen*!

The woman 'Queening this rude sty' makes it clear that Poet's 'summer love', manifested in 'songs in the honour / Of your white limbs' is of no use to her. Isolated 'on this barren hill / Imprisoned by those black and tearing winds' with a 'sapless stick' of an old man 'And an unshaven boy whose mind / Runs more on rhymes than the white limbs of women', she is sexually frustrated. Songs, visions and dreams cannot 'kill the weasel biting at the heart'.[87] She needs a man 'to keep [her] warm at nights'. The play's simple conflict is thus stated: sex in the flesh against sex in the head; idealistic male against pragmatic female; reality against illusion. It will be resolved only by violent death.

The old man's response to the conflict is a vision of

> Black horses thundering across the sky,
> Ridden by women with long, rippled hair
> Into a bloody and tremendous sun.

The women ride naked, their eyes 'love-crazed', they have a wild loveliness. The power and peril of sexual love are disturbingly evoked. The woman recognizes her destiny, but will not, cannot, be deflected from it:

> I would not change.
> I want a lover,
> The warm night's desecration in his arms,
> And to be queen in the cold light of day.

The poet has no answer except, for the last time, to make a song for her:

> Intellect and passion
> Violently mixed
> Have always vexed
> Unexultant hearts,
> Given great hurts.
> *But cannot keep the flesh upon the bone.*

The woman kisses him. The curtain falls.

The second scene opens in the cold, grey light of dawn. The woman has had her night of passion:

> In such strong arms so . . . clipped and caught,
> Who would have thought that dawn would ever come,
> Or daylight birds eclipse my warm heart's music?

In Yeats's words, 'All changed, changed utterly: / A terrible beauty is born':[88] the hovel is a throne-room, the woman a queen, robed and crowned, the old man a palace official. She calls for 'singers to enhance [her] glory' and a chorus sings that everything is created by desire:

> All our desire is crying for creation,
> Our blood for the forming of small bones,
> Our voices for the making of rich words,
> Our present to create a history.

The queen is arrogant in her satisfied sexuality.[89] Everything now exists 'to honour the great Queen' and 'the fierce weasel / Bites no longer at the desiring heart'.

Everything honours her except

> My poet.
> . . . the bitter scorner,
> He who would sing no more,
> He who foretold an agony to follow
> My night of love, my day of royalty.

She sends for him, she offers him 'all rewards' if he will sing, but, even under the threat of death, he refuses: 'To die is less than sing without the heart.' Blind in her arrogance, she calls for 'His head, that I may dance before it.'[90] When the head is set before her 'She looks at it with mounting horror' (the Chorus meanwhile, with heavy irony, singing of happy love) and realizes that, 'with the proud poet [she] has killed', she has lost everything. Red sunlight floods the scene and, casting off her royal robes, she dances away slowly into death. The old man speaks the final words:

> When all the fire of life is gone
> A bloodless man is left alone.
> *Passion and pride and pain.*

To many of those watching, the whole thing was a *roman à clef*, an extended supplement to the 'cold beauty', of 'Two poems',[91] her façade of 'bright disdain' shattered, her 'white coldness' marred by 'tenderness', and to the summer love of 'Three love poems'.[92] The play does tell us a good deal about the relationship between T. H. Jones and Rachel Roberts, but it reveals more about the poet than the man. 'No Muse-poet', according to Graves, 'grows conscious of the Muse except by experience of a woman in whom the Goddess is to some degree resident . . . every Muse-poet must . . . die for the Goddess whom he adores.'[93]

The Weasel at the Heart (what better emblem?[94]) is another version of the archetypal conflict between body and spirit, flesh and intellect, the forlorn effete poet ousted by his virile opposite. It foreshadows the revulsion against lust that T. H. Jones's Non-conformist conscience would impose when, from the safety of Australia, he wrote poems savaging the sexuality of the people of Llanafan and his own tragi-comic infidelities. It reveals his identi-fication with Neo-Romanticism, and this is underlined by the Apocalyptic, Expressionistic style of Nesbit's sets (derived from those of the Kurt Joos Ballet which established itself in Britain in the 1930s). Nesbit's painting was influenced by these, as was that of the better-known Cecil Collins at Dartington. Collins depicted the artist-figure as a Grail-less wanderer, a Bunyanesque pilgrim with the profile of a Picasso-like Neo-Classical head displaced amongst vast crags, waters and wilderness.

This alienated landscape resembles T. H. Jones's later representations of Llanafan, and Collins's 'Nature' is as textually influenced as his. The first major drawing produced by John Craxton, another painter of the New Apocalypse movement, 'Poet in a Landscape' (1941), depicts the reclusive poet buried in country solitude and is a visual realization of Herbert Read's free, anarchic poet-painter. The central motif of Neo-Romanticism, the relationship between a symbolic landscape with its myth of transcendence and a poet-figure who constructs organicist metaphors of a poeticized life to set against death is a central theme of T. H. Jones's poetry and prose of the late 1940s/early 1950s.[95] The connection between poetry and painting is by no means unusual (university lecture-courses have been devoted to it), and T. H. Jones was fascinated by painting, had friends and lovers who were painters, had his portrait painted at least three times and was married to an active artist who exhibited and socialized within communities of artists.

The Weasel at the Heart was a triumph. It was celebrated with a party at Portland Road: 'We got a lot of Winchester bottles full of John James's brew', Gwyn Alf Williams recalled, 'all labelled "poison".'[96] Jones, who dominated the group of historians he lived with, orchestrated a suitably ritualistic scene in which first Gwyn, then a succession of other history undergraduates, paid formal court to Ray. She sat in a chair and splayed her long red hair over the face of each in turn. 'Harri astonishingly waltzed around like a head-waiter, wearing an unheard-of tie and being dreadfully charming.'[97] Then he and Arge did their act, the latter playing his violin somewhat in the manner of *Peter and the Wolf* to illustrate Jones's raucous recitations with their brilliant improvisations. *The Weasel at the Heart* also starred John Edmunds and Gareth Jones (both to become BBC producers); Denise Ormond and Jim Smith each had a walk-on part.

Younger undergraduates in the drama circle regarded T. H. Jones as 'a heroic boozer and lecher',[98] a reputation enhanced when he moved to Borth to join Ted Richards at about the time of the birth of his first daughter, Sian.[99] Ted was a few years older than Jones, kept a fishing-boat, the *Spanish Lady*, and cultivated a 'former naval person' image with his polo-neck, long greatcoat and sea-boots. He is best remembered today for a number of characteristically Anglo-Welsh short stories, including the much-anthologized 'Worthy is the Lamb'. He too had been encouraged by 'Prof. Gwyn', who had published his work in the early pre-war days of *The Welsh Review*.

Borth, with its bleak, windswept shingle strand fronted by a single line of weather-beaten small guesthouses, cafés and fish-and-chip shops, gave Jones time and space to work seriously on his MA thesis and to draft poems for 'serious' publication in the wider world of literary magazines. By the end of 1948 he had had poems accepted by *Life and Letters*, *Wales* and *Dock Leaves*; *The Dublin Magazine* followed in 1949. Ted and Pam, his wife, were good critics and the best friends he was ever to make. He was able to earn badly needed money by working in their café, The Welsh Kitchen. Ray Roberts worked there too, that summer of 1948, before going up to RADA. Her bohemianism had taken a sour turn:

> There was no guidance, no home, no advice, no finance . . . I slept with Tom – rigidly – watched by his friends, Harri and Ted. I let Ted's old father kiss my vagina because I felt sorry for him. He was old and what did it matter to me. But none of this was unusual as my punitive, puritanical, harsh, masochistic temperament later imagined it. It wasn't as good as it should have been.[100]

In politics T. H. Jones remained on what would later be called the 'hard left' despite (or perhaps because of) his romantic nature. 'Harri was a dedicated left-winger. He would simply say, "Anybody who buys and sells things for a living ought to be put up against a wall and shot."'[101] At the Debates Union he supported the communist coup in Czechoslovakia: 'Some people call this rape! I call it sweet seduction.'[102] The boos were deafening. He usually saw eye-to-eye with Gwyn Alf, a man of the left to the end of his days, but could be perverse: 'We had a hell of a row once over Tito's expulsion from Cominform (1948). I was a Titoist, like Gwilym Prys-Dafis, the Welsh Republican, now a lord. Harri was then a Stalinist. This is, of course, meaningless. Most of us were some kind of Communist.'[103]

The summer that had been Aberystwyth ended. A number of people remember rows that left Madeleine crying on the beach while T. H. Jones escaped with Ted Richards aboard the *Spanish Lady* – always with a crate of booze. Jones began to think seriously about his future – a university lectureship, he intended, but first the MA must be completed. He moved to London to concentrate on the work and his marriage and to have access to the British Library.

The social side of the marriage was conducted largely in the pub, its more intimate side in the squalor of the Asylum Road flat with its paper-thin walls. 'We lived a short tram ride from the Old Vic, and the West End theatres were not much further', Madeleine remembers. 'We managed a lot of theatre- and cinema-going with an occasional concert at the Albert Hall or Queens Hall. The "gods" at the Old Vic cost 1/6 and the Royal Circle 4 shillings. Harri, I discovered, was not very interested in music.'[104] When Ray Roberts moved to London, 'she asked me for a bed while she searched for accommodation. A year later she was still with me. London went to her head and she led a wild life. We became good friends', Madeleine (Jones) Mitchell recalls.[105] T. H. Jones's youngest sister, Pat, remembers staying with them: 'Ray was often there with Madeleine . . . they slept with Harri in the bedroom, and I slept in the lounge . . . Harri took me to all the galleries and museums and I shocked my Mam by taking home pictures of naked Greek and Roman gods.'[106] Tom Sallis remembers, 'We did Harri's regular pub-crawl: Spaniards, Cheshire Cheese, and we finished up drunk at the Prospect of Whitby.'[107]

Madeleine tells us[108] that there were frequent visits to Trefelin during the London period.

> . . . a long journey from Paddington Station to Shrewsbury, where we changed to the little line which wound its way through the valleys and hills to Newbridge on Wye . . . From the station, unless we had luggage, which meant hiring the local car, we walked the hilly way to Trefelin, about two miles of lovely scenery. After a brief greeting to his mother, we always went to see his old grandfather who lived at Cross Roads, Llanafan, in a cottage, cared for by his only maiden daughter, Maggie. He was chairbound and almost blind, but the conversation flowed happily between these old and young Welshmen – I sensed that a deep love existed between them.

(Thomas Jones was in his ninety-seventh year when he died in June 1950. He had been without 'The comforting presence of Mari',[109] his wife, for twelve years.)

T. H. Jones was desperate for work, and hated London, but it was September 1949 before he put the finishing touches to the thesis. The Richardses had invited him back to Borth, and his reply, incomplete, is the only detailed evidence we have of his life at this time:

> Dearest people, alas and alas, it cannot be . . . Tomorrow I am going to Cambridge for a couple of weeks. We are looking after Madeleine's sister's house while she luckily cavorts in France. Madeleine and Sian [their daughter] have been there since last week, enabling me to have a last spurt at the thesis, working 18 hours a day on cigarettes and black coffee . . .
>
> 'The Shapes of Pity'[110] is in the next *Dublin Magazine* and Robert Herring[111] is publishing 'Back to the Loved Sky'[112] – 2 of my better efforts you may remember. Haven't written very much lately but one or two shorter pieces I am quite pleased with. And plenty of reviewing. Did Hamish Henderson's *Elegies from the Dead in Cyrenaica*, which is as good as the very best Alun Lewis and Sidney Keyes, for *Poetry Quarterly* and have half-a-dozen books for *Life and Letters*. Among them is *Welsh Country Upbringing* by D. Parry Jones. Have you seen it? I haven't read it yet, but it looks very interesting – a Cardigan farm 40 years ago. And illustrated with a hundred fine photographs, including one of the meeting of the three counties in the Towy valley and another of the basketmaker at Ffostrassol [*sic*].
>
> I am still jobless as well as penniless. I was on a short list at Manchester, and was afterwards informed that the committee had great difficulty in choosing the other man instead of me. There may be another vacancy there this month.
>
> I've been keeping the wolf, if not from the door, at least off the table by doing part-time tutoring – teaching English to foreigners – Siamese, Persian, Swiss and French. Quite interesting and easy money, though not enough of it.[113]

The thesis[114] is an attempt to show that Donne, Herbert, Marvell and, to a lesser extent, Vaughan and Crashaw, created images by 'deliberate ratiocinative processes rather than . . . unconscious association'. For Jones, metaphysical poetry is a constant examination and criticism, at the same time passionate and analytical, of experience. He is interested in the psychology of contrast and paradox: 'Its impulse is in inquiry and conflict and in its logical elucidation of the problems of experience, the imaginative function itself becomes analytical.' T. H. Jones is an interesting combination of poet and academic and his paradoxical exploration here of paradox itself says something about his particular quality of mind.

Jim Smith anxiously consulted T. H. Jones's thesis 'in case it ruled mine out. I decided I had something quite different in mind . . . Harri followed out the 30's line on Donne's psychological turmoil which didn't, and still doesn't, interest me at all.'[115] T. H. Jones sees Metaphysical poetry as both a product of the intellectual revolution of the seventeenth century and 'the survival of the medieval ideas of the unity of the universe into an age of critical and sceptical realism'. He defines its aim as 'the reduction of the multitude of phenomena to a noumenal unity'. Metaphysical poetry is both passionate and precise, its essence is tension derived from 'the search for certainty rather than the certainty itself . . . the exploration of experience rather than its conquest . . . an acute awareness of disparate worlds rather than of the unified sensibility'. At their best all metaphysical poets 'preserve an imaginative unity and decorum' and accept a responsibility to both 'subject and intention'. Donne is the master of the appropriate, 'organic' (growing with the poem's idea rather than decorating it) image, but at their best all metaphysical poets employ imagery that is more than mere conceit. The true metaphysical image 'is a symbol of an extremely subtle apprehension of the complexity of life'.

The thesis is very much of its time, looking back to the 1930s and building on the work that arose from the revival of interest in Donne aroused by Herbert Grierson's work. Its originality derives from Jones's sensitivity, as a poet, to the texts: he was to become, in Australia, a successful teaching academic capable of inspiring his students because his powerful intellect was preserved by his creative instinct from pedantry. His strengths as critic are founded on his practice as poet and creative insights characterize the thesis as they do his work as reviewer and critic. With closely focused discussion he demonstrates how metaphysical poetry reflects the socio-economic circumstances and aesthetic preconceptions of the age. He does not deny Donne's authorial individuality, however, and he uses the poet's psychological states to illuminate those crafted images whose discussion forms the main body of the thesis. T. H. Jones is typical of his time in perceiving Donne is as a performer in the theatre of doubt. The Montaignian scepticism that modern critics see as 'the only credible reaction to the flux of definition created by . . . the convulsions of the contemporary European mind'[116] was as apt to his time as to Donne's and the way that Donne wrote uncertainty into his texts through tonal shifts, reflexivity and deliberately implausible assertions of the male self is Jones's way also in much of his poetry. There is common ground between the Donne who exclaims that 'New Philosophy calls all in doubt' and the T. H. Jones who, uprooted by war, exile and the collapse of religious belief, suffers and is in the end destroyed by that fragility of self which forms the existential crisis of identity and loss of biographical continuity so typical of mid-twentieth-century man.

Madeleine was beginning to acquire a reputation for her ceramics. Most of her contemporaries at Camberwell chose painting, but

> I reasoned that there would be a surfeit of painters coming up and, along with three men and two women, I joined the group majoring in pottery/ceramics . . . A wise choice as . . . all six of us were offered jobs at art schools around England before we had completed our courses.[117]

Among her friends were Delia and John Glanville and, although they figure only briefly in T. H. Jones's life, their contribution is important. Delia was responsible for the *Black Book*, John for a bronze head that captures, better than any photograph, the beauty and power of T. H. Jones's face.

The *Black Book*, which Delia Granville presented to T. H. Jones in November 1949, is a leather-bound octavo volume into which, between 11 May 1950 and 26 September 1964, he copied every poem he wrote, with the date of entry. It contains over 400 poems, more than 200 of which have never been published. To say that it is a useful tool for the critic is enormously to understate its importance. It enables us, virtually day by day, over a period of fourteen years, to chart his development. It illuminates his interests, themes and preoccupations. It is a psychological as well as a literary document beyond price.

Unlike Dylan Thomas, T. H. Jones hardly ever redrafted. Many of the poems exist in single drafts with alterations, if any, limited to the occasional word, phrase or punctuation mark. One or two handwritten MSS display evidence of more extensive reworking, but Jones's normal practice appears to have been to work the poem out in his head, write it down and then try it out on his friends and make alterations according to their advice, where acceptable. The final versions would be copied into the *Black Book*, singly or in groups, with the date of copying noted under the individual poem or the last in a group. When the *Collected Poems* was being prepared, Julian Croft in a few cases used the *Black Book* variant instead of the published text, an action which he later regretted. The flyleaf of the book bears the inscription 'London, November 1949', the following page, 'Poems: London, May 1950. Portsmouth, June 1951. Newcastle N.S.W., June 1959' and the final page 'Newcastle N.S.W., September 1964'.

Many of the unpublished verses are witty occasional poems or short pieces akin to the *Pansies* or *Nettles* of D. H. Lawrence:

> The puritan, the profiteer, the pimp,
> Are all descendants of a certain imp
> Who, when expelled from heaven, made it his mission
> To make men joyless even in coition.[118]

or short tributes to Madeleine:

> What I have found between your thighs,
> The eager strain, the blessed rest,
> I will not try to poetize.
> Silence is best.[119]

John Glanville was Anglo-Irish and had served in the Dorset Regiment before being seconded to the King's African Rifles with whom he spent 'a very pleasant kind of Cook's Tour during the war, visiting Abyssinia, Madagascar, Ceylon, India and Burma'.[120] He first met T. H. Jones

> through Madeleine . . . at Camberwell School of Art, where I was doing sculpture. This would be around 1948. On discovering that Madeleine lived nearby in Peckham, I asked her and her husband to join me and my wife one evening. We got on very well together, although I found out later that Harri did not want to come, probably thinking it would be cocoa and biscuits, rather than Guinness and Irish Whisky . . .[121]

The two men discovered a mutual fondness for a drink. Jones still had a penchant for navy rum and both of them had learned the trick of supplementing NAAFI beer with whatever local concoction might be available. They spent much of the next year visiting the many local pubs to talk, smoke and drink – the world of grey flannels, tweed jackets, real ale and conversation was the one in which Jones always felt most at ease because he had been introduced to it at such an early age. Though short of money, he was smoking heavily at this time: Glanville remembers his 'unhygienic, but economical, procedure with his fag-ends – he preserved them in a large bowl, eventually breaking them down and with the aid of cigarette-papers turning them into new cigarettes'.[122]

Glanville had a grant to cover his college course, but Jones was 'stone broke, and it was a hard winter'.[123] He could not afford to buy much fuel: Glanville noticed that on the way home from the pub he would somehow manage to acquire a large lump of coal to supplement his store. Madeleine went to stay with her sister in South America,[124] so he was a bachelor again.

> Harri was not unduly lonely. Apart from me and my wife he had numerous friends, most of them Welsh, including John Elwyn Williams, who was starting a law career, a former Rugby Blue, Hugh Lloyd Davies, the nephew of a Cabinet Minister in the post-war Labour government who had made himself upopular in Union circles by defecting to Rugby League and Maggie Dulanty.[125]

'Poem for Madeleine', although entered in the *Black Book* in April 1951 under the title 'To Madeleine', may relate to this time. It stands first, with a whole section to itself, in T. H. Jones's first volume, *The Enemy in the Heart*,[126] opens with 'An ocean or embrace away', refers to 'the random air / Of absence' and 'Estranging time, estranging seas' and concludes with a tender apology:

> And grant me pardon, love, for pride
> Expert in disobedience.
> Forgive me that I could not reach
> You when your longing cried.
> And grant me pardon, love, for each
> Failure of will, deceit of sense.[127]

T. H. Jones's closest friend was still Ray Roberts. She had become very friendly with Delia Glanville

> who assisted in advising her on fashion and with tricky feminine activities such as hair dyeing and bleaching. Rachel was a jolly extrovert, always cheerful, friendly and full of zest. Everyone liked her, both men and women, which is rare. She was also in some respects quite amoral. In Dorothy Parker's famous phrase 'she was the good time that was had by all'.[128]

Two lyrics of the period show that Jones was finding it difficult to cope with this:

> Stare, stare, said the soldier,
> At ghosts in uniforms.
> Peer in the deeps, said the sailor,
> For those who died in storms.
>
> And stare, said my evil love,
> At the hole I made in the sky,
> Or in the mirror look at
> A man about to die.
>
> I saw the uniformed ghosts,
> And the bones on the bed of the sea,
> And when I looked in the mirror,
> My love murdered me.[129]

The music of this is wonderfully plangent, the mournful vowel-sounds enforced by alliteration ('bones on the bed of the sea') and repetition. The poet strikes an attitude in Donne's manner, but genuine feeling underpins it: this is the kind of lyric you write to lessen the pain by getting some of your own back. This is the second lyric:

> The moment has gone by
> When I could have stared
> Unwinking in your eye,
> And with assurance dared
> To love you till I die.
>
> Whether it was a lie
> Or not no longer matters.

> Only you and I
> Will know in what deep waters
> We threw our love to die.
>
> And only you and I
> Will ever have to dream
> Whether a lover's lie
> Might not have made it seem
> More difficult to die.[130]

Love, death and sea come together again and the music is similar except that the staccato 'Or not no longer matters' acts like a cold douche, emphasizing that the passion is over – only for the return of the former music in the final stanza to suggest that it never will be.

Although they did not bring in any significant income, the poems, reviews and story published in *Life and Letters Today* and elsewhere between September 1948 and May 1950 were establishing a minor reputation for T. H. Jones, even though the days when such figures as Aldous Huxley and Virginia Woolf had appeared in the magazine were long gone. Its editor, Robert Herring, had come to despair of Fitzrovia: 'War had destroyed all creativity, which was fleeing from London to the regions.' To him, 'poetry was returning to Scotland and Wales in order to revive'.[131] Dylan Thomas had certainly done this, but T. H. Jones was, by accident rather than design, one of the first to make the reverse trip.

His review of Austin Warren's 'Rage for order'[132] exemplifies his approach. 'Faced with the genius of a Hopkins, a Yeats, a Kafka, the academic critic can only retire behind his professional timidities until that genius has been illuminated and re-illuminated by critics who are themselves creative.' He accepts Warren's theories about 'intensity and violence' and the interrelated disciplines of poet, reader and critic, but he finds that, when applied to specific writers, they lead to 'dull *lectures expliquées*'. The most interesting essay is that on Edward Taylor, the most considerable of the New England metaphysicals, who had been recently discovered and a selection of his verse published for the first time in 1939. Taylor, now regarded as the most important of the pre-nineteenth-century American poets, was, for Jones, an early introduction to the field of writing that would be the focus of his critical interests during his final years. His interest is, again, that of a critic who is himself a practising poet: 'Perhaps academic critics should be restrained from publishing their neat little articles, their written-up lecture notes.' The relationship between poet and critic would be more appropriately explored in verse, in 1953, in the poem, 'Critical encounter'[133] which Jones interpreted for Ludovic Kennedy in connection with a radio broadcast as

> An expression, in more or less dramatic form, of the essential poet-critic dichotomy, but to me it goes deeper, in that the poet and the critic are two aspects of the same person, and the poem is therefore one version, by no means final, of an internal conflict.[134]

(He would return to the problem ten years later.[135])

Savaging the work of American professors at a safe distance was one thing; it was quite another, for a man applying for university lectureships, to tackle the work of current English academics. His review of Rosemary Freeman's *English Emblem Books*[136] is kinder (the subject was, of course, closer to his heart and recent critical endeavour). He finds her book 'patient and lucid' and devotes his review to an intelligent summary of the significance of the emblem as a manifestation of the seventeenth century's allegorical cast of mind. He reminds readers that 'the emblem rose out of the taste for metaphor and conceit, not vice versa' and that it was the growth of science and the rational mode of thought that killed the taste for allegory in all its forms.

Edwin Muir's *Essays on Literature and Society*[137] were very much to his taste. 'In these days when so much that passes for criticism is either the driest authoritarianism or mere shoddy, it is refreshing to read a volume of essays as sane and civilised as this.' He admires Muir's 'lucid prose style', praises his account of Burns, Henryson and Scott and considers that his 'virtue is that he assents to no current formula, academic, theological, or political, for the sale of being fashionable'. Like himself, Muir is a creative writer and thus 'more aware of tradition than are some of its more vociferous upholders' and he concludes that: 'For those who are concerned with literature as a manifestation of the human spirit this dignified and illuminating criticism will be one of the most important books recently published.'

We can now see his views as part of that fusion of nineteenth-century romanticism and twentieth-century developmental psychology that was to shape much post-war thinking about the creative arts, the way in which they are taught and their place in education as a whole. In an advanced industrialized society there is inevitably a conflict between art as a technique for making and appraising products that are of social value (or simply can be mass-produced and sold for profit) and art as therapeutic engagement with the inner self. For T. H. Jones poetry was often, and quite often assertively, a striving to make sense of the most sensitive, conflicting, mysterious and traumatic feelings – all his life, armed, like his own Mad Prince,[138] with nothing heavier than a way with words and images, he fought the dragons and the nightmares.

As a teacher of adolescents and later young adults his practice was in the tradition of expressive aestheticians like Marjorie Hourd, Susanne Langer and John Dixon. This practice was at the sometimes sentimental and frequently misunderstood heart of the creative-writing-driven English curriculum, and the mainstay of the thinking of the National Association for the Teaching of English, which came to dominate English teaching in Britain and Australia during the later 1960s and the 1970s. David Holbrook stressed that writing can enable children, adolescents in particular, to come to terms with traumatic feelings and experiences – what matters is the capacity of the creative process to give relief and understanding, not the intrinsic merit of the poem produced. T. H. Jones, like Holbrook, believed poetry to be a central process in education for emotional and spiritual maturity, and so it is, but there are traumas that lie too deep for words. At the time of his death he would be writing some of his finest poetry, but his own pain was not eased.

A review of three anthologies[139] highlights other interests. He is largely dismissive of the young writers in the American *New Directions*, criticizing their reliance on violence and their obsession with Faulkner and Hemingway. A short story by Tennessee Williams is uncertain in intention: the writer seems 'unable to decide whether to reflect the strain, the violence and the horror of contemporary life by strict realism or by symbolism'. The best piece is Mary McCarthy's 'ingenious, brilliant, almost convincing presentation of Americans as essentially non-materialist' – more accurate, he thinks, than Evelyn Waugh's *The Loved One*. He cannot forgive the poor translations of South American poetry, the misprints or the failure of the editor to correct them (he was meticulous himself). *New Road 5* is damned because it contains too much critical and too little creative writing, but Herbert Read's *A New Romantic Anthology* is highly praised: for the Mervyn Peake chapters (with fascinating illustrations) from *Titus Groane* and because of the Irish, Scottish and Welsh poetry presented as national rather than regional. 'Eliot, Sitwell and Auden excepted', he maintains, 'the best poetry in England today is being written by non-English poets.'

Non-English writers face a variety of problems when they write in English. The forms, whether poetic or prose, are English of England and have a long tradition attached to them. An African or Asian novelist has to cope not only with the existence of, say, Dickens, but also with an education based on colonialist assumptions and a sensitivity which may amount to anger at being obliged to use the language of the oppressor. When he produces a major work, the critical appreciation that matters most may be ignorantly wide of the mark because the established critics are English and American. A Welshman or Scot born in 1921 might well feel guilty about writing in English at all, but in both countries at that time he had little choice in the matter, since his education had made no significant concession to his nationality or its linguistic and literary traditions. Cultural imperialism is difficult to cope with. As we have seen, T. H. Jones's school education in mid-Wales was in most respects no different from that of a contemporary living in the Home Counties of England, and his university course, though run by a Welshman aware of the Anglo-Welsh tradition, was based on the Oxford model. Excluded by his language from a place in the Welsh and by his nationality from a comfortable one in the English tradition, Jones would increasingly seek to define his identity by means of what Foucault calls 'discourses on sexuality'.

The Anglo-Welsh writer of the post-war period faced serious practical problems. There was no established, wide-circulation literary magazine in Wales. If he could get a volume of his work published there it would almost certainly be ignored by English reviewers. If he published in England he would very likely be ignored in Wales – and to publish in England at all he might have to make concessions that betrayed his nationality (Richard Llewellyn's *How Green was my Valley* is an obvious example). One of the few magazines hospitable to the Anglo-Welsh at this time was *The Dublin Magazine*.

T. H. Jones had made contact with its editor, Seumas O'Sullivan, as early as May 1949: 'You, and your magazine, will always be remembered with honour by us, the Welsh who write in English, because of Alun Lewis.'[140] In addition to Lewis, he had published Glyn Jones, Brenda Chamberlain, Ted Richards and some of the earliest work of R. S. Thomas.[141] In December 1949 he published 'The shapes of pity'.[142]

This difficult poem in four eight-line stanzas of iambic pentameters irregularly rhymed is one of a number of intellectual/abstract exercises ('The country of hurt'[143] and 'The persuasion of light'[144] are other examples) typical of one of the 'voices' the developing poet tried out as he worked towards the voice distinctively his own. He would later describe such poems as '"intellectual" . . . or, in the good sense, "sophisticated"'.[145] 'The shapes of pity' is an interesting synthesis of the Auden of 'Paysage moralisé'[146] ('Marooned in that discoloured wilderness / Distractedly looking for the healing streams') and the Yeats of 'The Second Coming'[147] ('Across the desert wing the hideous birds' is uncomfortably close to his 'Reel shadows of the indignant desert birds') and the Eliot of *The Waste Land* ('The skeleton sprawled across the desert rock / Is smiling in its empty staring eyes'). Collage verse, an unkind critic might say, has succeeded college verse,[148] and although it deploys a great range of imagery, it does not say very much. But it does contains some beautiful lines: 'the faded past / Is crystal in the memory of a tear', and some that are strikingly provocative: 'All metaphors are murder; death is human / The one true pity, the undeceiving surprise.'

Much of the early poetry shows equally obvious signs of the very different influence of Dylan Thomas. Like him, T. H. Jones discovered modern poetry through a delight in its most obscure manifestations, particularly the distorted, reversed or inverted cliché ('once below a time'), the range of ironies covering anything from the bawdy *double entendre* upwards: the celebration, that is, of language as serious play (that overdue shattering of decorum that is the golden gift of the Modernists to their successors). Like that of Dylan Thomas (but also George Barker and David Gascoyne),

Jones's poetry begins and ends with the problem of personal identity (identities, rather – in the later poetry consciousness will be explicitly multiple, a postmodernist characteristic absent from Auden, despite his shifting of the self onto heroes, landscapes, friends, lovers, victims, and also from the Movement poets). Through this multiple consciousness will pass all Jones's meditations on contemporary life. His writing is to become increasingly disruptive of its own poise and will pre-empt any simple foreclosure of its self-generated disorders.

Barker and Gascoyne (whose surrealist poetry Jones disliked) and, to a lesser extent, Dylan Thomas have been accused of invasive egotism 'by reckless objectification of the body image in terms of violent organic processes, by insistent possessiveness towards whatever exists outside the self and by an unconsidered proliferation of imagery quite unlike Auden's calculated and orderly lists'.[149] These refusals, however, were concomitants of an imagination that concerned itself with the identity of opposites and the resemblances between different orders of existence, designed to represent the self as dramatic and participative rather than reflexive.

In 'Difference'[150] we find what appears to be a Yeatsian promotion of change through radical continuity:

> Under God's violent unsleeping eye
> My fathers laboured for three hundred years
> On the same farm, in the expected legend.

This is a typical distortion of biography: the Jones family, even on his father's side, were migrants from the west. Like Yeats, Jones saw history as essentially illusionary: the creative, fictive act was what mattered. The 'lie' is a poetic image; it cannot invalidate the truth of the poem's point: 'I inherit . . . But I know loneliness, unwatched by God.' In his introduction to the first edition (1940) of *The New Apocalypse*, J. F. Hendry had addressed the sense of deepening social crisis which 'mechanical' politics could no longer remedy and suggested that 'man stands forth as the ultimate reality'.[151] The most significant aspect of his polemic is its distinction between collective and individual myths of self, myth as social ideology and the mythic projections of self as personality into everyday life. His argument offered a rationale for the poetic style that reproduces the objective world within the projection of conscious and unconscious self. G. S. Fraser[152] defines this as a dialectical development of surrealism in which unconscious image is brought under conscious poetic control. In developing, through myth, a style of self (a characteristically Welsh preoccupation – we have seen it at its most assertive in 'A poem for Wales'[153]) Jones found a device to integrate the human world and the world of things, to attempt, at least, to encompass the sum of objective existence:

> The world is spinning and the world is named,
> Adam unribbed and waking to his dream,
> Five senses rule the world, and five
> Are lucky in the last and burning name.[154]

He could identify with the Yeats who echoed Douglas Hyde's view of the relationship between the inner nature of nationality and the national language. Like Yeats, he valued his country's legends, stories and folklore. This Neo-Romantic stance was based on a conscious rejection of scientific rationalism and far removed from the dominant view among Movement poets. He was entirely in sympathy with Yeats's rewriting of Ireland as a unified, organic culture, a society naturally grown together – it appealed to his emotional socialism. According to Yeats, poets seek the truth so that 'they may not be lost in a world of shadow and dream',[155] or, as he has it in 'Ego Dominus Tuus',[156]

> What portion of the world can the artist have
> Who has awakened from the common dream
> But dissipation and despair?

During his London period T. H. Jones became publicly embroiled in the late 1940s argument about regionalism.[157] Keidrych Rhys[158] had promoted the view that the war had made the Welsh realize themselves as a nation with a land, people, culture and tradition very different from England's to fight for. He could not but recognize that Wales was a divided society in all these respects, but felt that, somehow, regionalism might unite it. After all, progress was being made in Ireland (*The Bell, Irish Writing, The Dublin Magazine*[159]) and in Scotland (MacDiarmid,

Soutar, Garioch and the promotion of Gaelic). Regionalism had been advanced during the war by the publication, in *Argosy*, *Writing Today*, *Modern Writing* and other magazines, of regional short stories by Irish writers and Welsh writers such as Rhys Davies and Alun Lewis. And even though the market declined after the war, T. H. Jones would be able to place at least some of his own regional short stories.

Regionalists argued about the use of the actual, living language of the region, but the real argument was more to do with provincialism and the need for the aspiring writer to make his way to, and reputation in, London. This period of T. H. Jones's life has a good deal in common with Dylan Thomas's earlier sojourn in Fitzrovia. Thomas, living at this time a schizophrenic existence between London and Laugharne, had things, as usual, both ways: he attacked the London Welsh for setting up 'a little mock Wales of their own, an exiled Government of intellectuals dispossessed not only of their country but of their intellects' and flayed Welsh artists who remained in Wales as

> Giants in the dark behind the parish pump, pygmies in the nationalist sun endlessly sniping at the artists of other countries rather than attempting to raise the standard of art of their own country by working . . . at their own words, paint or music.[160]

Thomas managed to secure an international reputation, though arguably it cost him his life as well as his art. R. S. Thomas, little known outside Wales, was read in England as a regionalist. T. H. Jones debated publicly in London, Aberystwyth and in print with Aneirin Talfan Davies the contention later taken up by Bobi Jones that only through the Welsh language could any authentic experience of Welshness be communicated,[161] and he refers to one particular Fitzrovian debate in 'The Anglo-Welsh':[162]

> Remembering among the unlovely London voices
> A man who said, out of enthusiasm and love,
> 'You live upon your grandparents' memories',
> I am vexed and despondent; where my unruly heart rejoices
> I am tongue-tied, having not gratitude enough
> To speak my own language or to hold my peace.

Julian Croft argues that this poem shows Jones trying to unite the dualities of the Welsh experience, and sees this as the key to the 'heroic purpose' central to his poetry, with its pervading concern with 'duality and contrarieties'.[163]

> This is the struggle of self with self; out of this war
> What may emerge of richer rhetoric may seem
> To justify this treason and this bitterness.[164]

(The play here on Yeats's assertion that out of the quarrel with ourselves we make poetry and out of the quarrel with others rhetoric is very neat.) The poet-figure of the poem is haunted by 'ancestral summonses to a more splendid cause / Than making poems in the beautiful alien tongue'.

Other dualities inhabit the poem. The poet 'born of the mountains' is 'enamoured of the sea' and wonders what he is doing 'where mechanic roadways run / To merit that ancestral piety and pride'. Julian Croft sees the young T. H. Jones as 'an exile from his ancestors but able to hear their call, or unable to make deep human contact with another because he sees love as unresolved and unresolvable conflict.[165] With Madeleine and Sian in South America, he was unable to find a woman to give him the stability he always craved:

> Time coughs and threatens,
> Evil are the streets,
> And love is murdered nightly
> Between the loving sheets.[166]

The undated story, 'These rooms, this bed, this woman', may well relate to this period. It is about an unsatisfactory affair between a 'Mountainy boy . . . green lout of a poet raw from the hills, lost and poor in the metropolitan friendlessness' and a married woman whom he deserts without explanation:

> I had to run away from my love and from my failure, but I could not run home. Already I knew that the best place to run to is just around the corner . . . I ran around the corner, leaving my love, leaving my child, taking my failure.

A number of references in unpublished poems also seem relevant. 'Pale hands you love'[167] – the title is a quite extraordinary allusion to the sentimental song which begins 'Pale hands I loved beside the Shalimar, / Where are you now? Who lies beneath your spell?' by the aptly named Laurence Hope (Adela Florence Nicolson, 1865–1904) – refers to 'absence as a kind of slow decay / Rotting all tenderness and rage away' and makes the vain promise 'Now if you should come back, I think you'd find / The weather altered'. 'For Sian',[168] in the manner of Yeats, warns his still-infant daughter to 'learn before it is too late / Love's unpredictable violence'.

Madeleine and Sian came home. He was, again, husband and father, and it seemed to his friends that he was prepared to accept the disciplines of married love and rewrite his marriage into his poetry. 'For Madeleine'[169] certainly does this, and it is one of a cluster of poems entered into the *Black Book* in 1951, which contain lines such as

> Drunken in the meadows of your breast,
> Helpless with the delicacy of love,
> I remember forgotten beauty[170]

and

> the lovers walking
> Eternally two by two down the enchantment
> Of children's smiles.[171]

He gave up his university ambitions, applied for teaching jobs and, in spite of an attempt by MI5 to block it, secured one at the Dockyard School, Portsmouth.[172]

1951–1959

The Serpent in the Suburban Garden

It would take T. H. Jones nine years to recover from his failure to obtain a university appointment. At his Portsmouth interview he was told that he was overqualified, but, as an unemployed ex-naval man he could have the post if he really wanted it.[1] It was with some reluctance that he accepted. Teaching has never in recent times been well paid: in the 1950s the salary was an insult to anyone of ability, and housing was expensive and hard to find. Portsmouth had been heavily bombed and large areas of devastation remained: 'Portsmouth was very slow to re-develop itself. Plymouth . . . was completely re-built before Portsmouth even started.'[2] The cityscape was one of bomb sites, the city centre a wasteland. The Naval Dockyard was gearing down after the war, and there was little new private investment to reinvigorate the local economy.

More important, from T. H. Jones's point of view, even compared with other provincial cities it had little intellectual or artistic life. Though there were far fewer sailors now that the war was over, it remained very much a sailors' city:

> Ghosted with sailors, the sleeping city
> Waits by the water for an admiral
> To take her out to sea . . .
> The Pompey chimes ring out over seven seas
> Portsmouth is pointed for a long commission.[3]

It did have three theatres: the Hippodrome, home of local variety, where the matelots repaired for the occasional evening of tame striptease; the Theatre Royal, a solid repertory theatre, and the Kings, which ran a few pre-West End shows and a little experimental drama – T. H. Jones found nothing to inspire him.

The Dockyard School for naval engineering apprentices and potential naval architects lay outside the dockyard. A collection of prefabricated single-storey buildings, it resembled 'an old American army hospital'.[4] Jones was appointed to teach technical English, but in his second year a new headmaster, John Goss, believing that even apprentice engineers deserved a liberal education, encouraged him to develop literature courses. For Mike Thomson

> It was my awakening. At sixteen I had moved away from home to a completely new experience, to a world of hostels and digs. Harri had an enormous influence . . . we drank cheap wine . . . read Dylan Thomas . . . at my twenty-first birthday party, we performed *Under Milk Wood* . . .[5]

A whole generation of young naval men was introduced to esoteric magazines, *Botteghe Oscure*,[6] for example, which published a number of poems by T. H. Jones. It was here that the Italian poet, Roberto Sanesi, translator of Dylan Thomas and champion in Italy of Anglo-Welsh poetry, was first introduced to T. H. Jones's work. The two poets would become friends at the 1958 Salzburg Festival and T. H. Jones included versions of some of Sanesi's poems in *Songs of a Mad Prince*.[7]

Three years of being taught by T. H. Jones caused Thomson to lose interest in naval architecture and try for an adult scholarship to Oxbridge. He even wrote a thesis, 'The Sensible D. H. Lawrence', which survives with numerous annotations by Jones.

> Harri was a real enthusiast for Lawrence at this time and wrote on my behalf to Frank Leavis, but I was unsuccessful . . . I remember Harri as a frail man, he never seemed to enjoy good health. I suppose he drank too much and ate too little.[8]

T. H. Jones certainly cultivated the image of the poet: 'He was not by nature a patient man with the world. He always seemed to have a passionate concern about some subject or other, be it the quality of the local beer, or the unbalanced syllabus, lack of money and political claptrap.'[9] Teachers were expected to look like civil servants, but Jones used to wear 'what we would call an "Oxford suit" – that is, two sizes too big – and he would also affect a choker around his neck'.[10]

Ex-students still recall T. H. Jones's slight stoop, his angular face, mop of black hair and intense eyes. They remember his inner stillness and his unselfconscious high opinion of his own abilities. He reminded all and sundry that he was working class – but in possession of a first-class honours degree. Anthony Conran believes that, as far as getting a university lectureship is concerned, he was unlucky in his timing: the big expansion did not occur until the post-war bulge 'opened up the Oxbridge oyster'; at this time 'Leavisite and other techniques of making available high culture to scholarship boys from the provinces and suburbs were not yet established orthodoxy.'[11] He sees the MA as 'something of a class-badge' and believes that some of Jones's bitterness arose because 'he had been trained to a fashionable destiny' that was, in reality, a fiction put about by the closed shop of English department professionals.[12] This does not explain why the University of Wales turned its back on him. His friends speculated that it was something to do with his flaunted communism or a dislike on the part of Professor Gwyn Jones and J. M. Nosworthy of his ex-service arrogance. More likely Aberystwyth was aping the English attitude that an Oxbridge degree counted for everything, and there was no shortage of provincial Ph.D.s.

T. H. Jones encouraged his students to write poetry as well as read it, but criticized their work ruthlessly.

> Harri could be brutal, but he was always honest . . . never stood for sloppiness . . . he was excellent at suggesting ways of getting published. He managed to get me published in the *Kenyon Review*, and he told me, 'Decide on your name and stick to it.' He invented 'T. H. Jones', and would have hated the . . . use of 'T. Harri Jones'.[13]

Although an iron man in class, he went out of his way to help his students, ran a creative-writing group and encouraged them to send their poems to established authors. One student sent some work to T. S. Eliot and received a reply from the great man saying that he liked it.

Many modern writers began their careers as teachers, in some cases very good ones[14] – but most of them escaped early.

Lawrence, working-class like Jones, was a conscious role-model. Professionally trained, Lawrence was a strict disciplinarian yet intolerant, like Jones, of authority. His teaching methods were innovative also, designed, as far as the system would permit, to encourage creativity. T. H. Jones was fond of quoting, with approval, Lawrence's bitter lines: 'What is the point of this teaching of mine, and of this / Learning of theirs? It all goes down the same abyss.'[15] He agreed that the

> mongrel school teacher is in a vile and false position set up as a representative of an ideal which is all toffee, invested with an authority which has absolutely no base except in the teacher's own isolate will. He is sneered at by the idealists above and jeered at by the materialists below.[16]

A few love-lyrics apart, T. H. Jones's early poetry is difficult.[17] To some extent this is a young poet's way of demonstrating his craftsmanship and individuality, the apprentice bard asserting his qualification for admission to the circle. It may also relate to the unsettled circumstances of the period between demobilization and getting a regular job and settled home. At Portsmouth he decided that 'love . . . is often too abstract in my poetry'[18] and began to explore the possibilities of simpler forms familiar from his youth, hymn tunes and ballads. Norman Talbot finds the ballads and songs 'simply entertaining and euphonious' and compares them to the work of Charles Causley 'where the modernism is only image deep'.[19]

Like T. H. Jones, Causley has stood apart from the mainstream of contemporary poetry and been neglected. Causley's work is in the tradition of Housman, de la Mare and Graves. It is nationalistic in an English way and popular because of its use of traditional forms. Causley also had wartime naval experience: the title of his second volume, *Survivor's Leave* (1953) is echoed in 'Lucky Jonah' (1959).[20] This parallel suggests others: later poems by both of them deal similarly with childhood and bleak adulthood. Causley's 'By St Thomas Water', like T. H. Jones's 'A storm in childhood', explores the child's fall from innocence and in 'Trusham' he revisits the village of his grandfather and father and is expected to feel guilty about his inability to conform to its traditions. Causley's most recent work resembles Jones's later poetry in its concern about the relationship between past and present, the public face and painful personal crisis.

Two of the Portsmouth ballads, 'The pride of the morning'[21] and 'Song of the Dandy Bones',[22] seemed to his contemporaries particularly to capture the poet's personality at this time. The first, traditional in form, is another example of how 'my poems lie': it is a pastiche of Auden's 'As I walked out one evening',[23] itself 'pastiche of folksong',[24] and to say that it cannot be taken at face value is to understate what is required of the reader. 'The pride of the morning' goes to the tune of 'The bride of Armagh', better known as its American variant, 'The streets of Laredo'.[25] Jones's ballad presents the poet as the dandy, 'Too young to admire and too old to deride', walking 'Alone, with a strut and a dandified smile' through a city 'bonny with fire' where 'everyone else had suddenly died'. His pride is brought low and his heart 'shrivelled up' because there is nobody left 'to see and admire'.

'Song of the Dandy Bones' delights in 'windy weather', rejecting conventional values and 'woman's kindling heat' for 'The mocking horses of the tide': only in the unrest of storms can 'The peace unknown to lubber[26] mind' be found:

> Let lubber bones in graves forget
> The windy weather rocks me yet,
> But I am scavenged clean and free
> To feed the harvest of the sea,
> *Sang the dandy bones as they swung in the tides.*

Madeleine says that she and her husband were both francophiles and the *Black Book* contains a number of poems translated from and written in French. Like Baudelaire, T. H. Jones was very consciously the poet, and, although not a Christian, haunted by a Christian heredity which had planted in him a strong sense of evil, sin and guilt. 'I suspect', says Julian Croft,[27]

> that one of the strongest influences on the early T. H. Jones was the poet's well-thumbed copy of Baudelaire's *Les Fleurs du Mal*. We find it in the recurring lyrics of the persecuted individual questioning his own identity, in the powerful presence of evil in the world, and in the vision of love corrupted . . .

Llewelyn Jones had been a dandy, would-be womanizer and drinker and his son had inherited all three characteristics (though his dandyism was intellectual, not sartorial). Lachan Mackinon[28] argues that in Baudelaire's work there is little sense of the poem as an end in itself, rather it is a piece of testimony 'bearing witness to the quest on which he was engaged'. Mackinon uses the word 'dandy' to delineate the poet as hero of his own quest (this is very much how T. H. Jones presents himself in the two poems above): dandyism, like the knight's armour, signifies to the world what he is about.

Auden was very interested in folk and popular songs and wrote many ballads and songs of his own. 'Willy and reality'[29] shows T. H. Jones writing in the manner of Auden's 'Victor' or 'Miss Gee'. In 'For my grandfather', Jones claims a similar heritage: 'Ballad the idiom of my ancestry, / The beginning men on the hills of speech'[30] and when Auden wrote:

> The farmer's children
> Tiptoe past the shed
> Where the gelding knife is kept[31]

he evoked a world like that of Jones, for his favourite childhood landscape, though he was neither born nor brought up in it, was similar to that of Llanafan: 'height, / small burn and lonely shieling'. Looking back as a mature adult, he comes to a similar conclusion:

> To me, though, much: a vision,
> not (as perhaps at
> twelve I thought it) of Eden,
> still less of a new
>
> Jerusalem . . .[32]

T. H. Jones's ballads of the 1950s are, like Causley's, economical in their style: every adjective and verb conveys a charge of emotion. They move with deliberate regularity in the timeless tradition of folksong and their full, deliberately un-sophisticated rhymes give the texture of popular verse. The story seems to tell itself, but has an ironic subtext – identifiable also through a symbolism that is postmodernist in its commentary. The echoes of the vernacular point to the mature, colloquial voice of the later poetry, and like Causley, Frost and Auden he can achieve profundity by deceptively simple means:

> Time coughs and threatens,
>   Evil are the streets,
> And love is murdered nightly
>   Between the loving sheets.[33]

Alan Marshfield believes that T. H. Jones 'found the whole period . . . very frustrating' and alleges that 'He had few friends',[34] but Madeleine disagrees.[35] Ray Roberts and her husband, Alan Dobie were frequent visitors. Others included Dr Grieves, a teacher of French at the school, who was interested in art, history and music, and 'Stanley the Pole', Stanley Kowalski, a displaced person, his main drinking-companion. In December 1952 Jones wrote 'Workers of the world unite'[36] for him. This sarcastic poem, disillusioned equally with sex, capitalism and communism, was inspired by a pair of lovers 'fucking' (his word) in public in a Portsmouth park. The satire (which may owe something to Orwell's *Nineteen Eighty-Four* (1949) begins with the pun on 'unite'. The lovers are indifferent to the 'crowds that pass / And cast an eye',[37] but in 'the perfect workers state' they will be able to choose between 'beds of down . . . unexposed to public frown / And torch shone down' and 'a bit of love on grass' (in other words, have as free a choice as the bourgeoisie). There's a catch, though: they will require 'a pass':

> For the State must still ensure
> Even in such lusts divine
> That rutting comrades still make sure
> That their passions keep the pure
> Party line.

Coition is not 'just fun for lad and lass – It means fruition':

> servants of the State
> Severely look by night and day
> That the lovers consummate
> Their joys to benefit the state.

Not much of a choice, really, for the 'proles': the only alternative to the 'sneering eye' of the capitalist bourgeoisie is the regimentation of the communist state.

Wallace Stevens's *Selected Poems* were published in London in 1953. Between 16 and 18 April T. H. Jones, wrote his 'Homage to Wallace Stevens',[38] an important poem because of what it tells us of his early interest in American poetry and the influence of Stevens[39] on his thinking. In 'Le monocle de mon oncle' Stevens wrote that 'There is a substance in us that prevails. / But in our amours . . . such fluctuations'[40] and elsewhere that 'the poem is a nature created by the poet'. He distinguishes the world of poetry as the 'mundo of the imagination', a fusion of the real and the imagined, a kind of Supreme Fiction.

T. H. Jones's response centres on 'The man with the blue guitar', a poem of more than 300 free-verse couplets arranged in thirty-three sections, each a pool of astringent thoughts on the incessant conjunctioning between things as they are and things imagined. For Stevens there must be no untruths, 'In poetry at least the imagination must not detach itself from reality'. The poet is 'the intermediary between people and the world in which they live and also between people as between themselves; but not between people and some other world'.[41] In Stevens's poem the man bending over the blue guitar is 'A shearsman of sorts'. As anyone knows who has witnessed sheep-shearing, a shearsman strikingly transforms appearances. The image could not fail to appeal to the grandson of a shepherd, nor the diction, imagery and rhythm to the poet who had recommended 'Tarantella' to his sisters:

> The man bent over his guitar,
> A shearsman of sorts. The day was green.
>
> They said, 'You have a blue guitar,
> You do not play things as they are.'
>
> The man replied, 'Things as they are
> Are changed upon the blue guitar.'
>
> And they said then, 'But play, you must,
> A tune beyond us, yet ourselves,
>
> A tune upon the blue guitar
> Of things exactly as they are.'[42]

In Stevens's colour system, blue is for imagination, green for reality, a fact appreciated by Dylan Thomas, though he distorted it. The guitar must always refrain from falsifying the reality that is seen as 'the ultimate value'.[43] Humans are able to create order out of chaos and therefore the guitarist's tune must be representative of our true selves, but because the imagination is involved, the tune, the ultimate reality, is both beyond us and yet ourselves. In his own poem Jones adopts the persona, or mask, of a clown, a motley fool who rages 'for colours as they are',[44] but the colours are 'tricksy things' and the music at best an aid 'to find them as they are'. The 'original sea' is the 'sea of syllables', an alpha and omega of 'Primal oh-ho and last ironic ha'. Jones is clear that in the beginning was the word and that 'It is the colour of ourselves we seek'[45] in it (an idea he will explore further in 'The colour of cockcrowing').[46] Once we have heard the blue music played on the ultimate guitar 'we can discard ourselves, / Into the ordered raging of the sea'.[47] It is through poetry that we can 'know the colour of ourselves' but there can be no certainty because the colours remain 'tricksy things'.[48]

Another poem by Stevens, 'Mystic garden and middling beast', also seems to have influenced Jones's idea of the poet as a fiction-maker (liar) 'Happy rather than holy' because this is the joy that has to do the work of the 'old' Heaven and its construction, Earth the paradise garden. He responded to Stevens's ebullience, capacity for self-mockery and cynicism, and the influence is profound because Jones identified with his idea of the poet as a creator 'not so much by choice as by necessity'.[49] Stevens's persona appears to be the result of a process of reconciliation of the guilt he felt about his own artificiality, and cynicism, which he successfully transformed in his writing into a pole of thought. Jones had himself been trying on so many masks that he seems to have felt, like Yeats, that he was doomed to be a chameleon or, like Stevens, drawn towards too many 'jocular procreations of the dark'.[50] But Stevens had, to use Jones's favourite epithet for the process, 'come through',[51] aided by the conclusion that every self is many selves. In his journal for 27 April 1906 Stevens wrote 'There is a perfect root of characters in every man – and every man is like an actor's trunk, full of strange creatures, new and old. But an actor and his trunk are two different things.'[52] He is suggesting that we do not take on our roles deliberately, as actors do: the roles are latent in our nature. The multifaceted nature of personality is a controlling principle, and for Jones, like Stevens, the 'tricksy thing' of the poem.

A contrasting influence was Edwin Arlington Robinson. Alan Marshfield recalls 'Robinson's long Arthurian poems we read completely in one evening, together with W. S. Graham's "The Night of the Sheep" '.[53] It was not just the Arthurian material that appealed but also the pessimism and irony and the significance of these narrative poems as a bridge to the twentieth century. Naturally Jones, who did this himself, would be drawn to writers who straddled boundaries. Robinson's poems were very popular in their day and Jones was anxious that though poetry *could* be difficult it *should* be accessible.

In search of a more receptive audience and extra money to help pay the mortgage on the house they had found at 84 Battenburg Avenue, Jones began running WEA classes in Portsmouth and the Isle of Wight. He took enormous trouble over them. His 'Appreciation of literature', which ran in 1954 at Gosham Park House, Portsmouth, was designed as introductory

> to a three-year tutorial class in the study of literature . . . planned mainly on the lines of Raymond Williams's *Reading and Criticism*. Its aim is the intelligent and responsive reading of literature; and to this end it is proposed to limit theoretical discussion and to concentrate on practice, i.e. reading and criticism, as far as possible.[54]

As always, he has got the register right, but what the housewives and pensioners who formed the bulk of his clientele made of it can only be imagined.

He declared, further, that he aimed

> to show that bad reading and bad writing complement each other just as good reading and good writing do; to help students to realise for themselves that full value can be obtained from literature only by close, mature reading. Such reading involves criticism, that is, evaluation (of intention, means and adequacy), comparison and standards. It is hoped that the practical nature of the course will enable students to find out for themselves that intelligent reading leads them to the establishment of critical standards which are neither arbitrary nor subjective.[55]

This exercise in wish-fulfilment reads like an Open University course-book half a generation ahead of its time: he was compensating himself for the university work he had failed to secure.

The course included the analysis of non-literary material (newspapers and advertisements) as well as selected extracts in prose and verse, mainly drawn from *Reading and Criticism* and Denys Thompson's *Reading and Discrimination*. The texts were Joyce's 'The dead', Lawrence's 'The odour of chrysanthemums', T. F. Powys's 'Mr Pym and the holy crumb', Yeats's 'The tower' and a series of *Observer* articles on the subject 'Is the novel dead?', followed by two weeks each on a series of longer works: 'Heart of darkness' (Conrad), 'The words upon the window pane' (Yeats), 'St Mawr' (Lawrence), *The Horse's Mouth* (Cary) and *Under Milk Wood* (Dylan Thomas). An extensive booklist included *Dubliners*, *God's Eyes A-twinkle* and Yeats's *Collected Poems*. In the second year he hoped to extend the range of poetry to include Hopkins, yet more Yeats, some Eliot and Dylan Thomas, further stories by Joyce, Lawrence, Powys and Kipling and to introduce some modern drama. The novels were to be *The Rainbow* and *Ulysses* (!) and the drama *A Phoenix too Frequent* and *Murder in the Cathedral*. The third year was to introduce Shakespeare, the study of a specific period (possibly Elizabethan drama), Romantic poetry and detailed exploration of either Pope and Swift, Dickens and George Eliot or Lawrence and T. S. Eliot.

Only 102 poems were thought worthy of copying into the *Black Book* during the nearly eight years spent at Portsmouth. Poems were published, in a variety of literary periodicals, and in July 1953 two poems, 'A plea against armistice'[56] and 'Stanzas in a mirror'[57] were read on John Wain's monthly radio magazine of new writing, *First Reading*. The first explored marital disillusion, suggesting that 'The subtle vanity of bickering' is preferable to a reconciliation which allows time to brood on 'old ideals still decorating heaven'. The second, with its lilting rhythm, is one of a number of poems which explore what Yeats called the 'anti-self', a force which 'distract[s] me wholly / From perfection of the dream'. The schizophrenic element defined here:

> I see behind my eyes
> The man I may become
> Take possession of my dream
> With his assured lies.

will become more important in the poet's life and poems (we have touched upon it in 'Builth Wells'[58]).

In 1953 T. H. Jones was delighted to be asked to read poems on the *First Reading* broadcast of 25 October. He wrote to Pam Richards in a tone almost ecstatic:

> This has been a big day in the life of your little Jonesey – from now on to be addressed please as the South Sea Nightingale . . . I am reading my own poems . . . on the Third on October 25th – and since you can't hear it in Borth to invite you down here . . . I have had a day of pedagogy today (I imagine my calligraphy tells you that) – I had to go to town for a voice test – and what the hell, I rang up the Dulantys so that I wouldn't have to pay for my own lunch and who should they turn up with but – in a ghastly pair of brothel-creepers – your old man. This was very nice – the rest of the afternoon was a scintillating rapture of Celtic wit and 'Shut up, Maggie!'. These are the four poems I read on 25 October. Later on Ludovic Kennedy is doing some more of mine – including 'Song of the Dandy Bones' (it is dedicated to Ted) – you can imagine what that meant in brandy today.[59]

The poems were 'Critical encounter',[60] 'Portrait',[61] 'Dedicatory poem'[62] and 'Reflections on tragedy'.[63] Ludovic Kennedy, who had taken over from John Wain, had asked for some indication of what they were about and Jones supplied it (thus aligning himself with the Group poet, George Macbeth, rather than the modernist, T. S. Eliot):

> 'Critical Encounter' may be taken straightforwardly as what it extensively is, an expression, in more or less dramatic form, of the essential poet/critic dichotomy, but to me it goes deeper, in that the poet and the critic are two aspects of the same person and the poem is therefore one version, by no means final, of an internal conflict. 'Portrait' is a 'might-have-been' poem; it expresses the poet's occasional treacherous longings to be as other men and his grudging and qualified admiration for the man who has refused to be a poet – in other words, it is about the poet's own, other, suppressed half.[64] 'Dedicatory Poem' had a personal inspiration, but as I see it now it is any poet's partly ironic apologia to whatever woman he is currently taking as the incarnation of his muse[65] – as a poet, he knows she is flesh and temporary, as a man he believes she is eternal. Of 'Reflections on

Tragedy' the inspiration is, as the title says, almost purely literary. It is an expression of the feeling that life is tragic, but that tragedy misses the point unless it is put into the words of the tragedian.[66]

'Song of the Dandy Bones'[67] was to be broadcast in January 1954, and Jones also tried to get in 'Address to my face',[68] another alter-ego poem, 'The formulas',[69] and 'Poem: back to the loved sky and the humped hills',[70] but these were refused (Aneirin Talfan Davies used them later on the BBC Welsh Home Service). He also tried to involve Rachel Roberts in the reading of 'Song of the Dandy Bones':

> I think it must be read by two voices as that is the way it is written; and the two I would like are my own and that of a young Welsh actress, Rachel Roberts. Miss Roberts has broadcast frequently and is familiar with my poetry [*sic*].[71]

Kennedy replied:

> your ballad is being broadcast in the next issue of *First Reading*. I am sorry that you could not have done this yourself, but it was hardly worth getting you all the way up here for just the one poem. Incidentally, I saw the actress you mentioned in a review in Brighton last week, and thought she was absolutely excellent.[72]

Jones had the satisfaction of being heard in company with Charles Tomlinson, Dannie Abse, Donald Davie, Steven Tumin and Gamini Salgado.

Not surprisingly, there were almost five years between the birth of Sian and that of the Joneses' second daughter, Rhiannon, in 1953. Their financial position was improved when Madeleine

> picked up a job at the Portsmouth College of Art – in my case only a part-time position as by now Sian was four years old and Rhiannon a baby. I only taught in the evenings thanks to a good supply of baby-sitters and that we owned an Austin 8 car, one of only two cars in the whole of Battenburg Avenue.[73]

Ruth Myfanwy, their third and last child, was born in October 1954. Madeleine says that her mother-in-law, who had looked after Sian for six months in 1948, 'taught me a lot about babies' and adds that her husband had 'inherited her talent and was always infinitely patient and loving to his three daughters'.[74]

This is borne out by a number of poems from *c*.1948. 'My daughter asleep'[75] vividly evokes a young father's sense of the vulnerability a child brings its parents, and concludes:

> O morning miracle, O pride of peace,
> When you have grown to stature and to guilt,
> Look in the dance and agony of your days
> Upon your child and learn how love is spelt.

Ruth Myfanwy would have to wait until she was seven 'Before your father turns his verses on you',[76] but Rhiannon, aged three, is beautifully celebrated in 'Sunday on the beach':

> In the water's salt and blue,
> A baby laughed and ran,
> A blob with legs and arms,
> A blonde hullabaloo,
> Squealing for liberty . . .[77]

This quality of tenderness is another trait T. H. Jones shares with D. H. Lawrence, whose play with Frieda Weekley's young children awoke a love that, paradoxically, took her away from them.

'Sunday on the beach', however, like 'My daughter asleep' (and Yeats's 'A prayer for my daughter') shows the domestic in collision with the elemental. It opens with a gentle warning:

> The wind was clouting the beach
> With proper motherly slaps
> That did not hurt perhaps
> Though it seemed they were meant to teach
> Something how to behave
> In the presence of wind and wave.

and moves, after the beautiful picture of the child at play, to an enumeration of the threats to her innocence: 'the harms of the sea' and 'the harms of the crowd' and the fact 'That, however unique, my daughter / Will behave as the crowd behaves'. Robert Lowell's

'The Quaker Graveyard in Nantucket' is perhaps behind the darker threat ('That last and lurking shape / By the transfigured sea') which precedes a concluding paternal incantation no less sincere for so closely echoing Yeats's prayer for *his* daughter.[78]

> May she assume a rage
> Decrepitude or age
> Or mere external stain
> Are powerless to touch.
> Let her, like the sea,
> All her life retain
> Grace of body and mind
> No accident can smutch.
> As even the winter bough
> Recalls its glory of leaf,
> Let her, in spite of grief,
> Stay beautiful as now.

Our postmodernist has also borrowed the cadences of 'Easter 1916':

> I write it out in a verse,
> Macdonagh and Macbride,
> And Connolly and Pearse,
> Now and in time to be . . .[79]

Both poets, confronted by overmastering emotion, are obliged to substitute incantation for objective correlative.

Alan Marshfield was introduced to T. H. Jones by a friend of his brother who was attending Jones's WEA classes. Alan telephoned him and was astonished to find that he was teaching at his own former school.

Harri was . . . a figure from a different generation . . . likeable, but not extrovert. I cultivated him because I wanted to talk to a published poet about poetry. He became my mentor, philosopher and friend. I still remember how flattered I was when once he said of one of my poems that he wished he'd written it himself. I would drink with Harri in the pub at the end of Battenburg Avenue where he lived. The front room of his house was full of books and that is where he did his writing, and really it was the only room in the house I knew. The pattern was, we would go drinking, then I'd go back to his place and we would read and talk about poetry until the early hours of the morning . . . We both enjoyed the reading and it was something that I have never been able to regain again in any other company. It seems strange now, that after a few drinks we could sit there and talk about the importance of poetry and our love of it, and it seemed the most natural thing in the world somehow that all life should always be like this . . . [80]

These discussions in the mid-1950s centred on such topics as the quality of Ted Hughes's poetry and the respective values of the Group and Movement poets,

Harri being savagely anti-urbane and concerned to maintain things like the ballad form and the centrality of poets such as Yeats. I felt that Harri was trapped by Portsmouth and its limited literary life and that Harri was damaged at this time by not being part of a coterie.[81]

We suspect that T. H. Jones would not have wanted to belong to any coterie that would have had him as a member.

A substantial part of his life was devoted to solitary reading and writing, so he needed the escape of his customary social drinking,

But he didn't drink heavily. A couple of pints to free himself up. However, it was easy to see how this later could become hard drinking and alcoholism as it also happened to me. Harri used to say that he often needed a couple of drinks to start him off with his writing.[82]

He was sensitive at this time to his friends' suggestion that he was overinfluenced by Dylan Thomas and Yeats. Marshfield took him to task for overuse of the word 'rage' and T. H. Jones countered with an argument which is central to the understanding of his poetry: 'Somehow the speaking seemed to make it right.' He would not excise even obvious influences: by shaping them into his own work he had made them true for what he wished to say. In this he surely exemplifies T. S. Eliot's assertion that 'what happens when a new work of art is created is something that happens simultaneously to all the works of art which preceded it . . . the past . . . altered by the present as much as the present is directed by the past'.[83]

Jones's young friends had little contact with Madeleine. Marshfield remembers her as

> higher class . . . extremely sophisticated, socially totally in control, although sometimes she seemed worn by the three children and having to cope with Harri. There were always worried lines on her face and she wouldn't join in the poetry sessions and I sometimes think that Harri regretted that. And we would occasionally talk about the fact that a lot of his love-poetry was about the absence or the evanescence of love, and about constant lovers' quarrels.[84]

Even by the standards of the 1950s they felt that his attitude to women was chauvinistic. Marshfield remembers 'a woman friend . . . complaining about having too many children and that it was getting her down and Harri saying . . . that the best thing was . . . to shut up and have another one'.

He insisted on being 'masculine' and 'free'. He affected to be the malcontent, dreamer, predator/victim – the angry provincial young man discovered (or invented) by John Osborne,[85] the young Donne whose watchword was 'Let me love none, no, but the sport'. This comes across in the unpublished 'The way of the world':

> She that has sweated in my sweat
> Must find this little knowledge yet:
> Because one woman's true to me
> I must be true to two or three.[86]

This is an inversion of Donne's

> Though she were true, when you met her . . .
> Yet shee
> Will bee
> False, ere I come, to two or three.[87]

'We usually read poems about love', Marshfield says.

> everything was new to me and I was impressed by Harri's
> honesty and insight into his private life. In fact sometimes I think
> he was cruelly honest, not disguising some of the harshness and
> difficulties in his personal relationships, although outside of the
> poetry he was totally private about his marriage . . . In the male
> company in the pub, he would sometimes brag about women,
> and . . . we would speculate about whether he had a fairly open
> marriage. Certainly he used to impress us with his bohemian
> accounts of fondling and making love to women at parties.[88]

(A distasteful characteristic, recalling the voyeurism at Borth.)

There is no doubt that he loved his wife – the quality and nature
of that passion is defined and refined in more than two hundred
poems. Ten years later he would declare, 'I am an old-fashioned
poet / Writing over and over again, My love'.[89] Writing of Dylan
and Caitlin Thomas's stormy union, he says: 'Too many people
are only too eager to believe the worst of poets, as well as
apparently their wives . . . Thomas's marriage was one of the most
fundamentally important things that ever happened to him . . .
they remained deeply and genuinely in love.'[90] More than thirty
years after his death, Madeleine remembers how 'we continued
happily in our friendship/love-affair and enjoying seeing our
daughters grow up'.[91]

He is brutally honest, though, about how sex with a partner of
long standing can lose the excitement it always has with a new
one, how in marriage it often becomes a necessary release or
comfortable routine or turns to boredom, dislike, even hate. 'A
birthday poem for Madeleine'[92] is damned by Tony Conran for its
ordinariness.[93] By now T. H. Jones has achieved a mature voice
very different from that of the early years, and the poem's opening
is deceptively pedestrian:

> It was at first merely the inconvenience
> – Children, we thought, would interrupt our love,
> Our lovemaking, thwart our careers,
> Interfere with plans for foreign travel,
> Leave us less money for drink and cigarettes,
> And generally be a bloody nuisance.

It goes on to say that the arrival of three daughters only made them more in love than ever, but that as their children grow up he is oppressed by his responsibilities:

> I should be frightened, I should run away
> To sea, or to some childless woman's arms,
> Or to writing poems in a lonely room.

but its conclusion is the inevitable one:

> Then I see your smile upon the pillow,
> And, forgetting inconvenience, responsibility,
> I answer as I can to your sweet asking,
> And only hope these girls deserve their mother.

The discourse reflects perfectly both the nature of the marriage during the Portsmouth years, and the nature of the institution itself, with its community of shared myths, significant mutual experiences meaningless to the outsider, codes of dyadic language and hermetic culture. Conran seems embarrassed by the intimacies and misses the cruel irony of those first six lines. 'O come off it!' he exclaims and more or less abandons his reading with the throwaway comment 'unless there is some arcane meaning to it that I haven't spotted'.[94] It is precisely the absence of the arcane in those lines and the next four that enables the enforcement of meaning by a very different diction and technique in the three lines which follow:

> But now – three tall daughters growing taller
> Every day – who am I to boast I bear
> Such tall and triple responsibility?

Here, typically, a play of vowel-sounds (now/tall/daughters/day/I/boast/tall/triple) is emphasized by alliteration. Nor are the next three lines ('I should be frightened . . . a lonely room') 'A perfunctory fantasy about escaping his responsibility in the three odd ways mentioned'.[95] There is nothing 'odd' about them: anyone with children must feel the first and be tempted by the second, he has to some extent tried the third more than once and is temporarily engaged in the fourth, which is no escape anyway for a father who is also a poet. Indeed, with 'writing poems in a lonely room' the poem is turned ironically back upon itself. Married love survives on significant shared moments from the past – the recapitulation of 'inconvenience' underlines this – which enable the original passion to be re-enacted as it is in the final four lines of the poem. The cliché that clinches the poem is the final extraordinary touch of irony because it undermines any attempt to assume a cosy conclusion – there is no reason to suppose the poet less frightened, or less liable to run away in either of the directions suggested earlier. Despite Conran's strictures this is amongst the most anthologized of T. H. Jones's poems.

In March 1954 the Welsh Home Service broadcast 'In my returning'[96] and 'Poem on St David's Day'.[97] In June/July 1955 'My angel'[98] and 'Merlin's lament'[99] were used in their *Literary Review*. In February 1956 'Poet'[100] was used by Gwyn Thomas on *Present Indicative* and in March 1956 Raymond Garlick used 'A song of the days'.[101] But there had been no further broadcasts by BBC London, so in May 1956 T. H. Jones wrote to the 'eccentric and boozy'[102] producer, John Davenport:

> Forgive the strictly non-U approach. A few years ago you produced my reading of three of my poems in Ludovic Kennedy's programme. I would like to have some more poems on the Third, but am so out of touch, I turn to you as a person I know, and put my poems in your arms – you can always send them back, which you can't do with a baby. You did say you liked those three of mine, so I could almost absolve myself of boasting when I add that Rupert Hart-Davis is going to publish a volume of mine. If you can do anything about a broadcast, I shall be very grateful.[103]

But he had no further luck with the BBC. After a silence of nearly three years Carne-Ross writes, apologetically:

> I have been going through a number of my papers lately as I am on the point of leaving the Corporation and I find to my horror that I never returned the set of your poems which a colleague passed on to me a very long time ago.[104]

A number of Anglo-Welsh poets have written short stories – Glyn Jones, Alun Lewis and Dylan Thomas, for example. T. H. Jones tried his hand at school and continued to write them at intervals throughout his life, though he never had the confidence in his narrative skill that he felt in his poetry. Most of his stories were written during the 1950s: 'The riding strangers',[105] 'My grandfather would have me be a poet',[106] 'Holy deceptions',[107] 'Home'[108] and 'A day at the seaside'.[109] The rest of this group cannot be dated precisely, but we know that all but the last (probably 'These rooms, this bed, this woman'[110]) had been completed by 1956, when he wrote to Rupert Hart-Davis:

> After an indecent interval I send you my stories as promised. I am much more diffident and uncertain about these than about my poems – but I had better refrain from comment, except to say that half of them have appeared in magazines . . . and a couple are in editors' hands just now. I also have at least one more Gwilym story to write . . .[111]

In addition to the five listed above, he sent Hart-Davis the unpublished 'What's become of Waring', 'Knives' and 'Saturday night'. His inspiration was Dylan Thomas's very successful *Portrait of the Artist as a Young Dog*.[112] 'Gwilym', as we have seen, is borrowed from 'The peaches'.

In 'Knives', another 'rites of passage' tale, Gwilym cycles out with his schoolboy satchel each evening to practise heavily symbolic knife-throwing in a 'Sacred Grove': 'The wood was still . . . the sighing of the air, the stirring of the leaves, the movement and murmur of small animals, the sound of birds, the whirr of earth in space.' One day his rituals are disturbed by a young girl who offers herself as a partner and attempts to domesticate his knife-throwing into a music-hall act which will support their marriage. He kills her in the coldest of cold blood; tomorrow he will find another tree to throw at. Although it has a powerful atmosphere, the story is not particularly satisfactory, though its connection with Graves's 'domestic woman . . . who would have [the poet] turn into a domesticated man'[113] is clear. The one story which has no Gwilym character, 'What's become of Waring' is, in spite of an ironical title derived from Browning, the least satisfactory of all – a typical well-made 'twist-in-the-tail' fiction which recalls the ghost-stories of A. G. Prys-Jones. Hart-Davis was not interested.

Throughout the 1950s T. H. Jones's exile in Portsmouth had ensured that he received less recognition than Vernon Watkins,

Roland Mathias and Dannie Abse – not to mention R. S. Thomas. He had refrained from placing many of his poems with such Welsh magazines as were available and had preferred not to establish a connection with a small Welsh publisher as R. S. Thomas had done.[114] R. S. had been virtually unknown in Wales until *An Acre of Land* was published by the Montgomeryshire Printing Company, Newtown, in 1952. Rupert Hart-Davis published *Song at the Year's Turning* in 1955, thus giving Thomas a British platform and it was for this reason that T. H. Jones turned to him.

There are many parallels between his poetry and that of R. S. Thomas, a fact about which both of them could be sensitive. T. H. Jones's admiration of Thomas was never reciprocated, but Jones bore no grudge, even using Thomas's work as a touchstone in his criticism. Assessing a piece by the Australian poet, Robert D. Fitzgerald, in 1964 he wrote: 'it is one of the few poems one would care to match with something by R. S. Thomas or Robert Lowell.'[115]

Thomas imperiously dismissed T. H. Jones, Alun Lewis and others as 'minor writers' whom 'the small country'[116] is over-anxious to canonize. In 1958 he was unhappy that Hart-Davis was 'picking up' a Welsh voice which might distract from his own. Both of them attracted Hart-Davis as a counterbalance to Movement suburbanism. Even in domestic poems Jones often seeks out dark origins, primal myths: Celtic magic transfigures *his* suburban hearth. This characteristic prefigures what Ted Hughes and the later R. S. Thomas have described as the reclamation of the great metaphysical issues of traditional poetry and the reaffirmation of the romantic concept of the poet/artist.

The Enemy in the Heart opens with the dedicatory poem to Madeleine, which has section I to itself. Section II is titled 'Wales', section III 'Elsewhere', section IV 'Songs', and the untitled section V is a triple rededication: 'Dedicatory Poem'[117] for Madeleine, 'A wish for my eldest daughter'[118] for Sian and 'Sunday on the beach'[119] for Rhiannon. The wife is adjured to 'Be wise, / And listen to no other poet's lies'; he prays that the eldest daughter will never 'know extravagant despair / Because no poet finds her wholly fair' and that the youngest will 'in spite of grief, / Stay beautiful as now'. There are fifty-two poems in all, the earliest datable being the title poem (1946), the most recent, 'Sunday on the beach' (February 1956).

The eight poems in the 'Wales' section amount to a definition of the poet's heritage and an autobiography of his development from innocence to experience. To appreciate them fully we must remember that T. H. Jones grew up in a particular landscape and religious background, that he left it for a wider world and returned to re-evaluate landscape, childhood and religion in the light of experience. As a poet, he came under and then came to terms with the influence of Dylan Thomas. Merely listing some of the titles gives the broad picture: 'Ancestral', 'In my returning', 'Difference', 'The ballad of me', 'Gorse idyll' (early sexual experience) and 'Poem dedicated to the memory of Dylan Thomas'.

Llanafanfawr is 'a windy place' with 'curlews calling' and 'careful men' guarding their heritage from the 'brute inhabitants' of the 'fat plains'. People know who they are and what they believe in:

> the quiet men, the burdened women,
> Aloof as foxes, clung to the ferned hillsides,[120]
> The stubborn memory, the confidence of God.[121]

The initial reaction of the poet returning from the wars is ecstatic:

> Wales wears an air, a grace, as a loved face
> Motions to kisses on the letters of exile;
> And the intricate maps of farms
> Welcome me back to a singing service,
> A wonder of work, and the toil of love
> In the green cathedrals of the sea-lapped,
> Lovely, enduring landscape of fact and legend.[122]

It consciously echoes Thomas, in particular his even more beautifull 'Fern Hill'. 'Difference'[123] makes a contrasting pair with 'Ancestral', both poems being of the same length. The experienced poet sees the 'careful men' as subject to 'temptation, women, drink'. Sin, 'the original and withering worm / Was always with them' and he has inherited not merely the 'long arms and mountain face' but the withering worm also. The archetype is Eden before and after the Fall: the withering worm is also Blake's 'invisible worm'[124] and both of them the Serpent in the Garden. The poet, his inherited religious belief rejected, endures 'loneliness, unwatched by God'.

'Amends'[125] contrasts sharply with 'Ancestral' and very sharply with 'In my returning':

> Buzzard and carrion-crow controlled the air,
> The Weasel slinked bloodthirsty through the woods;
> The fox and badger plundered and ran free
> Where the grey winds made howling solitudes.

The harsh landscape of this fallen world is presided over by the 'jealous god' of the Old Testament, 'the ancient thunderer / Cloudy with terror of his images' and the poet's departure 'to find the city roads', motivated by dreams of 'hot sunlight' and 'older gods', has been no escape, but has brought him full circle back to 'the only god that was ever mine'.

'Poem: back to the loved sky and the humped hills'[126] makes the same kind of contrast with 'In my returning'. The poet recalls a 'fronded boyhood breaking like a tide', an adolescent's strong sexual and religious feelings ('rascal girls in the spilled calm of winter / Bridehaunted in that scriptural enchantment') and a young man's escape from the 'maggot-murdered Eden' to the 'far, complaining seas'. Again the escape is no escape at all: childhood innocence is recollected not in tranquillity but in the unforgiving light of experience. The pervasive echoes that inhabit the garden are of Dylan Thomas; the poem makes the most deliberate and postmodernist use of his work, and a virtual quotation from 'Fern Hill', 'in my green ruins / I sang like the rain', identifies its child with Thomas's: 'Time held me green and dying / Though I sang in my chains like the sea',[127] virtually demanding that we reread that poem in order to appreciate this one.

'The ballad of me'[128] also consciously exploits Dylan Thomas. Written in an exile where 'The streets break on my feet and my heart', it returns us to the Eden-before-the-Fall of childhood, the landscape where 'the eternal trees / Denied the fear of death, the flowers in their seasons / Were all immortal'. The child walked and dreamed in the paradise garden, 'heard the ancestral summons' of the sea and, supportive here,

> the preacher's sounding voice,
> The word, the beginning,
> God's tremendous breath.

Violence and death cannot be denied, but the preacher's voice is not to be silenced, nor the poet to be 'Nailed on a foreign street and an alien tongue' because, if only in the man's memory, the poet's act of creation,

> that lovely sky goes on
> To where all words are woven in one word,
> The first, immortal breath, the living breath
> Shadowed in trees and grass and poets' words.

The ironically titled song, 'Gorse idyll',[129] evokes an apparently joyful, innocent sexual experience. The woman has 'hair . . . like the sunlit gorse',[130] a body 'like the gorse on fire', but the 'content' of the lovers' mutual post-coital sigh is matched against the religious exhalation of the chapel deacon. On this hinge the poem swings towards familiar guilt, leaving the poet with 'a double heart': relish the sex as he may, he can never forget the deacon.

The section ends appropriately with the 'Poem dedicated to the memory of Dylan Thomas',[131] a last tribute to his important influence. As we have seen, in 'In my returning' and 'Poem: back to the loved sky and the humped hills', it is harnessed to Jones's own deliberate purposes. At first sight this poem appears dominated by Thomas, but it was written later (April 1954), and the pastiche is calculated. It is also – there is no other word for it – joyous: 'From gorse and cinder hills I Adamed out / To take to name to praise all things I breathe'. The poet presents himself as Adam, 'unribbed' and 'unparadised' (in the wrong job, married, two children to support, exiled in England) – but exuberantly aware of his poetic gift:

> The world is spinning and the world is named,
> Adam unribbed and waking to his dream,
> Five senses rule the world, and five
> Are lucky in the last and burning name.

The majority (31) of this first volume's poems are in Section III, 'Elsewhere' (which signifies anywhere but the beginning garden of Wales and childhood). It might more appropriately be called 'Songs and sonnets', for it contains three of the latter, nine short lyrics in quatrains and a variety of other lyrics in various forms, many of them about love. It opens with two more poems to his daughters. The first, 'My daughter asleep',[132] is a wonderful postmodernist concoction out of Shakespeare, Hopkins, Dylan Thomas and Yeats:

> Here is the blossom and the laboured print
> Not tempest-daunted yet, not by the beat and whirl
> Of winds and waters strifesodden, savourspent,
> Dragoned by days and nights to weary hell.

The second,[133] 'Out of Wales', employs a device of Auden's ('Remembering today the land . . .'[134]) to associate the child with remembered Wales.

We have dealt already with 'The enemy in the heart', 'For Rachel', 'The shapes of pity', 'Mediterranean: wartime', 'Stanzas in a mirror', 'Poet', 'Critical encounter' and 'Homage to Wallace Stevens', but merely listing them gives an idea of the variety of work included. Images of garden and sea are frequent, notably in 'The vocabulary of promise',[135] a transtextual poem, Audenesque in manner, that raises the problem of fictional assertion:

> The sailors on the boredom of the seas
> Forget the lovely city and their dream
> Of gardens . . . [136]

This poem both lies and reveals truth about literary and extra-literary reality, 'The children in the enchanted wood explode / Into monsters', and ultimately 'the helpless poets . . . Landfast within their private kingdoms', slaves to mere fashion, destroy 'The value of each unenduring word / In the demoded vocabulary of promise'. 'The need for pardon'[137] and 'The definitions of circumstance'[138] are equally sceptical about love's realities. 'The shapes of pity'[139] is seen to be one of a number of 'divided self' poems (the others are 'Stanzas in a mirror',[140] 'Portrait'[141] and 'Stare-in-the-face'[142]). 'Two'[143] combines Graves ('Deadlocked and still indubitably two') with Donne ('Each in the mirrors of the other's eyes').

Section IV is suitably titled 'Songs', in that eight of its nine poems have that word in their title. It is difficult to imagine 'Song for a time of trouble'[144] being sung, or indeed singable: 'When the lion brings to the broken city / The dialectic of hate'. 'Song of the

Dandy Bones'[145] and 'The pride of the morning', already discussed, lend themselves to well-known folk-tunes. There are some beautiful (and very singable) lines in other poems:

> O weathers, thunder, golden sun,
> Make me sad and numb,
> And all my singing branches dumb,
> To see my stolen countries gone.[146]

> On Tuesday it is the drumming
> Dazzle of words
> And the hurt tongue.
> On Tuesday it is the saying.[147]

Further evidence that the poet (self-confessedly tone-deaf) is playing games.

The beautiful 'Song, O who unribbed me where I lay'[148] is best taken alongside 'Dedicatory poem'.[149] The first is about loss of innocence, the 'fall' each of us has to experience in our development to manhood/womanhood whether or not, like Jones, we bear a religious background which has inculcated the myth of the Fall, the 'thunderer' god of the Old Testament and original sin. Jones admired *Paradise Lost* and habitually, and not only in love-poems, evokes the myth of the Fall (his attitude to women is reminiscent of Milton's 'He for God only, she for God in him').

The Creation myth teaches that all men descend from Adam and all women from Eve and that God created Adam directly and Eve from Adam's rib, putting Adam to sleep while he carried out the operation. The couplet which introduces and concludes the first of these two poems: 'O who unribbed me where I lay / Sleeping like Adam that bright day?' presents sexual intercourse ('lay') as a ritual wounding *for the man* and the physical pleasure of sex ('The dancing light, the dancing blood') as disappointing (we put off our pride when we give ourselves so completely, and the experience is rarely what 'ambitious verse' claims for it). 'Knowing' a man or woman in sex is unsatisfactory (in postlapsarian times) because it leaves us with

> the harsh smouldering to possess
> Some intimacy deeper than
> The touch of wavebright bone on bone

a knowledge, an identity with the loved one greatly desired, but impossible after the 'knowledge of good and evil' conferred by the Fall. That beautiful, resonant image – 'wavebright bone on bone' – does justice to sex as we know it, but evokes contradictory overtones of drowning.[150] We might call this fine poem a 'love-elegy', so plangent is its lament for what can never be.

Underpinning this poem is a reminder that Celtic pre-Christian culture venerated the female principle (carried over into the early Celtic Church, it survives in a much diluted form in Roman Catholicism). The female principle was virtually obliterated by Puritanism and is quite absent from the sinning-fields of Welsh Nonconformity. Yet for Jones, Eve opposes Adam in a drama of sexual politics and also in concepts of sexual difference mediated largely through a post-Freudian reading of Graves's *The White Goddess*:

> The reason why the hair stands on end, and the eyes water, the throat is constricted, the skin crawls and a shiver runs down the spine when one writes or reads a true poem is that a true poem is necessarily an invocation . . . of the Mother of All Living, the ancient power of fright and lust – the female spider or queen bee whose embrace is death.[151]

Graves identifies his Goddess with the Muse; she has a nest 'littered with the jawbones and entrails of poets'[152] (the male spider pays with his life for fertilizing the female; any strong human sexual relationship is potentially destructive; many men fear active female sexuality).

There is an interesting relationship between Jones's work and that of Sylvia Plath and her husband, Ted Hughes. Critics have identified a tension between the desire for and fear of frenzied female sexuality in the poetry of the latter and Judith Kroll's study of Plath, *Chapters in a Mythology*,[153] is a reading of her work largely through the mythography of *The White Goddess*. Jacqueline Rose suggests that there 'might be a problem for women in . . . [Graves's mythological scheme] it might function as male projection and fantasy . . . the archetype might be hellish, might be taken on . . . at considerable cost'.[154] Graves leaves no role for woman-as-poet: 'woman is not poetic, she is either a muse or nothing',[155] and this view appears to colour Jones's relationship with his wife and with other 'muses'. He shows women as inspiring him, neither writing poetry of their own nor writing themselves into his life (they are permitted to be artists with their hands, but not their heads). Reading Graves caused him to see the Portsmouth period as a struggle not to compromise his integrity as a poet by valuing any other range of experience above the poetic and also to avoid losing his personal White Goddess to enforced domesticity:

> the woman whom he took to be a Muse, or who was a Muse, turns into a domestic woman and would have him turn similarly into a domesticated man. Loyalty prevents him from parting company with her, especially if she is the mother of his children and is proud to be reckoned a good housewife; and as the Muse fades out, so does the poet . . . The White Goddess is anti-domestic; she is the perpetual 'other woman', and her part is difficult indeed for a woman of sensibility to play for more than a few years, because the temptation to commit suicide in simple domesticity lurks in every maenad's and muse's heart.[156]

The Enemy in the Heart was published on 15 February 1957 to good reviews. The anonymous *Times Literary Supplement* reviewer[157] contrasted it with Richard Church's *The Inheritors*, finding Jones 'turbulent, raging, ecstatic' and 'accomplished', but needing to 'put a brake on his rough force'. The 'essential Welshness' was praised, and the technical skill, but the tone of the volume was felt to be rather bitter: 'His turbulent quest of the ideal ends in restlessness, disillusion, despair, rage.' As Julian Croft points out, this reviewer is right to compare some of the songs to Blake's,[158] but the suggestion that they were dissimilar to Dylan Thomas's work because of lack of obscurity was a point that met with some derision in Wales. The conclusion is that Jones is a major find: his poetry is 'vigorous and genuine' and 'lends itself to rich development'.[159] Morwyth Rees, in *Dock Leaves*, was equally supportive and Padraic Fallon, in *The Dublin Magazine*,[160] made interesting comparisons between T. H. Jones and Thom Gunn, in particular over-emphasis on craft at the cost of 'artificialising experience'. 'Never invert the process', Fallon advised, 'by expecting language to do your thinking for you, or your feeling', a shrewd point endorsed by Julian Croft.[161]

T. H. Jones was a celebrity in Portsmouth for a while. He featured in the local newspaper under the headline 'HERE WE FIND A POET'S

CORNER' as the most interesting individual resident in Battenburg Avenue, North End:

> His main ambition has just been realised, for a collection of his poems have [*sic*] just been published in a book [*sic*] entitled *The Enemy in the Heart*. Mr Jones has a library of over 1500 volumes at home, and when I called there he told me it was thrilling to add one of his own to the collection.[162]

In August 1958 T. H. Jones attended the Annual Salzburg Seminar on American Literature: 'I am gloriously drunk with sunshine, wine, talk, the company of other Poets, beautiful women, no responsibilities.'[163] The American poet and *New Yorker* poetry-reviewer, Louise Bogan, was there and on 12 August Jones, ever the opportunist bard, celebrated her:

> You call yourself 'old lady' and the phrase
> Becomes a poem. We poets who have known
> You also love you. May our love be shown
> In many poems brightening out your days,
> And may your tough New England charm
> Be sheltered long from ordinary harm.[164]

Later she would publish him in the USA. Bogan recalls one session in a letter to her friend, May Sarton:

> Did I tell you about the Poetry Evening when about six nationalities read poems from their literatures, *plus* original poems? One large, shock-haired man who is a Dutch journalist by profession but a Frisian nationalist by avocation, arose and sang a long loud hymn *in* Frisian . . . and an Italian gave a translation of 'Medusa' into the finest Florentine.[165]

The 'Italian' was Roberto Sanesi, a close friend of Vernon Watkins and Ceri Richards, whom Jones had met for the first time at Watkins's home a few months earlier.[166] He and Jones immediately became friends and agreed on a project, outlined later to Hart-Davis:

> you will be pleased to learn I am broadcasting a little anthology of Anglo-Celtic (horrible word) poetry on B.B.C.'s European

Service at 5.45 next Sunday. The actual contents are not definitely fixed as yet, but there will be something by R. S. Thomas and . . . me. I had a letter last week from Roberto Sanesi in which he said he had proposed 'a cultural exchange' in the matter of translations to you. I assure you there was no collusion here. When I mentioned translations to you the other day, it was because I had been working on Sanesi's poetry that weekend, and my mind was full of it. Now that I have wrestled some more with the intractability of translation, I doubt if I could ever do a volume. But what I should like to do is to include some in my next volume. Anyway, I send you the best so far, and will send you some more when I have done some more polishing . . . A story I hope you will like. Sanesi was reported in an Italian newspaper as returning from Salzburg where he had been studying the English Poets, T. H. Jones, Walt Whitman and W. C. Williams. There must be a Latin tag that fits![167]

T. H. Jones made an impression at Salzburg, so his name was 'current' when Norman Jeffares was canvassing lecturers for the expanding Australian university system. He met Jones 'At a British American Conference in Wales . . . a pleasant, interesting, lively-minded man', he recalls.[168] Madeleine was an enthusiastic traveller and Jones was flattered to be offered a post. He wrote to his mother:

You will be surprised to be getting one of my rare letters . . . and you will be even more surprised when you know the reason. We are going to Australia for a few years. I have got a job in a university out there. It is a much better job than my present one in all ways – more interest, more money, better prospects, and University teaching is what I have always wanted to do.[169]

To Hart-Davis he wrote:

I am tremendously pleased to have a University job at last even if it is 11,000 miles away. We won't be sailing till April so I hope to have an opportunity of seeing you at least once before we leave.

Would you consider it premature if I gave you the manuscript of a second volume before I go. . . . I think I have enough for another volume – possibly a little thinner than *The Enemy* – this is one of the things . . . that I would very much like to do before I sail.[170]

The symbolism is clear: he wishes to make a clean break with an unsatisfactory period in his life, and assemble the remainder of the poems associated with it in a second volume, thus clearing the way for new developments. A similar symbolic gesture was the burning of a suitcase full of the early letters between himself and Madeleine. He wrote to Hart-Davis again on 16 February 1959:

> Here is the manuscript of my proposed second volume. I am sorry it is in somewhat untidy condition – but life is very rushed in these last weeks in the northern hemisphere . . .
>
> If you would like to discuss anything, I should be glad of an excuse to come to town sometime in the next few days . . .[171]

Hart-Davis had many reservations, but Jones was determined:

> I do agree with you quite a lot about these poems. (Some of them are, it is true, earlier work, but the majority have been written since *The Enemy* took shape). I did debate this with myself . . . Finally I decided that it was important to me to have them published now . . . I have been in a rut for so long – I feel that the adventure of this complete break will really trigger me off again as leaving the Navy did years ago . . . what I am stammering after is that if these poems, or most of them, are published, then the break has been made, my first phase is over, and I can really start off anew.[172]

The *Black Book* reveals that in this case it is not the poems that 'lie', but the prose. The most recent poem collected in *The Enemy in the Heart* had been dated 17 February 1956. Since that collection 'took shape', only twenty-three poems had been written. Six of these are translations from Sanesi; eleven of the remainder are in the new collection (fifty-one poems in all). Of the three 'Songs of a mad prince', one had been written in October 1955. Thirty-five of the poems in the collection had been available for inclusion, but not included, in *The Enemy in the Heart*. Seven of them were eight years old. In his need to 'make a clean break', T. H. Jones was scraping the barrel. In one sense the break was made already: between October 1958 ('Not lack of children only') and 15 June 1959 ('Bewilderment') not one original poem was written.

Reluctantly, Hart-Davis gave in. Jones was ecstatic:

Was ever a poet so blest in his publisher? . . . I do hope that I can justify this faith in me by writing you something really good[173] in the future. At the moment I expect to be in London for sure on Tuesday . . . I say for the moment because life is somewhat disorganised. What with no furniture and the children catching chicken pox. In case something does turn up to prevent my coming, one or two practical points. Can you add to the acknowledgements the *New Statesman* . . . and *Hot Dog* (Yes, it's a Manchester University thing I have been asked to contribute to by one of my Salzburg friends). . . Looking a long way ahead, may I suggest that when it does come out you send a review copy to the *New Yorker*, as Louise Bogan (Salzburg again) likes both me and my poems and I am sure will be delighted to review it.[174]

Although it would be 1960 before the new collection, *Songs of a Mad Prince*, appeared,[175] this, clearly, is the place to consider it. Julian Croft suggests that the reader is asked to see its unity in an unfolding of the personality of the Mad Prince (the 'Three songs', as a completed poem, bridges a period of twenty months) and that it evokes 'a wounded sensibility and a determinedly pessimistic world view' and makes a statement about the downside of marriage and the Portsmouth suburban experience.[176] There are no sections: the poems are arranged chronologically in order of composition, suggesting that T. H. Jones regarded them as a progression of some kind which he desired the reader to follow.

It is easier to approach this volume from the group of poems new enough not to have been available for *The Enemy in the Heart*. The translations, which Julian Croft and Don Dale-Jones considered unrepresentative of the pattern of Jones's output, were (as is now evident, wrongly) omitted from the *Collected Poems*. They are highly regarded by Italian critics and by Sanesi himself, and can be seen as analogous to 'Homage to Wallace Stevens' in the previous collection. Jones was open not merely to the influence of a wide range of English-language poets (Yeats, Eliot, Auden, Dylan Thomas, Hopkins, Graves), he quite deliberately used their contrasting and complementary influences to shape his own work. We have seen his openness to French influences, meeting French poets while stationed in Algiers, writing poems in French and translating from that language (which he spoke and read). An unpublished poem, 'For Roberto Sanesi, il miglior fabbro',[177] reveals what he drew from the Italian:

His eyes
Perceive reality and make us real.
He burns the torch, the taste, the scent, the feel
Of love and language. O tears and wounds
Of words let his truth speak beyond the daily lies.[178]

The phrase 'beyond the daily lies' is, amongst other things, a tribute to the liberating experience of Salzburg.[179]

Brief quotation from Jones's translation of 'The crab'[180] will be sufficient to illustrate both 'reality' and 'beyond the daily lies':

It was at the wave's foot the crab was scrabbling
With rusty pincers wet in the sand, the hidden
Labyrinths into the salt and August drowsiness of sun,
The quiet floss-sulking of the foams between
The sticks on the beach veined with small red grains . . .
Orpheus' wild beast has now transformed himself
In the free yoke of the water, repetition, future . . .

Even in translation, this is fine poetry; the original's combination of very real detail and powerful symbolism was understandably inspiring and instructive. The hint at the Eliot/Pound relationship raises interesting questions. Eliot saluted his friend's 'better craftsmanship' in acknowledgement of Pound's editing of *The Waste Land*; Jones, presumably, is complimenting Sanesi (though not, like Eliot, acknowledging this to the reader, since the poem was never published) on helping to shape his own future compositions. The second question is, how did Jones, who neither read nor spoke Italian, manage to translate complex and allusive Italian poetry? In the same intuitive manner as Pound translated Chinese poetry without speaking or reading that language? However achieved, Jones's translations are remarkable.

The first two 'Songs of a mad prince'[181] are modern ballads in the traditional metre. Their imagery hints at traditional ballad imagery ('Your delicate bones will make me pens') and at Auden ('mackerel fields . . . seas of barley'[182]). They evoke a love that is disappearing, a heart that is despairing, a death from which the lover who 'Murdered all the witness air / And epitaphed my heart' has the power 'if she learns to read' to resurrect her prince. They picture a man cruelly destroyed by his lover ('I saw my blood run

down the stairs . . . / My love danced on the landing') and cruelly
desiring to destroy her (a very *literary* murder) in return

> Your delicate bones will make me pens.
> And on your skin I'll write
> The song of the bloody river
>
> That runs all night.

In the third song,[183] in stanzas varying in length from four to
sixteen short lines, with the refrain 'Lie down, lie down in peace,
poor prince's daughter' the prince walks abroad in his kingdom
accompanied by his 'lost daughter'. The purpose of their walk is
'To show her her heritage, / Bright lands, blue water'. The Prince
asserts that their land is beautiful – 'Tall trees, green grass, flowers'
– rich and heroic, 'Our fathers here did deeds / Famous across far
seas', but on inspection it proves to be nothing of the kind. It is a
waste land,[184] the ground exhausted, the people starving:

> springs were foul and dry.
> We saw an old horse dying
> In a dirty place;
> A ravaged salmon lying
> In the cold water.

The horse and the salmon are powerful symbols in Celtic
mythology, the one an incarnation of the Spirit of the Solar Year,
the other associated with wisdom. Not surprisingly, the Prince's
daughter rejects the corrupted heritage:

> No heritage for me.
> Father, let me wander
> Across the beckoning sea
> To find another kingdom
> And a prince who loves me.

The move to a more promising land is retrospective: the daughter
has already 'gone far away / Over the water'. The father, left
behind, walks alone and looks at her heritage of 'Grey lands, cold
water'. There is nothing to be said except 'Lie down, lie down in

peace, poor prince's daughter'. The process which began in 'disappearing love' ends with the youth's flight from the waste land.

Other poems in this group express disillusion, disappointment and unhappiness. 'Poetic retrospect'[185] laments a summer that 'will not stay in mind or poem . . . nothing remains but bits of paper / In a cold wind blowing'. 'Not lack of children only'[186] portrays two lonely lovers who now share only

> the unsatisfied
>
> Longing to be neither
> Together nor apart,
> Not to hear the knocking
> Of either heart.

We may now return to the beginning of the collection and trace its main themes in the light of the conclusion just explored. Garden and wilderness imagery is important throughout. The concept of the lost garden paradise is carefully worked out in 'A song for you and me'.[187] The poem centres on the idea that the Fall induced by sex is inevitable: we cannot enjoy life's fulfilment without transgressing and being punished for it. Who, the poet rhetorically demands,

> would want to pardon
> The sunlight for infringing
> The protocol of night,
> Or disinfect the garden
> Of the lithe, estranging
> Serpent of delight?

and he makes creative use of the threatening overtones from Louis MacNeice.[188]

The discourse of 'Four'[189] assumes an understanding of the Book of Revelation and is a reading of the Four Horsemen of some personal Apocalypse defined in terms of the four corners of a suburban room. The room is a metaphor of security, but also a metonym of the prison that is marriage. There is an allusion to the angel with the flaming sword – 'archaic images of sin . . . each armed with blast and flame': the couple have been expelled from

Eden and it is guarded against their return. Love has laid waste the poet's heart; the 'doom' that will 'tear' him was 'studied in love's nursery'. Jung's particular concern was with adults who had achieved sexual identity through separation from their parents, but still endured a crisis of self in middle life. This poem defines similar territory: the images in the signification patterns of the text could be read as signposts on a journey towards psychic wholeness. Jung abandoned representational painting of his experiences for abstract circular designs, recognizing only later that these were mirror-images of the mandala used as instruments of contemplation in Tantric Yoga. He came to regard the 'four' as an archetypal symbol of self, the totality of which embraces the unconscious as well as the conscious psyche. Jones's use of four 'images of sin . . . after a shoddy mimicry of fame' can therefore be read as an attempt to integrate the discordant elements within the personality at the time of the threat of disintegration.

This is explored in 'Adam',[190] where he wonders:

> Did he dream that sweat of intercourse
> Or thought might stain and strain
> His bright prophetic body?
> . . . [and] God's wrath . . .
> . . . rob them of their innocent sleep?

'Villanelle'[191] asserts that

> Something there is not cured with a kiss . . .
>
> Nor is it cured when you hear the hiss
> The expiring serpent makes in his old age.

'Nursery Rhyme'[192] has Eve laughing with 'that serpentine clown' and Adam failing to see the joke, another example of the recurrent image of the false face, life as game. The symbolic opposites, Cain and Abel (who 'drove her mad'), parody man's ('originally') sinful nature and the wife/lover is warned

> . . . you, my dear, had better learn
> This game of great renown.
> Be good, my dear, be careful, for –
> *All fall down.*

The refrain's allusion to 'Ring a ring of roses' brings in sexual associations from a rhyme that, in its Celtic version, has nothing to do with the Black Death, being part of the pattern of circle-games to celebrate the renewal of fertility. These poems continue the exploration of what A. J. Hassall refers to as 'that other fall, from unity into multiplicity, from integrity of identity into hostile, irreconcileable and mutually destructive opposites'.[193] This can be seen in a whole series of 'mirror-poems' and such symbols as the enemy in the heart, the weasel at the heart and, later, the beast at the door.

'Lady in the garden'[194] is also addressed to an Eve, a woman 'Penned in the garden of her own disaster'.[195] 'The brilliant talking fellow' (Serpent/husband/other man) 'is gone', leaving a phallic after-image of 'suddenly tall' trees. The lady is 'alone with all her flowers', a naked goddess: Blodeuwedd, Eve, *a* woman, *the* woman, *Woman*. Seduced by the appeal to her pride, she feels the 'curl and lash of cold' and understands 'how it will be told' (her reputation will be made, and destroyed, by language). The final line, 'And sees night fall', derives from Milton's 'brought death into the world and all our woe',[196] and its bitter irony lies in the fact that *this* fallen Eve sinned through sex with a 'fellow' whose name she did not even ask.

'Love dies as a tree grows', T. H. Jones's only prose-poem,[197] centres on the Tree of Knowledge of Good and Evil. We never hear 'in the dark . . . the scream of the tortured roots', never feel ourselves 'drowning in the torrent of the sap'; when we wake, the tree and our love look unchanged, but they are not: growth and death are both there: 'Love dies as a tree grows: in the dark, softly, and with a terrible scream.'[198] The imagery is deliberately metaphysical, this is a 'vegetable love' that grows not 'Vaster than empires and more slow'[199] but to death. The scream hints at Donne's mandrake root but contradicts the associations of fertility.

'Old man's song'[200] is, in the words of its Yeatsian refrain, a meditation by 'the old man as he took off his clothes'. It deals specifically with original sin: 'Children', being innocent, not yet capable of reflection, instinctive, 'do not need to think / Precisely on original sin' any more than to 'read the clock', 'stare in mirrors' or care that 'dictionaries lack / The words to make their loving right'. They are spared 'urges to get drunk' or to commit suicide.

(The immediate effect of eating of the Tree of Knowledge of Good and Evil was to rob sex of its innocence by turning what had been instinctive into a subject for mental agonies centred in self-consciousness – Adam and Eve *knew* their nakedness, their sexuality and shame.) Because (in Wordsworth's phrase, though it is not acknowledged) 'The child is father to the man', however, the course of time and the wisdom of age may enable him to rediscover

> The childish meaning of I love
> And cease to read the brutal clock
> Or stare in mirrors at his fate

– prelapsarian innocence. But by then, presumably, impotence will have set in.

'A promise to my old age'[201] again juxtaposes youth and age. The strutting, arrogant young man, striding the earth like Adam before the Fall: 'like any rightful owner, and . . . pleased / To see tall trees reflect your arrogance' (phallic again) is adjured to remember in his old age that it is in 'This earlier brash hero' that 'his promise lies'.[202] The poet prays that his old age may be free of 'these terrors and desires / Of disobedient flesh'[203] and promises 'pride / Only in glories that have long been dead', but immediately, and ironically, undermines the vow with 'Whatever song or madness your last lust / May farrow'.

'The ring of language'[204] has two epigraphs, the first from W. J. Entwistle's *Aspects of Language* ('the speechless animals' are not necessarily disadvantaged by being, like children, excluded from 'concepts and representations' for if *they* are excluded from that world, *we* are incarcerated in it) and the second from Genesis. Adam's naming (before the creation of Eve) of the animals defines his loneliness:

> Adam had named the animals and knew
> His gift was also his despair for ever.
> Adam and all the animals he'd named
> Must live for ever separate and alone.

Language defines self, internalizes individuality. After the Fall, language defined nakedness (and thus shame and guilt). The creation of Eve had not eased Adam's aloneness, rather it exacerbated it: men and women, like Britain and the USA, are two countries divided by language. We have completed our circular journey to the prince's lost paradise in the third of the 'Songs of a mad prince'.[205]

R. S. Thomas, in the 1960s, also examined the relationship between well-tended garden and wilderness. Two poems from *The Bread of Truth* (1965) ('The untamed'[206] and 'The garden'[207]) make an interesting comparison with T. H. Jones's treatment of this theme. In the first, Thomas contrasts his love of the wild with his wife's delight in gardens. As he sees it, a formal garden encloses, limits our concept of peace; only in the wild can a 'stillness / Of the heart's passions' be achieved. The poem turns on the capacity of the garden and, by association, the woman whom to some degree it embodies, to hold 'the wild hawk of the mind'. It cannot do so for long: to the hawk it is a place for 'play' – by analogy the wife's capacity to 'hold' her husband is limited and uncertain. J. P. Ward suggests that Thomas, the introspective mystic, recognizes a lust in himself which he cannot bear openly to name, let alone explore as Jones does.[208]

In Thomas's later poems the dominating signifier is no longer Iago Prytherch, but the Puw family and reflections, analogous to T. H. Jones's, on the biblical and Miltonic Garden of Eden. All the female figures of the later poetry are reincarnations of the fallen Eve. Thomas appears to have a horror of describing the sexual act, often not because of its intrinsic nature (in his work the act is performed by others and only observed by the poet), but because it can produce children. J. P. Ward points out that Thomas represents women primarily in terms of their bodily hair. They are 'blondes', the woman in 'The boy's tale'[209] catches the sailor 'in her thin hair' and in 'The dance'[210] we find 'Let me smell / My youth again in your hair'. Thomas draws his references from the Old Testament and mythology, where hair is both feminine in its ability to entrap, and masculine in its delineation of power (in the Samson myth loss of hair brings loss of strength). Thomas's sexual feelings are far less close to the surface of his poetry than Jones's, but he does not deny them. He recognizes in his own procreation a reaffirmation of sin, but J. P. Ward is right to say that his theological view is essentially orthodox. Adam sinned out of boredom with Eden's perfection and Thomas argues that in consequence blood-lust was let loose into the world. For Jones, the world 'was always the colour of the cockcrow'.[211] Envy and jealousy lie close to the heart of creation; language and its fictions make them inevitable in the field of this world: 'did she make / The story up?', Adam wonders,[212] 'invent behind her eyes / The talking snake as one more pet illusion'.

Thomas differs from T. H. Jones in another major aspect, his belief in the Christian archetype of the figure nailed to the cross. In another perceptive reading of the former's work, J. P. Ward, following Derrida's contention that differentiation in writing demythologizes the modern world, suggests that he 'is writing this rupture, updating the theological myth into the act of writing itself'. In poetry located within the confines of the garden, 'Thomas winds a poem round, away from and then back to the figure of the hole in the side, or the tree on which the body is nailed, or the paradisal place into which elusive, shadowy humans come'.[213] Jones has only his fractured self: 'I am what I may be. / And whatever else is mine ineluctably'[214] with which to face 'The ineluctable and irate / Brag of the artillery of God'.[215]

When *Songs of a Mad Prince* appeared, the *Times Literary Supplement*[216] review was brief and imperceptive: 'Mr Jones is a poet partly in the Movement manner . . .', preferring Jones to Anthony Conran because 'As a Welsh romantic and patriot dodging the influence of Dylan Thomas by way, perhaps, of Pound and Yeats, his Christian attitude is less veiled than Conran's . . .' Roland Mathias questions T. H. Jones's seriousness:

> If I say 'After all, this is 1961,' I am not meaning thereby to imply progress. [Jones] overestimates gravely the value and effect of repetition; his poems start (and too often finish) with a phrase out of the air, a snatch, a catch; he yearns much after the ballad (without a subject for one) and the Donneish love poem (in which he is rather more resourceful) . . . Almost half the pieces in the book have the air of poetic exercises and could well have been discarded. I liked especially 'Love's Tautology', 'Child at Night' and 'Grandparents'.[217]

Douglas Phillips in the *Western Mail* was kinder. In the only totally positive review Jones ever received, 'A sweet tooth in the core of Eden's apple', he again shared attention with, and dominated, Conran's *Formal Poems*. Phillips saw Jones as

No roaring boy writing Alpha and Omega in an Authorised Book of Revelations, though he seems to have seen enough reality to make the most apocalyptic roar on to cringe and whimper . . . his only beast here is the unfabulous two-backed one. Its anatomy is delineated in language remarkable for its purity and sharpness . . . His poems are for the most part short, concise, highly disciplined, the work of a man of rare and acute intelligence shot through with the vein of sardonic humour that is black and bleak enough to scare the pants off anyone whose mind is wrapped in the grey flannel clichés of our admass world . . . Mr Jones's subject, briefly, is the core of Eden's apple . . . In controlled sharp stanzas he cuts through the luxurious fruit of loving to the bitter sweet seeds in the centre.

Phillips perceptively isolates and identifies the vision at the heart of the volume as being

as naked as Blake's in the *Songs of Experience,* with the same mastery of technique . . . I regard this as one of the most impressive books of new verse by a Welshman since *Deaths and Entrances* . . . Anthony Conran's poems, although interesting, do not stand comparison technically or in subject-matter . . . [218]

Here, perhaps, is the source of some of Conran's negative responses to T. H. Jones's poetry of this period. In his excellent evaluation of Anglo-Welsh poetry, *The Cost of Strangeness,*[219] he writes 'I would myself doubt if more than about two dozen of his pieces have much to offer us'. His criticism appears conditioned by a need to establish a positioning within an Anglo-Welsh hierarchy for T. H. Jones and to define his own considerable achievement against a concept of Jones as 'merely' a significant poet of *hiraeth* and exile – as if this were not a considerable achievement in its own right. In doing so he undervalues his own work as well as Jones's.

The last few weeks at Portsmouth hurried by. A tearful Ruth called to say goodbye. There was room for very few possessions: 'I feel dreadful about the suitcase of correspondence that we decided to burn', says Madeleine.[220] Jones's friend and fellow Anglo-Welsh writer, Robert Morgan, called in on T. H. Jones's last day in England: 'His house . . . where I had often visited him, was practically empty. I walked in through the open door and found him sitting on a packing-case writing a poem. This was the last time I saw him'.[221] His summing up of their relationship and T. H. Jones's character contains more than one ominous note for the future:

> Life seemed rather empty for a while after he left. We had much in common, especially our backgrounds, which were working class. We both left our Welsh environments, studied, qualified, but we could not forget from whence we came, and neither of us wanted to. Harri was often sombre and detached, but whenever we were in a pub together he would relax and become more than extrovert. This other persona was so different from the one he carried to work or displayed in a social gathering. He always had a deep longing for remote Breconshire where he spent the first 18 years of his life, and drew extensively from such memories of those early years.[222]

1959–1962

Taffy was Transported

T. H. Jones would express few doubts about what he ironically
styled his 'exile' in New South Wales, and it was in a mood of
powerful optimism and creativity that he boarded the MV *Oceania*
in April 1959. On 4 April Madeleine sent a postcard to her in-
laws: 'We are in summer dresses and hoping to visit Naples after
lunch. Very smoothly organised trip from London to Genoa,
where Harri's friend, Roberto [Sanesi], met us and spent a couple
of hours . . . on board.'[1] Sanesi noticed 'an instinctive change in
Harri, a new hope'.[2] This is confirmed in his letter the next day to
Pam and Ted Richards:

> Down the blooming Meddy again – just off Messina, in fact.
> Ship a bit different from what I am used to – very good, in fact,
> especially the food. We are all basking in unaccustomed luxury!
> And I am actually working quite hard on lectures on Milton
> which I have to give to the Honours students. If only I knew
> whether Wales won yesterday![3]

The voyage stimulated an upsurge of childhood and wartime
memories. Several new poems were drafted, among them 'Lucky
Jonah'.[4]

The New South Wales that awaited the Jones family was not the
almost virgin garden whose vision had fired the imagination of
Australia's first settlers:

> A land of evergreen trees, waxed leaves on edge to the sun and
> topsoil so loose it could be raked through the fingers . . . A land
> no wheel had marked, no leather heeled and no cloven hoof
> trodden. A land of kangaroo and wombat, a perpetual flower
> garden attended by native Aborigines in a near perfect symbiotic
> relationship with the earth itself.[5]

Something of this vision, and much of T. H. Jones's optimistic mood, however, is to be found in an exuberant poem much enjoyed by audiences at his poetry readings, 'The colour of cockcrowing'.[6] Foregrounding a magnificent catalogue of creation (fifty species in thirty-seven lines), it juxtaposes the creatures of the New World (moose, eland, okapi, jerboa, kangaroo, 'sun-daring eagle', vulture and 'laughing kookaburra') with the familiar ones of his own Old World (fox, badger, otter, seal, 'brawling sparrow'[7] and 'murderous Christmas robin') and unites man and the beasts, created together at the dawn of the world, named by Adam, in the knowledge that the world 'was always the colour of the cockcrow': 'They all looked out on their first morning / And knew at once the colour of cockcrowing.' Cockcrow is, most obviously, the sound that wakes us to each new day, itself an analogue of creation. It has also (see Lawrence's 'The escaped cock, a story of the Resurrection' and Jones's later bawdy poem, 'Keeping chooks':[8] 'I had a cock, and he was tall / My lady loved him dearly') sexual/fertility overtones. Finally, because Jones's Eden is never without its serpent, it reminds us of the Fall and Peter's betrayal, before the cock crowed twice, of Christ. The poem presents the world as an Eden, full of beauty, delight and fertility, but joyously postlapsarian: 'In the world we know it was always the colour of the cockcrow.'

The title inevitably invokes Dylan Thomas,[9] but this poem is quite different from the Sadean world of unstable, entropic, inter-changeable species of fish, crustacean, human and animal fused in his 'The ballad of the long-legged bait'. It reminds us instead of Ceri Richards's 'The cycle of nature', a celebration of Thomas's phantasmagoric drama, 'The force that through the green fuse drives the flower'. 'The colour of cockcrowing' is untypical of Jones's work: nostalgia for lost Eden is more than balanced by the exuberance, beauty and teeming life of the fallen world and its creatures. It is the poem of a man rejuvenated, freed to write by contact with a new world. In the later work the pervasive sense of sin/guilt/loss resembles that angst which Peter Watson saw as the essential characteristic of the Neo-Romantic painters of the 1940s: 'the world is a trap in which any idea of spiritual safety would be as audacious as the confidence of a mouse resting in the hollow of a human hand ready at an instant to crush it'.[10] Although Jones's affection for this poem would survive, the mood which inspired it could not.

Newcastle was no antipodean Eden, but a smokier version of Swansea, an industrial town with a glorious stretch of surfing-beach. It owed its foundation in 1804 to the abundant deposits of coal in the Hunter Valley, its iron and steel mills were built in 1915 and in the 1960s it was the largest coal port in the world. Britain's economic influence was waning and Australia was in a period of cultural transition. 'The U.S.A. had replaced the U.K. as Australia's main beef export market, and women had finally got legislation ensuring equal pay. However, there was also not much raw ethnicity.'[11] The movement away from old alliances was tentative: it was a time for introspection before the real shocks of the late 1960s hit the cosy world of white Australia.

University College, Newcastle, was embryonic in 1959.

When Harri arrived . . . the Faculties of Arts, Economics and Commerce, and the Library were still housed in an ex-machine-shop of the Technical College, with flimsy partitions dividing the offices, which were all shared, often by people from different disciplines. Noisy hammering from the next-door metal shop punctuated poetry readings. A spartan common-room allowed communal morning teas and lunches and the occasional evening sherry party.[12]

Even in 1961, when Clive Hart, later professor of English at the University of Essex, was recruiting, the library 'was virtually non-existent' and administrative facilities very limited: 'The Arts Faculty had one-and-a-half secretaries and of course the Xerox had hardly been invented.'[13] Staff shared offices; teaching was by formal lecture supplemented by the occasional individual seminar. There was also the Australian part-time system of day and evening lectures. Most of the students were from Newcastle itself or up-country New South Wales. A basic three-year first degree was available for full-time students, but the same qualification could be obtained through part-time study over five and many took this option. 'The evening sessions were normally 6–10 p.m. and as a lecturer you inevitably repeated your lectures, although the repeat was not always on the same day . . . sometimes the repeat was before the main lecture. Which could be confusing!'[14] The English course had a token Old English component, rather more Middle English, some linguistics and small amounts of Australian and American literature among the options.

Jones gave his first impressions in a letter to Pam and Ted Richards:

> Do not be too surprised getting a letter from this prolific correspondent – put it down to *hiraeth*. I met a Welshman the other day, fresh and green from the old country – none other, in fact, than G. B. Thomas of the *Western Mail*, over here with the Lions . . . They are playing here with New South Wales this afternoon but I have to content myself with a television view. This involves going to the pub, which as Madeleine points out is hard luck on me . . . I have a very reasonable lecturing programme – Milton and Yeats and an introductory course for poetry for first years this term, and next year Yeats and Eliot to third years and Byron, Shelley and Keats to second years. Next year I shall have some American literature with the Honours students.[15]

Of his new colleagues he writes:

> The senior English Lecturer is very easy to get on with, there are two not very important young men, and a charming young woman. Auchmuty, the Deputy Warden, is a friendly and garrulous Irishman, who likes whisky, rugby, and Yeats . . . The Head of the Arts Department is a Welshman named Newton John who has translated *Under Milk Wood* into German and played the part of the Narrator in a professional Melbourne production. He is also reputed to have left Melbourne . . . because of some leather couch work he had been doing. Life, you see, tends to be the same as elsewhere.[16]

Jill Stowell remembers family life:

> Most of us were young, nesting and producing babies far from our relatives. We became like families for one another. Maternity clothes and baby necessities were passed round. Advice was sought from already experienced parents like Madeleine and Harri. Harri loved babies and the whole birth business. He was . . . one of my first visitors when Vanessa was born . . . She was only a few hours old when he arrived, well before hospital neatness was re-established.[17]

A more ominous feature is 'one Jim Dodds, a wine shop proprietor and provider of booze to the staff. . . . We buy sherry by the half-gallon at twelve shillings, and red wine at six shillings the half-gallon and (expensively) nine shillings – Australian whisky at 23/6d. a bottle.'[18] He had mixed feelings about the city and its hinterland:

> Newcastle is a great sprawl of a place, a bit like South Wales now and again, with coal pits and railway lines, lots of ponies and rugger pitches round any corner. The country outside is magnificent and the weather – well, it's cold today – I have to wear a jacket.[19]

The *hiraeth* was considerable: 'We hope anyway to have a newsy letter from you some day to assure us that the land of my fathers still goes its dear old methodist, alcoholic, poetic way, that there are still pubs and preachers . . .'[20]

In September he sent Ted a copy of 'Lucky Jonah':[21]

> As 'the onlie begetter' of this, you had better have a copy. Read it aloud some time when the lamps are swinging. The second copy is for Maggie [Dulanty] if you'd pass it on to her sometime . . . We are all flourishing – the children all go to school now. Rhiannon has decided she wants to learn Welsh, so I will have to send her to Borth sometime. She has a fabulous reading age, and is the astonishment and delight of her teachers. I am very busy with reviews, articles, W.E.A. on top of my lectures. All very good fun, all very good for me and keeps me off the drink – part of the time, anyhow.[22]

Julian Croft reads 'Lucky Jonah' as another of the 'guilt poems', expressing 'a feeling of purposelessness and loneliness . . . it would be better to die than live . . . the impression is of a man at odds with the world . . . a man alienated by his failure to live up to the example set by others'.[23] It declares itself an elegy for friends killed on active service: the man who 'loved football and cards and girls – but had to die'; the schoolfellow met 'in a brazen bar / In Alexandria' who survived two shipwrecks only to die in a road-accident, three unnamed 'Jacks who are not jolly any more' and it concludes with a funeral knell:

> But I can hear ships' bells
> Strike the melancholy sound
> Of dead men's names, of sunk ships' names,
> The lullaby and catalogue of the drowned.[24]

It evokes unsparingly the horror of modern warfare at sea: 'The scalded stokers and the sick, singed smell'; the enemy sailor dying like a butchered sheep with the poet, looking on, unable to feel pity. And it contrasts the boy's golden dream of adventure with the reality of the man's experience. It contains the biographically ominous lines

> And all of life a long survivor's leave
> For lucky Jonah, spewed up from the maw
> To wait and wait and wait for death.

A 'Jonah' brings bad luck on others but survives himself, as the original did when he took ship for Tarshish to 'flee . . . from the presence of the Lord'[25] whom he had disobeyed. Such happiness as can be found in the poem lies in the past (the boy's dreams), the runs ashore for drink, socializing and brothels, and the rough humour. And in the fact that, however damaged, the sailor/poet *has* survived. 'Lucky Jonah' is the work of a man who has, in Lawrence's words, 'come through'[26] to a new period of creativity in a new land. Its wry epigraph, 'A man born to be hanged cannot be drowned', evokes *The Tempest*, thus positioning the poet as both shipwrecked mariner and Magus. Jones is taking the opportunity to craft his new world in words. By writing traumatic experience 'out in a verse'[27] a poet, even if he cannot heal, may at least come, if only temporarily, to terms with it. It is not unusual for T. H. Jones to leave us with an element of ambiguity: perhaps the whole thing turns on how we interpret 'long survivor's leave'. Survivors are given this compassionate leave to recover from wounds physical or mental before being returned to service and, likely enough, experience even more horrific. 'To wait and wait and wait for death' does not suggest rude psychic health. The letter does not help us much: its tone is robustly cheerful; 'when the lamps are swinging' suggests stormy weather; no further hint is offered. The one thing over which there can be no doubt at all is that the poem demands far more serious attention than it has so far received. This first manifestation of T. H. Jones's mature voice points forward to the remarkable longer poem of 1964, 'Cotton Mather remembers the trial of Elizabeth How'.[28]

Writing to Hart-Davis in November about the galley-proofs of *Songs of a Mad Prince*, Jones reveals more of his response to the new life:

we like Australia itself very much. It is easy to exaggerate the differences – where these are more than superficial, I tend to be in favour of the Australian way. The great exception to this is pubs – the hotels here don't compare with the peculiar institution of the English pub. On the other hand, wine and sherry are cheap enough for us to drink them without feeling extravagant. As far as I am concerned, the change from Technical College to University is really bigger than from one part of the world to another. And this, I am very happy about. I have had to work quite hard, but it is work I really enjoy doing. And it has stimulated me – I have not had time to do a great deal of writing, but I have, for example, written an article on Melville and Faulkner, and sold it to the leading 'cultural' (horrible word) magazine and got some (paid) reviewing to do on the strength of it. And I am bursting with ideas which I feel for the first time in years I can do something about. The poetry is another matter. I have written a poem,[29] long for me i.e. 90 plus lines which is rather different from anything I have done before and which appears to be admired by my colleagues.[30]

T. H. Jones naturally cultivated the Welsh expatriate community, among them Professor Dai Phillips at the Sydney College of the University of New South Wales, to whom he wrote on 30 November:

> I did enjoy meeting you the other day, and look forward to another talk sometime. Meanwhile, I send you some of my poems, including the Dydd Gwyl Dewi one[31] to admire. Did I tell you it was published in the *Western Mail?* The others are spare copies I thought you might like too. The title of my first volume was *The Enemy in the Heart* and it was published by Rupert Hart-Davis in 1957. . . The second volume I shall give you a copy of when it comes out.[32]

By the end of 1959, nine poems had been entered in the *Black Book*. 'Lucky Jonah' and 'The colour of cockcrowing' have been explored. Only one, 'Bewilderment',[33] appeared in a collection arranged by the author. It is about the restless perplexities of married love. The initial physical attraction gives no warning of 'how love could grow / To these proportions of bewilderment' and any hope that middle age might reduce this has proved fallacious.

Consequently, at this time 'when we might have been at peace' neither partner knows 'how to create / From our poor weathers of unease / Climates of unbewilderment'. A sense that old age threatens, and a questioning of the nature of married love will be important aspects of the poems of this period.

Of the others, two are occasional:[34] 'Excuse' (to Marlene)[35] and 'A Christmas poem' (for Audrey and Doug[36]), and one is a further translation from Sanesi.[37] 'In the light of ordinary evenings'[38] is about being afraid to face the 'unbearable white radiances of revelation',[39] 'The ditch of desire',[40] is a typical literary ballad about rejection by a proud beauty and 'Not when I came'[41] is a rather conventional lyric about sexual acceptance when male pride is completely humbled. Both of these latter are in Jones's pseudo-courtly love or Arthurian manner: 'your true man', 'With anger and tall drum', 'Weary with wounds'. There is much in the new work to justify the feelings of the letter: indeed, 'Lucky Jonah' alone would be more than enough to do so.

Songs of a Mad Prince appeared, as we have seen, in 1960 to the one enthusiastic review.[42] Jones was so pleased by this that he wrote to Douglas Phillips:

Thank you very much for the enthusiastic review in the Old Rag. It was so glowing to know that a stranger appreciates what one hopes one is managing to do . . . perhaps you will take it as a mark of how really pleased I was with what you said that it provided the following:

'The Same Story'

Always, it seems, I wanted to tell, compulsive
As that ancient mariner, the same story,
Careless of my listener's response
Or consideration of my own shame or glory.

The same story: the one of which I had intimations
In childhood when a cousin told a lie
And I was beaten for it. Another version
Was the war and watching my betters die.

And there were other versions too – that girl,
And perhaps those others, most certainly

The one I loved and most betrayed
By my failure to be anything but me.

But if you know better stories, or truer ones,
I might tell them as fairy-tales for my grandsons.[43]

Phillips had mentioned 'acute intelligence', 'sardonic humour that is black and bleak' and 'cutting through the luxurious fruit of loving to the bitter sweet seeds at the centre'. This sonnet demonstrates all three qualities. Coleridge's *Ancient Mariner* is about sin (the gratuitous destruction of innocence and beauty, the albatross an analogue of Christ), God's punishment of the Mariner and his shipmates, confession, contrition and absolution. Telling the story over and over again to reluctant listeners is the penance. Jones's sonnet places the boy whose unjust punishment makes him feel guilty in the position of the Mariner's shipmates, who did not themselves kill the bird, but failed to restrain the Mariner from doing so, and then in the position of the Mariner watching his shipmates die and feeling guilty about that.[44] Stanza three is more straightforwardly about sexual betrayal and guilt. In aligning himself with a character compelled 'Careless of my listener's response / Or consideration of my own shame or glory' T. H. Jones also, and with justice, claims kindred with confessional poets such as Lowell and Plath.

Clive Hart saw T. H. Jones as:

> A small, beetle-browed, stooped man with a shock of black hair that hung down over his angular, somewhat distorted face with its hooked nose . . . He looked like a difficult birth with his squeezed, asymmetrical teeth and, in his last years, a slightly slavering, loose mouth . . . usually he looked surly, and then he would smile his wonderfully broad, totally winning smile – it was totally engaging, totally seraphic . . . [45]

When Hart flew in from Perth, Jones was sent to meet him at the airport, but he was 'on an unexpected flight . . . and of course he didn't meet me'.[46] Although this was in no way his fault, 'Harri naturally got accused of spending the time in the pub: his reputation had already been established.' [47]

The University College still 'didn't feel like a University', but 'it was looking to grow right from the early days',[48] keen on achieving autonomy and anxious to improve its courses and standard of teaching. At first it was largely vocational/technical, its English Faculty small, and in some ways Jones found it rather a small step up from Portsmouth. Brin Newton John, head of Arts, was fated to be known to posterity as the father of beautiful daughters, Olivia in particular. A Cambridge graduate, he spoke with a 'deliberately plummy accent and wore a great moustache'.[49] There is a satirical portrtait of him in the unpublished 'One reason for disliking Englishmen':[50]

> 'Balls, old boy,' he said, and he spread
> His handlebar all over his face,
> And I had some very hirsute doubts about him . . .
> Poor bastard, he was, I believe, a Wing-Co,
> And dropped the appropriate weight of bomb . . .

Auchmuty, warden and later principal, tried to combine English and American academic traditions in his establishment: 'It was sherry in the office during the morning recession – sherry by the half-gallon', says Hart. It was easy to be drunk by one o'clock in the afternoon. One half of T. H. Jones, 'false gentrification', Julian Croft calls it, seems to have wished to cultivate this lifestyle and 'take over the living and clothes of this establishment group', the other to rebel. Madeleine, stereotyped as a 'Hampstead socialist', found herself easily accepted.

In setting up the Arts Faculty Auchmuty selected staff recruited in England, mainly by Norman Jeffares. Another transplant was the 'self-styled working-class poet, Norman Talbot',[51] between whom and Jones a half-friendly rivalry existed. 'Towards a homage to Norman Talbot'[52] evokes, Talbot says, 'a brilliant contrast to my actual shape':[53]

> A gentle man in a long wind
> – Think of him as tall . . .
> The fat wind wraps its rhymes about him.
>
> He would go gravely.
> But his far legs frolic . . .

Doug Muecke, head of English, had written interestingly about Dylan Thomas and initially the lecturers were Robyn Iverach

('The colour of cockcrowing' is dedicated to her) and Jones, supported by some part-time help. 'Students were extremely earnest', says Clive Hart.[54]

Hart confirms that T. H. Jones took great pleasure in being a university lecturer. He disliked all paperwork, however, and hated meetings. He lectured mainly on poetry, 'read criticism extensively, but always spoke and wrote about poetry as a practising poet'.[55] He gave many lectures outside the university in support of the WEA: 'They were very freewheeling. He would often just read a poem and say, "Isn't that a good poem?", then read another',[56] but he inspired in many people an understanding and love of poetry. Tony Hassall, another of his students, now professor of English at Queensland University, remembers his lectures for 'the most marvellous readings of poetry' and that 'Milton, Hopkins and Lowell [were] the poets he read with the greatest enthusiasm'. He was 'not a particularly academic lecturer'[57] but brought great passion and enthusiasm to his teaching: 'His reading voice was magnificent, and I remember poetry readings . . . where he and Brin Newton John both read poetry as only the Welsh can.'[58]

Alan Farrelly, another student, described T. H. Jones as a small, dark, intense man with the shock of characteristically untidy hair:

> His clothes were high quality casual, untidy also . . . I remember him starting out to quote a few lines to illustrate a lecture point, become immersed and read on oblivious, the class sitting mesmerised by that sonorous voice rolling out a new dimension to the words. Unusual obtuseness could provoke him, but generally he was patient with students. He was very helpful to budding undergraduate writers – poets and other-wise – and gave hours of time to helping, criticising and encouraging them. His lectures were always popular . . . he put an incredible amount of time into research and preparation and a high proportion of his material was original.[59]

The extremely well-received paper he later delivered to the first meeting of the Australia and New Zealand American Studies Association in Melbourne has survived to give us some impression of his lecturing style. Speaking on the 'Gilded age' of US literature (1865–1905), he begins with characteristically disingenuous self-depreciation: 'Without any disrespect to my brilliant predecessors

– indeed, as a mark of respect for them – I suggest that what we now need is a little light, even comic, relief. I take the task of providing that relief upon my shoulders.'[60] Disclaiming any credentials as a historian, he suggests that 'no period in the history of any country or any civilisation has been so be-ribboned or be-labelled'. It has been known variously as:

> the Great Barbecue, the Brown Decade, the Mauve Decade (very precise, that one – if you can remember which one), the Chromo Civilisation, the Buried Renaissance (my favourite metaphysical oxymoron), the Age of Innocence, the Gay Nineties (which sounds to me like another English hangover) and 'an age of guilt' (which is, of course, somebody's prescient hindsight).[61]

There follows a serio-comic survey illustrated by a wide range of quotations from such well-known writers as Mark Twain, Henry James, Emily Dickinson and Melville and such obscure ones as Lloyd Mifflin and Harry E. Mills. The quotations are skilfully chosen to demonstrate Jones's skill as a performer and the salient characteristics of the period – in that order – and the jokes are many and good. For background he uses the 'redolently nostalgic . . . Jeffersonianly colourful' opening pages of part I of volume 3 of Parrington's literary history: 'The pot was boiling briskly in America in the tumultuous post-war years', and he follows this with a quotation from a letter to her father by Mrs Henry Adams describing Henry James's visit to Washington in 1882: 'And a certain man came down to Jerusalem and fell among thieves . . . and they sprang up and choked him.' He then proceeds by way of *Slopes of Helicon and Other Poems*[62] ('A life-long labour spent upon the sod') and *Sod House in Heaven and Other Poems*[63] ('Bowed by the weight of centuries he leans / Upon his hoe') to the 'Robber barons', quoting the

> Yale sociologist . . . William Graham Sumner [who] said that the millionaire was the finest flower of a competitive society . . . Peter Dunne's Mr Dooley described John D. Rockefeller as 'a kind of society f'r the prevention of croolty to money. He looks after his own money and the money of other people. He takes it and puts it where it won't hurt them and they won't spoil it . . .'

He quotes Mark Twain's 'Ode to Stephen Dowling Bots, dec'd', which he compares to Dylan Thomas's Eli Jenkins poems, and reaches a climax with 'The fate of the frontiersman':[64]

> You may rip the cloud from the frescoed sky,
> But you can't tear me from the truth I cry,
> That life is loathsome and love a lie.
> She lifted me up to her bare, brown face,
> She cracked my ribs in her brown embrace,
> And there in the shanty, side by side,
> Each on the other's bosom died.

The paper concludes with a comparison between Walt Whitman ('I find Whitman almost as unreadable as Emerson') and 'poor old' Henry Adams, who would never have survived a House Committee: 'the corruption that troubled Adams was far less the corruption of the till than of the mind'. Perhaps, says Jones, bringing the whole thing back full circle to his own preoccupations 'this is what has been the trouble with all our Gilded Ages ever since Eve gave Adam that goddam apple'. Intellectually self-confident, humorous, wide-ranging and with a twist in the tail: we have seen this quality of mind before, in 'Visions', the eisteddfod prize-winning essay of 1941.

Another of T. H. Jones's pupils was Marion Halligan, a writer who transformed the landscape of short fiction in Australia. In her campus novel, *Self Possession*, she bases aspects of the poet/academic, Tom Lloyd, on Jones:

> Generations of students remembered him on the platform, clutching the lectern with both hands but still leaning alarmingly to one side, his scruffy, threadbare gown turning him into a rusty black academic scarecrow, occasionally shading his eyes from the searing light that bounced down on him from the lecture room's high windows, or his ears from the equally searing noises that penetrated from the scullery fastness. He would wince and shrink within his clothes, and hang even more alarmingly to one side, and then suddenly there would be Milton or Yeats or Hopkins as they had never conceived him before. And sensitive as his hangovers were to light or noise from outside, they never seemed to mind the reverberations of his own voice. His classes sat fascinated, absorbing, silent. Often they forgot to write

anything down, which was irritating afterwards, but they never forgot the experience. His Honours seminars were a great success too. They were held in his study, a bleak, barely functional room; above the desk, and the rough plastered wall was written in pencil, 'symbolism-Symbolisme', a reminder to some long ago class not to forget the difference. Always he would wander over to the wardrobe, with a small, complicit, let's-be-devils-just-this-once sort of smile, and bat around in the folds of his gown until he found a flagon of red wine. Then he'd look about, light upon half a dozen grimily rinsed glasses, and pour everybody some wine, with careful modest triumph.

They never finished after an hour, those seminars. They often repaired to The Brass Monkey but they didn't stop as a result of the move. Literature was Tom's only topic of conversation, apart from sex, and even that was a form of literature with him.[65]

Jones, the 'spoiled preacher', would frequently allege that proselytizing poetry was only a means to earning money to buy booze, but that was bravado. When he made the opposite claim, to be the poor colonial's Dylan Thomas, Clive Hart would tease him: 'You're more like a poor man's R. S. Thomas', but he remembers that 'He was . . . a tremendous boozer . . . I remember one afternoon Robyn, Harri and I drank a gallon of sherry in Harri's room and then Brin Newton John came downstairs with another gallon and we drank a third of that.'[66] Auchmuty, 'a tolerant Trinity, Dublin, man', kept the college on a loose rein:

> 'Harri is a poet. He drinks like a poet and if you try to stop him drinking you won't get anything out of him.' . . . There were sometimes some complaints from the more strait-laced mature students . . . Harri was utterly unreliable, but totally trustworthy.[67]

It was Brin who had to organize the inevitable 'drying-out' and 'Harri never forgave him for it!'

T. H. Jones's prediction that 'this complete break will really trigger me off again as leaving the Navy did years ago' had come true. By 1961 he was averaging ten poems a month. Always anxious not to be forgotten in Wales, he wrote to Raymond Garlick:

> It seems an awfully long time since I had any communication with *Dock Leaves* – I can't get used to your new title. Anyway, I

wrote this poem[68] only a couple of hours ago and thought immediately that you might like it . . . I have heard from Abelard Schuman about your proposed anthology – good luck with it, and with the *Review*.

The poem demonstrates how the new country was stirring the memories of his Welsh heartland that would dominate his Australian poems. He wonders if his 'daughter of the Mabinogion name', Rhiannon, who wants to be a poet, will find her imagination mediated by the Australian landscape:

> As in my mind and dreams these thirty years
> There stays the small hill, Allt-y-clych,
> The hill of bells, bedraggled with wet fern
> And stained with sheep, and holding like a threat
> The wild religion and the ancient tongue,
> All the defeated centuries of Wales.

That 'threat' is ominously prophetic.

As newcomers from the Old Country the Joneses were newsworthy. The *Newcastle Sunday Mirror* of 12 February 1961 displayed a large photograph of 'Grandma Scott' from London, visiting her grand-daughters before sailing to South Africa to visit her son. Madeleine was frequently photographed at exhibitions of her pottery, including a major show prior to a study-tour to Mexico. Another letter to Pam and Ted Richards reports progress:

> We are all thriving. Sian, with her horse (Cymro), Madeleine, beginning to make pots again, Ruth and Rhiannon with just being themselves. Me, I am writing a bit, getting a bit published . . . lots of public readings. A week or two ago we did a reading of *Under Milk Wood* – first voice, Brin Newton John, second voice and Reverend Eli, me – packed house, great success.[69]

It was naturally necessary to celebrate in the usual way: 'Appropriately, after the party I fell down my own steps and cracked or broke a rib or ribs.'

We have seen T. H. Jones write poetry for his beloved sisters, so it is not surprising that, as a loving father, he wrote poems for his daughters. None of these poems has been published, and they

were not entered into the *Black Book*. 'The girls of Llangamon' is
typical:

> Sian and Rhiannon live in Llangamon
> In a caravan covered with leather.
> They like it a lot in the cold and the hot
> And every sort of weather.

It continues with an account of adventures rather in the style of
Enid Blyton. There is a series of poems for Sian ('Sianni's ride',
'Sianni and the goldfish', 'Sianni's party') and a poem for Ruth,
'The bunster'. Jones seldom wrote home during the Australian
period. When he did, he had not changed from the son and
brother of the war period:

> This is to wish you a happy birthday and hope you are both very
> well. As you can see from the girls' letters, we are all well, and
> quite busy. It was very nice to meet Joss Davies again – he has
> come to the University of Sydney . . . How are Afan and Fred
> and Aunty Maggie? Please give them all my love, and of course
> Pat. What is happening about Glyn's job on the railway? I don't
> suppose I would recognise Trefelyn now that you have electricity.
> . . . Thank you for sending the cuttings about Rachel and about
> Pisgah, and for the photographs.[70]

Julian Croft, author of the only critical study of any length on
T. H. Jones, had met him during his first year at Newcastle. Croft,
eighteen years old at the time, was impressed less by the lecturer
than the man so completely committed, like the Tom Lloyd of
Marion Halligan's novel, to poetry.

> The flesh began to creep; she had never seen him like this in
> private, the words naked, framed and partly obliterated by the
> surrounding shadows; their turned, listening faces, half gilded,
> half dark, sat like a mannerist painting composed into a work of
> art by the power of Tom's voice.[71]

To Croft he seemed 'straight out of the Bohemian tradition of the
late nineteenth century, a Rimbaud or a figure from the Soho of
the twenties, thirties and forties'.[72] Wales had sent a second Dylan
Thomas to Australia, it seemed to the small group of undergraduates who became part of his circle; Jones was 'a breath of

fresh air in the Australia of the time', dominated by the bourgeois poets of classicism. But 'his teaching was never as stimulating as his actual presence because the booze quite soon got in the way'.[73]

Kessel and Walton, in their classic study of alcoholism,[74] stress that 'every alcoholic's history is unique'. Personal experience, psychological disturbance, social shifts and upheavals, physical illness, changes in drinking habits, singly or in combination, contribute to the sequence of events peculiar to each individual. There is a basic, underlying pattern, however, and usually it contains two transitions of special significance. The first is the move from excessive drinking to alcoholism proper: 'from then on the body is harmed';[75] the second is into chronic alcoholism, with its severe and persistent physical changes. Social drinking was part of the culture in which T. H. Jones had grown up. His father had always liked his pint and he himself had enjoyed a social drink with adolescent friends within the farming community. In the navy he had acquired a taste for the rum that has always been used as a prophylactic against boredom and the stress of combat. Attempting to cultivate the role of poet during the unhappy London years, he had asserted, in the pubs of Fitzrovia, that 'good writers are drinking writers'.[76] He spent more and more time, during the later Portsmouth years, in social drinking, but it was only in Australia that he began drinking to excess, typically drinking spirits when others drank beer. In Australia he drank partly to conform to a macho tradition, and partly to relieve the stress of work, but he was not the first poet to find that alcohol freed his mind for poetry and 'the sweat of poetry'[77] and relaxed him after a performance. Drink became a necessity and wrought its devastation on his career as it had on those of writers as diverse as Scott Fitzgerald, Faulkner, Hemingway and Dylan Thomas. He was never the sullen solitary drinker. For him drink was the social lubricant that gave relief from the solitary 'craft and sullen art'.[78]

As true dependence set in there was a disabling effect on his work, absenteeism and drunkenness in and around the university. There was no shortage of those who admired his wild behaviour; it became part of his public persona. The admirers did not have to live with him, however: 'it crucified Madeleine', Julian Croft says,[79] and almost forty years later she is 'still reluctant to write about Harri's alcoholism, which finally destroyed him, and feel guilty that I never mentioned' (to his parents) the battles he was waging.

His grandfather and father did not tolerate alcohol well, but they only had the market days at Builth to indulge it. The English Department at Newcastle University College was notorious for its drinking habits. Flagons of dry sherry and wine were kept in most of the lecturers' rooms, and the tippling often started in the morning. The social life in Newcastle was pretty high, which didn't help matters. However, for the first few years, I didn't recognize the problem . . .[80]

There were moments of savage self-analysis:

> Morning shall not torment and parch
> Him, fearful to sleep or wake,
> Nor ambiguity of nerves betray
> By wilful and beseeching shake
> He burns with the consuming fire
> That's fuel to its own desire.[81]

in a crapulous, stuttering world where, paradoxically, 'the word is all':

> twisted, winded, slur
> All words, stumble the cwm
> Wordbeat to home,
> Slur and fall
> The word is all.[82]

The unpublished 'Sonnets at forty'[83] evoke threat of age ('Not bald or impotent yet . . .') and 'forty years / Of blood sweat toil nightmares and tears'. The image of the sweaty nightmare becomes common. Clive Hart recalls:

I sometimes saw him scrawling in the pub when drunk. He would be lucid for part of every day, and that's when he really wrote. There was this party thing that moved around the university campus . . . Invitations were sent out to about forty or fifty people. In particular there was the Spring party season working up to the Australian Christmas, and if you were around and available you were expected to give a party. They were places where people got together to bitch about other people. It was a circumscribed community. All the Arts people from the University and other educational institutions got together with the cultural hangers-on . . . there were lots of painters. Newcastle seemed to have a large number of very good painters in the early sixties, and the best of them was Rae Richards, who for a while became Harri's Muse. Harri loved women.[84]

Inevitably we remember 'all of life a long survivor's leave'.

T. H. Jones, Llanafan always at the back of his mind, did indeed find Australia liberating. Although never part of the beach-culture, he identified with its hedonism. He did enjoy the company of women, including attractive students: the *frisson*, the tension, the poetic potential of life's sybaritic side:

> Then suddenly
> Your young breasts bring again
> The illusion of immortality.[85]

He sent the manuscript of this poem to Dai Phillips and wrote on it, 'This ought to be dedicated to my girl students, but I dare not'. Clive Hart suggests that 'Harri did not find himself early, and I think his early poetry was sometimes over-controlled because he had no self-control'.[86] The *Newcastle Evening Herald* printed a typically candid confession:

> I made up my mind several years ago not to make any more New Year resolutions, and my views can best be expressed in verse.
>
> > At the beginning of another year
> > After so many broken resolutions,
> > More in hope than confidence, my Deadly Dear,
> > I vow to be less faithless than before.[87]

The *Black Book* contains many candid short lyrics and occasional poems stimulated by casual affairs and passing fancies. The following is typical:

> Disorganised,
> And by a woman again,
> I try to bring myself
> To concentrate on something proper,
> Work, family, or even poems,
> Only to find that all I am doing
> Is murmuring, murmuring your name.[88]

Jill Stowell explains that this

> was part of his worship of women (perhaps 'woman'). This . . .
> was in the days when the White Goddess reigned supreme, when
> the Muse and the generative process were amalgamated. Harri
> loved women as he loved poetry. It was part of his literary
> persona to express admiration for all the goddess surrogates he
> met, both individually and collectively. There was nothing
> predatory or furtive about what were not so much affairs as
> conceits. Women friends basked in his regard. He dedicated
> poems to many of his female colleagues and the wives of his male
> colleagues. Maybe certain men . . . were jealous of the easy, guilt-
> free relations we all enjoyed, and found it hard to imagine from
> their own experiences that Harri's friendships were innocent of
> deceit. I am not aware that husbands bore him malice.[89]

Julian Croft confirms that Madeleine remained the stable factor
in Jones's life. She was also, in his view, 'a far better teacher than
Harri'.[90] She quickly established herself as a pre-eminent teacher
of ceramics and, over the next twenty years, had a profound
influence on the development of the art-form in New South Wales:

> She had a powerful presence both as a woman and as a creative
> person. She had a great sense of discipline and sense of order –
> all the things that Harri was the complementary opposite of . . .
> Ceramics was heavy work – you can't afford to make mistakes
> when you are firing, you have to be precise.[91]

Jones continued to be immensely productive, sometimes writing
two or three poems a day, but in Croft's view he lacked the
dedication and control of the true craftsman. He was regarded by
undergraduates as the Dionysian poet of Greek tradition.

> I remember being in a butcher's shop, and Harri went by on the
> way to the pub. Harri had long, flowing hair, and the wind was
> blowing, and the butcher said, 'God, I'm glad I'm not him.'
> Australia of this time was, by European standards, philistine,
> parochial and Calvinist.[92]

T. H. Jones's friends were officially informed that he had to cut
back on drinking and be 'dried out'. Told not to drink with him,

they did not know whether to 'lecture him on the evils of drink, or simply go off to the pub with him and try to limit his drinking'.[93] They were very supportive, but Australian men had their own bar-culture, and, as is graphically demonstrated in 'Absalom, Absalom',[94] his last story, a core of hardened drinkers, with whom Jones easily identified, could be found in any establishment.

Although initially much of his drinking was at the round of parties, even from the beginning he would drop into bars, often in the morning on the way to his first lecture.

> A typical pattern would be for him to say, 'Come and have a drink,' and he knew every early-opener in Newcastle. I once picked him up at about 7.45 a.m. and I wanted to get in early for a 9 o'clock lecture and Harri said, 'Just take us round the corner' . . . Harri himself never drove, and there was an early-opener for the dockers and at ten to eight in the morning he easily downed a couple of double vodkas.[95]

In the last two years he carried bottles around with him all the time.

In the pub at lunchtime he would often, as he had done at Aberystwyth, pull out a sheet of poems he had just finished and ask Hart, Croft or anyone who would listen, what they thought of them. 'I used to find this an impossible question to answer,' Hart says. 'What do you say to a poet? "I like it?" or "It's lousy?" I can't respond just like that.'[96] It is not even clear whether Jones really wanted a response or, if so, of what kind. From an early stage he had been *possessed* by poetry. The students were correct in comparing him to Dionysus, who taught civilization as well as the cultivation of the vine: *being* a poet, *living* poetry came first and had to be defended against every external threat. Even within his family circle mundane demands were hard to accept because they demanded compromises that undermined his poetic identity. He could behave very badly, make instinctive gestures that felt heroic at the time but later were perceived to be foolish, even criminal.

> Storms are one thing, but this is not a storm:
> Merely your incredible cool saying
> That you no longer feel the need for weighing
> How much I am now worth your keeping warm.

> The only answer to a tempest is a kiss:
> But how can I, creeping into middle age,
> Evoke the proper and very loving rage
> To say, Leave if you must, but not like this?[97]

The poem ends by begging the wife for sex because the one thing that sustains him against 'any storm' is the knowledge that 'We share each other in our separate pain', an honest but extremely ominous confession.

The worse and more threatening the present crisis of middle age in a foreign land, the more he was driven back on Wales and childhood: fallen Adam longing for paradise lost. 'Could I make that bare poem, / True as home, I could sing';[98] 'Love should have been as harsh and challenging / As the landscape of my childhood . . . And love turns out to be / This tender landscape under this blue sky',[99] he declares, lamenting the loss of an environment which could (or possibly might) hold a sinful man to the straight and narrow.

In his memoried childhood he attempted to rediscover proof of the power of self. The 'Gwilym' stories of the London and Portsmouth period show the child as father to the man and so, but in a more disturbing sense, does the one substantial story of the Australian period, 'The first Christmas'.[100] Although its setting is a farm, and its hero could be Gwilym, it is heavily allegorical, placing, and reshaping the Nativity in a landscape that might be Llanafan. It opens with 'the lucid parable of snow . . . the miracle of light'. The animals offer their love, the birds sing, the boy has a smile of peace on his innocent face: 'It seemed to him that the world had just been born, a flawless lamb dropped without blood or tearing from the womb of the sky.' We are in a version of Eden before the Fall.

The boy goes to the stable expecting to find there 'promised and loving gifts, and the strange delicacy and richness of Christmas food and drink to nourish and slake more than the body of this life'. Even as he turns in the door 'for a last look at the perfect world of snow', the black wings of a bird 'shut out for the moment all the clarity and peace of the heavenly light' and what he sees is an anti-Nativity. Mary is a 'thin negress', her eyes 'proud, stubborn, and uncomprehending', Joseph is absent. The baby seems to smile, and the mother smiles also, but the boy has left the door open. The stable's warmth is gone, and although he knows himself to blame, open it remains.

The Wise Men *are* present. The first, 'lean as a winter hazel', has abundant Celtic red hair and repeatedly tosses and catches one of the pile of golden coins he carries (gold as lucre, not gift). The second, 'short and dark and very fat, a killing-pig of a man', smokes a long-stemmed pipe (frankincense as drug). All that can be seen of the sinister third, 'obscured in the dark against the corner of the manger', is 'a briary old hand holding a large pewter pot' (myrrh – alcohol as death). The boy challenges their presence 'in our stable' and receives replies which are 'not what he had expected'. Although he retains his 'faith in the starred prediction', he has lost 'the certainty of the white and carolled mystery'. He asks what is, for him, 'the most important question in the world', what are the negress and her child doing here; she replies, '"Where else could I bear my baby?"' and it seems to him the answer to all questions. The momentary chill is dissipated, 'the stable . . . alive with happiness again . . . he was in another kingdom now'. Thus ends the first part of the story, which can be seen as a re-enactment, in contemporary, politically correct terms, of the Christ myth, and in conventional theological terms as its re-enactment in the heart of each Christian who 'finds Jesus Christ'. The second part opens shockingly with all creation fallen: a sky red with blood, a carrion smell in the air, 'All the snowed landscape . . . filled with animal whimperings and the cry of birds'. 'Across the dismayed and frantic wilderness fled a small boy with a face blinded by betrayal. He ran in a circle of panic.' The uneasy paradise of part one has been succeeded, for some reason, by the brutal world into which, after the Fall, Adam and Eve were driven out. 'On a low horizon hill a wooden cross made a stiff and awkward gesture of pain, a broken symbol of something he had forgotten. At its foot a dark woman crouched in an abandon of weeping, and three men argued over golden, spinning coins.' Death has been brought into the world, and all our woe. What mortal sin has accomplished this?

It is the boy's fault. He had been 'basking in the rich promise of life abundant' offered by the stable when the third Wise Man challenged from his dark corner with, 'It is the season of gifts, and you must give according to your nature in order that you may receive. What is your gift?' The cold draught returns, the wings of the black bird shut out the light of the heavens, the baby whimpers with pain. The boy knows that he must answer 'even though his answer break all history and his heart'. He takes the baby, says 'I bring you the only gift I can, my power to doubt and my will to break', kills it and drops the 'little corpse onto the dunged straw'. The world turns black. He tries

> to run away from himself and the blood and nightmare of his future. But however hard he ran, he could still see the cross and its attendant figures and the dirty stable where these things had begun, could still hear the sounds of pain from all the world and smell the carrion flesh and the sick blood.

Weary of running, he flings himself down in the snow. 'As the drifting, dirtied warmth [closes] over him' he analyses what he has done: 'he had been asked for a gift and forced to honesty, and his gift appalled himself and the world. A white time had died between his hands.' The afternoon has passed; night has come on. A bright star shines above the cross and 'his horror had given place to misery'. He hears the Wise Men debating, puzzled; hears them decide to depart 'with doubts and scruples and hesitations' for 'Another and more bitter journey'; hears them echo Eliot's 'Journey of the Magi': 'Birth? Death?'[101]

'The first Christmas' is, amongst other things (it is another complex 'signpost' work like 'Visions' and 'The enemy in the heart') a rites-of-passage story. We have already had one echo of Joyce's *Portrait of the Artist* ('my power to doubt and my will to break') and we now have another:

> he . . . knew that he had done what he had to do, and that there was no remedy or escape. He no longer wished to run away from himself. In the morning there had been a promise: he had looked for it and found it. The promise had turned to blood and horror, but even in the core of the nightmare there was another promise. He would seek that too, according to his nature.[102]

The story concludes with an echo of *The Waste Land*: 'He looked towards the house and decided to return. For a moment there was a ring of light in the burdened sky; then, with a trumpet of thunder it began to rain.'[103] In Eliot's poem the flash of lightning and the rain represent Peter's appalled realization of betrayal and the despairing tears of repentance that follow it, and what the thunder says is 'give, sympathise, control'. The boy returns home. He has crucified Christ twice over. The 'lucid parable of snow' is 'stained and staled to a puddled indifference on which his tears fell softly, like the horror of eternity dropped by gentle, callous hands into an open grave. / It was the first and the last Christmas.'

This appalling parable of paradise lost through pride-driven disobedience; of the world we live in made harsh by our sin and our lives nasty, brutish and short; of the Redeemer's love rewarded by crucifixion, and Christ recrucified anew by each proud sinner, is central to an understanding of T. H. Jones's life and work and it is particularly apt to the Australian years. The picture of the child facing his challenge alone (though the conflict the story depicts is one that can be resolved only in the heart and mind of the individual sinner) and coming to terms with it alone, suggests a loss of faith in the family and is a logical development of the earlier stories. Jones had believed that through academic success he could both reward his Mam and escape becoming a bank clerk or preacher. The escape was hard, its price guilt and its effect on him showed itself in intolerance and an inability to suffer fools gladly.

At Pisgah Sunday school, at morning and evening chapel services and in a home coloured by his mother's essentially Calvinist faith, he had been brought up to believe in a just and all-seeing male god who entered a catalogue of sins on one's personal tally against the Day of Judgement. Ruth was the most loving of mothers, but she believed, and taught, that hell-fire could be escaped only by good deeds and the acceptance of God's will. The seminal poem 'The Welshman in exile speaks',[104] dedicated to Brin Newton John, asks the central question:

> Being a boy from the hills, brought up
> Believing that fornication is a sin,
> Adultery abomination, what should I do
> But fornicate until I'm caught, and then
> Commit adultery in my dreams.

Its defiant conclusion, 'Boyo, if you come from a country like that / You can talk to me of sin and related matters', leaves us with little doubt about the stimulus that produced it. The assumption is that the adult *must* defy authority. The mere existence of a prohibition – the Tree of Knowledge in the Garden – ensures its defiance. Defiance underlines the boy's instinctive strangling of the baby in the stable; his self-respect, identity, his very survival depend on it.

By reliving and re-examining his childhood Jones achieved an understanding of those early dreams and ambitions that had done so much to make him what he had become: the dream of adventure and power on the sea, the academic distinction, fame as a poet and the repeatedly refreshed but never satisfied union, in woman after woman, with the Muse. He realized that in taking pains to please others, conforming to the stereotype of the responsible, hard-working family man, he had abandoned a freedom essential to his genius:

> Caught young, I grew to be a pretty boy,
> Fondled and dandled on many a lovely lap,
> Called precious and a pet as well as pretty,
> *But the green tree keeps on growing.*[105]

You have only to look at the damage growing trees inflict on suburban pavements, let alone on the foundations of a rural home, to appreciate that refrain.[106]

'Time held me green and dying', Dylan Thomas had written, 'Though I sang in my chains like the sea.'[107] Had there ever been a time without chains?

> Eating the bread of the world
> In the thin rain of time
> The child ignores the crow,
> The stoat, and worm who know
> What bread and child will come
> To, crumble to at last . . .
>
> A bible in his mind,
> A pulpit for his mouth,
> Should he seek further for
> The absence of the wind
> Or accommodating truth,
> Life's wound without a scar?[108]

'Spoiled preacher',[109] dedicated to 'many contemporaries, and some in especial', makes the definitive statement that he has abandoned forever the innocence of childhood. In his haunted, drunken sleep 'in the sweaty and stained night' the poet finds his recollections so freed by alcohol that he is almost physically one again with his parents: 'mother's / Flannel nightgown . . . father's dirthard shirt' and the thought comes to him:

> Suppose,
> You think, you had gone through with it,
> Suppose a war hadn't come conveniently,
> Suppose – this is the moment when your scream
> Awakes you to your own sweat and dirt . . .

The appalling thought is that of becoming a 'Pastor': baptism in the Chwefri, learning 'from the ghosts of Christmas Evans / And Evan Jones "the man from Eglwyswrw"'. Evans (1776–1838) was the son of a shoemaker who joined the Baptists in 1788, ministered for thirty years in Anglesey and wrote hymns; Jones (1777–1819), another Baptist, was born at Llandysul, but his family came from Eglwyswrw in Pembrokeshire; famous for his Calvinistic pamphlets, he was so accomplished a preacher that Christmas Evans would not preach after him, but he was excommunicated in 1810 for public drunkenness.

'How beautifully', Jones tells himself, 'you would have been able to thunder / Against sin (meaning only one thing, that thing) / To your thin and sinning congregation.' In appealing to these 'ghosts' Jones is resurrecting the real enough rulers of Caradoc Evans's Capel Sion and a whole world of priestly dictatorship and endemic sexual corruption carefully concealed beneath frock coats, kid gloves and hypocritical pulpit piety:

> Pastor you would have been – and what a hypocrite
> You would have been in the glory of the pulpit –
> Hair flowing all over the place, and hellfire texts
> All endlessly against fornication
> To a few thin and avaricious buggers
> Of both sexes heedfully laying up their treasure
> In the bank and whatever they thought was heaven.

The indictment is as unsparing as that of Caradoc Evans:

> But now you are emancipated – suppose
> Any of them should look upon you now –
> You could stand their contempt for your Sunday drinking
> And your tenderness for girl students and secretaries –
> They took Sunday School in their time, and for their reasons.

The use of the ambiguous 'took', with its implication that the pastor's lust for young female flesh, like his own, goes beyond the eyes, shows Jones happily associating himself with what Caradoc Evans's detractors called 'the literature of the sewer'.[110] Unlike Evans's, though, his intention is to identify himself as a product of the community: he could have dissembled in it as preacher no less competently than he now lies as poet:

> But suppose, suppose
> You had to preach a sermon on a thin belly,
> Hoping the big farmer would spare you an egg or two.

> I suppose
> I would have been a pretty good preacher,
> Getting properly hot against fornication,
> And getting my eggs.

Anthony Conran is right to regard this poem as among T. H. Jones's most important: 'We are witnessing', he writes,[111] 'the birthpangs of a real middle class out of the Welsh way of life. The new-born professional Welshman looks back in horror at the trap he has escaped: but the cost of his escape is exile and guilt.' Is it in any real sense escape at all? Anthony Giddens[112] argues that the achievement of privacy and the psychological needs associated with it that are primary features of postmodern life have led to a total fracture between childhood and adulthood. 'Childhood as a separate sphere becomes an infrastructure of the personality' and is capable of, and in personalities such as Jones's appears to require, constant reinvention. A psychological consequence is the increased prominence of shame associated with self-identity as compared with guilt. Guilt essentially depends on mechanisms extrinsic to the internally referential systems of modernity and is associated with moral transgression and anxiety derived from failing to satisfy a moral imperative. For Giddens, shame is more directly and pervasively related to basic trust than is guilt, because guilt concerns specific forms of behaviour or cognition. 'Unlike guilt, shame directly corrodes our sense of security in both self and surrounding social milieu.' The more internally referential self-identity becomes, the more the hold of tradition is broken, the more shame takes centre stage. Foucault notes the proliferation of the discourse that brings sexuality to the fore in the modern world and Giddens argues that 'eroticism conjoined to guilt was progressively replaced by an association of sexuality with self-identity and the propensity to shame'. Sexuality becomes *the*, in some cases the only, significant medium for self-realization.

Clive Hart considered T. H. Jones the most sexually alive man he had ever met. A member of the Jones's circle, and an inspiration, was Rae Richards. 'Beautiful, fascinating, a blonde Milton's Eve', she was also 'a very wonderful and talented painter and a marvellous mother'.[113] Jones seemed for a time to be head-over-heels in love with the idea of her: 'She was his Muse for a while and is the Eve for the sequence of Eve poems.' Jill Stowell remembers that 'she and Harri admired each other's art'.[114] Richards painted the final, and only extant of the three portraits of T. H. Jones: the wild, coal-black hair contrasts with a lurid background that might be hell-fire; the face is an extraordinary combination of innocent bliss and angst, the dark eyes are full of anguish, but the mouth is half blissfully smiling; neck and sideways shouldering torso suggest a powerful physical presence. This is the artist's comment; the poet's is found in 'On having my portrait painted':[115]

> My eyes were never right
> To see the colour and happiness of the world;
> My mouth was always twisted into wrongness.
> Still your patient labouring hands transform
> Them into something rich and strange.
> But though I'd recognise it anywhere
> *In the mirror I see a face*
> *You have not seen in any place.*

There is sad irony in the allusion to *The Tempest* where it is Ferdinand's wicked, supposedly drowned father who suffers the sea-change.

Marion Halligan gives a fictionalized insight into the relationship of poet and painter:[116]

> Tom Lloyd was there too, which wasn't surprising, with a beautiful woman, which wasn't surprising either. She was somewhat Spanish and called Concetta . . .They were a bizarre couple in the gloom of the bar, Tom stoutish and often abstracted, staring into his fat glass of white wine as though truth lurked in its murky depths, though only to be caught unaware, dropping sentences into the conversation every now and then with the comfortable certainty of being listened to, and casting libidinous sly beams upon Concetta, who glowed in the dark room.
>
> ' . . . She is Tom Lloyd's mistress. Well, mistress isn't actually the word . . . I mean they are lovers. Actually she . . . Says they are loving friends; that's rather nice, don't you think? They have been having an affair for years, she used to be a student of his, but it didn't start then, I gather, old Tom was rather scrupulous about that sort of thing.'

There is discussion among the artists about illuminating Concetta's poetry, then:

> 'Why don't you think of doing the same sort of thing with Tom's poems?'
> 'Of course, he hasn't asked me, for one thing and perhaps it's that there is something very stern, isolated, pure – what's the word – something complete about Tom's work. He can't imagine doing anything to it.'

Although Jones's friends feel this to be an accurate portrait, Halligan is careful to indicate reservations:

> You suggest that the character of Tom Lloyd is loosely based on Harri Jones. Yes, you could say that, but what does it mean? He is also based on other people . . . What I would say is really him is the poetry reading; he was marvellous in that respect. But note that Tom is a bachelor and walked around the college gardens like an abbot round a fish pond. Harri was very much married and liked being so and was certainly totally un-abbot-like. I remember him with immense affection; he taught me a lot of things.[117]

If a single Muse inspired 'Girl reading John Donne'[118] it was probably Marion, but there are other candidates. There is an insolent poise about this poem, a flexible control of form. It is reflexive, playful and the dramatic structure facilitates the controlled expression of powerful feelings reflected in tranquillity but not tranquilly. In a free-verse form which impishly hints at the blank verse of Donne, Jones constructs an ambiguous picture of the suspect but perhaps morally secure 'anonymous lecturer' playing the voyeur in the university library. The poem's superficial appeal lies in its arousal of familiar sexual perspectives in the male reader; to the female it appears to offer insight into the minds of men who have eyed her. The bored lecturer/poet is marking assignments and time while the unconsciously sensuous girl student, 'her arms bare and her eyes naked', is aroused by the power of erotic poetry. There are at least three specific references to Donne: 'The extasie', by reading which the student enters into the poet's seductive plea to release the 'great Prince' of sexual desire; 'The good morrow', where the sex act makes 'one little room an everywhere'; and 'To his mistress going to bed', where 'before, behind, between, above, below' becomes a rape of fair Australian virgin country.

Jones's poem is a 'metaphysically' witty *tour de force*: the girl reads and both intellectually and emotionally appreciates the poem; the almost anonymous lecturer in a rather different sense reads and appreciates assignments which might themselves be appreciations of poetry. The bored pedantry of marking which, hard as one tries to make it creative, is only too liable to descend to the cancelling of ampersands in the absence of anything interesting enough to be worth the effort of significant comment, is well done.

More interesting is the visual technique employed to structure the narrative code. The poem is primarily about ways of looking. The reader is positioned as knowledgeable (knowing) spectator of the scenes that unfold in the library and elsewhere; the writer/lecturer controls the pictured events from within the frame and outside it as the protagonists, the deliberately self-deprecating 'almost anonymous lecturer' and the young girl, perform. The first pleasure is the looking itself: we watch the watcher watching the watched. This is the scopophilic drive that predisposes us to subject others to a controlling and curious gaze.

The drive is narcissistic in form because the reader identifies with the figures represented, male voyeur or female victim depending on gender. There is a tension between voyeurism and fetishism. Laura Mulvey[119] argues that in cinematic terms voyeurism is an active mobile form associated with change and narrativization: 'It demands a story, depends on making something happen, forcing a change in another person, a battle of will and strength, victory/defeat, all occurring in linear times with a beginning and an end.' Voyeurism thus celebrates sexual difference in its attempt to demystify or punish women: it insists on the separation of the seer and the seen. It is the lecturer who has exercised his power to prescribe 'the text for her undoing'; he remembers 'how she crossed her legs in class'. Male fascination with the act of female display triggers intellectual insecurity. The poem centres on senses so aroused that they are stripped naked, here amongst the text that aroused them in the library. This arousal is triggered by poetry; the poem appears to suggest the notion of poetic text as fetish. What seems necessary for a particular object to become a fetish is that it should be constituted as a sexual signification by its articulation in a discourse of sexuality. The poem forces the girl to confess 'I am in love, I am in love' and it is the poem that says '"I love" to her exposed / And wanted flesh'. She is locked into a cyclic narrative form which forces her to re-enact scenarios of desire in which the reader ('Hypocrite lecteur, – mon semblable, – mon frère!'[120]), through a knowledge of Donne, can participate: he can enjoy her without her knowledge or consent. The reader is forced to ask what exactly it is that gives the girl pleasure.

The narrative is controlled through the persona adopted by the poet, the 'anonymous lecturer/great Prince' paradox. The poem reaffirms male power: the woman can escape neither the male poem she is reading (the seed) nor the womb of texts (the library in which she has been placed by the code of narration controlled by the watcher).

The poem's closing focus is on the 'marked' man who goes on marking, yet makes no progress ('It's marking time'). The poem itself is a discourse about male and female sexual pleasure and reaffirms Graves's view of poetry as female-inspired and offering its pleasure through the interrogation of the female principle. It is also a working out in Jungian terms of the resolution of the conflict of self. The poet persona is able to differentiate between the young woman and the image he projects on to her, the anima. The way has been opened for the internalization of emotional significance, true individuation. Poetry is presented as offering a symbolic solution, but we would do well not to forget the poem's typically ambiguous final line: 'a great Prince in prison *lies*'. A comparison between this quintessentially postmodern work and the early 'signpost' poem 'The enemy in the heart'[121] reveals T. H. Jones's maturity: here, with no apparent effort or straining after effect, he achieves great complexity of meaning in simple, colloquial language.

Halligan gives us an impression of T. H. Jones's style of poetry-reading:

> He took a book from the shelf behind him. 'Life is short, art is long, the crooked worm will have us in the end, and that's the way it should be,' he said. 'Listen to Dylan Thomas . . .' His rage against the dying of the light was not loud, but it was violent. On his beautiful voice went, his unashamed rhetorical rich voice, through Dylan's poems about death which shall have no dominion to 'The Refusal to Mourn the Death by Fire of a Child in London'. 'Deep with the first dead lies London's daughter . . .' He read slowly, and the words came so lovingly out of his mouth that it seemed as if he were inventing them. 'Secret by the unmourning water . . . After the first death, there is no other.'[122]

As epigraph to 'On a painting, "Sunk Lyonesse", by Rae Richards'[123] Jones quotes R. P. Blackmur: '*Perform* is a word of which we forget the singular beauty. Its meaning is: to furnish forth, to complete, to finish . . . performance is an enlightening name for one of our richest activities, rich with extra life.' The poem *is* a performance and it is *about* mutual performance, in art and in love: the word and the paint, the union of poetry and painting made flesh. Diction, imagery and rhythm are of an extraordinary beauty and it begins with a hint at Hardy's late Cornish poems:

> It was to make the words perform
> I laboured, and it was to make the paint
> Perform you toiled in sea-sunk Lyonesse.[124]

It is a conceit, an extended sea-image: the artists 'ride the ruffian storm[125] / Of our distress'; after 'all the long / Submergence . . . ride out the storm like birds' and:

> Now we have made our work complete.
> Now we have found the lovely form.
> Under green arches once more drown
> So that our labourings may meet
> Where our two languages go down
> To find and finish what we form.

This makes the same contrast with 'The enemy in the heart' whose symbolism the stanza recalls. There is a serenity here, a humility rare in Jones's poetry, derived from the coincidence of artistic and sexual satisfaction (the reader should never forget the strength – 'necessity' is hardly too strong a word – for him of the connection between sexual stimulation and poetic performance). It is Yeats who underwrites this poem, the echo augmenting its power, beauty and serenity:

> Labour is blossoming or dancing where
> The body is not bruised to pleasure soul,
> Nor beauty born out of its own despair,
> Nor blear-eyed wisdom out of midnight oil.
> O chestnut-tree, great-rooted blossomer,
> Are you the leaf, the blossom or the bole?
> O body swayed to music, O brightening glance,
> How can we know the dancer from the dance?[126]

To impressionable undergraduates Jones's repeated assertion that art is about processing what happens to you and being completely honest about it[127] had enormous appeal.

> He was always good company, never morbid, generous to a fault, and as free of personal malice as anyone I have ever met. He took a personal interest in his students . . . and he was not much concerned with the conventional distance between teacher and student.[128]

Some students thought that T. H. Jones's poetry was becoming influenced by the new focus of his critical attention, American poetry. To Croft it seemed not dissimilar to what Lowell was writing at the time: 'It was metaphysical in origin and influenced by New Criticism techniques.' The Canadian, Northrop Frye, was a seminal influence at the cognitive level, in particular his *Fearful*

Symmetry[129] in which he contended that the product of the imaginative life 'is most clearly seen in the work of art which is a unified mental vision of experience'. Perception is superior to abstraction, says Frye, and vision is 'the goal of all freedom, energy and wisdom'. Frye's standpoint is Christian and holistic, concerned with unity rather than dislocation: 'there is', he maintains, 'a single visionary conception which the mind of man is trying to express, a vision of a created and fallen world which has been redeemed by divine sacrifice'. This formulation was particularly attractive to Jones, the alienated exile.

The problem was how to achieve personal regeneration. Many of the poems of this period are consistent with such terms, current during the 1960s, as 'poems of experience', 'confessional', 'open', 'poetry of involvement'.[130] Lowell's *Life Studies* (1959) and *For the Union Dead* (1964) were the significant texts, but Jones had also lectured on and performed poetry by Roethke, Berryman and W. D. Snodgrass. His own mature poetry had now achieved simplicity, directness,[131] a language close to common speech; its preoccupation is often with psychological truths and obsessions and he reveals with wry regret intimate, sometimes sordid or humiliating details of a physical decline that included alcohol-induced impotence:

> Drunk on duty, not for the first time,
> Private Ianto stands limply to attention,
> Thankful that though being unable's a crime
> At least it can't be punished by detention.[132]

compulsive promiscuity:

> Waking with the taste still of your nipples
> In my mouth, I groan and stretch my empty arms,
> Remembering too well I have a member
> And rise reluctantly to write a poem.[133]

and more promiscuity:

> As malefactors once were branded, so
> I hoped your bites would stay upon my body
> That the whole envious world might know
> This was my guerdon when I served you nightly.[134]

The habit of self-scrutiny is central to American literature. At its purest it dominated the discourse of New England Puritanism; twentieth-century America wholly embraced its extension, psychoanalysis. The significance of language in the process of self-scrutiny has been discussed by Perry Miller:[135] 'the doctrine of regeneration caused the founders of New England to become experts in psychological dissection', he writes. Herbert Leibowitz says of Lowell's early poetry that 'his ambivalent attitude to the Puritans is central to an understanding of his poetry'.[136] Anthony Giddens suggests that Puritanism was one of the main stimuli for 'a take-off' into the more inclusive internally referenced ordering of society and nature.[137] Just as Lowell was preoccupied with the strange figure of Jonathan Edwards,[138] so T. H. Jones used characters like Cotton Mather and Frances Higginson to give perspective to puritanical Welsh characters, such as the referential Uncle Daniel Jones who influenced his childhood.

Students were 'amazed' by 'the social poems for birthdays, weddings, women friends, all within the framework of some well-worked stanza', says Julian Croft,[139] and Marion Halligan says,

> The bit in *Thrift* about going to W.E.A. classes is Harri, and so is the amazing, revolutionary effect he had in Newcastle; he put poetry on the map . . . you could say, and the city has never looked back. He would write poems . . . for special occasions, lovely poems, not great perhaps, but always to be treasured.[140]

Typical of one facet of this verse is 'For David Jonathan Power', written for his sister Pat's first-born son:

> May David be a big boy who
> Will be the biggest joy unto
> His mother and his family, especially his Mam,
> Who will be
> Always the reason he
> Will know what's what and who is who.
>
> May he like proper things, and women most,
> And have words to say his liking in.
> So, when he meets his old uncle's ghost,
> We can together put our two words in;

His mother and my sister. And no host of
Bad things can stand against our good word.

David, I hope sometime you will say
Though mother's brother could not pray,
He said some words for me; these words I heard,
And tell my mam my love today.[141]

Discussing poetry with Julian Croft, Jones professed a tension in his continuing love of the long line and detestation of the febrile short lines American poets were beginning to employ in the 1960s. 'He still seemed to have a natural affinity for the long declamatory line, the line of Milton.'[142] This allowed him to flirt with the conservative literary figures who had dominated Australian poetry in the 1950s, in particular the poets of the classical revival; A. D. Hope and James McAuley. Alec Hope, the grand old man of Australian poetry, whom Jones came to know and admire, was, at the time of their first meeting in 1959, in a sense 'the Australian Auden'.[143] Half a generation older than Jones (born 1907), he had had an isolated upbringing among Presbyterian Scots in Tasmania, respected traditional forms (his regret at the loss of the epic and ode was congenial) and was sceptical of the fashionable new. 'Cotton Mather',[144] the Browning-like dramatic monologue, and the Adam and Eve poems (the first of them[145] is dedicated to him) owe something to his influence. On the other hand, his disgust for romantic biographical poetry and his dismissal of the significance of place in Australian poetry, in particular the idea that only poetry generated by specific Australian landscape is truly Australian, appears the antithesis of Jones's philosophy of poetry. In his 1956 essay, 'Standards in Australian literature',[146] Hope had attacked the chauvinism exemplified by the Jindy Worobak Movement. Recently Les Murray has suggested that white settlers' assimilation of Aboriginal culture is a healthy 'creolizing influence'[147] and that the organic power of Australia's distinctive environment might bring together its diverse cultures.

It is interesting to compare Murray's comments on white settlers' respect for certain sites, Ayer's Rock in particular, which function as symbols of identity, with T. H. Jones's use of this icon in 'Rhiannon'.[148] Murray's view that 'after all human frenzies and efforts there remains the great land [that] does not finally permit imported attitudes that would make it simply a resource, a thing'[149] harmonizes perfectly with Jones's 'small hill, Allt-y-clych'. Murray is also interested in alternatives to the pervasive hierarchies of metropolitan culture: the reduction of British life to a London, Australian to a Melbourne or Sydney. Jones also maintains the primacy of the local and Murray's term 'vernacular republic'[150] applies aptly to many of the later poems.

This did not prevent him from accepting Hope's belief that Australian poetry, like British, derived from the Judaeo-Christian and Graeco-Roman traditions. It enabled him, as an incomer, to be also an insider.[151] For a polyglot mind like that of T. H. Jones, Hope's copious use of classical and biblical references and his referential employment of British and European poetry was a delight. In 1964 he wrote: 'Hope's romanticism is that of the *Roman de la Rose* and of Paolo and Francesca: he believes in the virtues of the flesh and is perhaps the first poet since Yeats to transmute that belief into poetry.'[152] In poems such as 'The death of the bird' and 'Imperial Adam' the tensions between domesticity, male machismo and female sexuality are expressed in the deceptively simple quatrains of the traditional ballad. Hope alternates comic grotesque and sexual angst:

> Adam had learned the jolly deed of kind;
> He took her in his arms, and there and then,
> Like the clean beasts, embracing from behind,
> Began in joy to found the breed of men.[153]

Hope's tough metaphysical dialectics, his scepticism, and, in particular, his intense male eroticism have, in recent years, encouraged younger Australian feminist critics to reassess his reputation downwards. Jones identified with the romantic/ phallocentric view – though he was not uncritical in his admiration:

Hope is the most gifted and the most disappointing of Australian poets. In many ways he is the John Dryden of Australian poetry. Technically the best equipped, he is the only modern poet I know who has written verse satire that does not look incompetent by eighteenth century standards . . . but he has ignored his roots . . . all his best poems could have been written by an equally intelligent, sensitive and gifted poet in Wales, America, or any other English-speaking country . . . If I accuse Hope of not being an R. S. Thomas or a Robert Lowell, it is for reasons I believe Hope might approve of.[154]

Hope responded by championing T. H. Jones's work and introducing him to James McAuley, editor of *Quadrant*, where he quickly established himself as a reviewer. McAuley, an incisive, provocative theorist, was strongly anti-modernist, concerned to restore the primacy of reason and a certain classical clarity. He deplored romantic portentousness and modernist formlessness. *Quadrant* was intensely conservative, the Australian equivalent of *Encounter*, even to the extent of accepting Central Intelligence Agency money at the same time as that magazine did so. Had Jones's socialism moderated sufficiently to accept the compromise? Was he unaware of or perhaps indifferent to *Quadrant*'s politics? As far as reviewing was concerned, he went his own way, championing radical poets like Judith Green and David Malouf[155] and castigating Geoffrey Dutton and Bruce Dawe for being suitable to 'fit snugly into an English anthology that contains Larkin and Enright' but 'embarrassing in an American one that contained Lowell and Berryman'.[156] His favourite younger Australian poet was Gwen Harwood who, he felt, had 'fire and irony . . . like other spoilt romantics she is better when she is at a distance from her subject as in her magnificent Professor Eisenbart poems'.[157] These satirical squibs at the pretentious, self-centred, uncreative academic, were the work of a poet who in 1979 could echo T. H. Jones, writing of her work that it expressed 'the continuity of self through memory and through descendants; I felt myself to be part of an unbroken chain of women'.[158] Jones disagreed sharply with McAuley about the great Australian romantic poet, Robert D. Fitzgerald,[159] finding him 'like Yeats in his care for his craft of poetry and his care for his past, for memory, for the living roots from which the sap of life and art rises'.[160] On the few occasions when they discussed politics, Julian Croft found Jones 'a sentimental socialist'[161] now; nothing of the Stalinist apart from a personal intolerance of those he disliked.

By March 1962 there were enough poems for a third volume (165 had entered the *Black Book* since *Songs of a Mad Prince*). Jones wrote to Hart-Davis on the 27 March:

You are probably more accustomed to the excuses of authors than I am to purveying them. But in fact I had a hell of a year . . . I was fairly overworked. On top of this I accepted a commission . . . to write a book on Dylan Thomas for the Writers and Critics series.[162]

Emphasizing his productivity and optimism, he continues:

The really important thing is that since I have been here I have written more – and more good – poetry in 3 years than I had in the previous 10.[163] I have been writing too quickly for my typewriter . . . I think I can say . . . that I already have a reputation in the antipodes . . . Are you prepared to lose more money on me? I honestly believe that I already have the makings of a better volume than either of the two you have published. And . . . I think that a third volume published at the same time as my book on Dylan Thomas might attract some attention.[164]

Hart-Davis was receptive, but it was November before Jones wrote again:

I am sending you under separate cover the MS for a possible third volume of poems,[165] *The Beast at the Door*. As you can see, I have really been prolific since my translation down here – this is about half my output in the last three years . . . .
  I have just finished correcting the galleys for my book on Dylan Thomas. Next year I shall be busy again as I will be temporarily in charge of the department while the Head is on sabbatical.[166]

There was a slight adjustment to the manuscript before the book was published. The latest poem to be included is dated 30 March 1963, and two others December 1962 and 9 March 1963. *The Beast at the Door* will be discussed in Chapter 8. This one concludes with the Dylan Thomas monograph.

It might be suggested that, in writing a critical study of his very influential older contemporary, T. H. Jones was taking the opportunity to write his influence into perspective. Except in his earliest work, however, and there only occasionally, although he *was* influenced, it was more a case of matching himself against Thomas than being overwhelmed by or merely imitating him. Five years' naval service had given him the time, the experience and the maturity to avoid being overinfluenced and, as we have seen, his use of the influence of other poets was always carefully calculated.

The cheaply priced Oliver & Boyd series became standard undergraduate texts, and this has caused what remains the best introduction to Thomas to be undervalued and it has long been out of print. The *Western Mail* was cordial:

> In this tidy, well-reasoned critical analysis Mr Jones claims that Thomas's value as a poet has been obscured by the sensationalism of his brassy life and alcoholic death. He demonstrates convincingly that Thomas's roots were firmly in Wales, most emphatically at home among the seascapes of Laugharne . . . Altogether this is a satisfying, revealing book, not wholly confined to the dryness of theoretical analysis.[167]

The book deserves reprinting as a short, accessible and wry reading of Thomas's craft by a poet who understands his challenge to his own work. Jones describes him as 'the most sensational poet of our time'.[168] He believes that Thomas achieved too early fame and notoriety

> not merely as a poet, but as some sort of heaven-sent or White-Goddess-given reply, the rejoinder, or antistrophe to what poetry-starved people felt to be the desolation and erudity of *The Waste Land*, the early 'Cantos' of Pound and the pyloned versions of these in the early poems of those writers whom Roy Campbell cruelly, but not unfairly, lumped together . . . as MacSpaunday.[169]

The context for the poetry, in Jones's view, is the life of a man who was hailed as a genius, denounced as a charlatan and died 'in another country, all too young, and in sordidly dramatic circumstances'.[170] The uniqueness of Thomas's poetry derives from his Welsh origins and his conception of poetry as 'the gift of the Gods' and 'the poet as an inspired seer expressing his individual experiences, emotions and *Weltanschauung*'.[171] Resuming his long-standing debate with Aneirin Talfan Davies,[172] he claims that 'no native English writer could so creatively have misused the English language in the peculiar fashion that characterises Thomas's poetry'.[173] He emphasizes, with a reflexive nod in his own direction, that Thomas's childhood was an imaginatively happy one. The poetry is seen as consciously classless in an age when poetry was expected to have social reference. Ironically,

> The writer about Dylan Thomas (and particularly one from a similar background) is tempted to say that the first fatal step which he took towards that premature death in New York was the one that put him, following the example of many other young men from the provinces and the Principality, on a train to London.[174]

Jones deals extensively with Thomas's role as a nature poet, his obsession with birth, copulation and what Alun Lewis called 'the single poetic theme of life and death'.[175] The book, however, is of continuing interest principally for its discussion of individual poems. The reading of 'Fern Hill' is a skilled deconstruction of Thomas's concept of time and childhood, celebrating what Robert Graves called

> The greatness, rareness, muchness,
> Fewness of this precious only
> Endless world . . .[176]

Starting with the last two lines

> time held me green and dying
> Though I sang in my chains like the sea.

Jones suggests that the theme, reduced to some such pedestrian statement as, 'Duw! man, the world was a wonderful place when I was a child. But alas! time passes',[177] is not the point. What signifies is the way in which Thomas gives a concrete quality to the child's world: apple barrels, house, grass, the dingle, wagons, trees, leaves, daisies, barley, barns, the yard, the farm, the sun, the calves, the foxes, the pebbles, the streams, the hayfields, the chimneys, the dew, the cock, the sky, the fields, peasants, clouds, hay and 'the swallow thronged loft'. What we experience is 'a suggestion of the breathless incoherence of a child recounting the glory and wonder of a day'.[178] He identifies different, but overlapping kinds of imagery. The first is the familiar phrase given a surprising twist: 'happy as the grass was green'. Second, there are childlike comparisons: 'I was huntsman and herdsman'. Then there is a childish sense of time: the idea that the farm goes away at night and returns only when the boy wakes up in the morning. Fourthly, there is chapel imagery reminiscently biblical: 'it was Adam and Maiden'.

Jones concludes that, to the very end, Dylan Thomas's poetry was characterized by a developing awareness of his own human nature and a developing ability to present the human nature of others. He endorses G. S. Fraser's view that the main elements of Thomas's complexity were 'the legendary sweet funny man and the fine solemn poet and the growing together'.[179] He defends Thomas against Grigson's assault on his 'obsessions', exclaiming: 'why an obsession with birth, death, and love should be a fault in a poet is not made clear – most poets have taken it to be an inevitability and, at the worst, a fate of virtue from necessity.'[180] For T. H. Jones, Thomas was a genius, but 'not a major poet . . . he was a good poet',[181] and, once more speaking from the heart:

> The true Thomas was not the anti-hero of a thousand sniggering tales or the retching wreck eventually passing into oblivion in a New York hospital, but the author of 'Fern Hill' and 'A Refusal to Mourn' and twenty or thirty other equally fine poems.[182]

Typically, he gives the last word to another poet, quoting the final lines of Vernon Watkins's tribute:

> The superhuman, crowned
> Saints must enter this drowned
> Tide-race of the mind
> To guess or understand
> The face of this cracked prophet
> Which from its patient pall
> I slowly take,
> Drop the envelope,
> Compel his disturbing shape,
> And write these words on a wall
>
> Maybe for a third man's sake.[183]

1963–1965

The Last Days – A Small Vision of Hell

The anonymous *Times Literary Supplement* review of *The Beast at the Door* appeared on 6 September 1963. Headlined 'For the most part gloomy', it stood alongside work by Tom Scott, Edwin Brock and Richard Weber. T. H. Jones was dismissed as an unhappy sheep-farmer with a 'macabre gift of putting his fantasies in order by bringing them face to face with the realities of his condition'. His subject-matter was seen as often trivial, and his style 'so consistent that one ends up wondering whether Mrs Jones looks like a wild crag or Alexander Pope was a secret drinker who took wry amusement out of having his portrait painted'. The first reference is to 'Cwmchwefri rocks',[1] a richly allusive poem inaccessible to superficial reading. The second, with unintentional irony which would have delighted the Augustan poet, is to 'Mr Pope',[2] which, in a form and style which could hardly be less 'consistent' with 'Cwmchwefri rocks', damns contemporary dunces:

> How we could use now his pain and his perfection
> When the stupid army's swollen even more,
> And literacy has become a means of rejection
> Of everything by which Mr Pope set store.

Jones does receive a grudging acknowledgement of his 'integrity', but Weber alone is considered 'a real poet' because (wonderful irony!) 'He can lie with aplomb'.

Glyn Jones reviewed the collection in the *Western Mail*,[3] alongside R. S. Thomas's *The Bread of Truth*. He saw Thomas's work as 'touched with greatness and compassion'; for him it was Thomas who dictated the dominant reading of T. H. Jones: 'Echoes and prose are the besetting menaces of his poetry and several of the poems here sound like R. S. Thomas, e.g. the fine

"Llanafan unrevisited".' 'Could so many punctual adjectives possibly be the work of R. S. Thomas?', though.[4] Glyn Jones singles out 'One memory',[5] untypical of T. H. Jones, and 'A man without eyelids'[6] as 'among the twenty or so poems that speak without mimicry and ventriloquism'. He pinpoints the post-modernism, but fails to understand it.

The Beast at the Door is the strongest of the four published volumes, the last to be shaped by the poet. As T. H. Jones points out,[7] the bulk of the poems, arranged in three sections ('Hiraeth', 'Eros', 'Owl and echo') are framed by 'a superb pair of bookends – my "Lucky Jonah" . . . and another bloody long Welshman at the other end'.

This is the title-poem. Comprising only twenty-eight lines, it is long only in its implications. 'The beast at the door'[8] is part of the sequence of related symbols of threat from within begun with 'The enemy in the heart'[9] and continued through *The Weasel at the Heart*.[10] The danger this time is the poet's Caliban-like 'Id', personified as an 'Amiably slavering', disingenuous, very masculine animal. Burrs and thorns cling to his 'pelt'. Assertively dirty, he wears 'wilful clots of dung . . . like medals'. His breath stinks. Like the poet in his nightmares, he reeks of sweat. His eyes are 'Small as a pig's, or mine' and the poet is at first happy to have him, 'Bald-rumped, big-pilled, wise', in the house to 'smell out my tricks / As he sniffed around for sex'. When he realizes the beast's true significance it is too late to shut the door and 'those white / Fangs were for me'. Disingenuous as ever, Jones implies that he is fully conscious of personal neuroses. 'The beast at the door' images the danger of being destroyed by an alter ego out of control. We think, surely, and with similar regret, of Sylvia Plath.

Jones has largely abandoned the reflexive biblical/Miltonic images of exile from the Garden. Reflexivity now undermines the certainty of knowledge and these poems often display an erratic dynamism. 'Hiraeth'[11] is redefined as a feature of high modernity or postmodernity, 'fertile ground for certainty and decon-struction'.[12] Tester suggests that nostalgia is impossible without movement and transformation. In relation to 'the reified past, the present is a reflexive achievement'.[13] Nostalgia is not merely a repudiation of where the I is presently located, it is a way of coming to terms with the present position, making 'the relentless struggle against reification even more resolute'. T. H. Jones does not look back to a halcyon past, he uses the past to reinforce the will to know. He defines his experiences in what Tonnies has described as the real and organic community (*Gemeinschaft*) as opposed to society as a merely mechanistic structure (*Gesellschaft*).[14] Tester argues that *Gemeinschaft* is based on natural, not calculating, rational will and says of Tonnies that 'he is torn between identification of a pastoral idyll and . . . identification of a tyranny of tradition'. The individual is released from the constraints of tradition, but into what kind of existence? For Durkheim, the reflexive individual has the potential to 'destroy every thing to which it might be possible to attach some meaning and some purpose'.[15] That potential is evident in these poems of Jones's middle age.

The 'Hiraeth' section is the heart of this volume as it is of Wales, the poet and his poetry. Of its twenty-one poems, only 'Swansea',[16] a tribute to Dylan Thomas, is not directly about Llanafan as landscape, people, family and the particular religion and way of life which shaped the poet, from whose constraints he has been physically released but whose influence he cannot and does not wish to escape. For Llanafan we may read Wales: to T. H. Jones, Llanafan *is* Wales. The final poem, 'Prayer to the steep Atlantick stream',[17] sums up. Although in Australia 'the golden blackmail of the day / Holds me in winterless security', neither Australia, nor anything else can 'stop that shouting in my ears / Of the cold waves that batter on the rocks / Of Wales'. Despite his 'surrender to the sun' (the exile's guilt is defined by 'blackmail' and 'surrender'), his desire/intention is to 'find a kind of peace, / And lie down with my fathers'.

Madeleine is the only compensation for exile. In 'Mr Jones as the transported poet'[18] 'the only exile is from her bed'. In 'Llanafan unrevisited'[19] 'I live in the good meadows, and I have / No emblem but your body', but 'am / Still a member of a narrow chapel'. In 'Land of my fathers',[20] although 'what happens between me and you' is of the greatest, continuing importance, 'Always I feel the cold and cutting blast / Of winds that blow about my native hills'. In the very fine 'Cwmchwefri rocks',[21] it is in the arms of Madeleine, identified with the Muse, Ceridwen, that 'I can forget / Cwmchwefri rocks and the stern face of God'. Forget, but only in the act of love, and even there but briefly.

The evocation of Llanafan/Wales is comprehensive. Most of the poems involve harsh landscape. 'In memoriam'[22] identifies with

Uncle Daniel, 'My grandmother died in the early hours of the morning'[23] portrays the grandfather with whom he had had so close a relationship as a boy. 'Ancestor, old lady'[24] and 'Portrait gallery'[25] present a family and people shaped by centuries of struggle for subsistence in such a landscape and 'The Welshman in exile speaks'[26] and 'In memoriam' exemplify a religion, a way of life and a tradition.

The 'Eros' section, appropriately placed *after* 'Hiraeth', contains twenty love-lyrics inspired by various women, sometimes named in the title or dedication. 'A confusion of bright women'[27] in a sense sums up:

> It was a confusion of bright women troubled
> Me this morning . . .
> Olwen, and Blodwen, Mary, Jane, and Anne,
> Megan and Deborah and Marguerite,
> Came back like ghosts to stir my ghostly blood.

To the woman with whom he is in bed at the time he offers the dubious compliment:

> If I should call you by some other name,
> What matter so that I hold you rightly
> And make this poem for you, only for you.

'Between nightmare and nightmare'[28] echoes 'Cwmchwefri rocks': the best defence against nightmare is the 'nightly care' of 'Your arms around me', but the comfort is limited by the guilt which is 'closer to me even than you'. 'Adam's song after paradise'[29] is a *felix culpa* poem which develops ideas embryonic in 'The ring of language'.[30] Adam, after naming the animals, is rewarded with the mixed blessing of Eve, 'Torn from my side and fashioned fair / To be my hope and my despair':[31] She has caused his 'lapse from innocence'. The couple now 'do furtively / The deed in open joy begun', but heartbreak is more than compensated for by 'Seductiveness of hair and eyes / The promised welcome of your breasts':

> I take again your guilty hand
> I look into your candid eyes

> And am content that I have lost
> That half-regretted Paradise
> To win your human smiles and tears
> To comfort my declining years.

To Jones the guilt associated with sex is more than half its attraction.

'A mirror of herself'[32] makes an interesting pair with the previous poem and shows that Jones has not forgotten Wallace Stevens (who provides the epigraph, 'And Eve made air a mirror of herself'). A witty reworking of Stevens's allegory,[33] it combines the *felix culpa* theme ('Praise be for fallen beauty everywhere') with the mirror symbolism of which Jones was so fond, making playful use of Stevens's colour symbolism: 'the air is blue about us everywhere' suggests recrimination; 'the blue mirror is a very fact' is, to say the least, paradoxical. The poem's paradigmatic patterns are metaphysical, 'A sharpening of my wits on some bright bone / To disentangle images from hair' playing with Donne's 'subtile wreath of haire' and 'bracelet of bright hair about the bone'[34]). The poem is witty in the metaphysical sense[35] and skilfully balanced: 'How fair she was whose daughters are so fair' / 'And praise her darkly whom I find most fair'.

The final section is titled 'Owl and echo' after the eponymous poem[36] with its epigraph from Dylan Thomas, 'I am the owl and the echo'. The highly reflexive poem, which has something in common with Ted Hughes's 'The thought-fox', appears to image the act of composition when, in meaningful darkness, the poet is 'undertaken' by 'overpowers' and, like the owl leaving its perch, goes 'Mousing down all the wordy heavens'. Under the 'naked and re-echoing stroke' of the Muse, possessed by her, he loses all superior wisdom, 'wise now only in my echo'. Lines from 'On having my portrait painted' are relevant:

> the owl
> Reminds me that our only wisdom
> Is to know the labour and the love we put
> Into our making[37]

and associate 'Owl and echo' with the mirror or divided-self poems: 'In the mirror I see a face / No one has seen in any place'.

The poems of this section explore aspects of the poet's fixated self. In 'The minstrel boy'[38] and 'Simply to write'[39] it is his capacities as professional and in 'Lines for a double christening'[40] as occasional poet. 'Fall of an empire',[41] 'The nightmare of King Theseus'[42] and 'A man without eyelids'[43] deal with various neuroses. 'Sea-faiths',[44]

> In countries where no sea-faiths were
> I would not want to live . . .

and the ominous 'The moods of the sea'[45] – 'we fail / Until we die and worship with the fish' – remind us how important the sea was as a source of inspiration.

The section is clinched with 'To my mother',[46] the 'One woman alone' who 'Cries I was born'. That word 'alone' tolls through five short stanzas which bring together the Llanafan landscape, rural toil:

> My scythe hissed drily
> Through the headland corn
> I mowed alone.
> Seagulls made clamour
> About my leaning plough . . . ,

the important symbolic thorn of the last-period poems and God's admonition against sin. Stunted hawthorns are a quintessential feature of the Llanafan landscape, but the symbol appears to derive from Christ's crown of thorns by way of the fable of the nightingale that sang so sweetly to its death against the thorn. Woman as sexual comforter 'In wood or meadow' is juxtaposed with woman as earth mother, and the poem concludes, God's voice a whisper, familiar landscape lost, with the anguished, triumphant cry of the woman delivered. Ambiguity again: 'cries' signifies both 'announces' and 'laments'. An impressive recording of this poem by Jones does full justice to Halligan's praise of him as performer.[47]

By 1963 T. H. Jones's drinking was out of control. 'There were three kids, they were poor, the money disappeared . . . and Madeleine had to take more and more responsibility for all things.'[48] A letter to Pam and Ted Richards contains more than a hint of *hiraeth*, disorganization, self-pity and risk-taking:

. . . with the probable exception of Ted, I am the world's worst correspondent. I do remember being – startled, I think is the mot juste – by a letter from Ted last (?) year about Joss coming here – but I had met Joss . . . before your letter arrived. By the time you get this you may well, I hope, have seen my first *book* – I distinguish between this and volumes of poetry, which happen. The book is on Dylan in the Writers and Critics series, written by invitation, and I suppose it means I can't come back to Wales – that, you recognise, is all balls – I am only angling (the word reminds me – give my bloody love to Jack) – I only want the Richardses to tell me what I tell myself – this is the best book yet written on Dylan.

I also have coming out soon my third, and best, volume of poems, *The Beast at the Door.* . .

This . . . is a disgustingly inadequate letter – and it's certainly no great consolation to you to know that whenever Davies and I have been together we have had too much once for ourselves and twice for our dear friends. . . . Oh, love, love, love, to you all from all of us, and especially love to my one and only Pam and Ted. [49]

For the first time in his life he forgot his mother's birthday and wrote, disingenuously, nearly three months after the event: 'I did not realise Madeleine hadn't written to you for so long. Neither, I think, did she – she has been very busy, as I have been too. You know that I am in charge of the department, which involves a lot of work.'[50] A letter to Pat, this time a month late, offers similar excuses: 'I am terribly sorry, Pat, I did not write to you at Christmas when I wrote to the other girls . . . This was very thoughtless and unkind of me, and I hope you will forgive me.'[51]

Croft and others of Jones's friends felt that his poetry had become more flexible. His continuing drive to reinvent himself certainly led to the adoption of new personae. He discovered new techniques for distancing art and love, poetry and sexuality, from personal preoccupations, but was very apprehensive that the cures forced upon him might cause the poetry to dry up, dependent as he felt it to be upon unconventional behaviour licensed by the Muse. Here again is the Dionysiac poet doomed to accelerated self-destruction as more alcohol is required to set his words free.

'It was a need, a neurosis',[52] Jones's personal fault-line, yet he managed to write his *Dylan Thomas*, carefully shape *The Beast at the Door* and lecture impressively, if erratically. The last short story,

'Absalom, Absalom',[53] set in a bar, is a compassionate, comic dramatic monologue which perfectly captures the broken torrent of pub-talk. The least personally focused of the stories, it evokes the character of the Irish Australian, O'Bannon, who has taken his prospective son-in-law out for the obligatory pre-nuptial chat:

> All right, now, all right, you've been courting Cathy for two and a bit years – first by stealth and then by permission – though let me tell you – well, it's a special occasion, same again – but I am not the man to let sentiment interfere with me principles . . .

It exposes the religious prejudices and assertive sexism of its boastful protagonist:

> It's a nice little place, here, now, d'you think? Ol' Shirl, there, best barmaid in town. Well, of course, you may think it's not so posh – but believe you me, my boy, I have imbibed in some of the best hostelries in the western hemisphere – were you ever in Jammet's now? Ah! I thought not. Well, you know, what was it the bard said
> 'Much have I travelled in the realms of gold,
> And many men and cities seen'[54]
> – and women, me boy, and women –

Inevitably O'Bannon's monologue circles back to his lost son:

> Sure, he had the limbs on him. You're not a bad-built young feller yourself, but my boy would have topped you by a couple of inches in any direction. And the daredevil look on him. You can imagine there wasn't a girl or a woman from Skibereen to Dundalk or from Erris Head to Rosslare who didn't feel weak at the knees from the mere sight of him . . .

The betrayal is no more than hinted at: Jones leaves us to infer it from our knowledge of the Bible[55] and Faulkner. The story concludes with the suitor manoeuvring his intoxicated prospective father-in-law away from the bar:

> What d'you mean, you're taking me home? O'Bannons are never drunk. What did you call me? Dad? Dad!

> You Pommie bastard, d'you think you'd be marrying one of the O'Bannon girls tomorrow if she ever had a brother?

In addition to a developing interest in American literature and a growing reputation as a critic of it which he felt would open up opportunities in American universities,[56] Jones had some idea of a return to Wales. Madeleine encouraged it as a potential escape from his personal problems. He kept in touch with Aneirin Talfan Davies, and wrote to him, in response to *Dylan: Druid of the Broken Body*:

> I must express my thanks for your illuminating essay on Dylan . . . I find your thesis completely convincing . . . it was always obvious to anybody with any sense and feeling that Dylan was essentially a religious poet – but you have made me see clearly for the first time how Christian he was and how he was Christian, and that he was . . . more inclined to Catholicism than Nonconformity. I think this comes out clearly if one compares his poems with those of R. S. Thomas or, I imagine, mine.[57]

A further letter following a period of drying out reveals a T. H. Jones more committed to Australia than ever before and looking forward to some time in the USA.

> I shall be reviewing your *Druid* . . . on the Saturday page of *The Australian*, our new national newspaper. How easily, after six years out here, one says 'our'. You ask if I might come back. In many ways I would like to – though I would probably stop writing hiraeth-laden poems then . . . but it's not only congeniality of life that keeps me here. I came here . . . because I could not get an academic job – this, like convicts in the old days, tends to be a one way traffic. And of course my children, despite their Welsh names, are thoroughly Australian.
>
> In 1966 I have a sabbatical year. I shall be going to the States . . . I shall probably be home for a short while at the end of that year.
>
> You mentioned my two volumes of verse. I hope you saw the third one . . . which came out last year . . . I send you a batch of recent poems and would be very pleased if you could have some of them broadcast – especially the Welsh ones. Still living on our grandparents, you see.[58]

Julian Croft's view of T. H. Jones as a 'great Prince' imprisoned by 'an ethical system that he found suffocating' who responded by creating 'an impressive vision of the deracinated post war man' in search of harmony in a 'permanent and satisfying myth'[59] is persuasive. In the early poetry he flamboyantly pursued a synthesis of personal and national identity and he was always a shape-shifter, a deft deviser of personae. In dealing, however, with the failure to secure a satisfactory system of values and the resultant depression, Croft underrates the essential playfulness, the metaphysical wit of the poetry if not the poet. His view is coloured by his having come to know Jones at the nadir of his existence. Anna Rutherford, recipient of a number of love-poems, found Croft's monograph 'disappointing as biography'.[60]

A. Alvarez has explored the stress and danger involved in containing passion within artistic form: 'the greater the insecurities, the greater the artistic effort . . . the greater the risks involved'.[61] Sylvia Plath is *the* case in point. Jones identified with Dylan Thomas, Brendan Behan, Malcolm Lowry, Berryman and Hemingway, and his own early concern with an elaboration of style which has been called 'artificiality'[62] we can now read as conscious formal reflexivity. A view of the work which suggests that 'In these early volumes the voice is changeable and uncertain . . . In the last two books his own voice . . . takes over assured, simpler, direct, and the poetry becomes less intellectual, less cluttered with poetic learning and distracted with echoes'[63] fails to take adequate account, on the one hand, of the calculated use of the appropriate persona and, on the other, of the no less calculated[64] employment of appropriate and focusing echoes. What such criticism fails to grasp is the unusual combination of a restless urge to experiment and a working within and around traditional forms[65] to prove that they are adaptable to twentieth-century requirements.[66] This historicity is a fundamental aspect of the institutional reflexivness of postmodernism and it generated creative tensions.

Jones's distaste for the Movement's middle-class, English celebration of the complacencies of suburban life had to do with the realities of his Llanafan Welsh working-class background and his decision to assert a 'bardic' persona within such a life. The move to Australia produced a creative upsurge because it was an escape from suburban imprisonment and because Newcastle provided him with the necessary grand stage for the persona that accompanied the generation of the text and performance of the poetry. Given his origins and education, what he regarded as the 'descent' into the avant-garde was no solution either. Alvarez suggests that part of the gift of the serious artist is 'a weird knack of sensing and expressing the strains of his time in advance of other people'.[67] This variety of 'poetic hero' became, in the twentieth century, both victim and scapegoat. The Yeatsian 'Savage God' on display to Jones throughout the Second World War, his instinctive peasant emotional conservatism, his contrasting intellectual Marxism, the personal turmoil and then, abruptly, the hothouse of Newcastle, contributed to his feelings of guilt, shame, hostility. An intensely *public* poet, he frankly shared the hostility with his audience and risked attempting to tightrope-walk a chasm too wide to span.

'Llanafan unrevisited', composed in July 1961, before despair and alienation became dominant,[68] demonstrates the problem. Reflexive as ever, he distances himself from the potential naturalisms of the text: 'I took for emblem the upland moors and the rocky / Slopes above them', then toys with the worlds of the two Thomases: parishes are 'bitter', the fox 'ragged', the preacher 'starved'. A small warmth arises from a 'hell that once had meaning'. The people are 'small' in all the Welsh senses of the word, tight with the *arian fach*,[69] unendearing but enduring. All the poet can find to clutch at among the Australian '*good* meadows', though, is the body of some anonymous woman which has, for a while, 'a surplus of . . . sunshine'. He remains the boy from the 'hungry parish' and the proverbial 'spoiled preacher' terrified of the hell he had externalized when he attempted to escape but could not because it was among the baggage that accompanied him to Australia. This poem and ten or so others of the period evoke not the schoolboy childhood of 'Fern Hill' but a Beckett-like past against a present sterility. In the technically dazzling 'Thinking to write an ode',[70] poised and deadly serious play, he defines his own 'mix' as a poet: he is a lyricist who would like to be more substantial and his lyricism comprehends Welsh elegy. Since lyrics begin as yells of pain, they are not always, or easily, transmutable into true poetry: 'you have to be satirical to keep sane'. And he is. And he does not.

He invites us to share something we already know, but to apprehend the unsayable. The advantage of genres is that within them the reader can feel a sense of security. The mythic level of the exile/*hiraeth* genre is an exchange through which Anglo-Welsh culture addresses itself. T. H. Jones's obsession with reworking the mythic/semiotic language generated by a deeply fictive Wales was his last line of defence, an attempt to reconcile capitalist values of possessive individualism with the ethic of shared social needs, goals and sense of community. These, he speculated, had once been reconciled in the Wales/Eden myth:

> But here the sun is warm on belly and back
> As I indulge in wine and memories
> And hear above the long Pacific swell
> Stern voices of my fathers saying I lack
> Their faith, their courage, their black certainties.[71]

The attempt failed.

'Welsh bastard',[72] dedicated to David Jones, is a sparse verbalization of 'The Lord of Venedotia' (1948) and 'The Annunciation in a Welsh hill setting' (1963/4). In the former the canvas is a palimpsest of distressed signs and surfaces, the scratched wax and chalk of the drawing connoting the bruised and dirty feudal patriarch, the Romano-Celtic warrior-chieftain. The classical order of civilization is unravelling into ragged skeins even as we read the canvas. The poem, deceptively simple in form and style, is perhaps even more apocalyptic:

> I was always defeated
> My dad died at Camlann
> And his dad at Catraeth . . .

What a fall from the innocent 'bardic fury' with which 'Poem for Wales',[73] had 'proclaimed . . . In me my fathers are not dead'. What a rise into maturity. In this song of bitter experience Jones, in the last year of his life, sick and disillusioned, creates the comfort of a timeless validity for his personal encounters with war, poetry and love.

The whole of Welsh history, from the fourth century ('Sarn Elen'[74]) to the fifteenth ('Agincourt') is called in aid. *He* has 'walked Sarn Elen', 'helped to make Blodeuwedd',[75] been 'Nest's[76] lover'. *He* 'was not absent from Glyn Dwr[77] . . . or Llewelyn[78] / Or the bloody-minded Tudor'[79] 'and *he* is to be looked for 'in the annals of defeat . . . Or now and again a bloody victory'. For Wales, as for T. H. Jones, there has always been the compensation of poetry; for him, the love in a sense *is* the poetry. The juxtaposition of 'her bright face' with the 'dark hall of Cynddylan' and 'the eagle of Pengwern' evokes the *Canu Heledd*,[80] an intensely emotional response to the destruction of Cynddylan's hall and the sufferings of ninth/tenth-century Powys. The 'eagle of Pengwern' refers to 'Eryr Pengwern', one of the poems that make up the *Canu Heledd*: it describes birds of prey feasting on fallen warriors. The choice of a woman as narrator appears to have been influenced by the ancient Celtic myth which held the land to be personified by a goddess – for Jones, the White Goddess. The deeper the poet's hurt, the more complex the response.

'A storm in childhood'[81] is the most satisfyingly complete of that series of poems which have addressed lost innocence. It is a powerful interplay of past and present, the experienced poet impelled by his present neurosis to relive the innocent child's past terror. He and his cousins disobediently take the long way home so as to have more time in their own, separate world, and a thunderstorm is, it appears to them in consequence, 'loosed for us, on us'. They are among trees[82] and Blodwen, 'oldest and wisest of us' says 'The lightning kills you when it strikes the trees'.

> We ran, between the trees and the trees,
> Five children hand-in-hand, afraid of God,
> Afraid of being among the lightning-fetching
> Trees, soaked, soaked with rain, with sweat, with tears . . .

The trees have both pagan and Christian significance. They are the trees of the Celtic Cad Goddeu,[83] the mythic path the initiate must pass in pursuit of wisdom, but also of Knowledge of Good and Evil. The 'loud voice and the lambent threat' remind us of Adam hiding among trees from the angry voice of the God he has disobeyed; Llanafan is mythologized as Eden after the Fall. The stumblings of the disobedient 'Children aware of our sins',[84] get worse as the 'older terror' of the trees gets worse. They are 'waiting to be struck by the flash' of death, sin's wages. The majestic tree imagery of the White Goddess, the alphabet of trees as record of the knowledge of the world's past history, is foregrounded, but a new God has replaced the old goddess, he blazes at the children, and their 'sins which seemed such pointless things to talk / About to mild Miss Davies on the hard Sunday benches' are made, by their recognition of good and evil, only too real.

Albert Camus declares[85] that a man's works derive their 'definitive significance only from his death'. At the moment of death it may be possible to 'make the air "echo" with sterile secrets he possesses'. T. H. Jones lays before us all his faults, all his betrayals. In these last poems he identifies more and more with what Alvarez calls extremism: 'the work of poets committed to psychic exploration out along the friable edge which divides the tolerable from the intolerable'.[86] Like Lowell, Hughes and Plath he is very much aware of the craft of poetry. Alvarez suggested that Plath, under the influence of Lowell's *Life Studies*, rejected her early artificial style so as systematically to explore 'the nexus of anger, guilt, rejection, love and destructiveness . . . for her poetry to be valid it must tackle head on . . . her own death'.[87] Jones confronted the reality of death, on the evidence of 'A storm in childhood' from an early age, certainly in young manhood on the Malta convoys. The poetic confrontation begins no later than 'Lucky Jonah', and the poems of the 1960s are increasingly obsessed by age. They deal directly with the frightening experiences that lurk in the dark corners of the psyche and are explorations of what Günter Grass calls 'the black witch', that dark *doppelgänger* that is the opposite of the White Goddess.

Two poems of 1964, 'Thorn'[88] and 'Mountain death',[89] are particularly relevant. Both employ the thorn image derived from the Llanafan landscape, the 'thorns also' that the earth, in consequence of Adam's sin, 'shall bring forth'[90] and Christ's crown of thorns. The 'bloody thorn' in the singer's breast has already been encountered, and there is another version of this in 'Cwmchefri rocks',[91] where Jahveh, symbolized as a buzzard, fails to pierce the child with his 'bloody thorn' which, however, 'Might mark you[92] if you dared to read his book'. The beast at the door has thorns in his pelt. In 'Thorn', arguably Jones's most frightening poem, the image is changed again: the solitary tree, 'punished' by the winds is 'Companion for a bitter mind / And the blood's dark' and the anguished poet prays to be 'relentless in the wind / As the thorn, as harsh / As the thrashed and lonely thorn'. This use of the image recurs in 'My grandfather going blind':[93] 'He had a thorny faith not to be beaten / Down by any wind or language'. All joy has gone, endurance only remains.[94] 'Mountain death'[95] takes the final step, from endurance of painful life ('to be born / Is to wear a keen thorn . . . Until death is due') to acceptance of death:

> Death is good on the taciturn
> Mountain, in the wind
> More close than a friend;
> Under a familiar thorn
> Pay for your birth
> On unrequiting earth.

T. H. Jones's last review appeared posthumously,[96] a very personal statement. It deals with *Penguin Modern Poets 6, Jack Clemo, Edward Lucie Smith and George Macbeth*[97] and the Penguin anthology, *Poetry of the Thirties*.[98] The 1930s was, he says, a period when those who grew up in it realized that 'we were growing up in a decade that was somehow important – a decade that would be remembered in, say, the way the year 1848 is remembered'. Retrospectively, the reader might agree that Auden's 'low, dishonest decade' was nevertheless a legendary one:

> Reading the book produced in me . . . a feeling of tremendous familiarity . . . like going home after a long absence and finding that nothing had changed . . . The 30's was the decade of depression, hunger marches, Communism as an inspiring faith, The Spanish Civil War, Hitler, The Left Book Club, the first Penguins . . . and the constant threat of the war that finally came. To most young people today it must seem as remote and fabulous as the pre-1914 world of secret Sassenachs and *Memoirs of a Fox-Hunting Man* did to us.

This was the decade dominated by Auden, Spender, Day Lewis and MacNeice, but also the one in which Dylan Thomas's poetry began to appear and, 'astonishing to realise', John Betjeman's. It was the decade of Michael Roberts's anthologies and Geoffrey Grigson's astringent periodical, *New Verse*:

> young poets, on the whole, were fierce in their social concerns and loud in their commitment. My own particular delight was to find again in this collection 'Carol' by John Short, about whom I know nothing except that he wrote this poem:

> There was a Boy bedded in bracken
> Like to a sleeping snake all curled he lay
> On his thin navel turned the spinning sphere
> Each feeble finger fetched seven suns away
> He was not dropped in good for lambing weather
> He took no suck when shook buds sing together
> But he is come in cold as workhouse weather
> Poor as a Salford child.

Allusive lyricism in strong, simple language. It might have been written by Jones himself.

He is very clear about the poetry he dislikes and the extent to which he has moved away from the English literary scene:

> I am out of touch with the movements and counter movements, groupings and re-groupings on the contemporary English literary scene, but I gather that Mr Lucie Smith is regarded as a poet of some importance. I cannot imagine why. His poems are formal exercises, correct, unexciting and dull. Of Mr Macbeth's poems perhaps all that needs to be said is that every one of the poems here has a note to explain to the reader what it is about. The note to 'The Son' is typical: 'a mortuary attendant rapes the body of a dead woman. He associates her with his mother, who died of a liver disease. He believes in a concrete form of resurrection by the power of love'. It would be impossible to deduce any of this from reading the poem . . .

It is with Jack Clemo that he identifies:

> A Cornishman, poor, suffering severe physical disabilities and . . . an uncompromising Calvinist . . . I share none of Mr Clemo's attitude, but I admire his poetry. It is hard, human poetry, making no concessions to the reader or to contemporary fashion, disturbing yet rewarding to read and re-read.

About Calvinism Jones protests too much; for the rest he has summarized his own achievement.

The body of T. H. Jones was found in the early evening of 29 January 1965, by two teenage boys who, walking along the cliffs about three-quarters of a mile from his home, saw it floating in the Bogey Hole. This is a bathing pool hewn for their officers out of the solid rock by transported convicts. It faces south into the swells booming in from the Pacific, and 'can be reached only by climbing down a steep ladder'.[99] The boys called the police, and Constable Ramsay, who, with their help and that of a colleague, recovered the body, suggested at the Coroner's Inquest that 'The dead man had apparently been walking at the foot of the steps leading down to the Bogey Hole when he had slipped and fallen into the water. Waves were washing to the foot of the steps.'[100]

During this summer holiday the Australian Association of American Studies ran a very successful summer school. T. H. Jones, as secretary, organized this and took a prominent part as lecturer and reader. At the end of the plenary session on the morning of the 29th, there was 'a conflagration . . . when Harri wanted to make a comment and the Chair of the Panel told him to refrain . . . By then Harri had had a couple of drinks but was not drunk. He was offended and angry and left the meeting in a huff.'[101] Clive Hart says that Jones departed muttering about friends who had deserted him; it appears that he went into town for a few more drinks.

Two friends brought him home in the later afternoon just as we were leaving to change library books for the long weekend coming up. When we returned home soon after, all the lights in the house had been turned off (unusual) and Harri had gone. I drove Richard[102] round the pubs but we never saw Harri again . . . At 11 p.m. Brin Newton John and his wife, Valerie, called round to . . . tell me that Harri was dead . . .[103]

A cable was sent to Jones's parents, and Madeleine wrote the same night:

you will have received a dreadful cable telling you of Harri's death. He was walking by a rock pool, a deep swimming pool, Ruth and Non's favourite haunt, yesterday evening after dusk, slipped and fell in and drowned . . . He had had a most successful week at the Summer School . . . last night he was pretty exhausted and decided to go for a walk in the fresh air and to look at the sea. Alas, alas by 11 p.m. I knew what had happened, the ghastly truth, and I had to tell Sian, Ruth and Non. They have all three been marvellous and recovered their equilibrium, they adored Harri as you know and he loved them as much as God knows how and God knows how I can replace his affection for them.[104]

For a time there was gossip. Inevitably, and most of all in Wales, suicide was suggested. Clive Hart believes that Jones had reached a crisis:

If one could know the state of Harri's mind on that night, then certain other mysteries about Harri's personality would be revealed. Until his death I would have said Harri was utterly unsuicidal and that after the death the question needed to be asked and I am still puzzled . . . But in his physical life he was such a careful operator, he avoided danger, he did not take risks, he was cautious.[105]

It is certain that he had been angry and felt slighted at the seminar; it is certain that he was drunk and that he switched the lights off before leaving the house. Was this out of pique because he felt, confusedly, that everyone had gone out *deliberately*, had 'deserted' him in an hour of need? Any man might, under the influence of drink, find it amusing, a challenge, a kind of revenge for some imagined slight, to do something dangerous that would 'serve "them" right'. Jones's lifelong obsession with the sea would make it natural for him then to walk close by it, hearing the sound of the waves, feeling the cleanness of their spray – and it is easy, when drunk, to slip, and hard to save yourself if you fall.[106] Lucky Jonah had met his death as ironically as the friend who survived two shipwrecks only to die in a road accident. 'Adrift'[107] is apposite here:

> I shun the foreign land,
> Content to share the waves
> With the ghosts I understand.
>
> Companioned so by ghosts
> I ride this burial sea
> Away from the living coasts.

And so remain dumbfound
With the sound of the sea, and the sea
Of the sound I sound.

Scandal was soon replaced with a sense of terrible loss. Norman Talbot wrote 'an eulogy that totally lacks any sense of balance'.[108] A gauche modern 'Lycidas', redolent of loss, it plays reflexively with signifiers of T. H. Jones's obsessions:

> The poetry he loved was sea – all seas
> The same – bones and the blubbered sway of the tide . . .
> He should have been stolen in a dolphin swoop
> But his death was the brief flat explosion of a face
> On the water in the black cliff's shadow
> And the longer indignity of breath bubbling
> Away, slippery, fished for in dark places
> Heaving and sinking with older urgencies.
> Then silence, then the edge-courting feet,
> Hauled, hobbled in by the midwife's belt . . .
> In the thick pubs, the fading conversations,
> He was haunted by his poetry; the mirror
> Of the eyes so wary he thought they were wild
> Showed poems racing like flood waters from mountains
> To the ceaseless dance of the undersea.[109]

John Stowell, in contrast, retained 'two outstanding memories: hearing the thunderous reading of Milton . . . and a kind of quiet, forgiving friendliness which made one glad to be with him'.[110]

The funeral was on 3 February:

> Your little Harri was cremated this afternoon and I hope to send the ashes to you to scatter in the churchyard at Llanfihangel. He was given a wonderful funeral in the Cathedral and every possible person in attendance – a great throng of sorrowing friends. Magnificent organ music and a marvellous sermon ending with his own Poem, 'Late Spring in Wales'[111] from *The Beast at the Door*.
> His coffin was draped with a Union Jack owing to his career in the Royal Navy and just one lovely wreath of flowers from his four women here, Madeleine, Sian, Rhiannon and Ruth . . . I feel so dreadful about Harri as I always felt he belonged to you and I must look after him well, alas, but you have three beautiful and

happy grand-daughters and they have a lot of Harri's charm and intelligence. He was very proud of them and they of him.[112]

Madeleine wrote to Aneirin Talfan Davies:

> I feel that you would be pleased at how delighted he was to know that you had arranged for some of his poems to be included in the anthology of poetry to be published as part of the Cardiff Commonwealth Arts Festival celebrations, and the editor, Mr John S. Williams, contacted him only last week, and Harri gave his permission – perhaps you would be kind enough to let him know of Harri's death. Perhaps you could let my parents-in-law be informed if any of Harri's poems are broadcast – he was their only son and, as you will only too fully understand, having suffered the same cruel fate not long ago, they are deeply grieved. To see or hear his work will please them.
>
>   . . . Harri left his bank account in the red – fashionable and easy to do these days – if he is paid for any poetry used for B.B.C. readings, he has three healthy young daughters with good appetites . . . he has unpublished poetry still here. Sad, but very good.[113]

Talfan Davies had already received the news and written to Pat Power:

> I was deeply shocked at the news of Harri's death which I read in the *South Wales Echo* on Saturday night. I only met him once but this once seemed to put an effect upon him, for he wrote two poems rising from the effect of our meeting. I happened to put his poetry on the air and was very glad some years ago to receive a copy of his first volume of poems signed by himself. This is a tragic loss to Wales and I hope to be able to arrange some kind of tribute to him in the future . . .[114]

Hart-Davis approached the Royal Literary Fund and, through her solicitors, Madeleine thanked him:

> We can assure you that the circumstances of this case are such as to be deserving . . . The inquest on Mr Jones concluded on Thursday 11th. instant and the finding of the court was that he died from asphyxia when he was accidentally drowned after apparently slipping on rocks on the sea shore.[115]

Talfan Davies's tribute was broadcast on 29 July, with contributions from Ted and Pam Richards, Pat Power, Talfan Davies, Joss Davies and the recorded voice of T. H. Jones himself, but the death went largely unnoticed in the literary community. Meic Stephens, reflecting in 1990 on the inaugural number of his *Poetry Wales* (Spring 1965) wrote:

> I knew perhaps a dozen young poets who in one way or another might have been dubbed Anglo-Welsh. Only three had volumes to their names and the only magazines that published their work were the *London Welshman* and the *Anglo-Welsh Review* . . . Indeed, most of the poets I had read were living in England at that time contributing to English literary reviews. It seemed that the brilliance of *Wales* whose brief revival had dazzled my undergraduate years was snuffed out for ever. Of the older generation David Jones was known only to a select few, Vernon Watkins and R. S. Thomas were established abroad but begrudged at home, and hardly a hair was turned when T. H. Jones whose three volumes were almost unknown among his own people was drowned in Australia.[116]

Madeleine proposed a final, posthumous volume, and had the manuscript ready by 12 August 1965, when she wrote to Hart-Davis:

> Here is the collection of Harri's poems that you have offered to consider for publication. They were nearly all written in 1964, apart from 'The Colour of Cockcrowing'. I have all of Harri's correspondence with you and realise that you were not keen to publish this poem and 'The Beast at the Door'. But it has always been popular with his friends and I wonder if you would be kind enough to include it in this more permanent form. Harri loved reading it!
>
> I hope that you will consent to its inclusion and perhaps we can make *The Colour of Cockcrowing* the title of the book.
>
> We have been fairly drastic in our eliminations with the advice of Doug Muecke and Harri's colleagues, Doctor Norman Talbot and Mr Clive Hart of Newcastle University.
>
> The poems have been checked and re-checked very carefully and we have only altered the punctuation, in a few cases where it appeared misleading. I hope that there are sufficient poems to make a volume, but if you do need extra material there are a few

poems from an earlier period that could be used. Doug Muecke, who is a Senior Lecturer in English at Monash University, Victoria, will be happy to have any suggestions concerning the Preface.[117]

In the event, *The Colour of Cockcrowing*, compiled by Madeleine and Jill Stowell with the aid of the small committee mentioned in her letter, and with a perceptive preface by Doug Muecke, contained only seven poems available for, but not included in *The Beast at the Door*. Fifty poems had been entered in the *Black Book* since publication of that volume, the last of these, 'Cotton Mather', filling it. A further nineteen existed in manuscript. Since *The Colour of Cockcrowing*, though it is a strong volume and contains some of Jones's best poems, was neither selected nor arranged by him,[118] we shall explore the most significant poems of the last twenty-one months of his life, which, as far as composition is concerned, appears to have ended in October 1964, and then deal briefly with the volume's critical reception. If Jones had not composed any poetry for three months this would have confirmed his worst fears and partially explain the mood in which he passed his final days.

Rather more than usual of the poems are occasional: a reflection upon someone's MA, someone else's marriage. Three more to Rae Richards indicate continuing mutual inspiration; one of them, 'Instructions to a painter: for her birthday',[119] with its Arthurian imagery is worthy of publication: it relates interestingly to 'Anoeth bid bedd i Arthur'.[120] References to drowning become more frequent in the sea-poems and poems of unhappy love are common. It is worth beginning with these two groups: all of the *hiraeth* poems[121] were rightly deemed worthy of inclusion.

'Unsuccessful attempt at suicide'[122] for the first time depicts the sea with no associations of adventure, danger – even interest. It is 'flat', it 'smugs' and 'oils' in. The poet looks for inspiration ('I dive for a word'), finds none, metaphorically comes up for the third time and is rescued by a woman who 'breathe[s] the flat verse / Of my limp body awake'. He promises to create, tomorrow, 'A kind of storm for your storm's sake'. 'Here is the peace of the fathers',[123] which *was* collected, may now be seen in a different light. Addressing drowned friends, 'Old talkers who now talk ghostlily well', it concludes:

> may the peace where your bones dwell
> Requite in all green undertows
> The bitter overtones
> Of my unpeaceful bones.

'Adrift'[124] similarly has the poet sharing the waves 'With the ghosts I understand', and 'Eyes, hair, sea, fall',[125] which typically compares the physical attractions of a woman to the sea, contains the lines 'Now I inherit my kingdom, the bonestrewn / Bottom of the sea my bones knew before'. Sex, sea and Wales, the three major themes of Jones's poetry, are brought together in 'But if it be a boy you shall put him to the sea':[126]

> The lecherous and griefless sea
> Was always more beckoning than gardens
> To a boy from bare, exciting mountains . . .
> The books did not tell me, nor your griefless flesh
> That oblivion can also be found in gardens . . .
>   the sea's obvious oblivion
> Because of some salt lecheries . . .
>   the last and salt oblivion.

The final word is 'My country, my grief'[127] with its echoes of 'Prayer to the steep Atlantick stream':

> Anguish is my country.
>   I would not recognize
> A land where only fair winds blow
>   And the sun shines.
>
> But the land where every wind
>   Is the breath of guilt
> Is home, and let the loud seas lash
>   Wherever I have slept.
>
> My paradise will be despair
>   And the cold winds that blow
> About the rocks, about your hair
>   And the grief I know.

Of the love-poems, 'Infidelity'[128] is a not entirely convincing excuse for adultery:

> I could not bear
>   not in that unsustaining air
> Your brutal absence, so I made,
> Breathless and afraid,
> A sort of image of you.
>   I didn't think you'd care
> That for a moment she was passing fair,
> Or dare to believe that I would dare.

'After the quarrel'[129] is disillusioned and self-pitying:

> The unforgiving door
> Will greet you on your soused return . . .
>   Your presence or your absence
> To her are merely animal . . .

and 'A failed marriage'[130] pictures a ghastly relationship devoid of physical, emotional and intellectual comfort:

> I crumple under the hurt hump of marriage,
> Burden too hard, the bound sticks
> Writhing, together and hostile, the belly empty,
> Sucked dry, wrinkled flat back to
> The backbone.
>   Disowned now that original glory,
> Dishevelled hair upon a procreant pillow.
>
> Not even the ignominy of love,
> Only unspeaking bodies that do not touch,
> And shivering minds huddled in separateness.

In 'A small vision of hell'[131] this 'most sexually alive man' finds that sex itself has turned, like his once-loved sea, to nightmare. All the archetypal ingredients are deployed: rotten 'apples', a hairless penis-turned-serpent, sexual disgust, guilt. The poet lampoons himself as Don Juan slavering at Woman exploded into erogenous fragments: 'hairy parts', 'navels, armpits, nipples'. Its conclusion reveals a frightening neurosis: 'The last thing I remember before waking, / I'd turned aside to eat the hairless snake.'

Most of the published poems show a love that endures and sustains:

A stammering repetition of your name
Can jerk me out of any waking nightmare . . .
Permit me stammer with my voice and hands
A little longer: homage, thanks, and prayer . . .
It is your bright hair's shadow by which I write.[132]

Of these, 'Anoeth bid bedd i Arthur' must be quoted in full because, apology and elegy, saddest of love-lyrics, it achieves such pathos:

'A grave for March, a grave for Gwythur
A grave for Gwgan Red-sword
A hidden thing is the grave of Arthur'
Old Welsh, *The Stanzas of the Graves*[133]

'*Anoeth* . . . refers to something difficult to acquire, hidden, precious, a wonder.'
David Jones, *Epoch and Artist*

And my grave, when you make it,
Will be hidden too,
Because, although a common man,
I married a princess,
Precious, a wonder.

So I would have my tomb unknown
But, wherever it is,
Quondam and *futurus*
Written on it
So I may hope when Arthur comes again
I may recover my lost princess.

It is craft of a high order that can so ennoble human imperfection. Welsh history and legend, above all the brief, bright, tragic glory of Arthur,[134] lost in darkness yet preserved in hope, enfold the pedestrian story. The singer leans on the thorn, but the song has no false note.

The compilers of *The Colour of Cockcrowing* appropriately placed 'Cotton Mather remembers the trial of Elizabeth How: Salem, Massachusetts, 30 June 1692'[135] in section II, after a group of poems of the kind that Jones himself titled 'Hiraeth' in *The Beast at the Door*. Although set in a previous century and a different country, 'Cotton Mather' belongs with the *hiraeth* poems because it is a religious poem which portrays a sensitive intellectual struggling to come to terms with evil and human imperfection. T. H. Jones said of Dylan Thomas that it was 'clear . . . that Thomas was essentially a religious poet',[136] and the same is true of himself. Anna Rutherford's impression was:

> Not a religious man in the conventional sense of the word, but in other ways . . . one of the most religious people I ever met. And his presence alongside me . . . made me very much aware of his desperate search for a faith, and the fear and defeat he felt in his inability to find it.[137]

We have seen in 'Spoiled preacher'[138] that the ministry had been a possible career. 'Cotton Mather' is the dramatic monologue of a troubled preacher, and Jones enters seriously into the part.[139]

The poem filled the last available pages of the *Black Book*. After copying it, Jones signed off: 'Newcastle. N.S.W. September 1964'. Its epigraph is taken from Marion L. Starkey's *The Devil in Massachusetts*, it comprises 172 lines in five sections and its form is a blank verse that echoes seventeenth-century diction. It is based on the actual words of its subject. In a concluding note Jones tells us: 'I have taken some liberty with Mather's language (see *The Wonders of the Invisible World*, 1693, and his *Diary*) and have anachronistically used some phrases from the *Magnalia Christi Americana*, 1702.' Mather (1663–1728) was the son of Increase Mather and the grandson of John Cotton and Richard Mather. He attended Harvard at the age of twelve and received his MA six years later from the hands of his father, then president of the college. A Congregational minister and the most famous of the New England Puritans, he was, like T. H. Jones, both intellectually brilliant and a divided personality, believing, on the one hand, in the existence of witchcraft and on the other in modern science.[140] He described his life as 'a continual conversation with heaven' and spent it alternately rejoicing in his salvation and agonizing over his damnation.

The Salem Witch Trials occupied almost the whole of 1692 and the episode was brought to an end only by the Superior Court in

1693. It was a period of extreme religious hysteria set off by the strange symptoms exhibited initially by two girls aged nine and eleven respectively. Their 'possession' included blasphemous screaming and trance-like episodes and the minister and his parishioners concluded that the girls had been taken over by the devil. Twenty people, most of them women, were hanged as witches. When Elizabeth How was examined on 31 May she pleaded 'If it was the last moment I was to live, God knows I am innocent . . .', but she was executed on 19 July. Anyone whose behaviour or views offended against the conventions or social order of the time was vulnerable and Mather, some of whose views were certainly unconventional, was deeply upset. He joined his father in warning judges against the evidence of individuals who claimed to have been attacked by spectres of people they knew and, in Arthur Miller's interpretation,[141] had a grudge against:

> For my own part, I was always afraid
> Of condemnation on feeble evidence
> Of spectral representings, and testified so
> In public and in private . . .

But he did believe in possession by the devil. He had endeavoured, however, to persuade the community 'To try without more bitter methods prayer / And fasting to end these heavy trials' and was deeply distressed to be regarded later as 'A prosecutor in the time of witchcraft'.

He was present at the trial of Elizabeth How, and, as the epigraph puts it, his

> . . . righteous indignation that such things could be was unconsciously submerged in the thrill of having been present as spectator at a collision between heaven and hell . . . So far as he was concerned, the delirium might begin again with full force tomorrow.

As a devout Puritan, Mather considers that

> The chief task
> Of history is to record, as I have done,
> Men's Christ-given virtues, and instil

> The fear of sin and infamy, of evil
> Words and deeds.

He naturally regards the episode as heaven's dreadful judgement: he was a traditionalist who fought all his life against the complacency and decline from spirituality of his community and believed that, as in the case of Job, God had given the devil permission to afflict Salem. He took an active, spiritual part in the whole affair, praying, fasting, visiting the court, preaching to the accused in prison; although he 'could not allow some principles / Some of the Judges had espoused', he defends them as sincere men, striving in 'agony of soul' to carry out God's will.

The superstitious furore was resolved not by God but by Governor Phips, who dissolved the court and set up the Superior Court. Those who had not been hanged or pressed to death were brought to trial in May 1693. There were no further convictions. Looking back, Mather can hardly believe it all happened:

> Were these things here in Salem? Did help come?
> Is God's good wilderness now purified?
> Or must we fear and go in constant sorrow
> That we are still afflicted, that tomorrow
> May bring back to Salem that delirium?

Or, as Milton put it, 'Good and evil, we know, in the field of this world, grow up together, almost inseparably; and the knowledge of good is so involved and interwoven with the knowledge of evil'.[142]

There is nothing here of the exuberant rejoicing in a fallen but teemingly beautiful world that had characterized 'The colour of cockcrowing' five years earlier. There is, indeed, no joy at all in 'Cotton Mather', only the nightmare of witch-hysteria and the agonies of a divided man. T. H. Jones saw parallels between the New England colony and the small, chapel-haunted community that had shaped his own divided psyche: he believed emotionally, and disbelieved intellectually, in a vindictive God, just as Mather was prepared to suffer for both scientific progress[143] and traditional Puritan dogma.

There is no joy, either, in 'Improbable land',[144] the opening poem of *The Colour of Cockcrowing*. This Petrarchan sonnet is about the way 'that incessant fall falls through my veins'. Its octave characterizes Wales as 'my improbable land', a harsh place of 'stone and rain'; the sestet contrasts with this the 'sunbright day' of Australia in whose light the poet, his bones 'hewn from that sad rock', sees more plainly some of the 'strains and stains'. There is even less in 'On re-reading the Twenty Third Psalm':[145]

> No uncompanionable divinity
> Comforts me now beside these unstill waters,
> Nor in this shadow do I want to shout green praises . . .

This poem symbolizes Wales as a rotten Eden, a place of half-dead trees and maggotty sheep,[146] the font and origin of all the lies: 'the family lie, the pastor's lie / And all the lies that I have told myself'. The contrast he makes with the beautiful, consolatory language of the Twenty-third Psalm could not be more savage:

> what I remember, is a dead sheep
> Stinking in what we called a meadow, a pastor
> Gutsily taking more than a proper tithe,
> And three crows, indolently flapping
> Back to a rotten, thunder-riven oak
> When I disturbed their happy rotten luncheon.

It is hardly necessary to add 'I walk / In the valley of the shadow and am not comforted'. It is some consolation that his daughters, 'who never knew my God', have escaped.

The opening lines of 'Welsh pastoral elegy'[147] exemplify the religious conflict:

> You could, I suppose, make some parable
> About Dai, stone and story him in a way,
> What the Lord giveth, and so on, but I
> Don't believe in these sermons which I love.

It goes on to evoke the backbreaking toil of farm-work and the antagonism between the two friends who 'quietly killed each other, / Slicing the tops off swedes with frozen fingers'. 'Welsh childhood'[148] pictures the man with 'A bible in his mind, / A pulpit for his mouth' who 'will never be out of the wind, / As long as he has breath'. 'With a distant bow to Mrs Hemans',[149] 'My grandfather going blind'[150] and 'For my grandfather'[151] all celebrate 'Old Crogau' and show how obsessively his grandson's mind had turned back to childhood and ancestry. The first regrets personal inadequacy: 'I had not bulk enough to fill the chair / Grandfather left me when he died . . . I try to fill your chair with all my shame'. The second echoes this with 'could not speak his language' and 'Lacked his mountain skills' and concludes

> The old names still resound
> For me of farms, men, ponies, dogs,
> The old names that are all that I possess
> Of my own language, proud then
> And prouder now to call myself only
> Young Crogau, old Crogau's grandson

throwing us back to the fictions of childhood, in particular the extraordinary, virile, happy old pagan of 'My grandfather would have me be a poet',[152] and the boy who loved him. The third evokes Llanafan and exile:

> No fire spoke to me out of a thornbush,
> No true Book pleached or preached me on the hills,
> I went down to the sea, to the great waters,
> Rhymed in the antipodes of language,
> But talk with a shepherd in the winds above Cwmcrogau.

'Taffy was transported'[153] uses the ballad form for a lighter comment on exile. The poem is reminiscent of Dylan Thomas's Eli Jenkins poems, which Jones liked, or Sankey and Moody's hymns which, unlike Lawrence, he claimed he did not:

> Over there, the hills of Sion
>   Tempt with their peculiar light,
> Eternal beacons to the pilgrim
>   Stumbling in this southern night.
>
> With his eyes on heavenly mansions,
>   Treading where his fathers trod,
> Knowing that he's even further
>   From the comfort of his God . . .

And the lost sheep find salvation
Underneath a crooked star.

The famous 'Back?',[154] dedicated to an unsympathetic R. S. Thomas, recalls the 'old country that sings and kills' of 'Land of my fathers', listing many reasons for staying away from Wales – 'the narrow path', 'shamed memories', 'chapel . . . charade', 'ingrowing quarrels' – before, with typical panache,[155] bursting into

Of course I'd go back if somebody'd pay me
To live in my own country
Like a bloody Englishman.

He concludes that he will have to be content

with the curlew's cry
And the salmon's taut belly

And the waves, of water and of fern
And words, that beat unendingly
On the rocks of my mind's country.

'The solitary wanderer'[156] identifies Wales as the paradise lost and portrays the poet as an exiled, solitary, Christless pilgrim pursuing the never-to-be-met Godot. The postlapsarian earth 'snarls'; it is full of thistles, burrs and thorns; his progress is followed by the 'evil eye of the toad'; he goes 'stoutly armed', carrying a 'twisted stick'. The interface between himself and nature is defined in a sound-image calculated to set the reader's teeth on edge: 'the drawn, hinged grinding of a gate'. Here is the cosmic terror that Mikhail Bakhtin called 'the heritage of man's ancient impotence in the presence of nature'.[157]

Poems like this one, 'Thorn'[158] and 'Mountain death'[159] mirror the despair at moral evil felt by writers such as William Golding and Mervyn Peake. T. H. Jones particularly admired the latter, whose:

Out of the chaos of my doubt
And the chaos of my art
I turn to you inevitably.[160]

might have been written by himself. More significantly, they enter the territory explored by Graham Sutherland in his studies of twisted trees and thorns in Wales, later synthesized in his extraordinary *Crucifixion* for St Matthew's church, Northampton. Here the tortured Christ is pierced with thorns of light and arc-ed with wire: the infamous post-Belsen Christ of no resurrection. The imagery of the lapsed Nonconformist thus coincides with that of the Catholic obsessed with the violence of mankind and the inevitable decay of nature. 'A Welsh poet finds a proper story'[161] returns to Llanafan's 'beginning garden' to ask forgiveness; seduced, like Adam, by sexual attraction, fallen, the poet takes a final defiant look back at 'sinful joy':

> In a garden beginning he finds a proper story
> And lets the paper bellow, bark and build it
> For him while he cradles in the treetop in Wales
> His silence and the serpent and the woman
> And all that glory.

The publication of *The Colour of Cockcrowing* met the usual mixed response. Elizabeth Jennings noted that:[162] 'His last verses were sombre and pulsing with life. The two qualities, as Jones demonstrated, are not incompatible.' Bernard Bergonzi[163] felt that the poems contained predictable echoes of Dylan Thomas

> but a more noticeable influence is R. S. Thomas . . . They share an unidealistic view of Wales and the Welsh which, nevertheless, stops some way short of cynicism or rejection . . . of the two, Jones is the more energetic and restless writer. He is at his best in 'A Storm in Childhood', a wonderfully successful poem which looks back on childhood without any softening nostalgia, and with a firmness and flexibility of rhythm that mark his late style . . . Another effective poem, of a more sophisticated kind, is 'Girl Reading John Donne', which wearily exploits the male academic's ambiguous feelings about a girl student. Jones was an excellent poet who was clearly moving into a new phase of maturity at the time of his tragic death.

Herbert Williams[164] felt that the best poems were the 'colloquial . . . conversational ones'. He found Jones a 'striking and original talent'.

The most challenging review, typically acerbic, was by Terence Hawkes.[165] He found Muecke's preface vague, large-gestured and mummifying:

> Breathes there a Welsh poet writing in English who doesn't search for unity, who doesn't write about love, sex, sin and religion (one word, surely?), who doesn't arrange (to call again on Mr Muecke) for land and sea motifs to alternate in his work, perhaps as by-products to the 'gift of the rhythmic musicality' and as prelude to the frequent appearance of The Garden of Eden and The Paradise Lost themes and the sense of exile, not only from Wales, but also from religion.

Hawkes finds the poems 'less terrifying and more true to the complexities of life in Wales than their surface . . . or their author's bardic persona suggest' and sees Jones as

> steering between these, the Scylla and Charybdis of Anglo-Welsh poetry (perhaps, in a larger sense, of Welsh culture: the two Thomases have it in them to embody the polarities of body and soul, disorder and order, boozer and Bethel, Saturday night and Sunday morning).

Hawkes says that Jones's problem was the search for his own voice and he praises most the poetry that exemplifies the search; 'here and in many places Mr Jones seems to me to engage fruitfully and honestly with a genuine problem of his culture . . . significantly these are poems about breaking free from the past and its demands'. He praises 'Back?', finding it more complicated than it at first appears in that it recognizes the decay in the Welsh Eden as having an internal origin, 'the spectacle of his own culture reaching out for an alien one, and desiring it', and says that T. H. Jones's dilemma was how to avoid the Thomases as the best way of keeping up with the Joneses. He concludes that Jones's death has meant the loss of an original Welsh poet almost at birth.

Norman Talbot,[166] attempting a retrospective assessment, was right to emphasize that Jones treats the lapsed state as preferable to primal innocence. '"I can't imagine what a good poet would write about if he didn't have Original Sin", Harri once said.'[167] Talbot captures the essence when he says that the poetry involves a genuine and humorous delight in the temptation towards somewhat less original sins and the rather (Manichean) guilty self-recognitions in the mirror or in the nightmare are often mocking, especially when linked to the realisation that middle age is approaching fast.

Jones's modern, sophisticated myths concern masculinity and femininity, the family, success and failure of the search for identity, but they are, in aggregate, a pilgrimage to nowhere. For Barthes,[168] a myth is a culture's way of thinking about something important, making meaning from fragments of disparate realities. Jones mythologizes factual and fictional characters, places and events, to examine through his poetry the distinctions between dominant and counter myths. The poems about Wales and the Welsh evoke an alternative vision focused on the boundaries of historical time: between the first and second flowering; between the loss of identity and its partial recovery. As the poet of actual exile, his mythologizing of its semiotic definition at least is concerned to produce a discourse of cultural self-identity which is the site of the struggle for more than Welsh cultural hegemony.

Anthony Giddens[169] says that the theme of the decentring of the subject should not lead to the disappearance of self as agent. Structuralism and post-structuralism have certainly de-emphasized the knowledgeability of human behaviour. Lévi-Strauss[170] has shown 'not how men think in myths, but how myths operate in men's minds without their being aware of the fact'. The 'I' as a continuous selfhood has been overthrown by Barthes and Lacan. Raymond Williams has stressed that the defining characteristic of the kind of work Jones was struggling to produce was its explicit and self-conscious knowledgeability and its intertextuality. As Lowell has said, 'A poem needs to contain a man's contradictions' and Jones was self-divided most obviously in his inability to shake off the chapel ethics of his childhood – 'a God / Renounced but not forgotten'.[171] Meaning is not constructed merely by the interplay of signifiers in these texts, but, as Giddens has suggested, by the intersection of the production of signifiers with objects and events in the world focused and organized via the acting individual. T. H. Jones would himself stress in his writing Marx's contention that people make history, but not that of their own choosing. In Australia Jones remade his personal history, but could not escape the destiny he so often attempted to deny:

> I thought here, now,
> Said the old poet
> To get rid of my chains . . .
> And the convict said to the poet,
> You never had any chains, son.
> And the poet replied,
> You haven't noticed the way I write.[172]

Roy Pascall,[173] reflecting on the idea of truth in autobiography, recalls how Jean Cocteau, asked to contribute to a volume about autobiography, asserted that 'every line we write, every blot, composes our self-portrait and denounces us', whilst Gertrude Stein thought autobiography easy to write. Pascall[174] concluded: 'anyone may write memoirs; true autobiography can only be written by men and women pledged to their innermost selves'. Paradoxically, T. H. Jones's most elaborate 'lies' confirm this important truth.

1966–2000

It was Always the Colour of the Cockrow

O ver the next decade T. H. Jones's reputation declined in both Australia and Wales. An award in his memory was established in Newcastle and its first winner was, appropriately, the Chatterton of Australian poetry, Michael Dransfield, 'who from precocious adolescence to his death at the age of twenty-four seems to have rejected all possible solutions except extinction'.[1] Jones did not feature in the key defining anthology of Anglo-Welsh poetry, *Welsh Voices*,[2] and had only a single poem[3] in *This World of Wales*.[4] He had five poems in *The Lilting House*[5] and fourteen in *Twelve Modern Anglo-Welsh Poets*,[6] but was not one of the poets in *Ten Anglo-Welsh Poets*.[7] In 1976 Meic Stephens, a consistent admirer, commissioned the monograph by Julian Croft[8] and out of this, also at Meic Stephens's instigation, arose the *Collected Poems*.[9] The translations of poems by Roberto Sanesi which had appeared in *Songs of a Mad Prince* were omitted to save space and because the editors considered that they had been included in that weakest of the four volumes largely to bulk it out.[10] Julian Croft was able, as a result, to make a selection of twenty-nine previously uncollected poems from the *Black Book*.[11]

A typical 1970s assessment is that of Roland Mathias:

> At first over-impressed by Dylan Thomas, and later by all kinds of literary concepts, Harri gradually leaves the artificial virtuoso performance of his second book, *Songs of a Mad Prince* (which reads very much as though it consisted of rejects from his first), for a clearer personal statement. Because he was rarely able, even towards the end, to treat love without some literary as well as physical posturing, his most impressive poems are about his childhood, about Wales and guilt, about the impossibility of going back, the unsatisfactoriness of going faithless on.[12]

To others it was his nationalism that appealed. Harri Webb was interested enough to write 'In memory of Harri Jones',[13] one of his best poems:

> From Irfon, guilty water
> And up the Chwefri[14] where
> A dead prince and a dead poet
> Called me the road leads
> From Epynt[15] where all words
> Fail in the witless wind.
> You did well to get out of
> This hole in the middle of Wales,
> Only there is nowhere else
> Anywhere. I went on:
> Dylife,[16] broken teeth
> Snarling, Clywedog,[17] a wound
> Laying bare the black Silurian
> Bedrock of rotten bone.
> Were you perhaps lucky
> Not to come back to this land
> Of dead villages and ruined harvests?

Webb has left accounts of how the poem came to be written which give us an indication of how T. H. Jones was viewed in contemporary literary circles in Wales:

I never knew him personally but heard a lot about him as a larger-than-life sort of character who'd had a blazing affair with Rachel Roberts, the actress, when they were contemporaries at Aberystwyth; he lived a very conspicuously 'poetic' life up to and, I suppose, including his suicide [*sic*] in Australia . . . The journey described, through empty, dead country, so much at odds with the vital character of the poet, was taken on July 29th 1965 with John Howell.[18] The Clywedog dam was then a-building, and the black Silurian rock exposed, nasty and rotten.[19]

This account is supplemented by a letter to Julian Croft which creates for Jones a personality suitably reductive and ecological:

the rape of the Epynt Mountains as an English Army training-ground and the uprooting and destruction of a Welsh speaking community. The hole in the middle of Wales is partly the colloquialism, 'What a hole!' and partly a reference to the birth of economic or other activity . . . rich water resources of the area [were] being impounded for the benefit of the distant cities of England and their expanding population of cosmopolitans, and, as we see it, parasites, instead of being used for the benefit of the countryside in which the incessant rain actually falls. The foundations of the dam were visible down to the bedrock, which is geological salient and black, but also stands for the historic Silures after whom the rocks were originally named, and the suggestion is that these formidable tribesmen of the past have by now gone rotten and friable like the rocks. The amazing thing, to me, was that such a vivid poet should have come out of all this. This is what I find so paradoxical. On such a day as the poem describes, with sodden stooks floating in the flooded fields, one could only wish him good luck in a sunnier clime. And yet, to people of my way of thinking, that is not an option and his early death in a much more favoured country had a certain irony about it. I have a feeling that his personal problems were those of the nation . . . I have a feeling that the temperamental peculiarities of the Welsh and everybody else if it comes to that are irreducibly clinical or medical, and arise from diet or the chemicals in the water supply or whatever; certainly English kids, brought up in Wales, get to look Welsh before they leave school, and there is some psychic (though not supernatural or mystic or anything like that) element in the environment.[20]

This analysis, with its echoes of T. H. Jones's *hiraeth* poetry, shows the difference between the practical political nationalist and the romantic one. 'Like a bloody Englishman'[21] is the closest Jones ever gets to Webb's position.

By the time this letter was written T. H. Jones had become obscure enough for some readers to think him an invention of the poet's:

> There is so little about him, here in Wales at any rate, things may be different in Australia. Indeed, in a not very good article on my own work in the *Anglo-Welsh Review*, the impression was somehow created, about the poem of mine you quoted, that I had invented him, a sort of ghostly Iago Prytherch . . .[22]

Harri Webb, a candidate for the position of people's remembrancer for whom it was important to register that events actually happened as described, that the description is accurate, that the character existed, was in some ways the heir of T. H. Jones, but it was R. S. Thomas who came to dominate and to embody the condition and identity of Wales. T. H. Jones, published in England, dead in the antipodes, was marginalized into a transitional figure.

The year 1985 marked the twentieth anniversary of T. H. Jones's death. Pat Power, always her brother's greatest supporter, keeper of the family archive, readily welcomed the idea of Ben Jones, a sculptor from Llanwrtyd Wells, to create in his memory a piece of public art as the first exhibit on a proposed Powys sculpture trail. Pat suggested that there was enough archive material to mount a small exhibition at the Wyeside Arts Centre in Builth Wells to coincide with the unveiling of the statue. Bernard Jones chaired a fund-raising committee and a mochette of a recumbent naked river-god, Cephasus,[23] was presented to it by Ben Jones. Despite reservations about the design and proposed location of the sculpture at the busy Wye bridge junction opposite the Arts Centre,[24] the committee agreed to put it to the Planning Committee of Brecknock District Council, which promptly rejected it on the grounds of the nudity. This stiffened the resolve of the fund-raising committee and united them behind the cause of Cephasus. A series of events now unfolded which would have gladdened T. H. Jones's heart and sharpened his pen. There was coverage in the local press and on radio and even interest from 'national'[25] tabloids and television.

Following a vigorous campaign by the Jones family, the council relented. After a convivial evening of poetry and pints, the statue was unveiled before a small crowd and a shocked party of civil dignitaries. Ben Jones had modelled from life, using a superbly well-endowed young man who, during his brief sojourn at Builth, had impressed a number of local women. Many spectators could not understand why their local poet had been presented naked and stood so erect on that savagely cold mid-Wales evening. The mayor, in an equivocal speech, praised the sculpture as little as possible and dissociated the council as far as possible from its erection – to cries of 'Shame' from the back of the crowd, who then dispersed to resume their drinking and continue the debate.

The pubs never really close in Builth. In the early hours of the morning a group of young men emerged from the Fountain, one of T. H. Jones's watering-holes, and hacked off Cephasus's phallus.

There was more tabloid interest over the emasculation than had been provoked by the erection. Ben Jones carried out a penile transplant and the television crews and newspaper journalists returned. Most of the locals who were interviewed said that they hated the sculpture; there were further attacks on the genitalia and a price, it is rumoured, was put on the head.

That winter was as wet and cold as any T. H. Jones had written about. Water penetrated through the damaged penis, froze, and began to destroy the torso as surely as the pox. Or, ironically, as relentlessly as alcohol had destroyed the poet. Ben Jones, disillusioned, withdrew his creation, ostensibly to effect major repairs. Cephasus never returned: an offer had been made by a rich local hotelier with an eye for an interesting piece of work and a bargain.

Today Cephasus surveys the waters at the upmarket Lake Country House Hotel in Llangammarch Wells, a celebration not of the poet but of small-town politics and the accumulated wealth of post-colonial 'bloody Englishmen'. A tribute also, as T. H. Jones's predecessor, Thomas Jeffery Llewelyn Prichard had prophesied, to 'the most apathetic and indescribable indifference . . . to everything except the accumulation of property'[26] of the people of his homeland. Jones, seated in his more plebeian pub, would have damned the politics, laughed at the hypocrisy, downed another pint and waited for the next incarnation of the Muse to walk through the door.

In contrast, the exhibition of photographs documenting T. H. Jones's life and illustrating aspects of his poetry[27] was a huge success. The Welsh Arts Council commissioned Robert Greetham to rephotograph and remount it as a major exhibition at Oriel[28] in 1986. Subsequently the National Library of Wales featured the material in its bicentenary celebration of links between Wales and Australia. Meic Stephens suggested that further research might lead to publication of a volume in the Arts Council's series of photographic biographies, *Bro a Bywyd/Writer's World*, and Pat Power edited the text and photographs prepared by Bernard Jones and Liz Fleming Williams.[29]

Thomas Henry Jones invented the designation T. H. Jones under which all of his published work appeared. He did so to dare comparison with W. B. Yeats, T. S. Eliot and W. H. Auden and to resist submersion in Dylan Thomas.[30] Only to family and friends[31] was he known as Harri. We may broadly summarize his achievement in terms of the signpost works which mark its progress. 'The Welsh hills',[32] the schoolboy essay which first claims the Llanafan landscape as his own; 'Visions',[33] the undergraduate eisteddfod essay which shows the awakening intellect, the already wide reading and the Marxist/Blakean idealism. 'The enemy in the heart',[34] technical *tour de force* and first clear statement of the dangers of passionate love. 'Poem for Wales'[35] and other associated nationalistic declarations mark his return from the war and reassert Welsh nationality as the basis of his writing. 'Lucky Jonah',[36] requiem for the war years, elegy for lost companions but, unfortunately, no exorcism of the nightmares, is literally transitional, written on passage to Australia. 'The colour of cockcrowing',[37] one of the few wholehearted celebrations of the beauty, life, sexuality of the postlapsarian world which is the only one we know. 'The first Christmas'[38] is an unflinching assertion of individual identity even in the face of God, and acceptance of the consequences of sin; in contrast, 'Girl reading John Donne'[39] and 'Welsh bastard'[40] may stand together to exemplify the 'concealed art' of the many mature poems in which deceptively easy colloquial language and an apparently casual deployment of allusions convey a wealth of postmodernist significance. 'Cotton Mather'[41] moves to a bleak exploration of the man caught between a rigorous religion, a sense of human frailty and an awareness of change.

> the land where every wind
>   Is a breath of guilt
> Is home . . .

> My paradise will be despair
>   And the cold winds that blow
> About the rocks, about your hair
>   And the grief I know.[42]

> Crow, cock, until this woman and this man
> Return to dust, crow until their children
> And their children's children too are dust,
> Crow until God revokes his first decree
> That Earth and all the inhabitants thereof
> Should wear forever the colour of cockcrowing.
> In the world we know it was always the colour of the cockcrow.[43]

Viewed from the millennium T. H. Jones is neither transitional nor marginal even though he was, or made himself, most unjustly marginalized. In his distinctive Anglo-Welshness, he ranks with Dylan and R. S. Thomas, sharing the romanticism of the one, the intellect and sense of Wales of the other. All three are, in quite different ways, religious poets; all three are, also in quite different ways, international in their appeal and relevance. They remind us that writing out of the myth of a small nation is no bar to universality: Yeats is their paradigm, each his own justification. As a love-poet T. H. Jones is unique among Welsh writers who have written in English. That his private imagination was dismantled by war, that he was never quite able to rebuild for himself a sense of the unfractured home he desired, is as certain as that final feeling of futility which caused him to cry out

> Put not your trust in words or anything.
> Put not your trust in really saying enough.
> Birds in the hand can't be compelled to sing.
> Despair suffices. Love's something else, ah! something.[44]

Notes

Prologue

[1] Edward Richards, *Homage to a Poet*, unpublished script recorded BBC, 24 June 1965. Version transmitted 29 July 1965 (TCF 50821).

[2] T. H. Jones, 'Rhiannon', *CP* 116.

[3] T. H. Jones, 'For my grandfather', *Collected Poems of T. H. Jones*, (hereafter *CP*), ed. Julian Croft and Don Dale-Jones (Llandysul, Gomer Press, 1977), 190.

[4] T. H. Jones, 'The Welshman in exile speaks', *CP* 118.

[5] T. H. Jones, 'Builth Wells', *CP* 116.

[6] Theophilus Jones, *A History of the County of Brecknock*, vol. 1 (Brecknock, 1909), 225–6.

[7] Ibid.

[8] Jacques Derrida, *The Ear of the Other: Otobiography, Transference, Translations* (texts and discussions with Derrida), trans. Peggy Kamuf, ed. Christie V. Macdonald (New York, Schocken Books, 1985), 44–5.

[9] Thomas Price, *The Literary Remains of Thomas Price, Carnhuanawc, with a Memoir of his Life by Jane Williams, Ysgafell* (hereafter *JWTP*), vol. 2 (Llandovery, 1855), 8–9.

[10] Ibid., 28.

[11] Emyr Humphreys, *The Taliesin Tradition* (Bridgend, Seren Books, 1983), 130.

[12] *JWTP*, vol. 2, 36.

[13] 'Being then very young and always modest and unpretending he was accustomed nevertheless to take great delight in listening to the discussions held by the most intelligent of the elder boys upon various points suggested by their lessons. Whenever any of them chanced to deviate from the true course of argument he would gravely interpose saying, "Stop, stop, multum in parvo."' Ibid., 39.

[14] T. H. Jones, 'Cwmchwefri', *CP* 130.

[15] Ibid.

[16] William Wordsworth, *The Poems*, vol. 1 (London, Penguin Books, 1977), 554.

[17] T. H. Jones, 'A rule of three sum wrong', *CP* 117.

[18] *JWTP*, vol. 2, 46: 'When bad weather prevented excursions he used to resort to a neighbouring cottage, where he fitted up for himself a little workshop, and occupied his leisure time with a few old tools in the construction of various instruments. One of the first that he ever made was a sort of lyre, which with very impartial and candid acknowledgement of its defects he declared to bear at least more resemblance to a harp than a harrow. Thus early did he manifest at once his ingenuity and his ingenuousness while framing a rude imitation of that graceful national instrument which proved to be through life the favourite idol of his fancy.'

[19] Ibid., 52.

[20] T. H. Jones, 'The Anglo Welsh', *Dock Leaves*, 4/11, (1953), 26.

[21] Glyn Davies, interview by P. Bernard Jones, 16 July 1992.

[22] *JWTP*, vol. 2, 46.

[23] Ibid., 48.

[24] William Blake, 'The garden of love', *The Complete Poems of William Blake*, ed. Alicia Ostriker (London, Penguin Books, 1977), 127.

[25] T. H. Jones, 'A Welsh poet finds a proper story', *CP* 223.

[26] Thomas Jeffrey Llewelyn Prichard, *The Adventures and Vagaries of Twm Shon Catti, descriptive of Life in Wales* (Aberystwyth, 1828).

[27] Sam Adams, 'Thomas Jeffery Llewelyn Prichard', *Brycheiniog*, 21 (1984–5), 59.

[28] Ibid., 59.

[29] Thomas Jeffery Llewelyn Prichard, Preface to *Heroines of Welsh History* (London, 1854), 6.

[30] Ibid.

[31] Emyr Humphreys, *The Taliesin Tradition* (Bridgend, Seren Books, 1983), 130.

[32] *The Cambrian* (22 November 1861), 5.

[33] *JWTP*, vol. 2, 67. A seizure in 1848 had weakened Price's constitution. He had over-exerted himself during a career of extraordinary energy that had included the establishing of Welsh-medium schools, the Welsh Minstrelsy Society and the Welsh Manuscripts Society as well as the writing of a *Hanes Cymru* and the championship of Pan-Celticism. After organizing the Abergavenny Eisteddfod, he collapsed at his home at Crickhowell, was bled and died shortly thereafter. 'On the morning of Monday 13th. November, 1848, by coincidence the festival day of St Afan, the mountain streamlets of Cwmddu rippled glittering in sunshine and the landscape with its faded and half fallen foliage shone forth in the parting glory of a Martinmass summer. The blue sky was

cloudless and a solemn stillness pervaded the air, broken only by the heavy sound of a funeral peal from the muffled bells of the parish church.'

Chapter 1

1 Patricia Power (née Jones), interview with P. B. Jones, 6 February 1989.

2 Gwyn A. Williams, *When was Wales?* (London, Penguin Books, 1985), 252.

3 'My grandfather going blind', 4 October 1964, *CP* 189.

4 Donald Jones, interview with P. B. Jones, 4 November 1989.

5 *The County Times and Brecon and Radnorshire Gazette* (16 August 1914).

6 Jack Jones, *Unfinished Journey* (London, Hamish Hamilton, 1937), 119. Note the emphasis on 'home made' and 'home cured'.

7 T. H. Jones, 'Home', *The Dublin Magazine, 30/2*, 1954, 24–33.

8 Harri Webb, 'In memory of Harri Jones', *Collected Poems* (Llandysul, Gomer Press, 1998).

9 Glyn Davies, interview with P. B. Jones, 16 July 1992.

10 John Berger, *Selected Essays and Articles: The Look of Things* (London, Penguin Books, 1972), 178–82.

11 Ibid.

12 For a detailed photographic record, see Pat Power, Liz Felgate and P. B. Jones, *T. Harri Jones 1921–1965* (Cardiff, Welsh Arts Council, 1987). The photographs in this book were assembled originally for the exhibition commemorating the twentieth anniversary of the poet's death. They derive mainly from the archive of Pat Power, T. H. Jones's youngest sister. Family photographs are supplemented by photographs taken by Liz Fleming Williams, David Power and P. B. Jones.

13 The destruction, in the 1960s, of the Abery Studio Collection was an act of vandalism. The National Library of Wales holds a representative sample only of the work of mid-Wales's greatest photographer.

14 T. H. Jones, 'The Welshman in exile speaks', *CP* 118.

15 Idem, 'A refusal to write autobiography', unpublished essay written at Portsmouth, *c*.1954/5.

16 'Ancestral', *CP* 3.

17 'Poem', *CP* 7.

18 'Cwmchwefri rocks', *CP* 134.

19 'A Welsh poet finds a proper story', *CP* 223.

[20] *CP* 170.

[21] 'Cwmchwefri rocks', 22 September 1962, *CP* 134.

[22] 'Cwmchwefri', 15 March 1962, *CP* 130.

[23] T. H. Jones , 'My grandfather would have me be a poet', *Life and Letters*, 64, 30–8.

[24] Ethel Hammonds (née Lewis), interview with P. B. Jones, 13 May 1988.

[25] T. H. Jones, 'A refusal to write autobiography'.

[26] D. H. Lawrence, Introduction to *The Dragon of the Apocalypse*. Quoted in Jeffrey Meyers, *D. H. Lawrence* (London, Macmillan, 1990), 27.

[27] Madeleine Jones (née Scott), unpublished letter to Pat Power, 30 July 1965.

Chapter 2

[1] T. H. Jones , 'A Welsh poet finds a proper story', *CP* 223.

[2] See *The Wyeside* (Summer 1938).

[3] See *The Dublin Magazine*, 30/2 (1954), 24–33.

[4] Iago Prytherch, R. S. Thomas's persona in some twenty poems written between 1946 and 1970, would have been known to T. H. Jones. Prytherch epitomizes the farmers and farm-labourers of the mid-Welsh hill country.

[5] 'My grandfather growing blind', 4 October 1964, *CP* 189.

[6] 'There is a comfort in the strength of love; / 'Twill make a thing endurable which else / Will overset the brain, or break the heart', Wordsworth writes as his rustic hero approaches, undaunted, the end of his sufferings.

[7] *CP* 125.

[8] 'In memoriam', 9 August 1962, *CP* 133.

[9] Ibid.

[10] J. P. Ward, *The Poetry of R. S. Thomas* (Bridgend, Poetry Wales Press, 1987), 13.

[11] 'The Welshman in exile speaks', 13 April 1961, *CP* 118.

[12] Keith Tester, *The Life and Times of Post Modernity* (London, Routledge, 1993), 7.

[13] 'In memoriam', *CP* 133.

[14] Ibid.

[15] See 'Spoiled preacher', *CP* 175.

[16] 'Difference' (1950), *CP* 5.

[17] *CP* 118.

[18] *CP* 123.

[19] London and Edinburgh, Oliver & Boyd, 1963.

[20] Ibid., 43–4.

[21] Ibid.

[22] 'My grandfather would have me be a poet'.

[23] Julian Croft, *T. H. Jones* (Cardiff, University of Wales Press, 1976), 5.

[24] 'My grandfather would have me be a poet'.

[25] James Joyce, letter to Grant Richards in *Selected Letters of James Joyce*, ed. Richard Ellman (London, 1975), 83.

[26] 'My grandfather would have me be a poet'.

[27] *Dock Leaves*, 15 (Winter 1954), 7–12.

[28] See Matthew 7: 9.

[29] *CP* 112.

Chapter 3

[1] Robert Gibbings, *Coming down the Wye* (London, The Travel Book Club, 1942), 54.

[2] Ibid.

[3] T. H. Jones, 'The River Wye', *The Wyeside*, 17 (Easter 1935), 4–6.

[4] Idem, 'The castle ruins and the streamlet', *The Wyeside*, 19 (Christmas 1935), 16–7.

[5] 11 February 1964, *CP* 186.

[6] 'How oft, in spirit, have I turned to thee, O sylvan Wye!' ('Lines composed a few miles above Tintern Abbey').

[7] Had T. H. Jones read Algernon Sidney, who, in *Discourses on Government*, observed that 'Liars ought to have good memories'? It is not impossible.

[8] P. G. Davies, *Annual Governors' Report Minutes*, vol. 3, 31 July 1930, 31 (Builth Wells High School Archive).

[9] F. J. Anthony, interview with P. B. Jones, 11 May 1989. Anthony added, 'But it was a friendly school. We were on Christian name terms with pupils, unusual at the time . . .'

[10] P. G. Davies, *Headmaster's Log and Builth County School Headmaster's Reports*, July 1931 (Builth Wells High School Archive).

[11] *Builth County School Governors' Minutes*, vol. 3, 15 June 1933, 82.

[12] See Colin Hughes, 'A study of the development of secondary education in Builth, 1889–1949', unpublished M.Ed. dissertation, University College Aberystwyth, 1983.

[13] Gwanwyn Lewis, interview with P. B. Jones, 23 July 1989.

14 Ibid.

15 Gwyn A.Williams, *When was Wales?* (London, Penguin Books, 1985), 252.

16 Robson Davies, interview with P. B. Jones, 3 February 1989.

17 Ibid.

18 'The stand-off half', *The Wyeside*, 22 (Christmas 1936), 6.

19 Interview, 3 February 1989.

20 Ibid.

21 Ibid.

22 F. J. Anthony, interview, 11 May 1989.

23 Ibid.

24 Gwanwyn Lewis, interview, 23 July 1989.

25 F. J. Anthony, interview, 11 May 1989.

26 Ibid.

27 Robson Davies, interview, 3 February 1989.

28 'The River Wye', *The Wyeside*, 17, Easter 1935, 4–6.

29 Ibid.

30 Interview, 11 May 1989.

31 *The Wyeside*, 17 (Easter 1935), 16.

32 Ibid.

33 Ibid., 16–17.

34 Gwanwyn Lewis, interview, 23 July 1989.

35 'The poet', *The Wyeside*, 21 (Summer 1936), 15–17.

36 F. J. Anthony, interview, 11 May 1989.

37 *The Wyeside*, 24 (Summer 1937), 11.

38 F. J. Anthony, interview, 11 May 1989.

39 Ibid.

40 *The Wyeside*, 24 (Summer 1937), 21.

41 See, for example, 'My grandmother died in the early hours of the morning' (*CP* 125); 'My grandfather going blind' (*CP* 189); 'For my grandfather' (*CP* 190).

42 *The Wyeside*, 24 (Summer 1937), 21.

43 *The Wyeside*, 25 (Christmas 1937), 13.

44 Ibid.

45 Provenance unknown. The poem was handwritten into an exercise book by Jones and also exists in a scrapbook cutting from an un-identified newspaper.

46 Provenance unknown. The poem exists only as a handwritten copy.

47 Provenance unknown. Exists as handwritten copy and scrapbook cutting.

48 Julian Croft, *T. H. Jones* (Cardiff, University of Wales Press, 1976), 9.

[49] See 'A refusal to write autobiography'.

[50] In contrast with practice in England, where the English Association's *Poems of Today* or *The Poet's Tongue* (Auden and Garret) were used in more enlightened schools from the 1920s. As late as 1963 pupils in Wales regularly studied at O level *The Golden Treasury* selections from William Morris, Cowper and Marvell.

[51] Croft, *T. H. Jones*, 9.

[52] *The Wyeside*, 26 (Easter 1938), 23.

[53] 'What's become of Waring', unpublished short story, *c.*1951–2.

[54] R. A. Sayce, 'Vienna in March', *The Wyeside*, 27 (Summer 1938), 9–11: 'I arrived in Vienna on Wednesday night, the 16th March . . . the posters had all been torn, but it was still easy to read them. Most dealt with the achievements of Schuschnigg's Government; they seemed already strangely distant. The most touching was a photograph of the murdered Chancellor Dollfuss with the words *Auf das er Lebe, stimmen wir mit er*. Often a picture of Hitler had been stuck on top of the poster, otherwise the photograph was so torn as to be unrecognisable . . . then there were the scrubbing parties. On the Ring in broad daylight you would see a crowd gathered round a few Jews and others who were being made to scrub the pavements or wash down the official cars.'

[55] F. J. Anthony, interview, 11 May 1989.

[56] *The Wyeside*, 27 (Summer 1938), 14–16.

[57] 'A refusal to write autobiography'.

[58] By February 1938 Penguin Books had published such Specials as *Germany Puts the Clock Back*, *Mussolini's Roman Empire* and *Blackmail or War*.

[59] Donald Jones, interview, 4 November 1989.

[60] Published in *Planet*, 69 (June/July 1988), 77–82.

[61] Ibid.

[62] Ibid.

[63] Ibid.

[64] Ibid.

[65] Ibid.

[66] F. J. Anthony, interview, 11 May 1989.

[67] Robson Davies, interview, 3 February 1989.

[68] Gerwyn Price, interview, 30 June 1990.

[69] *The Dublin Magazine*, 26/1 (1950), 21–4.

[70] See above, pp. 23ff.

[71] *The Glass* (Summer 1950), 13–7. Anthony Borrow and Madge Hales, co-editors of this small magazine, invited writers 'to explore and, if possible, universalise any aspect of myth or of personal struggle towards mystery'.

[72] Ibid.

[73] John 1: 1.

[74] T. H. Jones, 'Holy deceptions'.

[75] Myra Jones, interview with David Power, 12 October 1988.

[76] Croft, *T. H. Jones*, 6.

[77] *The Wyeside* (Easter 1938).

[78] *The Wyeside*, 27 (Summer 1938), 22.

[79] *The Wyeside* (Summer 1939).

[80] Robson Davies, interview, 3 February 1989.

Chapter 4

[1] Myra Jones, interview with David Power, 12 October 1988.

[2] Gerwyn Price, interview with P. B. Jones, 13 June 1990.

[3] 'Sonnet on a lost mistress', unpublished, undated holograph, bearing, on reverse, 'submitted by Henry Jones, Trefelin'.

[4] *Things to Come*, Alexander Korda, 1936. Described by the *Sunday Times* as 'A leviathan among films . . . a stupendous spectacle . . . staggering to eye, mind and spirit'.

[5] Gwen Davies, 'Builth during the Second World War', unpublished memoir, 1990, 2.

[6] Ibid.

[7] Ibid.

[8] Caradoc Evans, *Caradoc's Journal*, in Oliver Sandys, *Caradoc Evans* (London, Hurst & Blackett), 125.

[9] Tom Sallis, interview with P. B. Jones, 8 April 1988.

[10] Caradoc Evans, *Journal*.

[11] Pat Power, interview with P. B. Jones, 6 February 1989.

[12] Gwyn A. Williams, *When was Wales?* (London, Penguin Books, 1985), 260.

[13] Dyfnallt Morgan, 'Editorial', *The Dragon*, 62/1 (Michaelmas Term 1939), 42.

[14] Ibid.

[15] Sigmund Freud, *Reflections on War and Death* (1915), trans. A. A. Brill and A. B. Kuttner (New York, W. W. Norton, 1950).

[16] Wendon Mostyn, *The Dragon*, 62/2 (Lent 1940), 22.

[17] Ibid.

[18] 'Quotes', *The Dragon*, 62/1 (Michaelmas Term 1939), 23.

[19] 'Quot Counter-Quot', *The Dragon*, 62/3 (Easter 1940), 29.

[20] T. H. Jones, 'Labour Club notes', *The Dragon*, 62/2 (Lent 1940), 45.

21 Ibid., 10.
22 Anon., 'Open platform', *The Dragon*, 62/3 (Easter 1940), 23.
23 T. H. Jones, 'Labour Club notes', *The Dragon*, 62/2 (Lent 1940), 45.
24 Thus inviting comparison with W. B. (Yeats), T. S. (Eliot), W. H. (Auden) and R. S. (Thomas) rather than Dylan (Thomas).
25 Unpublished holograph on Central Welsh Board examination paper, dated January–March 1940.
26 Tom Sallis, interview, 8 April 1988.
27 Gwen Davies, 'Builth during the Second World War', 3.
28 Ibid.
29 See *The Dragon*, 63/1 (Michaelmas 1940), 16.
30 Anon., 'Open platform', *The Dragon*, 62/3 (Easter 1940), 25.
31 Ibid., 24.
32 Tom Sallis, interview, 17 April 1988.
33 Anon., 'Open platform', 24.
34 Ibid.
35 'Then seek the truth', *The Dragon*, 63/1 (Michaelmas 1940), 17.
36 Roy Evans, 'Fellow students', *The Dragon*, 63/1 (Michaelmas 1940), 17.
37 'Quotes', *The Dragon*, 63/2 (Lent 1941), 27.
38 Eric Corfield, interview with P. B. Jones, 18 June 1985.
39 Tom Sallis, interview, 8 April 1989.
40 Ibid.
41 Vera Brittain, *Diary 1939–45: Wartime Chronicle*, ed. Paul Bishop and Alan Bennett (London, Gollancz, 1989), 82.
42 Ibid.
43 T. H. Jones, 'Visions', *The Dragon*, 63/3 (Summer 1941), 8–9.
44 'Poem XXX' ('Sir, no man's enemy . . . '), *Poems 1930* and *Collected Shorter Poems* (1950), but subsequently not reprinted.
45 T. H. Jones, unpublished short story written *c.*1960.
46 T. H. Jones, *CP* 16. Published by Gwyn Jones in the *Welsh Review* in 1946, T. H. Jones's first appearance in a literary magazine.
47 *CP* 171.
48 T. H. Jones, unpublished letter to Ruth and Llewelyn Jones, January 1942.
49 Idem, unpublished letter to Ruth and Llewelyn Jones from HM Signal School, Petersfield, Hants., 30 January 1942.
50 Idem, unpublished letter to Ruth and Llewelyn Jones from HM Signal School, Petersfield, undated (February/March 1942).
51 Ibid.
52 T. H. Jones, unpublished letter to Ruth and Llewelyn Jones from Petersfield, undated (February/March 1942).

[53] Idem, unpublished letter from RN Barracks, Portsmouth, undated (March 1942).

[54] Idem, unpublished letter from unnamed troopship, undated (early April 1942).

[55] See, for example, 'A day at the seaside' and 'Lucky Jonah' (*CP* 112): 'A small boy in a small Welsh school / Dreamed over books that he would go to sea'.

[56] T. H. Jones, unpublished letter to Ruth and Llewelyn Jones from unnamed troopship, 20 April 1942.

[57] Idem, letter to Myra Jones, same date.

[58] Idem, letter to Ruth and Llewelyn Jones, 11 June 1942.

[59] Madeleine (Jones) Mitchell, hereafter 'Madeleine', unpublished letter to Don Dale-Jones, 6 April 1993.

[60] Peter Calvocaressi, Guy Wint and John Pritchard, *Total War*, vol. 1 (London, Penguin Books, 1989), 379–80.

[61] Madeleine, unpublished memoir, 1998.

[62] March 1963 in T. H. Jones's *Black Book*, holograph collection of fair copies of all poems written between 20 May 1950 and 25–6 September 1964.

[63] See above pp. 34ff.

[64] T. H. Jones, 12 September 1959, *CP* 112.

[65] Ibid., 89.

[66] Ronnie Roantree, interview with P. B. Jones, 2 July 1987.

[67] This monthly magazine of contemporary writing, edited by John Lehmann, had commenced publication in 1940. It would give Jones access to the work of Auden, Spender, MacNeice, Day Lewis and Laurie Lee.

[68] Edited by Gwyn Jones (Professor of English at Aberystwyth from 1940), February–November 1939 and March 1944–December 1948. Caradoc Evans and Alun Lewis were regular contributors and contributors from outside Wales included T. S. Eliot.

[69] Edited by Cyril Connolly from 1940–50, *Horizon* featured the work of Auden, Lee, Grigson and Orwell, among others.

[70] Roantree, interview with P. B. Jones.

[71] Madeleine, unpublished letter to Don Dale-Jones, 6 April 1993.

[72] *The Dragon*, 69/2 (Lent 1947), 3.

[73] Dylan Thomas, in *New World Writing* (New York, Mentor, 1955), 134–5, quoted in T. H. Jones, *Dylan Thomas* (London, Oliver & Boyd, 1963), 54.

[74] Roantree, interview with P. B. Jones.

[75] Unpublished letter to Ruth and Llewelyn Jones, 25 September 1942.

[76] Roantree, interview with P. B. Jones.

[77] Tom Sallis, interview, 8 April 1988.

[78] David O. Selznick, 1939: this is only the second film that T. H. Jones is known to have seen. The letter is dated 20 February 1943.

[79] Unpublished letter to Ruth and Llewelyn Jones, 7 June 1943.

[80] Unpublished letter to Ruth and Llewelyn Jones, 3 June 1944.

[81] Roantree, interview with P. B. Jones.

[82] Unpublished letter to Donald Jones, 7 June 1945.

[83] Unpublished, undated, untitled poem written in pencil on the back of a 'Naval Message' sheet.

[84] Two drafts and a final version in pencil on both sides of a 'Naval Message' sheet.

[85] Pencil draft, dated '11/2/43' on 'Naval Message' sheet.

[86] Untitled poem, ink on a sheet of cheap exercise-book paper, with address ('from Tel. T. H. Jones, P/J X279998, HMS Seaham [crossed through] Hannibal, c/o G.P.O. London').

[87] Pencil draft on 'Naval Message' sheet.

[88] Untitled lyric on small sheet of flimsy paper, dated 'Algiers Xmas 43'.

[89] On sheet from a cheap writing-pad, together with three-line fragment. Dated 'Naples Oct '44'.

[90] T. S. Eliot, 'Portrait of a lady', *Collected Poems 1909–62* (London, Faber & Faber, 1965), 19.

[91] 11 June 1942.

[92] Unpublished letter to Ruth and Llewelyn Jones, 30 August 1942.

[93] Unpublished letter to Ruth and Llewelyn Jones, 23 June 1944.

[94] Unpublished letter to Ruth and Llewelyn Jones, 29 September 1942.

[95] Unpublished letter to Ruth and Llewelyn Jones, 29 October 1942.

[96] Unpublished letter to Ruth and Llewelyn Jones, 6 March 1943.

[97] Unpublished letter to Ruth and Llewelyn Jones, 29 March 1943.

[98] 'Late spring in Wales', 12 January 1962, *CP* 126.

[99] Unpublished letter to Ruth and Llewelyn Jones, 25 July 1943.

[100] Unpublished letter to Ruth and Llewelyn Jones, 23 June 1944.

[101] Unpublished letter to Ruth and Llewelyn Jones, 7 November 1942.

[102] Unpublished letter to Ruth and Llewelyn Jones, 13 December 1942.

[103] 12 September 1959, *CP* 112.

[104] Ronnie Roantree, interview with P. B. Jones, 2 July 1987.

[105] Ibid.

[106] 'Lucky Jonah'.

[107] Ibid., epigraph.

[108] *CP* 24.

[109] 'Sailor', 19 February 1954, *CP* 89.

[110] 'Voyages', 30 September 1952, *CP* 74.

[111] 'Adrift', 30 March 1963, *CP* 174.

[112] Ronnie Roantree.

[113] Madeleine, unpublished memoir, 1998.

[114] Unpublished letter to Ruth and Llewelyn Jones, 9 July 1944.

[115] Untitled, in pencil on reverse of 'Naval Message' sheet.

[116] Untitled, on cheap exercise-book paper with *Seaham* (crossed out), *Hannibal* address on reverse.

[117] Incomplete poem (first sheet lost?) on cheap exercise-book paper, *Hannibal* address on reverse.

[118] Untitled, in pencil on reverse of 'Naval Message' sheet.

[119] *The Dragon*, 69/2 (Lent 1947), 3.

[120] W. H. Auden, *Collected Shorter Poems 1927–1957* (London, Faber & Faber, 1966), 148.

[121] Unpublished typescript in the possession of Donald Jones, to whom it was read by the poet in the public bar of the Lion Hotel, Builth Wells, in 1948. Composed 1944?

[122] Compare 'The Welshman in exile speaks', 13 April 1961, *CP* 118: 'Being a boy from the hills, brought up / Believing that fornication is a sin, / Adultery abomination, what should I do / But fornicate until I'm caught, and then / Commit adultery in my dreams.'

[123] W. B. Yeats, 'Among school children', *Collected Poems* (London, Macmillan, 1958), 245: 'O chestnut-tree, great-rooted blossomer, / Are you the leaf, the blossom or the bole? / O body swayed to music, O brightening glance, / How can we know the dancer from the dance?'

[124] Idem, 'Byzantium', ibid., 280.

[125] W. H. Auden, 'As I walked out one evening', *Collected Shorter Poems 1927–1957* (London, Faber & Faber, 1966), 86.

[126] In *Wales*.

[127] W. B. Yeats, 'The second coming', *Collected Poems*, 210. Written in 1919, in reaction to the horrors of the First World War.

[128] T. H. Jones, *The Enemy in the Heart* (London, Rupert Hart-Davis, 1957).

[129] Unpublished letter to Ruth and Llewelyn Jones, 9 July 1944.

[130] T. H. Jones, 'Poem, In the mean parishes of my desire', unpublished typescript dated 15 January 1945.

[131] Idem, unpublished letter to (Donald) John Jones from 'Mess 44, HMS *Westminster*', 7 June 1945.

[132] T. H. Jones, verse-letter to Valerie and Pat Jones from HMS *Collingwood*, Fareham, Hants., 28 December 1945.

[133] For example, *New Year Letter*, 1941.

[134] W. H. Auden, *New Year Letter* (London, Faber & Faber, 1941), lines 1087–94.

Chapter 5

[1] Madeleine, unpublished memoir, 1998.

[2] Ibid.

[3] London, Rupert Hart-Davis, 1957.

[4] *CP* 2.

[5] This is a leather-bound manuscript notebook into which T. H. Jones entered fair copies of all the poems he completed between 20 May 1950 and 26 September 1964.

[6] 22 September 1962, *CP* 134.

[7] Robert Graves, *The White Goddess* (London, Faber & Faber, 1961), 490–1. It is worth pointing out that Graves bases the 'argument' of this book 'on a detailed examination of two extraordinary Welsh minstrel poems of the thirteenth century'.

[8] Roy Fuller, quoted in Andrew Sinclair, *War like a Wasp* (London, Hamish Hamilton, 1939), 236.

[9] See above pp. 85–6.

[10] *The Dragon*, 68 (Easter 1946), 13.

[11] *The Dragon*, 63/3 (Summer 1941), 8–9. See above pp. 64ff..

[12] Peter Richmond, 'The wanderer returns', *The Dragon*, 69/1 (Michaelmas 1946), 2.

[13] Tom Sallis, interview with P. B. Jones, 8 April 1988.

[14] Ibid.

[15] Ibid.

[16] Ibid.

[17] Ibid.

[18] *The Dragon, 69* (Michaelmas 1946), 3.

[19] *Welsh Review* (Autumn 1946).

[20] Tom Sallis, interview, 8 April 1988.

[21] Gwyn Jones, 'Editorial', *Welsh Review*, (February 1939).

[22] Gwyn Jones, interview with P. B. Jones, 16 July 1989.

[23] Ibid.

[24] *CP* 16.

[25] 'The last enemy that shall be destroyed is death', 1 Corinthians 26.

[26] *Deaths and Entrances*, his fourth volume of poetry, was published in 1946.

27 Clive Hart, interview with P. B. Jones, 4 September 1991.

28 *Dylan Thomas* (Edinburgh and London, Oliver & Boyd, 1963).

29 Madeleine, unpublished letter to Don Dale-Jones, 6 May 1994.

30 Pat Power, interview with P. B. Jones, 6 February 1989.

31 Ibid.

32 It links Peckham High Street with the Old Kent Road.

33 Madeleine, unpublished memoir, 1998.

34 'Coming shortly', *The Dragon*, 68 (Easter 1946), 11.

35 Tom Sallis, interview, 8 April 1988.

36 'Idyll' (6 June 1946) opens with 'The long legs of my love were walking like swans / In the green legend where I was happy once'.

37 Brian Evans, in Alexander Walker, *The Journals of Rachel Roberts: No Bells on Sunday* (London, Pavilion Books, 1984), 31.

38 Mansell Prothero, ibid., 31.

39 Mrs Bill Anthony-Jones, interview with P. B. Jones, 2 August 1987.

40 Walker, *Journals of Rachel Roberts*, 38.

41 'Coming shortly', *The Dragon*, 68 (Easter 1946), 11.

42 Tom Sallis, interview, 8 April 1988.

43 *The Dragon*, 68 (Easter 1946), 11.

44 *The Dragon*, 69/3 (Summer 1947), 9.

45 *The Dragon*, 69 (Michaelmas 1946), 3.

46 *The Dragon*, 69 (Michaelmas 1946), 21.

47 G. M. Hopkins, poem 65 ('No worst, there is none'), *Poems of Gerard Manley Hopkins*, ed. W. H. Gardner and N. H. Mackenzie (London, Oxford University Press, 1967), 100.

48 Haydn Williams, letter to P. B. Jones, 2 January 1990.

49 Published by both *The Dragon* (Michaelmas Term 1947, by which time T. H. Jones was its editor) and *Welsh Review* (Winter 1947). *CP* 4.

50 24 October 1961, *CP* 123.

51 30 March 1963, 'Welsh pastoral elegy', *CP* 173.

52 3 September 1963, 'Welsh childhood', *CP* 177.

53 'Editorial', *The Dragon*, 69/2 (Lent 1947), 3.

54 Tom Sallis, interview, 8 April 1988.

55 Bill Adams, 'I believe', *The Dragon*, 69/2 (Lent 1947), 2.

56 Ibid.

57 *The Dragon*, 69/3 (Summer 1947).

58 See, for example, 'Eyes, hair, sea, fall', 15 July 1963, *CP* 206.

59 'In my craft or sullen art' (Thomas) / 'will his negative inversion' (Auden).

60 Tom Sallis, interview, 8 April 1988.

61 Gwyn A. Williams, letter to P. B. Jones, 14 January 1990.

62 Tom Sallis, interview, 8 April 1988.

63 Ibid.

64 Haydn Williams, letter to P. B. Jones, 2 January 1990.

65 Ibid: 'admiration and sympathy for the Roman Catholic Church . . . dislike of Nonconformity' is an acute comment on the man who, all his life, could neither accept nor escape his religious heritage.

66 T. H. Jones and Joss Davies, 'Proceedings of the Honourable Philosophical and Philological Society', *The Dragon*, 70/1 (Michaelmas 1947), 22.

67 Jim Smith, unpublished letter to P. B. Jones, 26 May 1991.

68 T. H. Jones, undated, unpublished letter to Mair Jones (she dates it *c.*July 1947).

69 J.B.E., 'Review drama – *Juno and the Paycock*', *The Dragon*, 69/3 (Summer 1947), 17.

70 Rachel Roberts in Walker, *Journals of Rachel Roberts,* 38.

71 T. H. Jones, '*Juno and the Paycock*', in *The Dragon*, 70/1 (Michaelmas 1947), 22.

72 Idem, '*Ghosts*', in *The Dragon*, (Lent 1948), 11.

73 See above pp. 110ff.

74 Ronnie Cass, interview with P. B. Jones, 23 October 1990.

75 Gwyn A.Williams, unpublished letter to P. B. Jones, 14 January 1990.

76 Ronnie Cass, interview, 23 October 1990.

77 Among the borrowings from Yeats are these lines (derived from the 'complexities of mire or blood' of 'Byzantium'): 'Complexity of passion / Makes a song / From the tumult of dung, / Raises a flower / From blood and mire'.

78 John Edmunds, unpublished letter to P. B. Jones, 11 February 1993.

79 Tom Sallis, interview, 8 April 1988.

80 Madeleine, unpublished memoir, 1998.

81 Julian Croft, *T. H. Jones* (Cardiff, University of Wales Press, 1976), 17.

82 George Jean Nathan, *The World in Falseface* (New York, Knopf, 1923), 62–6.

83 W. B. Yeats, 'The second coming', *Collected Poems* (London, Macmillan, 1958), 210–11.

84 See above pp. 105–6.

85 Robert Graves, *The White Goddess*, (London, Faber & Faber, 1948; 3rd edn., 1967) 9 and pp. 9–15 *passim*.

86 Above, pp. 103–4.

87 Compare 'The enemy in the heart': 'In the heart alone is the last enemy / The fatal friend'.

88 W. B. Yeats, 'Easter 1916', *Collected Poems* (London, Macmillan, 1958), 204. This poem also contains the question 'what if excess of

love / Bewildered them till they died?', which is apposite even though in context Yeats means love of one's country.

89 Compare 'Words for music perhaps', VI, 'Crazy Jane talks with the Bishop', ibid., 295: 'A woman can be proud and stiff / When on love intent'.

90 The (obvious) source of this image of female sexual arrogance is the adulterous Herodias (Matthew 14) who obtained the head of John the Baptist 'in a charger' in revenge for his criticism of her misconduct.

91 Above, pp. 113–14.

92 Above, pp. 116–17.

93 Graves, *White Goddess*, 490, 489.

94 The weasel is a feature of the Llanafan landscape of the early poetry: 'The weasel slinked bloodthirsty through the woods' ('Amends', 1950, *CP* 6); 'Slinked animals . . . on hillsides . . . Weasel . . . ' ('The ballad of me', 1952, *CP* 9).

95 For example, 'The houseless poet, ploughman without friend' ('Poem', *The Dragon*, 70/2 (Lent 1948) 18); 'Everything dies / Into legend like Troy' ('Apologia pro carmine Suo', *The Dragon*, 70/2 (Lent 1948), 9).

96 Gwyn A. Williams, unpublished letter to P. B. Jones, 14 January 1990.

97 Ibid.

98 Jim Smith, unpublished letter to P. B. Jones, 26 May 1991.

99 May 1948.

100 Rachel Roberts, in Walker, *Journals of Rachel Roberts*, 38.

101 Tom Sallis, interview, 8 April 1988.

102 Gwyn A. Williams, unpublished letter to P. B. Jones, 14 January 1990.

103 Ibid.

104 Madeleine, unpublished memoir, 1998.

105 Letter to Bernard Jones, 12 June 2000.

106 Pat Power, interview with P. B. Jones, 22 February 1992.

107 Interview with P. B. Jones, 8 April 1988, but 'Tom Sallis' memory is faulty', says Madeleine. 'The two-bedroomed flat . . . was no palace, but it quickly became the rendezvous for our many friends. The main room had two divans – plenty of books and a few fine paintings, the second room was the kitchen plus nursery.'

108 Madeleine, unpublished memoir, 1998.

109 T. H. Jones, 'My grandfather going blind', 4 October 1964, *CP* 189.

110 *CP* 19.

111 Editor of *Life and Letters Today*, (in 1928–33 this monthly periodical, founded by Desmond MacCarthy in 1928, had been titled simply *Life and Letters*).

[112] 'Poem', *CP* 7.

[113] T. H. Jones, unpublished letter to Ted and Pam Richards, *c.*September 1949.

[114] Idem., 'The imagery of the metaphysical poets of the seventeenth century', unpublished MA thesis, University of Wales, Aberystwyth, 1949, 182.

[115] Jim Smith, unpublished letter to P. B. Jones, 26 May 1991.

[116] Stevie Davies, *John Donne* (London, Northcote House, 1994), 16.

[117] Madeleine, unpublished memoir, 1998.

[118] *Black Book*, 21 April 1951.

[119] Ibid., 22 August 1959.

[120] John Glanville, unpublished letter to P. B. Jones, 17 July 1993.

[121] Ibid.

[122] Ibid.

[123] Ibid.

[124] '[Ray Roberts] stayed on to keep Harri company when I went to Rio with Sian. My sister, Peg . . . was depressed and battling with three tiny kids . . . as Harri was still looking for a job, we decided that I could go . . . for a couple of months. This turned into a year as I developed typhoid fever and was very ill.' Madeleine, unpublished memoir, 1998.

[125] 'Margot (known as Maggie) Dulanty came from New England and moved to London to do a degree at the School of Economics. Brian was a solicitor, the son of the Irish Ambassador to the Court of St James. They were most generous friends and introduced Harri to interesting people. He was well entertained during my absence . . . [she was] most encouraging to Harri in his writing.' Ibid.

[126] London, Rupert Hart-Davis, 1957.

[127] T. H. Jones, *CP* 2.

[128] John Glanville, unpublished letter to P. B. Jones, 17 July 1993.

[129] 'Song for Rachel', 21 January 1949, *Black Book*.

[130] 'For Rachel', 15 June 1950, *CP* 17.

[131] Sinclair, *War like a Wasp*, 189.

[132] *Life and Letters Today*, 1 (1949), 180–2.

[133] 4 January 1953, *CP* 33.

[134] T. H. Jones, unpublished letter to Ludovic Kennedy, 5 October 1953, BBC MS 1826.

[135] In 'The second critical encounter', 30 March 1963, *CP* 203.

[136] *Life and Letters Today*, 2 (1949), 172–3.

[137] *Life and Letters Today*, 4 (1949), 162–4.

[138] See 'Three songs of a mad prince', *CP* 105–10.

[139] 'Three volumes of poetry', *Life and Letters Today*, 4 (1949), 185–8.

[140] T. H. Jones, unpublished letter to Seumas O'Sullivan, 16 May 1949, Trinity College Manuscripts, 4630–49, 2426.

[141] See Richard Burnham, 'The Dublin Magazine's Welsh poets', *Anglo-Welsh Review*, 27/60 (1978), 49–63.

[142] T. H. Jones, *CP* 18.

[143] Unpublished, 5 February 1949.

[144] 14 June 1950, published in *Dock Leaves* (May 1951).

[145] Unpublished letter to Ludovic Kennedy, 5 October 1953, BBC Archive.

[146] W. H. Auden, *Collected Shorter Poems 1927–1957*, 71.

[147] W. B. Yeats, *Collected Poems* (London, Macmillan, 1958), 210.

[148] On the other hand, such eclecticism is further evidence of Jones's postmodernity.

[149] Andrew Crozier, 'Styles of self', in *A Paradise Lost: The Neo-Romantic Imagination in Britain 1935–55* (London, Lund Humphries/Barbican Art Gallery, 1987), 114–16.

[150] *Dublin Magazine* (September 1950); *CP* 5.

[151] Crozier, 'Styles', 116.

[152] See *The Modern Writer and his World* (London, Penguin Books, 1964), 325.

[153] See above pp. 105–6.

[154] 'Poem dedicated to the memory of Dylan Thomas', April 1954, *CP* 12.

[155] W. B. Yeats, *Uncollected Prose*, ed. J. P. Fayne and C. Johnson, vol. 1 (London, Macmillan, 1970), 81.

[156] W. B. Yeats, *Collected Poems*, 182.

[157] See Sinclair, *War like a Wasp*, 267–8.

[158] William Ronald Rees Jones (Keidrych Rhys, 1915–87) founded the periodical *Wales* in 1937. Published in 1937–39/40, 1943–9 and 1958–60, it set out to be 'an independent pamphlet of creative work by the younger progressive Welsh writers' and Rhys asserted that 'though we write in English, we are rooted in Wales'.

[159] See Robert Welch, *Changing States: Transformations in Modern Irish Writing* (London, Routledge, 1993). Welch contends that what unites the major Irish writers is their attempt to respond to the transformation of Irish life from that reading of the world provided by the Gaelic language to post-industrial English culture. There is a close parallel between the reaction of Synge, Joyce, Heaney and Friel and the sense of loss, the understanding of the power of the craft of language, the uncertainties of self, and the redefinition of the nature of change in

response to the presence of history that is the focus of the work of R. S. Thomas and T. H. Jones.

160 See Sinclair, *War like a Wasp* 267–8.

161 See Bobi Jones, 'The Anglo-Welsh', *Dock Leaves*, 4/10 (1953), 23–8; 'Anglo-Welsh, more definitions', *Planet*, 16 (1973), 11–23; 'Order, purpose and resurgence in poetry', *Poetry Wales*, 11/ 1 (1975), 118–22. 'Bypassing London may also save one from the fate I sometimes have nightmares about . . . that I was once an Anglo-Welsh writer, and, what is worse, an Anglo-Welsh critic whining about the dangers of introversion, parochialism and overindulgence in "engagement".'

162 Published in *Dock Leaves*, 4/11 (Summer 1953), 26.

163 Julian Croft, *T. H. Jones* (Cardiff, University of Wales Press, 1976), 54–5.

164 'The Anglo Welsh'.

165 Croft, *T. H. Jones*, 54–5. Anthony Conran has suggested ('Anglo Welsh revisited', *Planet*, 108 (Dec./Jan. 1994–5), 28–34) that 'For Dylan Thomas's generation in Swansea in the Thirties there was no Anglo Welsh problem . . . they were exotic recruits to English literature. But by the Fifties . . . Even poets like T. Harri [*sic*] Jones or Leslie Norris . . . in their work show divided loyalties.'

166 T. H. Jones, 'Love', 5 December 1950, *CP* 35.

167 *Black Book*, 27 February 1950.

168 Ibid., 20 May 1950.

169 April 1951, *CP* 2. See also above pp. 103–4.

170 Untitled, *Black Book*, 1 April 1951.

171 'The vocabulary of promise', *Black Book*, 1 April 1951, *CP* 15.

172 ' . . . owing to [his] left wing activities while a student . . . Maggie . . . pulled the necessary strings.' Madeleine, unpublished memoir.

Chapter 6

1 E. George, former principal of the Dockyard School, interview with David Power, 22 August 1989.

2 Mike Thomson, interview with P. B. Jones, 13 June 1991.

3 T. H. Jones, 'Portsmouth at night', *Black Book*, 19 June 1957.

4 Mike Thomson, interview, 13 June 1991.

5 Ibid.

6 Literally 'Dark shops', established in Rome in 1949 by Marguerite Caetani, who edited it until it ceased publication in 1960. A leading international periodical, it published the work of, for example, Dylan

Thomas, W. H. Auden, Günter Grass and Albert Camus in their own languages.

7 London, Rupert Hart-Davis, 1960. T. H. Jones translated in all eight poems, of which seven were printed here. Unfortunately these were excluded from the *Collected Poems*.

8 Mike Thomson, interview, 13 June 1991.

9 Captain Roy Lee, 'an ignorant science student', letter to Pat Power, 12 December 1986.

10 Ibid.

11 Anthony Conran, *The Cost of Strangeness: Essays on English Poets in Wales* (Llandysul, Gomer Press, 1982), 277.

12 Ibid.

13 Mike Thomson, interview, 13 June 1991. Even the catalogue of the National Library of Wales employs this inaccurate usage arising, probably, from the Welsh habit of referring even to strangers by the Christian name ('Dylan', 'Prof. Gwyn'). Only to family and close friends was the poet happy to be known as 'Harri'.

14 For example, Joyce, Eliot, Waugh, D. H. Lawrence, Auden. Lawrence and Auden were gifted teachers.

15 D. H. Lawrence, 'Last lesson of the afternoon', *D. H. Lawrence: The Complete Poems*, vol. 1 (Phoenix Edition; London, Heinemann, 1957), 51.

16 Idem, quoted in Jeffrey Meyers, *D. H. Lawrence* (London, Macmillan, 1990), 53.

17 See the discussion of 'The enemy in the heart', above pp.110–11.

18 Alan Marshfield, interview, 16 July 1988.

19 Norman Talbot, 'To write simply: the poetry of T. H. Jones', *Quadrant* (Australia), 5 (1965), 35–42.

20 'And all of life a long survivor's leave', *CP* 114. Like Causley's, Jones's 'naval' poems are realistic and full of naval slang. Like Causley and Alan Ross, he shows no hatred of the enemy.

21 30 September 1952, *CP* 53.

22 19 October 1952, *CP* 52.

23 W. H. Auden, *Collected Shorter Poems 1927–1957* (London, Faber & Faber, 1966), 85.

24 Auden's description, see *The Poetry of W. H. Auden: The Disenchanted Island* (New York, Oxford University Press, 1968), 110.

25 Named after the opening line ('As I walked out in the streets of Laredo') of 'The cowboy's lament', which tells the sad story of the dashing young cowboy, brought low by drink and gambling, who knows he has 'done wrong'.

26 Contraction of 'landlubber', the seaman's contemptuous term for the landsman. We have already heard of T. H. Jones's preference for rough seas.

27 Julian Croft, *T. H. Jones* (Cardiff, University of Wales Press, 1976), 26.

28 See *Eliot, Auden, Lowell: Aspects of the Baudelairean Inheritance* (London, Macmillan, 1983), 2.

29 19 April 1952, *Black Book*.

30 11 October 1964, T. H. Jones, *CP* 190.

31 'Lost', *Collected Poems*, Edward Mendelson (London, Faber & Faber, 1976), 540.

32 W. H. Auden, 'Amor loci', *City without Walls* (London, Faber & Faber, 1969), 41.

33 'Love', 5 December 1950, *CP* 35. The reader needs to know his Auden ('Time watches from the shadow / And coughs when you would kiss') to appreciate the effect.

34 Interview, 16 July 1988.

35 'He had more than most people, and his . . . family life made his life busy . . . he had a great talent and patience with children'. Letter to P. B. Jones, 12 June 2000.

36 8 December 1952, *CP* 77.

37 'Cast a cold eye / On life, on death': W. B. Yeats, 'Under Ben Bulben', *CP* (London, Macmillan, 1958), 401.

38 T. H. Jones, *CP* 43.

39 Stevens may later have influenced R. S. Thomas also.

40 Wallace Stevens, *Collected Poems* (London, Faber & Faber, 1971), 15.

41 Idem, 'Adagia', *Opus Posthumus* (London, Faber & Faber, 1959), 161.

42 Stevens, 'The man with the blue guitar', *Collected Poems*, 165.

43 See Frank Kermode, *Wallace Stevens* (London, Oliver & Boyd, 1960), 62–72.

44 T. H. Jones, *CP* 43. Subsequent quotations same page.

45 Ibid., 44.

46 2 December 1959, ibid., 224: 'In the world we know it was always the colour of the cockcrow.'

47 Ibid., 45.

48 Ibid. (both quotations).

49 See Kermode, *Wallace Stevens*, 62–72.

50 See Richard Ellman, 'How Wallace Stevens saw himself', in *Along the Riverrun: Selected Essays* (London, Penguin Books, 1989), 204–20.

51 A Lawrentian phrase.

52 Kermode, 62–72. 'The true hero is the human fictive power applied to reality.'

[53] Alan Marshfield, interview, 16 July 1988.

[54] T. H. Jones, 'Syllabus for a first-year tutorial course of twenty-four lectures on the appreciation of literature', WEA/University of Southampton, 1954. Unpublished MS.

[55] Ibid.

[56] 26 October 1951, *CP* 34.

[57] 8 December 1952, *CP* 28.

[58] See above, pp. 40ff.

[59] T. H. Jones, unpublished letter to Pam Richards, 5 October 1953.

[60] 4 January 1953, *CP* 33.

[61] 27 August 1950, *CP* 30.

[62] 19 April 1952, *CP* 56.

[63] 18 July 1951, *CP* 64.

[64] Compare 'Stanzas in a mirror', *CP* 28.

[65] Compare Graves, *The White Goddess*, 490: 'the individual woman whom the Goddess may make her instrument for a month, a year, seven years, or even more'.

[66] T. H. Jones, unpublished letter to Ludovic Kennedy, 5 October 1953.

[67] 19 October 1962, *CP* 52.

[68] 6 January 1952, 68.

[69] 25 November 1951, 67.

[70] 1950, *Life and Letters Today*.

[71] T. H. Jones, letter to Kennedy, 5 October 1953.

[72] Ludovic Kennedy, unpublished letter, 22 December 1953, BBC MS, unnumbered.

[73] Madeleine, unpublished memoir, 1998.

[74] Ibid. The wartime letters reveal that he was a very loving brother to his four sisters.

[75] *CP* 13.

[76] 6 June 1961, *CP* 120.

[77] 17 February 1956, *CP* 58.

[78] W. B. Yeats, 'A prayer for my daughter', *Collected Poems* (London, Macmillan, 1958), 211.

[79] Ibid., 202.

[80] Alan Marshfield, interview, 16 July 1988.

[81] Ibid.

[82] Ibid.

[83] T. S. Eliot, 'Tradition and the individual talent', *Selected Essays* (London, Faber & Faber, 1963), 15.

[84] Alan Marshfield, interview, 16 July 1988.

[85] In *Look Back in Anger*, 1956.

86 13 August 1952, *Black Book*.
87 'Song, Goe, and catche a falling starre', *Selected Poems* (London, Penguin Books, 1950), 11.
88 Alan Marshfield, interview, 16 July 1988.
89 'Are there any modern poets?', dedicated 'for Madeleine', 21 March 1961, *CP* 233.
90 T. H. Jones, *Dylan Thomas* (London and Edinburgh, Oliver & Boyd, 1963), 33.
91 Unpublished memoir, 1998.
92 August 1961, after fifteen years of marrriage, *CP* 147.
93 In *The Cost of Strangeness: Essays on English Poets in Wales* (Llandysul, Gomer Press, 1982).
94 Ibid., 281–2.
95 Ibid.
96 *Welsh Review* (Winter 1947).
97 1 March 1951, *Western Mail*.
98 Date uncertain, *CP* 31.
99 September 1954, *CP* 46.
100 27 August 1951, *CP* 32.
101 21 September 1953, *CP* 55.
102 Ludovic Kennedy, *On my Way to the Club* (London, Collins, 1989), 228.
103 T. H. Jones, unpublished letter to John Davenport, 9 May 1956, BBC MS.
104 Donald Carne-Ross, unpublished letter to T. H. Jones, 29 May 1959, BBC MS.
105 Published in the *Dublin Magazine* (January 1950).
106 *Life and Letters Today* (January 1950).
107 *The Glass* (1953).
108 *Dublin Magazine* (June 1954).
109 *Dock Leaves* (Winter 1954).
110 Unpublished.
111 Unpublished, 7 August 1956.
112 London, Dent, 1940.
113 Robert Graves, *The White Goddess* (London, Faber & Faber, 1961) 449.
114 His first volume of poetry was published, in 1946, by the Druid Press, Carmarthen; his second by the Montgomeryshire Printing Company, Newtown.
115 'Able to be romantic', *Quadrant* 8/2 (June/July 1964), 73–6.
116 Conversation with P. B. Jones, Hay-on-Wye Literature Festival, 22 May 1994.

[117]   19 April 1952, *CP* 56.

[118]   Undated (Sian Jones was born in May 1948), *CP* 57.

[119]   17 February 1956, *CP* 58.

[120]   This juxtaposition was found significant by Dylan Thomas, who employs it in both the poem 'After the funeral' ('In a room with a stuffed fox and a stale fern') and the short story 'The peaches' ('stuffed fox . . . fern-pot').

[121]   'Ancestral', *CP* 3.

[122]   Published 1947, 'In my returning', *CP* 4.

[123]   Published September 1950, *CP* 5.

[124]   William Blake, 'The sick rose', *Selected Poems* (London, Penguin Books, 1958), 48. 'The invisible worm . . . Does thy life destroy.'

[125]   T. H. Jones, *CP* 6.

[126]   Published 1950, *CP* 7.

[127]   Dylan Thomas, 'Fern Hill', *Collected Poems 1934–1952* (London, Dent, 1962), 159. What better quarry, in prose or verse, for any writer, let alone a young Anglo-Welsh one, to exploit for childhood material?

[128]   Published June 1952, T. H. Jones, *CP* 9.

[129]   19 April 1952, *CP* 11.

[130]   Ironically evoking Blodeuwedd. One of the flowers from which she was created was broom. The essential difference between this and gorse is the abundant prickles.

[131]   Ibid., 12.

[132]   Ibid., 13.

[133]   Date unknown, ibid.,14.

[134]   Cf. 'Taller today, we remember similar evenings . . .', W. H. Auden, *Collected Shorter Poems 1927–1957* (London, Faber & Faber, 1966), 20.

[135]   Published March 1953, T. H. Jones, *CP* 15.

[136]   See 'Paysage Moralisé', *Collected Shorter Poems*, 71.

[137]   Date unknown, T. H. Jones, *CP* 22.

[138]   31 July 1971, *CP* 26.

[139]   Published 1949, 19.

[140]   8 December 1952, *CP* 28.

[141]   27 August 1950, *CP* 30.

[142]   19 October 1952, *CP* 38.

[143]   19 October 1952, *CP* 40.

[144]   Date unknown, *CP* 47.

[145]   19 October 1952, *CP* 52.

[146]   'Song, Ten weathers at my finger-tips', published 1948, *CP* 48.

[147]   21 September 1953, *CP* 55.

[148] Date unknown, T. H. Jones, *CP* 49.

[149] 19 April 1952, *CP* 56.

[150] The metaphorical death of orgasm clashes with a real death by water.

[151] Robert Graves, *The White Goddess*, 24–5. Graves's disgust with the sexuality of 'liberated' women is much in evidence: 'An English or American woman in a nervous breakdown of sexual origin will instinctively reproduce in faithful and disgusting detail much of ancient Dionysiac ritual. I have witnessed it myself in helpless terror' (Ibid., 458).

[152] Ibid., 442–62.

[153] New York, Harper & Row, 1976.

[154] Jacqueline Rose, *The Haunting of Sylvia Plath* (London, Virago Press, 1991), 152.

[155] Cited in ibid., 154.

[156] Robert Graves, *The White Goddess*, 449.

[157] 22 April 1957, p. 228.

[158] Julian Croft, *T. H. Jones* (Cardiff, University of Wales Press, 1976), 12.

[159] *Times Literary Supplement* (22 April 1957), 228.

[160] *The Dublin Magazine* (July–September 1957), 46–7.

[161] *T. H. Jones*, 13.

[162] 'Down your street', *Hampshire Telegraph and Post* (Friday 22 February 1957).

[163] Unpublished letter to Pam and Ted Richards, 2 August 1958.

[164] *Black Book*.

[165] 12 August 1958, in *What the Woman Lives: Selected Letters of Louise Bogan 1920–1970*, ed. Ruth Limmer (New York, Harcourt Brace Jovanovich, 1973), 312.

[166] Roberto Sanesi, 'Introduction' to *The Graphic Works of Ceri Richards* (Milan, Cerastico Milano, 1973), 5.

[167] Unpublished letter, 28 September 1958.

[168] Norman Jeffares, unpublished letter to P. B. Jones, 10 August 1990.

[169] Unpublished letter to Ruth and Llewelyn Jones, 19 November 1958.

[170] Unpublished letter, 19 November 1958.

[171] Unpublished letter, 16 February 1959.

[172] 15 March 1959.

[173] A revealing phrase.

[174] T. H. Jones, unpublished letter to Rupert Hart-Davis, 18 March 1959.

[175] London, Rupert Hart-Davis, 1960.

[176] Croft, *T. H. Jones*, 27.

[177] A deliberate use of T. S. Eliot's homage to Ezra Pound in the epigraph to *The Waste Land*.

[178] 14 August 1958, *Black Book*.

[179] A distinguishing feature of Anglo-Welsh writers is their interest in and desire to be part of European culture.

[180] October 1958, *Black Book*.

[181] October 1955 and 19 June 1957, *CP* 105–7.

[182] W. H. Auden, 'As I walked out one evening', *Collected Shorter Poems 1927–1957* (London, Faber & Faber, 1966), 85.

[183] 31 August 1958, *CP* 108.

[184] As Croft's 'wounded prince' implies, we are in the world of fertility myth.

[185] 3 October 1956, *CP* 97.

[186] October 1958, *CP* 104.

[187] 16 October 1951, *CP* 65.

[188] See *Poetry of the Thirties* (London, Penguin Books, 1964), 273: 'The sunlight on the garden . . . We cannot beg for pardon . . . We shall have no time for dances.'

[189] 6 October 1951, T. H. Jones, *CP* 66.

[190] 4 July 1952, *CP* 73.

[191] 8 December 1952, *CP* 76.

[192] 4 January 1953, *CP* 79.

[193] A. J. Hassall, 'A Welsh poet in exile', *Southerly*, 38/1 (1978), 113–17.

[194] 19 April 1953, T. H. Jones, *CP* 82.

[195] Compare 'Your delicate bones will make me pens'.

[196] *Paradise Lost,* book 1.

[197] 'Possibly in imitation of Baudelaire and Mallarmé', Croft, *T. H. Jones*, 35.

[198] *CP* 83.

[199] Andrew Marvell, 'To his coy mistress'.

[200] 19 February 1954, *CP* 87.

[201] September 1955, *CP* 92.

[202] A bitterly ironic ambiguity.

[203] Remembering Yeats's 'A prayer for old age' and 'The wild old wicked man'.

[204] 3 October 1956, *CP* 98.

[205] *CP* 108–10.

[206] R. S. Thomas, 'The untamed', *Selected Poems of R. S. Thomas* (Newcastle, Bloodaxe, 1986), 79.

[207] Ibid., 80.

[208] J. P. Ward, *The Poetry of R. S. Thomas* (Bridgend, Poetry Wales Press, 1987), 71–4.

[209] R. S. Thomas, 'The untamed', 80.

[210] Quoted in Ward, *Poetry of R. S. Thomas*, 71–4.

[211] 'The colour of cockcrowing', 2 December 1959, *CP* 224.

[212] October 1964, *CP* 221.

[213] Ward, *Poetry of R.S. Thomas*, 82–4.

[214] 26 October 1961, *CP* 240.

[215] October 1964, 220.

[216] Anon., 'Alive and kicking', 12 August 1960, 514.

[217] Roland Mathias, *Anglo-Welsh Review*, 11/27 (1961), 52–3.

[218] Douglas Phillips, 'A sweet tooth at the core of Eden's apple', 13 August 1960.

[219] Llandysul, Gomer Press, 1982, 275–95.

[220] Unpublished letter to Don Dale-Jones, 6 May 1993.

[221] Robert Morgan, 'Farewell to darkness', *Poetry Wales*, 24/4 (Spring 1989), 3–7.

[222] Ibid.

Chapter 7

[1] Unpublished, 4 April 1959.

[2] Roberto Sanesi, interview with P. B. Jones, 26 May 1991.

[3] Unpublished, 5 April 1959.

[4] Andrew Gurr notes (*Writers in Exile: The Identity of Home in Modern Literature* (Brighton, Harvester Press, 1981), 17) that 'Freedom to write is a major stimulus to exile, and creates a kind of isolation which is the nearest thing to freedom that a twentieth century artist is likely to obtain.'

[5] Ross Gittins, 'The state of New South Wales', in *That Place Called New South Wales* (Australia, The Fairfax Library, 1987), 66–71.

[6] 2 December 1959, *CP* 224.

[7] W. B. Yeats, 'The brawling of a sparrow in the eaves': 'The sorrow of love', *Collected Poems* (London, Macmillan, 1958), 45.

[8] Unpublished, *Black Book*, 1 May 1961.

[9] For example, 'Once it was the colour of saying'.

[10] Peter Watson, quoted in David Mellor, 'The body and the land', see *A Paradise Lost: The Neo-Romantic Imagination in Britain 1935–55* (London, Lund Humphries, 1987), 40–5.

[11] Ross Gittins, 'New South Wales'.

[12] Jill Stowell, letter to the authors, January 2001.

[13] Clive Hart, interview with P. B. Jones, 4 September 1991.

[14] Ibid.

[15] Unpublished, 30 May 1959.

[16] Ibid.

[17] Jill Stowell, letter.

[18] T. H. Jones, unpublished letter to Pam and Ted Richards, 30 May 1959.

[19] Ibid.

[20] Ibid.

[21] 12 September 1959, *CP* 112.

[22] Unpublished letter, 25 September 1959.

[23] Julian Croft, *T. H. Jones* (Cardiff, University of Wales Press, 1976), 61.

[24] *CP* 112, 114, 115.

[25] Jonah, 1: 3.

[26] *Look! We Have Come Through* is the title of the volume of poetry published after Lawrence's elopement with Frieda von Richthofen.

[27] See W. B. Yeats, 'Easter 1916', *Collected Poems* (London, Macmillan, 1958), 202.

[28] 26 September 1964, *CP* 193.

[29] 'Lucky Jonah'.

[30] T. H. Jones, unpublished letter to Rupert Hart-Davis, 2 November 1959.

[31] 'Poem on St David's Day'.

[32] T. H. Jones, unpublished letter to Dai Phillips, 30 November 1959. Mrs Phillips kindly provided Pat Power with the eighteen poems in MS which Jones sent to her husband. In a birthday card to Ruth in May 1960, he wrote, 'We are all liking Australia very much – but as my friend Professor Dai Phillips (who was down the mines in Aberdare at the age of 9) says – it's not bloody Wales boy.'

[33] 15 June 1959, *CP* 138.

[34] There will be many of these, in the tradition of the Bardd Gwlad, celebrating, for example, births, marriages, 'local' (that is, to the academic community of Newcastle) events.

[35] 14 October 1959, *CP* 200.

[36] 24 December 1959, *Black Book*: the poem contains a light-hearted use of the 'thorn' image – 'I lean my breast upon a bloody thorn / (Which austral friends say is pure metaphor)'.

[37] 'Taut rigidity of the senses', 14 October 1959, *Black Book*. The last of the series, 'Italian baroque music' would be entered into the *Black Book* in January 1960.

[38] 15 June 1959, *Black Book*.

[39] Compare Shelley's 'stain the white radiance of eternity'.

[40] 15 June 1959, *Black Book*.

[41] 15 June 1959, *CP* 228.

[42] See above, pp. 185–6.

[43] T. H. Jones, unpublished letter, 23 August 1960.

[44] 'Lucky Jonah'.

[45] Clive Hart, interview with P. B. Jones, 23 August 1991.

[46] Ibid.

[47] Ibid.

[48] Ibid.

[49] Julian Croft, interview with P. B. Jones, 16 August 1991.

[50] 30 March 1963, *Black Book*.

[51] Julian Croft, interview, 16 August 1991. Talbot would play a significant part in the making of the T. H. Jones myth, publishing a long obituary, two important articles on the poetry and the poem, 'The seafolding of Harri Jones'.

[52] 1 October 1964, *CP* 215.

[53] Norman Talbot, 'Poet as exile', *Quadrant* (January/February 1979), 82–3.

[54] Clive Hart, interview, 4 September 1991.

[55] Ibid.

[56] Ibid.

[57] A. J. Hassall, unpublished letter to P. B. Jones, 1 November 1988.

[58] Ibid.

[59] Alan Farrelly, 'The Welshman and the beast', *Newcastle Morning Herald* (13 March 1965).

[60] T. H. Jones, 'The literature of the gilded age', unpublished paper given at the inaugural meeting of the Australian and New Zealand American Studies Association, Melbourne, August 1964.

[61] Ibid.

[62] Lloyd Mifflin, Boston, 1898.

[63] Harry E. Mills, Topeka, 1892.

[64] Bayard Taylor, 'with some collaboration from Joaquin Miller', 1812.

[65] Marion Halligan, *Self Possession* (Australia, University of Queensland Press, 1987), 71.

[66] Clive Hart, interview, 4 September 1991.

[67] Ibid.

[68] He enclosed a copy of 'Rhiannon', 19 February 1960, *CP* 116.

[69] T. H. Jones, unpublished letter to Pam and Ted Richards, undated (probably Christmas 1961).

[70] T. H. Jones, unpublished letter to Ruth and Llewelyn Jones, undated.

[71] Halligan, *Self Possession*, 72–3.

[72] Julian Croft, interview with P. B. Jones, 16 August 1991.

[73] Ibid.

[74] Neil Kessel and Henry Walton, *Alcoholism* (London, Penguin Books, 1989), 2–6.

[75] Ibid.

[76] John Glanville, unpublished letter to P. B. Jones, 17 July 1993.

[77] His memorable phrase for poetry-reading, quoted by Jean Rigley, unpublished letter to Ruth Jones, 9 February 1965.

[78] Dylan Thomas, 'In my craft or sullen art', *Collected Poems 1934–1952* (London, Dent, 1952).

[79] Julian Croft, interview, 16 August 1991.

[80] Madeleine, unpublished memoir, 1998.

[81] 'Lines for the death of an alcoholic', September 1962, *CP* 165.

[82] 4 October 1964, *CP* 188.

[83] 1 December 1960, *Black Book*.

[84] Clive Hart, interview, 4 September 1991.

[85] 'Not young any longer', 16 March 1961, *CP* 139.

[86] Clive Hart, interview, 4 September 1991.

[87] 1 January 1962.

[88] 'Disorganised', 6 May 1961.

[89] Stowell, letter.

[90] Julian Croft, interview, 16 August 1991.

[91] Ibid.

[92] Ibid.

[93] Clive Hart, interview, 4 September 1991.

[94] T. H. Jones, 'Absalom, Absalom', *The Australian Highway* (Autumn 1965).

[95] Clive Hart, interview, 4 September 1991.

[96] Ibid.

[97] 'Storms etc.', 11 November 1961, *CP* 241.

[98] 'Word is all', 4 October 1964, *CP* 188.

[99] 'Love is different from what you think it is', 6 May 1961, *Black Book*.

[100] Unpublished, *c*.1962. The stimulus for this story may well have been Jones's rereading of Dylan Thomas in preparation for his 'Writers and Critics' monograph. The poem, 'A winter's tale', is described there as 'one of Thomas's greatest technical triumphs', is read as a 'White Goddess' poem ('the midwinter and rebirth myth . . . is its narrative core' and is said to give 'a complete visual and tactile impression of whiteness, cold, and stillness': see T. H. Jones, *Dylan Thomas* (London and Edinburgh, Oliver & Boyd, 1963), 74–6).

[101] Compare 'were we led all that way for / Birth or Death? . . . I had seen birth and death, / But had thought they were different; this Birth was

Hard and bitter agony for us, like Death, our death.', 'Journey of the Magi', T. S. Eliot, *Collected Poems 1909–1962* (London, Faber & Faber, 1965), 109.

[102] Compare 'I will not serve . . . I am not afraid to make a mistake, even a great mistake, a lifelong mistake, and perhaps as long as eternity too', James Joyce, *Portrait of the Artist* (London, Penguin Books, 1960), 247.

[103] Compare 'In a flash of lightning. Then a damp gust / Bringing rain . . . Then spoke the thunder . . .', T. S. Eliot, *Collected Poems 1909–1962* (London, Faber & Faber, 1965), 78.

[104] 13 April 1961, *CP* 118.

[105] 'The green tree', 28 April 1962, *CP* 245.

[106] And compare 'Love dies as a tree grows', *CP* 83.

[107] 'Fern Hill', *Collected Poems 1934–1952* (London, Dent, 1952), 161.

[108] 'Welsh childhood', 3 September 1963, *CP* 177.

[109] 30 March 1963, *CP* 175.

[110] See John Harris, Introduction to *My People* (Bridgend, Seren Books, 1987), 7–47.

[111] In *The Cost of Strangeness* (Llandysul, Gomer Press, 1982), 293.

[112] See *Modernity and Self Identity* (London, Polity Press, 1991), 153.

[113] Clive Hart, interview, 4 September 1991.

[114] Jill Stowell, letter.

[115] 4 September 1960, *CP* 157.

[116] *Self Possession*, 144–5.

[117] Marion Halligan, unpublished letter to P. B. Jones, 6 July 1992.

[118] 11 October 1964, *CP* 219.

[119] See 'Visual pleasure and narrative cinema', *Screen*, 16/3 (Autumn 1975), 6–18.

[120] Charles Baudelaire, 'Au lecteur', prefatory poem to *Les Fleurs du mal* (Paris, Le Livre Club du Libraire, 1956), 14. Baudelaire was a powerful influence on modernist poets and T. S. Eliot uses a similar technique, foregrounding it with this quotation, in *The Waste Land*.

[121] *Welsh Review* (1946), and see above pp. 110–11.

[122] *Self Possession*, 99–100.

[123] August 1960, *CP* 155.

[124] For example, 'And would sigh at the tale / Of sunk Lyonnesse' in 'I found her out there' from *Satires of Circumstance* (1914).

[125] Hints at the agony of the hero in *King Lear*, especially Act III, Scene 2.

[126] See 'Among school children', *CP* (London, Macmillan, 1958), 242.

[127] All artists 'process' life-experience; most critics, rightly, are more concerned with the process than the experience (for them in any case

irretrievable) that initiated it. The end-product of the processing is invariably and inevitably deceptive ('all . . . poems lie') of a biographical approach. Jones appears to have aligned himself rather with Wordsworth's 'spontaneous overflow of powerful feeling . . . recollected in tranquillity' than with Eliot's 'The more perfect the artist, the more completely separate in him will be the man who suffers and the mind which creates'. Or has he?

128 Julian Croft, interview, 16 August 1991. T. H. Jones was not likely to think, let alone say, 'After all, s/he was only an undergraduate.' See above p. 110.

129 Northrop Frye, *Fearful Symmetry: A Study of William Blake* (Princeton, Princeton University Press, 1947). The three quotations which follow are from this work.

130 Ibid.

131 The comparison, above, between 'The enemy in the heart' and 'Girl reading John Donne' indicates the sense in which 'simplicity' and 'directness' are employed here: beneath the surface the later poetry can be extremely complex.

132 'Drunk on duty', 27 June 1961, *Black Book*. Gurr (20) suggests that 'the allusiveness and the imagism which are poetry's responses to alienation are too obscure for the true exile'. The increasing directness of this later poetry may therefore be attributed to the impact of exile. A comment of Joyce's is also illuminating: 'If I can get to the heart of Dublin I can get to the heart of all the cities in the world' (for 'Dublin' read 'Llanafan').

133 'Who'd be an erotic poet anyway', 6 June 1961, *Black Book*.

134 'She bit me, but not in anger', 17 April 1961, *Black Book*.

135 *The New England Mind: The Seventeenth Century* (Cambridge, MA, Harvard University Press, 1939).

136 Herbert Leibowitz, 'Robert Lowell: ancestral voices', in *Robert Lowell: A Portrait of the Artist in His Own Time*, ed. Michael London and Robert Boyers (New York, David Lewis, 1970), 199–221.

137 *Modernity and Self Identity*, 155.

138 *For the Union Dead*: discussed in Katherine Wallingford, *Robert Lowell's Language of Self* (Durham, NC, University of North Carolina Press, 1988).

139 Julian Croft, interview, 16 August 1991.

140 Halligan, *Self Possession*.

141 T. H. Jones, unpublished letter to Pat Power, July 1964.

142 Julian Croft, interview, 16 August 1991. Croft might have added 'and Yeats'.

[143] Judith Wright, *Preoccupations in Australian Poetry* (Melbourne, Oxford University Press, 1965).

[144] 'Cotton Mather remembers the trial of Elizabeth How: Salem, Massachusetts, 30 June 1692', 26 September 1964, *CP* 193.

[145] 'Adam's song after paradise', 27 July 1961, *CP* 145. Others are 'Adam and Eve hear the thunder', *CP* 220; 'Adam wonders about Eve', *CP* 221; 'Against wantonness', *CP* 222; all written in October 1964.

[146] Discussed in Ken Goodwin, *A History of Australian Literature* (London, Macmillan, 1986), 20.

[147] Les Murray, 'The trade in images', in *The Paperbark Tree* (Manchester, Carcanet Books, 1992), 295–301.

[148] 19 February 1960, *CP* 116.

[149] Les Murray, 'The trade in images', 298.

[150] See also idem, 'A folk inferno', *Paperbark Tree*, 317–28.

[151] A precedent in Wales was Raymond Garlick's adoption, as an English incomer, of Wales as the basis of his inspiration. Like Garlick, Jones felt that Welsh poetry in English needed the European and international dimensions as well as the local.

[152] T. H. Jones, 'Able to be romantic', *Quadrant* 8/2 (June/July 1964), 73–6.

[153] A. D. Hope, 'Imperial Adam', *Penguin Book of Australian Verse*, ed. John Thomson, Kenneth Slessor and R. G. Howarth (London, Penguin Books, 1958), 122–3.

[154] T. H. Jones, 'Able to be romantic'.

[155] Idem, 'Four poets', *Quadrant*, 7/2 (963), 90–1.

[156] T. H. Jones, 'Flowers and fury', *Quadrant*, 7/1 (1963), 93–6.

[157] T. H. Jones, 'Able to be romantic', 73–6.

[158] See Ken Goodwin, *A History of Australian Literature*, 210.

[159] McAuley called his work 'toneless and unmusical . . . with phonetic structures that were coarse and abrasive'. Ibid., 117.

[160] T. H. Jones, 'Able to be romantic'.

[161] Interview with P. B. Jones, 16 August 1991. 'However, after a few pints, in discussing the poems that explicitly referred to his naval life he still could become animated and angry about what he regarded as the way in which the naval ratings had been regarded as expendable by the middle and upper class officers.'

[162] T. H. Jones, unpublished letter to Rupert Hart-Davis, 27 March 1962.

[163] True: roughly 140 poems had been composed in those years.

[164] Ibid.

[165] By now he had thirty-four more to choose from.

[166] T. H. Jones, unpublished letter to Rupert Hart-Davis, 12 November 1962.

[167] John Carr, 'Dylan resurrected', *Western Mail* (1 June 1963).

[168] T. H. Jones, *Dylan Thomas* (London and Edinburgh, Oliver & Boyd, 1963), 1. This acute and lucid study is essential reading for the insight it gives into Jones's own art.

[169] Ibid.

[170] Ibid.

[171] Ibid.

[172] See above, p. 142–3.

[173] T. H. Jones, *Dylan Thomas*, 5.

[174] Ibid., 12.

[175] Quoted by Robert Graves in *The White Goddess* (London, Faber, 1961), 21.

[176] Robert Graves, 'Warning to children', in *Robert Graves: Selected by Himself* (London, Penguin Books, 1957), 47.

[177] T. H. Jones, *Dylan Thomas*, 70.

[178] Ibid.

[179] Ibid., 110 and see G. S. Fraser, *Dylan Thomas* (London and New York, Longmans, 1957).

[180] T. H. Jones, *Dylan Thomas*, 109.

[181] Ibid., 111.

[182] Ibid.

[183] Ibid., 112.

Chapter 8

[1] 22 September 1962, *CP* 134.

[2] August 1961, *CP* 162.

[3] Glyn Jones, 'Poetry rooted in suffering', *Western Mail* (12 October 1963).

[4] Indeed they could – 'dark', 'lonely', 'slow' to name but a few.

[5] 22 March 1963, *CP* 154.

[6] 30 March 1963, *CP* 166.

[7] Unpublished letter to Pam and Ted Richards, 3 July 1963.

[8] 13 February 1962, *CP* 168.

[9] 1946, *CP* 16. For a discussion, see above, pp. 110–11.

[10] 1948, unpublished. For discussion, see above, pp. 120–6.

[11] '. . . nostalgia for childhood, youth, native district or country, or else a yearning for an ideal spiritual state or emotional experience in the

future, usually beyond place and time', *The New Companion to the Literature of Wales*, ed. Meic Stephens (Cardiff, University of Wales Press, 1998), 317.

[12] Keith Tester, *The Life and Times of Post Modernity* (London, Routledge, 1993), 72.

[13] Ibid., 64.

[14] Ferdinand Tonnies, *Community and Association* (London, Routledge, 1955), 39.

[15] Tester, *Post Modernity*, 72.

[16] 28 September 1962, *CP* 136.

[17] 9 March 1963, *CP* 137. The title is taken from Milton's 'pastoral drama', *Comus* ('the gilded car of day, / His glowing axle doth allay / In the steep Atlantick stream') and the poem is dedicated 'for the natives of Borth'. It goes without saying that the significance of this extends further than the fact that Borth is on the Irish Sea coast.

[18] 27 June 1961, *CP* 121.

[19] 27 July 1961, *CP* 122.

[20] 26 October 1961, *CP* 124.

[21] 22 September 1962, *CP* 134.

[22] 9 August 1962, *CP* 133.

[23] 10 December 1961, *CP* 125. This poem provides a coda to the short story, 'My grandfather would have me be a poet'. Above, 31ff.

[24] 12 January 1962, *CP* 127.

[25] 24 October 1961, *CP* 123.

[26] 13 April 1961, *CP* 118.

[27] 22 July 1961, *CP* 144.

[28] May 1961, *CP* 143.

[29] 27 July 1961, *CP* 145.

[30] *CP* 98, and see above pp. 183–4.

[31] The Donne-like pun on 'hope' is intentional: the poem is dedicated to A. D. Hope.

[32] 28 July 1961, *CP* 146.

[33] Wallace Stevens, 'Notes toward a supreme fiction', *Collected Poems* (London, Faber & Faber, 1955), 383.

[34] John Donne, 'The funerall' and 'The relique', *John Donne* (London, Penguin Books, 1950), 61 and 64.

[35] A complete understanding of this complex poem would begin with the sentence of which Jones's epigraph is a part: 'Adam / In Eden was the father of Descartes / And Eve made air the mirror of herself, / Of her sons and of her daughters.' One reason for Stevens's appeal is to be found in the following quotation from 'An ironic romantic: three

readings in Wallace Stevens' by Malcolm Bradbury (in *American Poetry* (Stratford-upon-Avon Studies, 7, London, Arnold, 1965), 155–73): 'Stevens proposes an imaginative ritual in which poetry affords the meaning, shape and design in the world formerly associated with religion.' Stevens believed that 'After one has abandoned a belief in god, poetry is that essence which takes its places as life's reality' (*Opus Posthumus*, 158).

[36] 11 November 1961, *CP* 163.

[37] *CP* 157.

[38] 28 April 1962, *CP* 163.

[39] 16 June 1962, *CP* 164.

[40] 30 June 1962, *CP* 165.

[41] 17 November 1960, *CP* 160.

[42] 11 October 1962, *CP* 166.

[43] 30 March 1963, *CP* 166.

[44] 3 November 1960, *CP* 159. This poem also has an epigraph from Thomas.

[45] 17 April 1961, *CP* 161.

[46] December 1962, *CP* 167.

[47] The sinister contrast of boom and hiss set up in the opening stanza with 'thorn – scythe hissed – corn – alone' is maintained through to the final stanza's 'thorn – whisper – alone – born'.

[48] Julian Croft, interview with P. B. Jones, 16 August 1991.

[49] T. H. Jones, unpublished letter to Pam and Ted Richards, 5 July 1963.

[50] Unpublished letter to Ruth Jones, 13 August 1963.

[51] Unpublished letter to Pat Power, 1 February 1964.

[52] Clive Hart, interview, 4 September 1991.

[53] Published posthumously in *The Australian Highway* (Autumn 1965), 28. The title sends us to William Faulkner: in his story the black prospective husband of the white girl provokes and is shot by her brother.

[54] A neat travesty of the first two lines of Keats's 'On first looking into Chapman's Homer': 'Much have I travell'd in the realms of gold / And many goodly states and kingdoms seen'. T. H. Jones's last jibe at Palgrave? (the sonnet heads 'Book Fourth' of the anthology damned in the 'Refusal to write autobiography').

[55] 2 Samuel, 18: King David's handsome, charismatic son rose in rebellion against his father, lost his life and was famously lamented.

[56] In his letter to Pat Power on 1 February 1964 he reveals that 'I have just been made Secretary of an organisation for American studies in all Australian universities – actually I started it going.'

[57] Unpublished letter, 24 September 1964.

[58] Unpublished letter, 17 November 1964.

[59] Julian Croft, *T. H. Jones* (University of Wales Press, 1976), 115.

[60] Anna Rutherford, 'Harri Jones: a tribute', *Planet*, 49–50 (1980), 128–34. In 'A sailor who reads books sends a Christmas card to his dead sweetheart', Jones, in the persona of the sailor, says to Anna, 'Darling, in that private place, / Do you hang toys upon the trees/As you used to hang your breasts to please / My unaccommodating face . . .?'

[61] A. Alvarez, *The Savage God: A Study of Suicide* (London, Penguin Books, 1971), 257–83.

[62] 'The enemy in the heart' (the poem) demonstrates that we must be careful to distinguish between this and artifice.

[63] Glyn Jones and John Rowlands, *Profiles: An Account of Welsh and English Writers in Wales Today* (Llandysul, Gomer Press, 1980), 236–328. This is a 'visitor's guide' to writing in twentieth-century Wales.

[64] See, for example, 'Girl reading John Donne'.

[65] The number of formal sonnets, both Shakespearean and Petrarchan, and of ballads throughout his work is indicative.

[66] Auden had taught him in, for example, 'As I walked out one evening', a favourite poem also of Dylan Thomas's, how the traditional ballad could be employed.

[67] Alvarez, *Savage God*.

[68] 27 July 1961, *CP* 122.

[69] Best translated as 'pennies'.

[70] 24 August 1960, *CP* 229.

[71] 'Wales–New South Wales', May 1961, *CP* 119. Raymond Williams, *The Country and the City* (London, Chatto & Windus, 1973), suggests that nostalgia is a response to the experience of the urban, so that the sense of futurity attaches to the city, whilst the sense of nostalgia is associated with the country.

[72] 26 January 1964, *CP* 182.

[73] *The Dragon*, 68 (Easter 1946), 13. See above, pp. 105ff.

[74] Sections of Roman road which survived in Breconshire (among other counties) were wrongly associated, in popular legend, with Elen Luyddog (Elen of the Hosts), heroine of the fourth-century tale *The Dream of Macsen Wledig*. A cottage known as 'Sarn Helen' sits at a significant crossroads in Llanafanfawr.

[75] Blodeuwedd, the beautiful, unfaithful wife of Lleu Llawgyffes, created by magic from the flowers of oak, broom and meadowsweet in the Fourth Branch of the *Mabinogion*.

[76] 'The Helen of Wales', daughter of Rhys ap Tewdwr, fl. 1100–20. She had many lovers.

77 Owain Glyndŵr (*c*.1354–1416), prince of Wales and national hero. The rising he led was eventually suppressed in 1413.

78 Llywelyn (ap Gruffydd), Y Llyw Olaf ('the last prince', *c*.1225–82), killed by English troops at Cilmeri, near Builth Wells.

79 It is not clear whether this is Henry VII, the Welshman who became king of England, or his more famous son, Henry VIII (for whom the epithet 'bloody-minded' appears equally, if not more appropriate).

80 The ninth- or tenth-century cycle of poems.

81 Composed after 26 September 1964, when the *Black Book* was full. *CP* 191.

82 A very old metaphor for falling into error. See, for example, Spenser's *Faerie Queene*, book 1, where the Red Cross Knight goes astray in the forest.

83 The 'battle of the trees', The first of the *Three Futile Battles of the Isle of Britain*. Robert Graves (*The White Goddess*, 341) says that it was fought between the White Goddess and the man who challenged her power.

84 Compare Auden's 'Children afraid of the dark / Who have never been happy or good'.

85 Albert Camus, *The Myth of Sisyphus*, trans. Justin O'Brien (London, Penguin Books, 1975), 95, 96.

86 *Savage God*, 257–8.

87 Ibid., 20–56.

88 Written after 26 September 1964, *CP* 186.

89 October 1964, *CP* 187.

90 Genesis 3:18.

91 22 September 1962, *CP* 134.

92 The poet.

93 4 October 1964, *CP* 189.

94 We are in the world of Macbeth: 'They have tied me to a stake; I cannot fly. / But bear-like I must fight the course.'

95 October 1964, *CP* 187.

96 'Looking back on heroes and dragons: the poets of a self-conscious decade', *The Australian* (6 February 1965).

97 London, Penguin Books, 1964.

98 London, Penguin Books, 1964.

99 Julian Croft, interview with P. B. Jones, 16 August 1991.

100 'Constable praised at inquest', *Newcastle Herald* (12 March 1965).

101 Madeleine, unpublished letter to Don Dale-Jones, 4 July 1998.

102 Richard Murphy, a friend of Madeleine's who was staying with them at the time.

[103] Madeleine, letter, 4 July 1998.

[104] Idem, unpublished letter to Ruth Jones, 29 January 1965.

[105] Clive Hart, interview. Professor Lewis Leary of the University of Columbia raises a similar point. He was a great friend of T. H. Jones and had arranged for him to spend a year's sabbatical there in 1966. His poem, 'Harri never jumped but he was pushed', was inspired by a conviction that Jones was *psychologically driven* to his death.

[106] Two lines from Yeats's 'Easter 1916' are apposite: 'what if excess of love / Bewildered [him] till [he] died?'

[107] 30 March 1963, *CP* 174.

[108] Julian Croft, interview, 16 August 1991.

[109] Norman Talbot, *The Seafolding of Harri Jones* (Nimrod Pamphlets, No. 2, 1965).

[110] Email to P. B. Jones, 8 October 2000.

[111] 'It was a curt cuckooing and the wind / Soon turned and all the girls were gone, / But a good time in which we should have sinned / When the eloquent and searocked skeleton / Of Wales put on a sensual covering . . . '.

[112] Madeleine, unpublished letter to Ruth Jones, 3 February 1965.

[113] Madeleine, unpublished letter to Aneirin Talfan Davies, 5 February 1965.

[114] Aneirin Talfan Davies, unpublished letter to Pat Power, 15 February 1965.

[115] Madeleine, unpublished letter to Rupert Hart-Davies, 16 March 1965.

[116] Meic Stephens, 'The second flowering', in Cary Archard (ed.), *Poetry Wales 25 Years* (Bridgend, Seren Books, 1990), 20–9.

[117] Unpublished letter, 12 August 1965.

[118] The reader, and, indeed, the critic attempting an appraisal of Jones's oeuvre is in a complex and rather difficult position in the absence of a *Complete Poems* (long overdue: the *Collected Poems* has a number of serious deficiencies). Many of the best and most crucial poems are in an arrangement that he did not control and the (inaccessible) *Black Book* contains other important, unpublished work, and, much more important, a complete chronology from 20 May 1950 to 26 September 1964.

[119] 3 September 1963: '"Kynge Arthur Ys Nat Dede', you know, / But sleeps, his gold outbraving grey'.

[120] See below 255.

[121] That is, relating to Wales and the poet's childhood.

[122] June 1964, *Black Book*.

¹²³ June 1964, *CP* 213. The title is a quotation from Hart Crane.

¹²⁴ 30 March 1963, *CP* 174.

¹²⁵ 15 July 1963, *CP* 206.

¹²⁶ 11 October 1962, *CP* 171.

¹²⁷ 1 January 1964, *CP* 180.

¹²⁸ 30 March 1963, *Black Book*.

¹²⁹ September 1964, *Black Book*.

¹³⁰ September 1964, *Black Book*.

¹³¹ 15 July 1963, *CP* 208.

¹³² 'In the shadow of your hair', 28 June 1963, *CP* 205.

¹³³ *Englynion y Beddau*, collections of lyrical, elegiac early Welsh poetry naming the graves of heroes.

¹³⁴ In identifying himself with Arthur, Jones invokes both the tragic love for Guinevere and the war to preserve a civilization, thus reminding us that he is a champion of his country as well as an unlucky lover.

¹³⁵ 26 September 1964, *CP* 193.

¹³⁶ *Dylan Thomas* (Edinburgh and London, Oliver & Boyd, 1963), 66.

¹³⁷ 'Harri Jones: a tribute'.

¹³⁸ Above pp. 214–16.

¹³⁹ Jones's admiration of Wallace Stevens may account for his interest in Mather. Stevens's 'The blue buildings in the summer air', *Collected Poems* (London, Faber & Faber, 1955) 216, is about him and contains the lines 'There was always the doubt, / That made him preach the louder'.

¹⁴⁰ He got into serious trouble with his congregation when he vaccinated his son against smallpox.

¹⁴¹ *The Crucible* (1952).

¹⁴² In *Areopagitica*.

¹⁴³ A bomb was thrown through his window during the smallpox controversy.

¹⁴⁴ 23 April 1962, *CP* 170.

¹⁴⁵ 15 February 1963, *CP* 172.

¹⁴⁶ Compare the third 'Song of a mad prince', *CP* 108.

¹⁴⁷ 30 March 1963, *CP* 173.

¹⁴⁸ 3 September 1963, *CP* 177.

¹⁴⁹ 19 September 1963, *CP* 178.

¹⁵⁰ 4 October 1964, *CP* 189.

¹⁵¹ 11 October 1964, *CP* 190.

¹⁵² See above, pp. 29ff.

¹⁵³ 19 September 1963, *CP* 179.

¹⁵⁴ 14 January 1964, *CP* 181.

155 Not, of course, to be taken in any simple sense. Compare 'I say, putting on a bit more accent, / And of course prefacing what I have to say / With that disarming and dishonest "of course"': 'Mr Jones as the transported poet', *CP* 121.

156 11 February 1964, *CP* 185.

157 Mikhail Bakhtin, *The Dialogic Imagination*, ed. M. Holquist, trans. Caryl Emerson and Michael Holquist (Austin, TX, University of Texas Press, 1981).

158 Late 1964, *CP* 186.

159 October 1964, *CP* 187.

160 Mervyn Peake, 'Out of the chaos of my doubt', *Selected Poems* (London, Faber, 1972), 10.

161 4 October 1964, *CP* 223.

162 'Poetry, a new selection', *Daily Telegraph* (26 January 1967).

163 'Exiles', *Manchester Guardian* (27 January 1966).

164 Herbert Williams, 'The ghost of Dylan', *Western Mail* (16 July 1966).

165 *Anglo-Welsh Review*, 16/38 (1967).

166 Norman Talbot, 'To write simply: the poetry of T. H. Jones', *Quadrant*, 9/5 (1965), 35–42.

167 Ibid.

168 Roland Barthes, *Mythologies* (St Albans, Paladin Books, 1973).

169 Anthony Giddens, *Central Problems in Social Theory* (London, Macmillan, 1979) and *Social Theory and Modern Sociology* (Cambridge, Polity Press, 1987).

170 Lévi-Strauss, *The Savage Mind* (Chicago, University of Chicago Press, 1966).

171 'On re-reading the Twenty-Third Psalm', *CP* 172.

172 'Not on this Continent', 28 May 1964, *CP* 251.

173 *Design and Truth in Autobiography* (London, Hutchinson, 1957), 67.

174 Ibid.

Epilogue

1 Ken Goodwin, *A History of Australian Literature* (London, Macmillan, 1986), 231.

2 Ed. Bryn Griffiths (London, J. M. Dent & Sons, 1967).

3 'Stormy night in Newcastle N.S.W.'.

4 Ed. Gerald Morgan (Cardiff, University of Wales Press, 1968).

5 Ed. John Stuart Williams and Meic Stephens (London and Llandybïe, J. M Dent and Christopher Davies, 1969).

6   Don Dale-Jones and W. Randal Jenkins (London, University of London Press, 1975). Pat Power, her sister, Valerie, and Harri Webb attended the launching of this intended companion to *Ten Modern Scottish Poets,* but (perhaps because it was by a London publisher?) it sank without trace.

7   Sam Adams (Manchester, Carcanet, 1974).

8   *T. H. Jones* (Cardiff, University of Wales Press, 1976).

9   Julian Croft and Don Dale-Jones (Llandysul, Gomer Press, 1977). Reprinted in paperback, 1987.

10 As we have indicated earlier, this was a mistake. That Sanesi is a fine contemporary poet to whom T. H. Jones does full justice ought to have been reason enough for their inclusion. More important, however, the fact that he chose to translate these poems helps the reader understand Jones's development and his postmodernism.

11 See pages 131ff. The dates of their composition range from 15 June 1959 to 28 May 1964.

12 Roland Mathias, *Anglo-Welsh Review,* 59 (1974). Mathias gives a condensed version of his assessment in *Anglo-Welsh Literature: An Illustrated History* (Bridgend, Poetry Wales Press, 1986), 92. Like Glyn Jones earlier, he senses the postmodernism.

13 Originally 'Epynt', 1965. See *Harri Webb Collected Poems,* ed. Meic Stephens (Llandysul, Gomer Press, 1995), 74.

14 This river runs under Cwmchwefri rocks and Allt-y-clych and through Llanafanfawr before joining the Irfon at Builth Wells.

15 A tract of hill-country, now a military range, between Brecon and Builth.

16 Abandoned lead-mining village in northern Powys.

17 Reservoir supplying water to Birmingham.

18 A leading member of Plaid Cymru, the Welsh Nationalist party.

19 Harri Webb. See *Harri Webb Collected Poems,* 401.

20 Harri Webb, unpublished letter to Julian Croft, 4 April 1977.

21 See 'Back', *CP* 181.

22 Harri Webb, letter, 4 April 1977.

23 Cephisus (or Cephissus) is a Greek river mentioned in the *Iliad.*

24 To 'lie', it might be said, with 'all my poems'.

25 That is, English.

26 Preface to *Heroines of Welsh History,* 6.

27 Assembled by Bernard Jones, Pat Power and Liz Fleming Williams.

28 Then the Arts Council's bookshop and gallery.

29 *T. Harri Jones 1921–1965* (Cardiff, Welsh Arts Council, 1987).

30 All four were influences upon his postmodernist development.

31   Among them the National Library.

32   *The Wyeside* (Summer 1938).

33   *The Dragon* (Summer 1941).

34   *Welsh Review* (1946). *CP* 16.

35   *The Dragon* (Easter 1946).

36   12 September 1959, *CP* 112.

37   2 December 1959, *CP* 224.

38   Unpublished, *c.*1962.

39   11 October 1964, *CP* 219.

40   26 January 1964, *CP* 182.

41   26 September 1964, *CP* 193.

42   'My country, my grief', 1 January 1964, *CP* 180.

43   'The colour of cockcrowing'.

44   'Useless advice to a young man hopelessly in love', 14 June 1962, *CP* 247.

Bibliography

A1. Poetry, Stories and Drama by T. H. Jones

Poetry

The Enemy in the Heart (London, Rupert Hart-Davis, 1957).

Songs of a Mad Prince (London, Rupert Hart-Davis, 1960).

The Beast at the Door (London, Rupert Hart-Davis, 1963).

The Colour of Cockcrowing (London, Rupert Hart-Davis, 1966).

The Collected Poems of T. Harri [*sic*] *Jones*, ed. Julian Croft and Don Dale-Jones (Llandysul, Gomer Press, 1977). The editors omitted the 'Versions from the Italian of Roberto Sanesi' published in *Songs of a Mad Prince*, and Julian Croft, who checked the published poetry against the holograph versions in the *Black Book*, made a number of minor textual emendations.

The Black Book, unpublished holograph containing all poems thought worthy of preservation between 20 May 1950 and 26 September 1964.

Stories

'My grandfather would have me be a poet', *Life and Letters* (January 1950), 30–8.

'The riding strangers', *The Dublin Magazine*, 26/1 (January 1950), 21–4.

'Holy deceptions', *The Glass*, 5/1 (1952), 24–7.

'Home', *The Dublin Magazine*, 30/2 (June 1954), 24–33.

'A day at the seaside', *Dock Leaves*, 5/15 (Winter 1954), 7–12.

'Absalom, Absalom', *The Australian Highway* (Autumn 1965).

'Saturday night', *Planet* (June/July 1988) 77–81.

'These rooms, this bed, this woman', unpublished ?1951.

'What's become of Waring?', unpublished ?1952.

'Knives', unpublished ?1954.

'The first Christmas', unpublished ?1962.

Drama

The Weasel at the Heart, verse-play performed at Aberystwyth 1948.

A2. Other Writings

'Visions', *The Dragon* (Summer 1941).

Review of *Elizabethan and Metaphysical Imagery* by Rosemon Tuve, *Life and Letters* (1948), 3.

Review of *Rage for Order* by Austin Warren, *Life and Letters* (1949), 1.

Review of *English Emblem Books* by Rosemary Freeman, *Life and Letters* (1949), 2.

Review of *Essays on Literature and Society* by Edwin Muir, *Life and Letters* (1949), 3.

Review of four volumes of poetry (*New Directions, 10; New Road, 5; A New Romantic Anthology; Since 1939, 2*), *Life and Letters* (1949), 3.

'The imagery of the Metaphysical poets of the seventeenth century', unpublished MA thesis, University College of Wales, Aberystwyth, 1949.

Review of *Skelton* by H. L. R. Edwards, *Life and Letters* (1950), 2.

Syllabus for 'A first-year tutorial course of twenty-four lectures on the appreciation of literature', WEA, University of Southampton, 1954.

'A refusal to write autobiography', unpublished ?1955.

'Fathers, daughters and poems', unpublished ?1958.

Review of *Lantana Lane* by Eleanor Dark, *Quadrant*, 4/2 (Summer 1959/ 60).

Review of *A Bachelor's Children* by Hal Porter and *The Tame Ox* by Jack Cope, *Quadrant*, 6/1 (1962).

Review of *Flowers and Fury* by Geoffrey Dutton and *No Fixed Address* by Bruce Dawe, *Quadrant*, 7/1 (1963).

Dylan Thomas (Edinburgh and London, Oliver & Boyd (Writers and Critics Series), 1963).

Review of *Four Poets* (Judith Green, Rodney Hall, David Malouf and Don Maynard), *Quadrant*, 7/2, (1963).

'Able to be romantic', review of *Australian Poets: A. D. Hope, Australian Poets: Robert D. Fitzgerald, In Light and Darkness* by Chris Wallace-Crabbe and *Poems* by Gwen Harwood, *Quadrant*, 8/2 (June/July 1964).

'Looking back on heroes and dragons: the poets of a self-conscious decade', review of *Poetry of the Thirties*, ed. Robin Skelton, *The Australian* (6 February 1965).

Review of *Penguin Modern Poets*, 6 (Jack Clemo, Edward Lucie-Smith and

George Macbeth), *The Australian*, 6 February 1965.

'The literature of the Gilded Age', unpublished paper delivered to the Australian and New Zealand American Studies Association, Melbourne, August 1964.

B1. Books on T. H. Jones

Croft, Julian, *T. H. Jones* (Cardiff: University of Wales Press (Writers of Wales), 1976).

Power, Pat, Jones, P. Bernard and Felgate, Liz, *T. Harri [sic] Jones 1921–1965* (Cardiff, Welsh Arts Council (Writer's World), 1987).

B2. Articles on T. H. Jones

Anonymous, 'Alive and kicking', *Times Literary Supplement* (12 August 1960), 514.

Anonymous, 'For the most part gloomy', *Times Literary Supplement* (6 September 1963), 674.

Anonymous, 'Down your street', *Hampshire Telegraph and Post* (Friday 22 February 1957).

Carr, John, 'Dylan resurrected', *Western Mail* (1 June 1963).

Conran, Anthony, in *The Cost of Strangeness: Essays on English Poets in Wales* (Llandysul, Gomer Press, 1982).

Croft, Julian, 'A word not lightly said', *Poetry Magazine Sydney*, 2 (1965), 3–7.

Dale-Jones, Don, 'Companion for a bitter mind', unpublished paper delivered to Association for the Study of Welsh Writing in English, Gregynog, 1993.

Dale-Jones, Don, 'The trouble with Harri, some thoughts on two writers for our time, Harri Webb (1920–94) and T. Harri [sic] Jones (1921–65)', in Sam Adams (ed.) *Seeing Wales Whole: Essays on the Literature of Wales* (In Honour of Meic Stephens), (Cardiff, University of Wales Press, 1998), 55–76.

Dale-Jones, Don, 'Reintroducing T. H. Jones', *Poetry Wales*, 33/4 (April 1998), 24–9.

Dale-Jones, Don, 'A Welsh poet's war', *New Welsh Review*, 45 (12/1), (Summer 1999), (50–56).

Davies, Aneirin Talfan, 'Ar ymyl y dalen' (On the edge of the page), *Barn* (Chwefror 1968), 88–90.

Farrelly, Alan, 'The Welshman and the beast', *Newcastle Morning Herald* (13 March 1965).

Hassal, A. J., 'A Welsh poet in exile', *Southerly* 38/1 (1978).

Hawkes, Terence, 'The colour of cockcrowing', *Anglo-Welsh Review*, 16/38 (1967).

Jennings, Elizabeth, 'Poetry, a new selection', *Daily Telegraph* (26 January 1967).

Jones, Glyn, 'Poetry rooted in suffering', *Western Mail* (12 October 1963).

Jones, P. Bernard, 'The anonymous lecturer', *Planet*, 69 (June/July 1988), 82–7.

Jones, P. Bernard, 'The Black Book of T. H. Jones', *Poetry Wales*, 33/4 (April 1988), 29–32.

Mathias, Roland, in *Anglo-Welsh Review*, 11/27, 52–3.

Morgan, Robert, 'Death of a poet', *London Welshman* (July/August 1965), 3–4.

Morgan, Robert, 'Farewell to darkness', *Poetry Wales*, 24/4 (Spring 1989), 3–7.

Phillips, Douglas, 'A sweet tooth in the core of Eden's apple', *Western Mail* (13 August 1960).

Rutherford, Anna, 'Harri Jones, a tribute', *Planet*, 49–50 (1980), 128–34.

Smith, Peter, 'The dissatisfaction of T. Harri Jones', *Planet*, 69 (June/July 1988), 88–92.

Talbot, Norman, *The Seafolding of Harri Jones* (Australia, Newcastle, NSW, Nimrod Pamphlets No. 2, 1965).

Talbot, Norman, 'To write simply: the poetry of T. H. Jones', *Quadrant* (Australia), 11/5, 1965, 35–42.

Williams, Herbert Lloyd, 'Ghost of Dylan Thomas?', *Western Mail* (16 July 1966).

B3. Radio Programmes

'Homage to a Poet', script by Edward (Ted) Richards. A version of this was broadcast (BBC Wales Radio) 29 July 1965. Ref. TCF 50821.

B4. Interviews carried out by P. B. Jones and others

In all but three cases (indicated by *) these were recorded, on cassette, on a Sony TC-D3. The interviewee was encouraged to tell her/his story rather than respond to a series of standard questions. The three exceptions were written up from notes taken at the time.

Anthony, Frank (F. J.), Llanelli, 11 May 1989.

Cass, Ronnie, Llandeilo, 23 October 1990.

Croft, Julian, London (British Museum), 16 August 1991.

Davies, Glyn, Llanafan, Powys, 16 July 1992.

Davies, Gwen, Builth Wells, 17 June 1989.

George, E., interviewed by David Power, Portsmouth, 22 August 1989.

Hammonds (née Lewis), Ethel, Builth Wells, 13 May 1988.

Hart, Clive, Thorpe Lee Soken, Essex, 4 September 1991.

Jones, Brenda, interviewed by Michael and Pat Power, Builth Wells, 19 May 1988.

Jones, Donald, Builth Wells, 4 November 1989.

Jones, Gwyn, Aberystwyth, 22 July 1989.

Jones, M. A., interviewer anonymous, Welsh Folk Museum Archive, St Fagans.

Jones, Myra, interviewed by Pat and Michael Power, Builth Wells, 12 October 1988.

Jones, William Anthony, interviewed by P. B. Jones and Pat Power, 2 August 1987.

Jones-Anthony, Bill and Mrs, interviewed by P. B. Jones and Pat Power, Aberystwyth, 2 August 1987.

Kowalski, Stanley, interviewed by David Power, Portsmouth, 22 August 1989.

Lewis, Gwanwyn, Brecon, 23 July 1989.

Llewelyn, Mair, Bangor, 21 December 1990.

Marshfield, Alan, London, 16 June 1989.

*Mitchell, Madeleine (née Scott), widow of T. H. Jones, New Quay, Ceredigion, 8 September 1989.

Phillips, Dorothea, London, 20 December 1992.

Power, Patricia, Builth Wells, 6 February 1989.

Price, Gerwyn, Rhayader, 13 June 1990.

Richards, Pamela, Borth, 7 August 1987.

Roantree, Ronnie, Torquay, 2 July 1987.

Roberts, B. H., Brecon, 7 November 1987.

Sallis, Tom, Porth, 8 April 1988.

*Sanesi, Roberto, Hay-on-Wye, 26 May 1991.

*Thomas, R. S., Hay-on-Wye, 29 May 1994.

Thomson, Michael, Dylife, 8 September 1990.

C. Background Reading

Abse, Dannie, *White Coat, Purple Coat: Collected Poems 1948–88* (London: Hutchinson, 1989).

Adams, Sam, 'Jeffrey Llewelyn Prichard', in *Brycheiniog*, 21 (1984–5).

Alvarez, A., *The Savage God: A Study of Suicide* (London, Penguin Books, 1971).

Auden, W. H., *Collected Poems*, ed. Edward Mendelson (London, Faber, 1976).

Auden, W. H., *Collected Shorter Poems 1927–1957* (London, Faber, 1966).

Auden, W. H., *New Year Letter* (London, Faber, 1941).

Auden, W. H., *City Without Walls* (London, Faber, 1949).

Bakhtin, Mikhail, *The Dialogic Imagination*, ed. M. Holquist, trans. Caryl Evans and M. Holquist (Austin, TX, University of Texas Press, 1981).

Barnes, Julian, *Flaubert's Parrot* (London: Jonathan Cape, 1984).

Barthes, Roland, *Mythologies* (St Albans, Paladin Books, 1973).

Baudelaire, Charles, *Les Fleurs du mal* (Paris, Le Livre Club du Libraire, 1956).

Benjamin, Walter, *Illuminations* (London, Collins, 1973).

Berger, John, 'Understanding a photograph,' in *Selected Essays and Articles: The Look of Things* (London, Penguin Books, 1972).

Bianchi, Tony, 'R. S. Thomas and his readers', in Tony Curtis (ed.), *Wales, the Imagined Nation: Essays in Cultural Identity* (Bridgend, Poetry Wales Press, 1986), 71–92.

Blackmur, R. P., *Language as Gesture* (London, Allen & Unwin, 1954).

Blake, William, *The Collected Poems of William Blake*, ed. Alicia Ostriker (London, Penguin Books, 1977).

Blake, William, *Selected Poems* (London, Penguin Books, 1958).

Bogan, Louise, *What the Woman Lived: Selected Letters of Louise Bogan 1920–70*, ed. Ruth Limmer (New York, Harcourt Brace Jovanovich, 1973).

Bradbury, Malcolm, 'An ironic romantic: three readings of Wallace Stevens', in *American Poetry* (Stratford-upon-Avon Studies, 7; London, Arnold, 1965), 155–73.

Bradury, Malcolm (ed.), *The Novel Today* (London, Fontana, 1977).

Brecht, Bertolt, *Brecht on Theatre, The Development of an Aesthetic*, ed. J. Willett (London, Methuen, 1978).

Brittain, Vera, *Wartime Chronicle: Vera Brittain's Diary 1939–45*, ed. Paul Bishop and Alan Bennett (London, Gollancz, 1989).

Burnham, Richard, 'The Dublin Magazine's Welsh poets', *Anglo-Welsh Review*, 27/60 (1978), 49–63.

Calvocaressi, Peter, Wint, Guy and Pritchard, John, *Total War*, vol.1 (London, Penguin Books, 1989).

Cambrian, The (22 November 1861).

Camus, Albert, *The Myth of Sisyphus*, trans. Justin O'Brien (London, Penguin Books, 1975).

Conran, Anthony, 'Anglo-Welsh revisited', *Planet*, 108 (December 1994/ January 1995).

Tony Curtis (ed.), *Wales the Imagined Nation: Essays in Cultural and National Identity* (Bridgend, Poetry Wales Press, 1986).

Dale-Jones, Don, *A. G. Prys-Jones*, Writers of Wales series (Cardiff, University of Wales Press, 1992).

Davies, Gwen, 'Builth Wells during the Second World War', unpublished memoir, 1990.

Davies, John, *A History of Wales* (London, Allen Lane, The Penguin Press, 1990).

Davies, Stevie, *John Donne* (London, Northcote House, 1994).

Derrida, Jacques, *The Ear of the Other, Otobiography, Transference, Translation*, texts and discussions with Jacques Derrida trans. by Peggy Kamuf, ed. by Christie V. Macdonald (New York, Schocken Books, 1985).

Donne, John, *Selected Poems* (London, Penguin Books, 1950).

Dragon, The, magazine of UCW, Aberystwyth.

Durkheim, E., *Moral Education* (New York, New York Free Press, 1961).

Eagleton, Terry, *Literary Theory* (London, Blackwell, 1983).

Eliot, T. S., *Collected Poems 1909–62* (London, Faber, 1965).

Eliot, T. S., 'Tradition and the individual talent', in *Selected Essays* (London, Faber, 1963).

Ellman, Richard, *Along the Riverrun: Selected Essays* (London, Penguin Books, 1989).

Evans, Caradoc, *Pilgrims in a Foreign Land* (London, Andrew Dakers, 1942).

Evans, Caradoc, *My People* (Bridgend, Seren Books, 1987).

Evans, Caradoc, *Caradoc's Journal* in *Caradoc Evans*, ed. Oliver Sandys (London: Hurst & Blackett, n.d.).

Fraser, G. S., *Dylan Thomas*, Writers and their Work (London and New York, Longmans, 1957).

Fraser, G. S., *The Modern Writer and his World* (London, Penguin Books, 1964).

Freud, Sigmund, *Reflections on War and Death*, trans. by A. A. Brill and A. B. Kuttner (New York, W. W. Norton, 1950).

Frost, Robert, *Poems Selected by Himself* (London, Penguin Books, 1955).

Frye, Northrop, *Fearful Symmetry: A Study of William Blake* (Princeton, Princeton University Press, 1947).

Gibbings, Robert, *Coming Down the Wye* (London, The Travel Book Club, 1942).

Giddens, Anthony, *Central Problems in Social Theory* (London, Macmillan, 1979).

Giddens, Anthony, *Social Theory and Modern Sociology* (Cambridge, Polity Press, 1987).

Giddens, Anthony, *Modernity and Self Identity* (London, Polity Press, 1991).

Gittins, Ross, *That Place Called New South Wales* (Sydney, The Fairfax Library, 1987).

Goodwin, Ken, *A History of Australian Literature* (London, Macmillan, 1986).

Graves, Robert, *The White Goddess* (London, Faber, 1961).

Graves, Robert, *Poems Selected by Himself* (London, Penguin Books, 1957).

Gurr, Andrew, *Writers in Exile: The Identity of Home in Modern Literature* (Brighton, The Harvester Press, 1981).

Halligan, Marion, *Self Possession* (Australia, University of Queensland Press, 1987).

Hamilton, Ian, *Keepers of the Flame: Literary States and the Rise of Autobiography* (London, Hutchinson, 1992).

Hargreaves, David H., *The Challenge for the Comprehensive School* (London: Routledge & Kegan Paul, 1982).

Hawthorn, Jeremy, *Unlocking the Text* (London, Arnold, 1987).

Heaney, Seamus, *Preoccupations: Selected Prose 1968–1978* (London, Faber, 1980).

Hewitt, Leah D., *Autobiographical Tightropes* (Lincoln, NE, and London, University of Nebraska Press, 1990).

Hopkins, Gerard Manley, *The Poems of Gerard Manley Hopkins*, ed. W. H. Gardner and W. H. Mackenzie (London, Oxford University Press, 1967).

Hooker, Jeremy, 'R. S. Thomas', in *Poetry Wales*, 7 (Spring 1972).

Hughes, C., 'A study of the development of secondary education in Builth, 1889–1949', unpublished M.Ed. dissertation, UCW, Aberystwyth, 1983.

Humphreys, Emyr, *The Taliesin Tradition* (Bridgend, Seren Books, 1983).

Jones, Bobi, 'The Anglo-Welsh', *Dock Leaves*, 4/10 (1953).

Jones, Bobi, 'Anglo-Welsh, more definitions', *Planet*, 16 (1973), 11–23.

Jones, Bobi, 'Order, purpose and resurgence in poetry', *Poetry Wales*, 11/1 (1975), 118–22.

Jones, Glyn and Rowlands, John, *Profiles: An Account of Welsh and English Language Writers in Wales Today* (Llandysul, Gomer Press, 1980).

Jones, Jack, *Unfinished Journey* (London, Hamish Hamilton, 1937).

Jones, Theophilus, *A History of the County of Brecknock*, vol. 1 (Edwin Davies, Brecknock, 1809).

Joyce, James, *Selected Letters of James Joyce*, ed. Richard Ellman (London, Faber & Faber, 1975).

Joyce, James, *Portrait of the Artist* (London, Penguin Books, 1960).

Kennedy, Ludovic, *On my Way to the Club* (London, Collins, 1989).

Kermode, Frank, *Wallace Stevens* (London, Oliver & Boyd, 1960).

Kessel, Neil and Walton, Henry, *Alcoholism* (London, Penguin Books, 1989).

Kristeva, Julia, *Powers of Horror* (New York, Columbia University Press, 1982).

Kroll, Judith, *Chapters in a Mythology: The Poetry of Sylvia Plath* (New York, Harper & Row, 1976).

Kunitz, Stanley, 'Talk with Robert Lowell', in *Profile of Robert Lowell*, ed. Jerome Mazzaro (Columbus, OH, Charles E. Merrill, 1971).

Lawrence, D. H., *The Complete Poems of D. H. Lawrence*, vol. 1 (London, Heinemann, 1957).

Leibowitz, Herbert, 'Robert Lowell, ancestral voices', in Michael London and Robert Boyers (eds.), *Robert Lowell: A Portrait of the Artist in his Own Time* (New York, David Lewis, 1970), 199–221.

Lévi-Strauss, Claude, *The Savage Mind* (Chicago, University of Chicago Press, 1966).

Lowell, Robert, *For the Union Dead* (London, Faber, 1965).

Lowell, Robert, *Life Studies* (London, Faber, 1965).

Mackinon, Lachan, *Eliot, Auden, Lowell: Aspects of the Baudelairean Influence* (London, Macmillan, 1983).

Maffesoli, Michel, 'The sociology of everyday life,' in *Current Sociology*, 37/1 (1989).

Maranda, Pierre (ed.), *Mythology: Selected Readings* (London, Penguin Books, 1972).

Mellor, David, 'The body and the land', in *A Paradise Lost: The Neo-Romantic Imagination in Britain, 1935–55* (London, Lund Humphries, 1987), 30.

Meyers, Jeffrey, *D. H. Lawrence* (London, Macmillan, 1990).

Miller, Perry, *The New England Mind: The Seventeenth Century* (Cambridge, MA, Harvard University Press, 1939).

Mulvey, Laura, 'Visual pleasure and narrative cinema', in *Screen*, 16/3 (Autumn 1975), 6–18.

Murray, Les, *The Paperbark Tree* (Manchester, Carcanet, 1992).

Nathan, George Jean, *The World in Falseface* (New York, Knopf, 1923).

Palgrave, F. T., *The Golden Treasury* (London, Oxford University Press, 1896).

Pascall, Roy, *Design and Truth in Autobiography* (London, Hutchinson, 1957).

Peake, Mervyn, *Selected Poems* (London, Faber, 1972).

Price, Thomas, *The Literary Remains of Thomas Price, Carnhuanawc, with a Memoir of his Life by Jane Williams, Ysgafell*, vol. 2 (Llandovery, William Rees, 1855).

Prichard, Thomas Jeffery Llewellyn, 'The land beneath the sea, or Cantrev y Gwaelod', in *Welsh Minstrelsy* (London, John and H. L. Hunt, 1824).

Prichard, Thomas Jeffery Llewellyn, *The Adventures and Vagaries of Twm Shon Catti, Descriptive of Life in Wales* (Aberystwyth, John Cox, 1828).

Prichard, Thomas Jeffery Llewellyn, 'Preface' to *Heroines of Welsh History* (London, W. and F. G. Cash, 1854).

Rose, Jacqueline, *The Haunting of Sylvia Plath* (London, Virago Press, 1991).

Sanesi, Roberto, 'Introduction' to *The Graphic Works of Ceri Richards* (Milan, Cerastico Milano, 1973).

Sinclair, Andrew, *War like a Wasp* (London, Penguin Books, 1989).

Sinfield, Alan, *Literature, Politics and Culture in Post-War Britain* (Oxford, Blackwell, 1989).

Skelton, Robin (ed.), *Poetry of the Thirties* (London, Penguin Books, 1964).

Skura, Meredith Anne, *The Literary Use of the Psychoanalytical Process* (Worcester, MA, Yale University Press, 1981).

Spears, Monroe K., *Dionysius and the City* (New York, Oxford University Press, 1970).

Spears, Monroe K., *The Poetry of W. H. Auden: The Disenchanted Island* (New York, Oxford University Press, 1963).

Sprinkler, Michael, 'Fictions of the self, the end of autobiography', in James Olney (ed.), *Autobiography, Essays Theoretical and Critical* (Princeton, Princeton University Press, 1980).

Stephens, Meic, 'The second flowering', in Cary Archard (ed.), *Poetry Wales 25 Years* (Bridgend, Seren Books, 1990), 20–9.

Stephens, Meic, *The New Companion to the Literature of Wales* (Cardiff, University of Wales Press, 1998).

Stevens, Wallace, *Collected Poems* (London, Faber, 1955).

Stevens, Wallace, *Opus Posthumous* (London, Faber, 1969).

Talbot, Norman, 'Poets and critics', *Quadrant* (January/February 1979).

Tester, Keith, *The Life and Times of Post Modernity* (London, Routledge, 1993).

Thomas, Dylan, *Collected Poems 1934–1952* (London, Dent, 1952).

Thomas, Dylan, *Portrait of the Artist as a Young Dog* (London, Dent, 1940).

Thomas, Dylan, *The Collected Letters of Dylan Thomas* (London, Grafton Books, 1985).

Thomas, R. S., *Selected Poems of R. S. Thomas* (Newcastle, Bloodaxe, 1986).

Thompson, John, Slessor, Kenneth, and Howarth, R. G. (eds.), *Australian Verse* (London, Penguin Books, 1958).

Tonnies, Ferdinand, *Community and Association* (London, Routledge & Kegan Paul, 1955).

'Twm Shon Catti, Byegones', *Oswestry Gazette* (December 1881).

Van Peer, Willie, *The Taming of the Text: Explorations in Language, Literature and Culture* (London, Routledge, 1989).

Walker, Alexander, *The Journals of Rachel Roberts: No Bells on Sunday* (London, Pavilion Books, 1984).

Wallingford, Katherine, *Robert Lowell's Language of Self* (Durham, NC, University of North Carolina Press, 1988).

Ward, J. P., *The Poetry of R. S. Thomas* (Bridgend, Poetry Wales Press, 1987).

Webb, Harri, *Collected Poems*, ed. Meic Stephens (Llandysul, Gomer Press, 1998).

Welch, Robert, *Changing States: Transformations in Modern Irish Writing* (London, Routledge, 1993).

Williams, Gwyn A., *When was Wales?* (London, Penguin Books, 1985).

Williams, Phil, 'That's what poets are for', in *Planet*, 107 (October/November 1994).

Williams, Raymond, *The Country and the City* (London, Chatto & Windus, 1973).

Wordsworth, William, *The Poems*, vol. 1 (London, Penguin Books, 1977).

Wright, Judith, *Preoccupations in Australian Poetry* (Melbourne, Oxford University Press, 1965).

Wyeside, The, magazine of Builth Wells County School, Builth Wells High School Archive.

Yeats, W. B., *Collected Poems* (London, Macmillan, 1958).

Yeats, W. B., *Uncollected Prose*, ed. J. P. Fayne (London, Macmillan, 1970).

INDEX